北京市高等教育精品教材立项项目

应用化学专业英语

第二版

万有志　王幸宜 ▎主编

纪红兵 ▎主审

化学工业出版社

·北京·

《应用化学专业英语》第二版是北京高等教育精品教材,是根据大学英语教学大纲(理工科本科用)的专业阅读部分的要求,受"全国部分高校化工类及相关专业大学英语专业阅读教材编审委员会"委托而编写的,旨在为应用化学专业师生提供一本较系统的专业英语教学用书。

本教材具有以下特点:一、内容选自近年来国外英文原版高等院校化学和化工类教学用书及化学专著,能体现当代专业英语的篇章结构特点和词汇特点;二、题材新颖,文体各异;三、围绕本专业若干重点内容精选阅读材料,覆盖本专业主要研究领域及发展历史、发展趋势;四、内容丰富,共包括五部分24个单元,每单元含精读课文、专业词汇(附音标)、课文注释、多种形式的练习和泛读课文。

本教材供已通过大学英语四级的应用化学专业学生及相关专业学生、同等英语水平和相关专业的科技人员使用。

图书在版编目(CIP)数据

应用化学专业英语/万有志,王幸宜主编.—2版.—北京:化学工业出版社,2008.3(2025.2重印)
北京高等教育精品教材
ISBN 978-7-122-02158-8

Ⅰ.应… Ⅱ.①万…②王… Ⅲ.应用化学-英语-高等学校-教材 Ⅳ.H31

中国版本图书馆 CIP 数据核字(2008)第 022595 号

责任编辑:刘俊之　　　　　　　　文字编辑:颜克俭
责任校对:洪雅姝　　　　　　　　装帧设计:关　飞

出版发行:化学工业出版社(北京市东城区青年湖南街13号　邮政编码100011)
印　　装:河北延风印务有限公司
787mm×1092mm　1/16　印张15¼　字数453千字　2025年2月北京第2版第19次印刷

购书咨询:010-64518888　　　售后服务:010-64518899
网　　址:http://www.cip.com.cn
凡购买本书,如有缺损质量问题,本社销售中心负责调换。

定　　价:39.00元　　　　　　　　　　　　　　　　　　版权所有　违者必究

前言

《应用化学专业英语》自出版以来,承蒙广大读者厚爱已重印 8 次。本教材第二版已经获得"北京高等教育精品教材"建设项目立项。笔者在教学过程中不断地探索、总结,多方收集用书教师和学生的意见和建议。为了适应不断变化的教学要求,紧跟科技发展的步伐,同时也弥补初版时的疏漏之处,笔者对初版教材进行了修订,现作为第二版出版发行。修改主要在以下几个方面。

1. 保持原版的编写体例和风格,对素材进行了更新。

2. 增加了化学专业类文章,删减了诺贝尔化学奖颁奖致辞及类似体裁的内容。部分章节的内容进行了修订。考虑到近年来学生英语水平的提高,也删除了一些难度较低的文章。

3. 课后练习中增加了英文原版教材中的练习题,旨在使学生尝试以英文思维方式解决化学问题,加强语感训练。

4. 修订了原版中的部分错漏。

5. 几位教师为本书编写了配套的教师手册(非出版物),供使用该教材的教师参考。内含课文注释相关材料、参考译文、习题参考答案和试题库。用书教师可直接和本书责任编辑(010-64519157)或笔者(yzhwan@mail.buct.edu.cn)联系。

第二版第 1~11 单元由万有志修订,12~15 单元由张丽娟修订,16~24 单元由王幸宜修订,全书由万有志统稿,纪红兵主审。

本书的修订得到同仁及化学工业出版社的鼎力支持,北京化工大学王探宇、史汝金、栗婷婷等参与了部分工作,特此致谢。虽然笔者倾力而为,但囿于水平,错漏之处在所难免,敬请广大读者批评指正。

万有志
2008 年 4 月

第一版前言

组织编审出版系列的专业英语教材，是许多院校多年来共同的愿望。在高等教育面向21世纪的改革中，学生的基本素质和实际工作能力的培养受到了空前重视。对非英语专业的学生而言，英语水平和能力的培养不仅是文化素质的重要部分，在很大程度上也是能力的补充和延伸。在此背景下，教育部（原国家教委）几次组织会议研究加强外语教学问题，制定有关规范，使外语教学更加受到重视。教材是教学的基本要素之一，与基础英语相比，专业英语教学的教材问题此时显得尤为突出。

国家主管部门的重视和广大院校的呼吁引起了化学工业出版社的关注，他们及时向原化工部教育主管部门和全国化工类专业教学指导委员会请示后，组织全国十余所院校成立了大学英语专业阅读教材编委会。在经过必要的调研后，根据学校需求，编委会优先从各院校教学（交流）讲义中确定选题，同时组织力量开展编审工作。本套教材涉及的专业主要包括化学工程与工艺、石油化工、机械工程、信息工程、生产过程自动化、应用化学及精细化工、生化工程、环境工程、制药工程、材料科学与工程、化工商贸等。

高等学校理工科本科《大学英语教学大纲》规定，高等学校理工科本科生在完成《大学英语教学大纲》所规定的大学英语基础阶段学习后，从第五学期起要开设必修的专业阅读课。基础英语是专业英语的基础，但专业英语在词汇、语法、句法及文风等诸方面又都带有各自专业的特色。为了使学生毕业后能够更快和更有效地应用英语这一工具为自己的专业工作服务，在授完基础英语之后，再开设相应的专业英语课程是非常必要的。认真总结多年从事专业英语教学的经验，结合本专业的特点，编写出针对性强、质量较高的教材，以提高这门课程的教学质量和教学效率，是当前专业英语教学中亟待解决的问题之一。

本书旨在为应用化学专业提供一本比较系统的专业英语教学用书。在选编课文时，从纵、横两个方面覆盖本专业的相关内容（本专业的发展历史和发展趋势、本专业的知识面和研究领域），体裁包括一般专业论文、著作的前言、鸣谢、颁奖会致辞等。通过阅读该教材，可以对本专业概貌有一个相对全面的了解，包括专业内容和文章体裁。

每单元包括精读课文、词汇表（附音标）、课文注释、练习、阅读材料等。其中精读课文和阅读材料选自近年来国外原版的化学化工类和相关专业的教学用书及专著，内容准确，具有一定概括性，文字流畅，难度适中，能体现现代专业英语的篇章结构特点和词汇特点，使学生在学完本教程之后能顺利阅读应用化学专业的英语资料。

本教材分五部分，共25个单元，内容涉及化学发展史，无机化学（元素及周期表、命名、络合物等），有机化学（有机合成、命名等），物理化学（热力学、动力学、结构化学），专业基础（结晶、蒸馏、物料衡算）等，并附有专业词缀和总词汇表等。内容既注重对专业知识面的覆盖，又照顾专业的历史发展资料，并反映当前最新发展状况和若干重要科技领域（如能源、环保等）。目的是为学生提供阅读素材，通过大量阅读，提高学生阅读英语资料的能力。

高等学校理工科本科《大学英语教学大纲》规定，专业英语阅读阶段的主要任务是："指导学生阅读有关专业的英文书刊和文选，进一步提高阅读英语资料的能力，并能以英语为工具，获取专业所需要的信息。"因此，本书以阅读为中心，以获取课文提供的信息为目的，注重对内容理解的准确性。

本书第1~6单元、8~15单元由万有志（北京化工大学）编写，第7单元由张丽娟（北京化工大学）编写，第16~25单元由王幸宜、荣国斌（华东理工大学）编写。全书由万有志统稿，钟理（华南理工大学）主审。

本书在编写过程中，许多同志提出了宝贵建议，并得到他们的鼎力支持和热情帮助，华东理工大学王秀环同志参与了第16~25单元的材料收集、编排以及练习、注释的编写等工作，特此表示真挚的谢意。

本教材获"北京化工大学化新教材建设基金"资助。

虽经多次补充和完善，但限于编者水平，书中谬误、不足之处在所难免，恳请广大读者指正。

编 者
2000年2月

CONTENTS

PART ONE　CHEMISTRY AND SOCIETY
Unit 1　The Roots of Chemistry ·· 1
　　　　Reading Material　What is Modern Molecular Structure About ···························· 6
Unit 2　Hot Springs and Fool's Gold ··· 10
　　　　Reading Material　How Chemistry Came to Life ··· 15
Unit 3　Fullerene Frenzy ·· 19
　　　　Reading Material　Crystals That Flow ··· 23
Unit 4　Drinking Water Quality and Health ·· 27
　　　　Reading Material　Modern CO_2 Applications ·· 33

PART TWO　THE FUNDAMENTALS OF CHEMISTRY
Unit 5　The Periodic Table ·· 37
　　　　Reading Material　The Halogens ·· 42
Unit 6　Nucleophilic Substitution: The S_N2 and S_N1 Reactions ································· 47
　　　　Reading Material　Competition with the Substitution: The E1 and E2 Reactions ····· 53
Unit 7　The Nomenclature of Inorganic Substances ··· 56
　　　　Reading Material　Chemical Bonds ·· 62
Unit 8　Hard and Soft Acids and Bases ·· 66
　　　　Reading Material　Valence Shell Electron Pair Repulsion Theory ······················· 70
Unit 9　Chemical Kinetics: Basic Principles ··· 74
　　　　Reading Material　Chemical Thermodynamics ·· 79
Unit 10　Nomenclature of Hydrocarbons ··· 83
　　　　Reading Material　Nomenclature of Derivative ··· 89
Unit 11　Carboxylic Acids and Their Derivatives ··· 95
　　　　Reading Material　Esters ·· 100

PART THREE　ANALYTICAL TECHNOLOGY FOR SAMPLE
Unit 12　What Is Analytical Chemistry ·· 104
　　　　Reading Material　Sample Preparation ··· 109
Unit 13　Ultraviolet and Visible Molecular Spectroscopy ·· 113
　　　　Reading Material　Structural Analysis (IR) ·· 118
Unit 14　The Chemical Shift ·· 121
　　　　Reading Material　Experimental Methods (NMR) ·· 126
Unit 15　Mass Spectrometry ··· 130
　　　　Reading Material　Introduction to Chromatography ·· 135

PART FOUR UNIT OPERATION

Unit 16 Techniques of Thin-Layer Chromatography in Food and Agricultural
Analysis ·· 140
      Reading Material Development of Thin-layer Chromatography ············· 145
Unit 17 Crystallisation ·· 149
      Reading Material Crystallisation Equipment ·· 153
Unit 18 Distillation ·· 157
      Reading Material Typical Distillation Equipment ···································· 163
Unit 19 Solvent Extraction ·· 166
      Reading Material The Application of Extraction ····································· 171
Unit 20 Supercritical Fluid Technology ·· 176
      Reading Material Supercritical Fluid Extraction of Nutraceuticals from Plants ······ 181

PART FIVE FINE CHEMICALS AND PROCESS

Unit 21 Catalysis ·· 186
      Reading Material Catalyzed Reactions ·· 190
Unit 22 Cosmetics Introduction ··· 194
      Reading Material The History of Perfumery ·· 199
Unit 23 Research of Vitamin E ··· 203
      Reading Material Vitamin E and Antioxidant ··· 208
Unit 24 The Benefits of Pesticides ·· 212
      Reading Material Pesticides and Children ·· 218

PREFIX AND SUFFIX ·· 222
VOCABULARY ·· 225

PART ONE
CHEMISTRY AND SOCIETY

Unit 1 The Roots of Chemistry

Chemistry can be broadly defined as the science of molecules and their transformations. In contrast to mathematics, chemistry is older than people. The appearance of life and people on our planet (Earth) is most probably the end result of specific chemical processes. Chemical processes have been present in the lives of people from the dawn of history until the present time. Initially, these processes were not under our control, for instance, the fermentation of fruit juice, the rotting of meat and fish, and the burning of wood. Later on we learned to control chemical processes and to use them to prepare a variety of different products such as food, metals, ceramics and leather. In the development of chemistry, four periods may be distinguished: prehistoric chemistry, Greek chemistry, alchemy, and scientific chemistry.

The early beginnings of chemistry were clearly motivated by the practical needs of people. The discovery of fire offered the first opportunity to prehistoric people to carry out controlled chemical processes. They learned to prepare objects made of copper, bronze and other materials that were readily available. Since the use of chemical processes by these early people predates writing there are no written records about their chemical skills. One can judge their chemical abilities only from the archeological discoveries of various artifacts. What has been found indicates clearly that practical needs influenced the early development of chemistry, as was the case for the early development of mathematics. [1]But chemistry and mathematics at this stage probably did not interact. If they did, there is no record to establish this.

Greek chemistry was based mainly on speculation rather than on experiment. This was a common trait of all Greek science in antiquity. The Greek scientist of antiquity was in fact the Greek philosopher, and so it is not surprising that the Greeks were much more interested in contemplating than in experimenting. Actually they seldom performed experiments outside of the thought experiment. This was a good approach for mathematics but hardly one to recommend itself for the physical, chemical or biological sciences. Nevertheless, because the Greeks thought a lot about the nature and structure of matter, they can be considered as the creators of the first chemical theories.

The Greeks introduced the concept of the element and proposed in all four elements. Thales (625—547 BC) of Miletus thought that all things were formed from one elementary substance, namely water. Anaximenes (ca 585—ca 528 BC), also from Miletus, accepted the idea of element, but he believed that the single element from which all things are made is air. Heraclitus (ca 540—480 BC) of Ephesus, who considered that the fundamental characteristic of the universe is continuous change, regarded fire as the element that embodied perpetual change. Empedocles (ca 490—ca430 BC), from the Greek city of Akragas in Sicily, abandoned the idea of a single element and introduced the principle of four elements: water, air, fire and earth, and the two forces of attraction and repulsion that operate between them. Empedocles is also known for his experimental proof that air is a material body.

The term "element" was first used by Plato (428—347 BC) who assumed that the particles of each element have a specific shape, even though such particle are too small to be seen. Thus, the smallest particle of fire had the shape of a regular tetrahedron; of air a regular octahedron; of water a regular icosahedron, and of earth a cube (or regular hexahedron).[2] The regular tetrahedron, the regular octahedron, the regular icosahedron and the cube are examples of regular polyhedra, and there are in all five of them; the fifth is the regular dodecahedron. In regular polyhedra the surfaces are bounded by congruent regular polygons and the vertices are symmetrically equivalent to one another.

Fire was thought to be the smallest, most pointed and lightest among the elements because it can easily attack and destroy. It seemed a natural choice that the regular tetrahedron (which consists of four regular triangles) be taken as the shape of fire, since it is the smallest and most pointed among the regular polyhedra. Water was the largest, smoothest and heaviest, because it always flows smoothly into the valleys of the Earth. Therefore, it appeared a natural choice that the regular icosahedron, composed of twenty regular triangles, was taken as its shape. Air is between fire and water and so it appeared natural to assign the regular octahedron (which consists of eight regular triangles) to air. The regular octahedron has the same faces, viz. the regular triangles, as the regular tetrahedron and the regular octahedron. Its numbers of faces is between the numbers of faces of those two. From the fact that the tetrahedron, octahedron and icosahedron could be decomposed into regular triangles which could be reassembled to form the other polyhedra, Plato concluded that fire, air and water could also be mutually transformed, that is, water could be transformed by fire into air, whereas when air loses fire in the upper atmosphere it becomes water in the form of rain or snow. The last element was earth which is heavy and stable, and this was assumed to take the shape of a cube, composed of six squares. Since it was not possible to reduce the cube into regular triangles, but only into squares, Plato concluded that earth could not be transformed into fire, air or water. This is discussed in Plato's dialogue *Timaeus*. In the dodecahedron, because, of all the regular polyhedra, its volume most nearly approaches that of the sphere, Plato saw the outer shape of the universe. The *Timaeus* also contains discussion on the composition of organic and inorganic bodies and may be considered as a rudimentary treatise on chemistry. At this point it should be perhaps emphasized that Plato taught that the idea, the form, was the truly fundamental pattern behind phenomena, that is to say, ideas are more fundamental than objects.

Plato's description of the shapes of the four elements was perhaps the first mathematical model used in chemistry, since regular polyhedra are mathematical objects. The regularity that exists between the numbers of vertices V, edges E and faces F, was discovered by Euler (1707—1783) and is thus called the Euler theorem.

This states that:

$$V+F-E=2$$

Which is considered by some to be the second most beautiful mathematical theorem? It is of interest to speculate why the Greeks did not discover Euler's theorem. Perhaps the simplest explanation is that Greek mathematics was two thousand years away from topology.

Topology ("rubber sheet geometry") is the part of mathematics that deals with the way objects are connected, without regard to "straightness" and metric.

A generalization of the above ideas on elements was put forward by Aristotle (384—322 BC). He accepted the idea of four elements, but introduced the concept of transmutation of elements. Aristotle thought that the elements could be obtained by combining the pairs of opposing fundamental properties of matter. These properties were hotness, coldness, moistness and dryness. The combination of hotness and moistness produced air. Moistness and coldness gave water and, similarly, coldness and dryness produced earth. Aristotle added the fifth element or quintessence, ether. The sky and heavenly bodies were supposedly made up of this fifth element. Aristotle defined an element as simple body that other bodies can be decomposed into but one that is not itself capable of being divided into simpler bodies.[3] He classified several chemical processes, first mentioned mercury and was familiar with the technique of distillation.[4] Aristotle's ideas dominated science for almost two thousand years.

There was another theory on the structure of matter put forward by Greek thinkers. This was concerned with the divisibility of matter. The first Greek philosopher to think about this problem appears to have been Leucippus (ca 470—420 BC) from Miletus. He came up with the proposition that matter cannot be divided endlessly, for in the process of dividing matter one will sooner or later come to a piece not divisible into smaller parts. His pupil Democritus (ca 460—ca 370 BC), from Abdera, continued to develop the ideas of Leucippus. He named these ultimately small pieces of matter $\alpha\tau o\mu o\sigma$ (atomos), meaning indivisible. This is the origin of our term atom. The concept of the atom is the basis of the atomic theory of the structure of matter and the philosophy of materialism. Most Greek philosophers, and particularly Aristotle, did not accept the atomistic teachings of Leucippus and Democritus. Atomism, however, did not die out because Epicurus (ca 342—270 BC) made atomism part of his philosophy, and Epicureanism won many followers over the next few centuries. One of these was the Roman poet and philosopher Lucretius (ca 96—55 BC), who wrote a fine didactic poem entitled *De Rerum Natura* (On the Nature of Things) in which he expounded the atomistic teachings of Democritus and Epicurus. Most of the works by Democritus and Epicurus are lost, but Lucretius's poem has survived intact and has served to convey the atomistic teachings of the Greeks to modern times. The splitting of the atom and the advent of the atomic bomb have surely confirmed what an excellent model of reality atomistic theory was.

The philosophy of idealism and the philosophy of materialism were opposed throughout history. From a chemical point of view the philosophy of materialism affords a basis for an understanding of the structure of compounds. However, the collective properties of compounds such as their smell or color or taste can also be interpreted in terms of Plato's ideas, which are particularly well suited for studying the mathematical properties of chemical structures. If we link the philosophy of materialism with experimental work in chemistry and likewise the philosophy of idealism with theoretical work, it is clear that both philosophies as well as both experiment and theory are needed to advance chemistry. This is of course also true for other sciences.

Alchemy is a type of chemistry that existed from about 300 BC until the second half of the seventeenth century. This constitutes a less interesting period for our purposes, since alchemists were practical people who did not care much for theories and mathematics. The alchemists had two main objectives: (ⅰ) to turn base metals into gold and (ⅱ) to discover the elixir of life. The origins of alchemy can be traced back to the ancient Egyptians.

There was a lot of magic involved in the work of alchemists and their symbols were difficult to decipher. However, the coding systems used by various alchemists are really cryptograms and as such possess a mathematical basis.

It is important to stress that chemistry as a science started only in the second half of the seventeenth century when alchemy gradually transformed itself into the science now known as chemistry following the appearance of the book *The Sceptical Chymist* (London, 1661) by Boyle (1627—1691).[5] The transition period from alchemy to chemistry lasted more than a century. It started with Boyle's book and ended with the book *Traité Élémentaire de Chimie* (Elementary Treatise on Chemistry, Paris, 1789) by Lavoisier (1742—1794). During this period appeared the first unifying chemical theory, namely, the phlogiston theory. The term phlogiston is derived from the Greek word $\phi\lambda o\gamma\iota\sigma\tau o\sigma$, which means flammable.

Now, most dictionaries define chemistry as *the science that deals with the composition, structure, and properties of substances and the reactions by which one substance is converted into another*. Knowing the definition of chemistry, however, is not the same as understanding what it means. In essence, *chemistry is an experimental science*. Experiment serves two important roles. It forms the basis of observations that define the problems that theories must explain, and it provides a way of checking the validity of new theories. This text emphasizes an experimental approach to chemistry. As often as possible, it presents the experimental basis of chemistry before the theoretical explanations of these observations.

From *Concepts in Chemistry* by N. Trinajstic
and *Chemistry: Structure and Dynamics* by James N. Spencer

New Words and Expressions

fermentation [ˌfəːmenˈteiʃən] n. 发酵
ceramics [siˈræmiks] n. 制陶术,陶瓷学,陶瓷制品
leather [ˈleðə] n. 皮革,皮革制品
alchemy [ˈælkimi] n. 炼金术,炼丹术
bronze [brɔnz] n. 青铜（一种铜锡合金）,青铜制品
archeological [ˌɑːkiəˈlɔdʒikəl] a. 考古学的
artifact [ˈɑːtifækt] n. 人工制品
speculation [ˌspekjuˈleiʃən] n. 思索,推测
antiquity [ænˈtikwiti] n. 古代,古人,古迹
Thales [ˈθeiliːz] n. 泰利斯（古希腊哲学家,数学家,天文学家）
tetrahedron [ˈtetrəˈhedrən] n. 四面体
octahedron [ˌɔktəˈhedrən] n. 八面体
icosahedron [ˌaikəusəˈhedrən] n. 二十面体
hexahedron [ˌheksəˈhedrən] n. 六面体
polyhedra [ˌpɔliˈhiːdrə] (polyhedron 的复数形式) n. 多面体
theorem [ˈθiərəm] n. 定理,原则
topology [təˈpɔlədʒi] n. 拓扑学,拓扑
Aristotle [ˈæristɔtl] n. 亚里士多德（古希腊哲学家）
elixir [iˈliksə] n. 长生药,万能药
decipher [diˈsaifə] v. 解开（疑团）,破译（密码）
cryptogram [ˈkriptəugræm] n. 密码,暗记,暗号

flammable [ˈflæməbl]　　n. 易燃物　　a. 易燃的，可燃的
phlogiston [fləˈdʒistən]　　n. 燃素

Notes

1. as 作关系代词时可代替整个主句或一件事（上文或下文所说的事），并在从句中作主语、宾语或表语。as 引出的定语从句为非限制性定语从句。本句在从句中作主语。参考译文：已有事实清楚地表明：正如早期数学的发展一样，实际需要影响着化学的发展。

2. of air 与 a regular octahedron 之间、of water 与 a regular icosahedron 之间、and of earth 与 a cube 之间均省略 had the shape of。参考译文：所以，火的最小微粒具有正四面体形状，气的最小微粒具有正二十面体的形状，土的最小微粒具有立方体（或正六面体）形状。

3. 参考译文：亚里士多德把元素定义成一个简单的物体，其他的物体能被分解成元素，而元素本身不能被分解成更简单的物体。

4. 句中 classified, mentioned, was familiar with 为并列成分，主语均为 He。参考译文：他对数种化学过程进行了分类，第一个论及汞，并通晓蒸馏技术。

5. 参考译文：化学是在 17 世纪后半叶才开始被称为一门科学的，强调这一点很重要。因为当时炼金术才逐渐将其本身转变为科学，随着 Boyle（1627—1691）所著的书 *The Sceptical Chymist*（1661 年，伦敦）的出现。这种科学被看作是化学。

Exercises

Ⅰ. Comprehension

1. It can be inferred from this article which one of the following items is not mainly based on practical use ____.
   A. prehistoric chemistry and alchemy   B. alchemy and chemistry
   C. Greek chemistry   D. Greek chemistry and chemistry

2. It was ____ who first introduced the idea that all things are not formed from just one element.
   A. Aristotle   B. Empedocles   C. Theatetos   D. Theodoros

3. In the development of Greek chemistry, ____ was the first one definiting the ultimately constituents of matter?
   A. Plato   B. Aristotle   C. Leucippus   D. Democritus

4. According to Plato, there are ____ "elements" whose faces are constituted by regular polygons.
   A. 3   B. 4   C. 5   D. 6

5. In the last paragraph, authors think that experiment ____.
   A. can examine whether the assumption is right
   B. can be used to check the new theories
   C. can be carried out by the chemist
   D. can deal with the reactions by which one substance is converted into another

Ⅱ. Make a sentence out of each item by rearranging the words in brackets

1. The purification (is usually/a matter of considerable difficulty, /often/of an organic compound/for this purpose/to employ various methods/it is/necessary/and).

2. Science is (is generated/and systematized knowledge/an ever-increasing body of accumulated/and is also an activity/by which knowledge).

3. Life, after all, is (in fact, /a small example of chemistry/observed on a single, /only chemistry, /mundane planet).

4. People (some of the molecules/are made of molecules; /in people are rather simple/are/highly complex/whereas others).

5. Chemistry is (from birth to death/ever present in our lives/there is neither life nor death/because without chemistry).

6. Mathematics appears (and also permeates/to be almost as humankind/all aspects of human life, /are not fully/although many of us/aware of this).

III. Translation

1. (a) 化学过程；(b) 自然科学；(c) 蒸馏技术。
2. 正是原子构成了铁、水、氧等。
3. 化学具有悠久的历史，事实上，人类的化学活动可追溯到无记录时代以前。
4. 根据水的蒸发现象，人们认识到液体在一定条件下可以变成气体。
5. 在你使用这种材料之前，你必须弄清它的各种性质。

IV. Translation

Chemistry is one of three fundamental natural sciences, the other two being physics and biology. Chemical processes have continually unfolded since the Big Bang and are probably responsible for the appearance of life on the planet Earth. One might consider that life is the end result of an evolutionary process in three steps, the first step being very fast and the other two rather slow. These steps are (i) physical evolution (the formation of chemical elements); (ii) chemical evolution (the formation of molecules and biomolecules); and (iii) biological evolution (the formation and development of organisms).

V. Problem

(1) The absolute mass of a ^{1}H atom is 1.6735×10^{-24} grams, whereas the absolute mass of a ^{12}C atom is 1.9926×10^{-23} grams. Calculate the ratio of the mass of a ^{1}H atom to that of a ^{12}C atom when the masses are measured in units of grams. Use this ratio to calculate the mass of a ^{1}H atom in units of amu if the mass of a ^{12}C atom is exactly 12 amu.

(2) A bone taken from a garbage pile found buried deep under a Turkish hillside had a ^{14}C/^{12}C ratio 0.477 times the ratio in a living plant or animal. What was the date of the prehistoric village in which the bone was discovered?

Reading Material

What is Modern Molecular Structure About

One of the more fundamental issues chemistry addresses is molecular structure, which means how the molecule's atoms are linked together by bonds and what the interatomic distances and angles are.[1] Another component of structure analysis relates to what the electrons are doing in the molecule; that is, how the molecule's orbitals are occupied and in which electronic state the molecule exists. For example, in the arginine molecule shown in Fig. 1.1, a HOOC— carboxylic acid group is linked to an adjacent carbon atom which itself is bonded to an —NH$_2$ amino group. Also connected to the α-carbon atom are a chain of three methylene —CH$_2$— groups, an —NH— group, then a carbon atom attached both by a double bond to an imine —NH group and to an amino —NH$_2$ group.

The connectivity among the atoms in arginine is dictated by the well-known valence preferences displayed by H, C, O and N atoms. The internal bond angles are, to a large

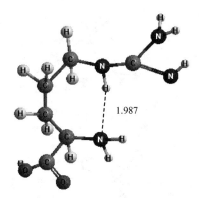

Fig. 1.1 the arginine molecule in its non-zwitterion form with dotted hydrogen bond

extent, also determined by the valences of the constituent atoms (i.e., the sp^3 or sp^2 nature of the bonding orbitals). However, there are other interactions among the several functional groups in arginine that also contribute to its ultimate structure. In particular, the hydrogen bond linking the α-amino group's nitrogen atom to the —NH— group's hydrogen atom causes this molecule to fold into a less extended structure than it otherwise might.

What does theory have to do with issues of molecular structure and why is knowledge of structure so important? It is important because the structure of a molecule has a very important role in determining the kinds of reactions that molecule will undergo, what kind of radiation it will absorb and emit, and to what "active sites" in neighboring molecules or nearby materials it will bind. A molecule's shape (e.g., rod-like, flat, globular, etc.) is one of the first things a chemist thinks of when trying to predict where, at another molecule or on a surface or a cell, the molecule will "fit" and be able to bind and perhaps react. The presence of lone pairs of electrons (which act as Lewis base sites), of π orbitals (which can act as electron donor and electron acceptor sites), and of highly polar or ionic groups guide the chemist further in determining where on the molecule's framework various reactant species (e.g., electrophilic or nucleophilic or radical) will be most strongly attracted. Clearly, molecular structure is a crucial aspect of the chemists' toolbox.

How does theory relate to molecular structure? As we discussed in the Background Material, the Born-Oppenheimer approximation leads us to use quantum mechanics to predict the energy E of a molecule for any positions ($\{R(a)\}$) of its nuclei given the number of electrons N_e in the molecule (or ion). This means, for example, that the energy of the arginine molecule in its lowest electronic state (i.e., with the electrons occupying the lowest energy orbitals) can be determined for any location of the nuclei if the Schrödinger equation governing the movements of the electrons can be solved.

It often turns out that a molecule has more than one stable structure (isomer) for a given electronic state. Moreover, the geometries that pertain to stable structures of excited electronic states are different than those obtained for the ground state (because the orbital occupancy and thus the nature of the bonding is different).[2] Again using arginine as an example, its ground electronic state also has the structure shown in Fig. 1.2 as a stable isomer. Notice that this isomer and that shown earlier have the atoms linked together in identical manners, but in the second structure the α-amino group is involved in two hydrogen bonds while it is involved in only one in the former. In principle, the relative energies of these two geometrical isomers can be determined by solving the electronic Schrödinger equation while placing the constituent nuclei in the locations described in the two figures.

If the arginine molecule is excited to another electronic state, for example, by promo-

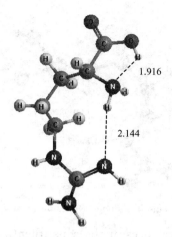

Fig. 1.2　another stable structure for the arginine molecule

ting a non-bonding electron on its C=O oxygen atom into the neighboring C—O π^* orbital, its stable structures will not be the same as in the ground electronic state. In particular, the corresponding C—O distance will be longer than in the ground state, but other internal geometrical parameters may also be modified (albeit probably less so than the C—O distance). Moreover, the chemical reactivity of this excited state of arginine will be different than that of the ground state because the two states have different orbitals available to react with attacking reagents.

In summary, by solving the electronic Schrödinger equation at a variety of geometries and searching for geometries where the gradient vanishes and the Hessian matrix has all positive eigenvalues, one can find stable structures of molecules (and ions).[3] The Schrödinger equation is a necessary aspect of this process because the movement of the electrons is governed by this equation rather than by Newtonian classical equations. The information gained after carrying out such a geometry optimization process includes (ⅰ) all of the interatomic distances and internal angles needed to specify the equilibrium geometry and (ⅱ) the total electronic energy E at this particular geometry.

From *An Introduction to Theoretical Chemistry* by Jack, Simons

New Words and Expressions

arginine ['ɑːdʒini(ː)n]　*n.* 精氨酸
carboxylic [ˌkɑːbɔk'silik]　*a.* 羧基的
adjacent [ə'dʒeisənt]　*a.* 邻近的，接近的
methylene ['meθiliːn, -lin]　*n.* 亚甲基
imine ['imiːn, -in; i'miːn]　*n.* 亚胺
amino ['æminəu]　*a.* 氨基的
zwitterions ['tsvitəraiən]　*n.* 两性离子
electrophilic [iˌlektrəu'filik]　*a.* 亲电（子）的
nucleophilic [ˌnjuːkliəu'filik]　*a.* 亲核的，亲质子的
isomer ['aisəumə]　*n.* 异构体
gradient ['greidiənt]　*n.* 梯度，倾斜度
vanish ['væniʃ]　*vi.* 消失，变成零
matrix ['meitriks]　*n.* 矩阵

eigenvalue [ˈaigənˌvælju:]　*n*. 特征值
Newtonian [nju:ˈtəunjən, -niən]　*a*. 牛顿的，牛顿学说的

Notes

1. 这是一个名词性从句，which 引导的句子用来说明 molecular structure。参考译文：很多化学文章讨论的基本论点之一就是分子结构，也就是说，分子中原子是怎样通过化学键、分子间距和键角连接在一起的。

2. 参考译文：然而，用于描述电子激发态稳定结构的几何学与那些用于描述基态几何学是不相同的（因为占据轨道与成键的性质是不同的）。

3. solving 和 searching 是并列成分。参考译文：总体上说，通过对不同几何构型的电子薛定谔方程求解，寻找梯度变为零和赫赛函数矩阵均具有正特征值的几何构型，可以找出分子（和离子）的稳定结构。

Unit 2 Hot Springs and Fool's Gold

  To make organic molecules from inorganic gases requires an energy source to drive the reactions—atmospheric lightning, volcanoes or ultraviolet light are all candidates. But these sources have the potential to destroy delicate organic molecules too. Another, very different proposal for the prebiotic synthesis of amino acids invokes an energy source that lies at great depths beneath the sea, where the products would be shielded from the inclement conditions at the planet's surface.

  In the 1970s, automated bathymetric vessels lowered to the floor of the Pacific Ocean revealed hot springs that were ejecting water at great temperatures sometimes exceeding 300 degrees Celsius (the water remains liquid only by virtue of the great pressures at these depths, which raise the boiling point). These springs, called hydrothermal vents, are formed when seawater transported down through cracks and pores in the rocks of the Earth's crust is heated by magma inside the Earth and rises back to the seafloor under pressure. Vents are therefore common in regions where undersea volcanic activity is strong, such as at "mid-ocean ridges". Here molten rock wells up from deep within the Earth's mantle to form new oceanic crust. The hot water issuing from a vent is generally rich in minerals, which are deposited to form tall chimney-like structures. The vent fluid is rendered turbid and opaque, like smoke, by its load of small mineral particles.

  John Corliss from NASA's[1] Goddard Space Flight Center in Maryland was amongst the team that discovered hydrothermal vents. He and his fellow researchers found that the vent chimneys were swarming with communities of creatures such as clams, marine worms and bacteria. These bacteria derive their energy and nourishment at least in part from sulfur-containing compounds formed in the volcanic environment and emitted from the vents.[2] They are representatives of a very primitive class, called archaebacteria, which bask happily in hot surroundings and have no need of oxygen—characteristics that would have been necessary in the earliest organisms.

  Far from being unpleasantly hot, hydrothermal vents therefore apparently provide a comfortable environment for living creatures. Corliss proposed that they might have been ideal locations for life to begin. The volcanic gases that are mixed in with the hot effluent of the vent are comprised largely of the simple chemical compounds, such as H_2, N_2, hydrogen sulfide, carbon monoxide and carbon dioxide, from which more complex organics may be formed. Here too was a source energy (the heat of the vent waters) to drive prebiotic chemistry. And there would be nutrients aplenty, in the form of minerals, to sustain the primitive organisms that might develop. (Inorganic nutrients are still an important part of the diet of today's marine microorganisms.) If creatures took up residence *inside* the vents, Corliss suggested that they would be protected from the worst of the natural catastrophes that the young Earth experienced, such as giant meteorite impacts. Corliss's vent hypothesis renders curiously prophetic the words of the Greek Archelaus in the fifth century BC: "When the Earth was first being warmed, in the lower part where the warm and cold were mingled together, many living creatures appeared, deriving their sustenance from the slime."

  Some researchers, Stanley Miller amongst them, have little time for[3] the vent hypothesis. Miller points out those temperatures in most vent fluids are so high that they would be more likely to destroy organic molecules than to create them. As a volume of water equivalent to the entire ocean is cycled through vents and mid-ocean ridges every 8 to 10 million years, Miller argues that subsea volcanism might have acted to frustrate the appearance of life, by burning up organic compounds formed elsewhere in the sea, rather than promoting it. It is certainly hard to imagine that the sort of chemistry that might generate living organisms can carry on amidst temperatures of hundreds of degrees: any amino acids and sugars formed in this environment would survive for scarcely a minute or so before falling apart again in the heat.

Supporters of the vent theory counter this by pointing out that further from the direct outflow; temperatures are milder while the waters are still rich in volcanic gases and nutrients. Geologists from the University of Glasgow in Scotland have reported that "minivents" made of iron pyrites, emitting waters at less than 150 degrees Celsius, can form on the seafloor close to vent systems. They suggest that the chemical environment within these mineral structures would have been ideal for the formation and the joining together of simple organic molecules. The hydrothermal vent scenario seems likely to continue to provoke lively debate, but it cannot be denied that it remains a speculative idea for which the precise details of how it might work are not clear.

One of the protagonists for the vent model is A. G. Cairns-Smith, a chemist from Glasgow who has for many years advanced an alternative theory for the origin of life which borders on the bizarre. He proposes that the first self-replicating "organisms" may not have been made of organic molecules at all, but was instead inorganic crystals. For all the peculiarity of this idea, it is based on principles similar to those that direct the replication of DNA[4] molecules, and has been considered sufficiently intriguing to be afforded serious attention. Cairns-Smith points out that crystals grow via a kind of template-directed process in which the crystal surface acts as a guiding framework for assembly of a new layer, just as a single strand of DNA provides a template on which a new strand can be built.[5] Many crystals can be fractured quite easily along the planes of atoms. The growth and subsequent fracturing of crystals might, Cairns-Smith suggests, be regarded as a kind of replication, like cell growth and division. Moreover, different crystal faces are known generally to grow at different rates, while the speed of growth is also influenced by the presence of irregularities and defects in the perfect crystal structure. This could provide a means by *which* slightly different crystal shapes might mutate and compete with each other in an evolutionary sense.[6]

Cairns-Smith suggests that clay minerals are particularly good candidates for primitive inorganic replicators. These substances are multidecker sandwiches of negatively charged aluminosilicate sheets stuffed with water and metal ions.[7] The metal ions between layers can be exchanged with others quite easily; ion exchange in clays is exploited in some water-purification processes to remove toxic metals from solution. Cairns-Smith proposes that clays might use different sequences of metals between layers as primitive "gene banks" that pass on advantageous traits to new crystals.

There is little doubt that the idea of clay replicators is far-fetched, but Cairns-Smith does not propose that these systems could ever be considered as living organisms (or even "inorganisms"). Rather, he thinks that they might have evolved to a stage at which they were able to facilitate the formation of organic molecules. Initially the organics would have been mere slaves, created because they help the crystals to replicate; but eventually they would have become adept at replication themselves. In support of the idea, we might note that clay minerals are sometimes rather good catalysts for reactions involving organic compounds, and because of their variable layer spacing they can show a degree of catalytic specificity reminiscent of that of zeolites. Furthermore, some organic molecules are known to act as growth inhibitors or promoters which engineer preferential growth of certain crystal faces. This kind of control of mineral growth is crucial to the formation of biominerals such as tooth and bone, which is orchestrated very skillfully by proteins.

Minerals lie also at the heart of the recent addition to origin-of-life scenarios put forward by the German Gunter Wächtershäuser, a one-time organic chemist now turned patent lawyer.[8] His theory focuses largely on the energy source that might have driven prebiotic chemistry, rather than being concerned with the details of the molecules so formed. In most biochemical reactions, energy means electrons: the reactions are often assisted by enzymes that are good at supplying electrons to, or extracting them from, the reactants. This is something that inorganic chemistry can do too, and Wächtershäuser singles out in particular iron pyrites—fool's gold, or FeS_2—as a potential electron source; this compound is the very constituent of the "minivents" identified by the Glasgow geologists. Wächtershäuser suggests that iron pyrites might have acted as a kind of battery to drive the metabolism of primitive precellular organisms consisting of layers of organic molecules attached to the positively charged surface of the mineral. Iron and its other principal sulfide FeS could have been sequestered by these "surface metabolists" and transformed into FeS_2 with the concomitant release of an electron for use in the "organism's" metabolic processes.

Wächtershäuser is the first to admit that his theory is highly speculative. But it gains a certain degree of respectability from the existence of a rare type of bacteria that do in fact seem to use tiny particles of iron pyrites for metabolism. If Wächtershäuser's "surface metabolists" were able to break free of the mineral surface and close up their organic membranous coat to form a sac with a tiny lump of iron pyrites inside,[9] they could be considered to represent a very crude kind of organism—protocells containing their own batteries.

From *Designing the Molecular World* by G. M. Rawlins

New Words and Expressions

ultraviolet [ˈʌltrəˈvaiəlit]   *a.* 紫外（线）的   *n.* 紫外线辐射
delicate [ˈdelikit]   *a.* 精巧的，精致的，脆弱的，微妙的
prebiotic [ˌpriːbaiˈɔtik]   *a.* 生命起源以前的
invoke [inˈvəuk]   *v.* 求助，借助
inclement [inˈklemənt]   *a.* 险恶的，严酷的
bathymetric [ˌbæθiˈmetrik]   *a.* （海洋）深测术的
crack [kræk]   *n.* 裂缝
pore [pɔː]   *n.* 毛孔，小孔，气孔
magma [ˈmægmə]   *n.* 岩浆
vent [vent]   *n.* 通风孔，出烟孔，出口
mantle [ˈmæntl]   *n.* 覆盖物
Earth's mantle   地幔
turbid [ˈtəːbid]   *a.* 浑浊的，雾重的
hydrothermal [ˌhaidrəuˈθəːməl]   *a.* 热水的，热液的
marine [məˈriːn]   *a.* 海的，海产的，航海的
archaebacteria [ˌɑːkibækˈtiəriə]   *n.* 太古细菌，原始细菌
nutrient [ˈnjuːtriənt]   *a.* 有营养的
catastrophe [kəˈtæstrəfi]   *n.* 大灾难，大祸
pyrites [paiˈraitiːz]   *n.* 硫化铁矿

scenario [siˈnɑːriəu] n. 剧情
provoke [prəˈvəuk] vt. 引起,惹起,驱使
protagonist [prəuˈtægənist] n. (戏剧,小说中的)主角,领导者
peculiarity [piˌkjuːliˈæriti] n. 特性,怪癖
intriguing [inˈtriːɡiŋ] a. 引起兴趣(或好奇心)的,迷人的
fracture [ˈfræktʃə] v. (使)分裂,(使)破裂
multideck [ˈmʌltidek] n. 多层(板)
aluminosilicate [əˌljuːmənəuˈsilikeit] n. 铝硅酸盐
far-fetched [fɑːˈfetʃt] a. 牵强的,勉强的
facilitate [fəˈsiliteit] vt. 使便利,推动,促进
reminiscent [remiˈnis(ə)nt] a. 回忆往事的
inhibitor [inˈhibitə(r)] n. 抑制剂,抑制者
precellular [ˌpriːˈseljulə] n. 前细胞的
concomitant [kənˈkɔmitənt] a. 伴随的;n. 伴随物
metabolic [ˌmetəˈbɔlik] a. 新陈代谢的
speculative [ˈspekjulətiv] a. 推测的,投机的
metabolist [meˈtæbəlist] n. 新陈代谢者

Notes

1. NASA: National Aeronautics and Space Administration 美国国家航空航天局

2. 句中 sulfur-containing compounds 是 from 的宾语,formed in the volcanic environment and emitted from the vents 为 sulfur-containing compounds 的定语。参考译文:这些细菌获得的能量和养料至少有一部分是形成于火山环境、并从火山口中喷出的含硫化合物。

3. have little time for sth:对某事不感兴趣

4. DNA: deoxyribonucleic acid 脱氧核糖核酸

5. 句中 in which 引导定语从句,修饰 process。just as 引导的定语从句修饰 guiding framework。on which 引导介词从句修饰 template。参考译文:Cairns-Smith 指出晶体的生长经由一种模板导向的过程,在这个过程中晶体表面充当一个新层面形成的指导框架,就像单股 DNA 为形成新股 DNA 提供的模板一样。

6. 句中 This 是形式主语,指代上文中的 different crystal faces are known generally to grow at different rates。which 指代 means。参考译文:不同的晶体表面一般按照不同的速度生长可以提供一种途径。通过这一途径,具有微小差别的晶体类型就可以发生变异,并与其他的晶体类型按照进化论的观点竞争生长。

7. 参考译文:这种物质有类似三明治的多层结构,在带负电荷的硅酸铝层中充满了水和金属离子。

8. 参考译文:由一位德国有机化学家(现转行做了专利律师)提出的矿石假说,最近成为生命起源论的热点。

9. 如果 Wächtershäuser 的"表面代谢生物"能够不受矿物表面的约束而贴近它们的有机膜外表形成一个内有一小团黄铁矿的液囊,……

Exercises

Ⅰ. Comprehension

1. We can find the " hot springs " at ____.
   A. the floor of pacific ocean
   B. undersea where volcanic activity is strong
   C. the cracks and the pores in the rock under the sea

D. undersea where the seawater was heated by magma inside the earth

2. John Corliss thought that the hydrothermal vents were the places where living creatures appeared because that ____.

A. they had found the creatures such as clams, marine worms and bacteria in the hydrothermal vents

B. the hydrothermal vents provided a comfortable environment for living creatures

C. in hydrothermal vents, there had some chemical compounds to form organics and energy to drive that react

D. the hydrothermal vents had the same natural environment like that of the young earth

3. Which of the following is not true? ____

A. Stanley Miller didn't admit the vent theory.

B. "Minivents" made of iron pyrites could provide the mineral to form organic molecules.

C. Amino acids and sugars would fall apart at high temperature.

D. The debate of the vent theory will last.

4. According to paragraph 7 and 8, we can know that ____.

A. A. G. Cairns-Smith was a supporter of the vent model

B. Smith suggested that the organisms growed up via self-replicating by organic molecules

C. the structure of clay could be described as layers aluminosilicate between water and metal ions

D. crystals could be fractured easily either along or cross the planes of atoms

5. Clay minerals are sometimes good catalysts for reactions forming organic molecules because ____.

A. they can help the crystals to replicate

B. they can self-replicate

C. they have variable layer spacing and special constituent

D. they can control the growth of organisms

6. According to Wächtershäuser's theory, we can know all except ____.

A. it didn't concern the details of how molecules had formed but the energy which had driven the prebiotic chemistry

B. FeS_2 is a potential electron source because it might act as a kind of battery

C. the energy which has driven prebiotic chemistry is electron

D. his theory is speculative and there has no example to support it

II. Fill in the blanks with the appropriate forms of the verbs given in the brackets

1. Perhaps the only thing we can be sure of is that there ____ never ____ (be) any lack of ideas ban how organic compounds ____ (appear) on Earth to seed the beginning of life.

2. Many geologists now ____ (believe) that meteorites ____ (supply) substantial amounts of organic matter to the early Earth.

3. Much of what we know about extraterrestrial organic chemistry ____ (derive) from analyses of the rocky objects that find their way to Earth in the form of meteorites.

4. In the spectra of interstellar gas clouds, astronomers ____ (read) the signature of simple organics such as methanol.

5. There is nevertheless no doubt that its raw materials-Organic molecules-____ (form) in space.

6. The Swedish chemist ____ (propose) in 1908 that the seeds of life ____ (sow) by deep-frozen spores from another world, blown to earth by the radiation pressure of the stars.

III. Translation
1. 化学革命是周围变革中人们最不理解的变革。
2. 因此，我们要想了解世界，就得弄清什么是化学。
3. 机器的这一部分的材质是熟铁。
4. 从传导性的观点来看，铝是做电线的好材料。
5. 这种溶液马上就要沸腾起来了。

IV. Translation

In the 1950s the American chemist Harold Urey and his student Stanley Miller, working at the University of Chicago, set out to test this hypothesis. Miller proposed that the best way of testing whether organics could really have formed in the primitive atmosphere was to carry out an experiment that simulated the conditions on earth at that time (as far as these were known). Urey and Miller circulated a mixture of methane, ammonia, water and hydrogen (thought to mimic the composition of the early atmosphere) through a reaction vessel, heating the brew in one part of the cycle and allowing it to cool and condense in another, while in the gaseous state, an electrical discharge was passed through the mixture to simulated lightning. After running the experiment for a week, Urey and Miller found a mixture of organic compounds dissolved in the water that condensed in the cool part of the cycle, amongst which were substantial quantities of simple amino acids such as glycine and alanine.

V. Problem

(1) A liter of water contains 0.10 mole of solid FeS. Another contains 0.10 mole of solid HgS. What concentration of H_3O^+ is necessary to dissolve completely the precipitate in each case? Assume the total volumes remain at 1 liter. (K_{sp} for FeS is 3.7×10^{-19}; K_{sp} for HgS is 1×10^{-19}.)

(2) Calculate the concentrations of all solute species present in a solution made up of 0.10 mole of mole of H_2S in 1.00 liter of water ($K_{a1} = 9.1 \times 10^{-8}$, $K_{a2} = 1.0 \times 10^{-14}$).

Reading Material

How Chemistry Came to Life

It is a long way from granite to the oyster…

Ralph Waldo Emerson

The American chemist Julius Rebek has said that "once there was physics and there was chemistry but there was no biology". In other words, unless you are inclined to take a more biblical view, there seems to be no avoiding the conclusion that the former two begat the latter. While evolution from primitive to complex life is the concern of the biologist, the initial appearance of life on Earth sets a puzzle that physical science must solve. In earlier ages the fundamental question was: can life arise from chemistry alone? But now that we understand, in considerable measure, the replicating mechanism of DNA, the manufacture of protein, the chemical basis of photosynthesis, cell metabolism, immune responses and the host of other molecular processes on which life depends, few scientists would doubt that this question can be met with a resounding affirmative.[1] The issue has instead become that of *how* these exquisitely tuned (bio)chemical systems could have arisen spontaneously on a planet of rock, water and a mixture of simple gases. We don't yet have all the answers, but this chapter will look at how far we have come, and how far we have yet to go, in attempting to formulate a scientific account of the origin of life on Earth.

Some people view such attempts with distaste, even if they do not have a strong predilection for theological alternatives.[2] They may suggest that, if we achieve a purely scientific explanation for life and its origins, we will have somehow stripped our existence of any spiritual content. Curiously, this point of view seems to assume implicitly that such a complete understanding is possible—the argument is that we should not inquire too deeply, that we should knowingly and purposefully leave unexplored some of the mysteries of life *even though* such mysteries would in principle yield to rational investigation. Nothing, it seems to me, could be more damaging to the human spirit than to impose boundaries on the questions that we are permitted to ask or the territories that we may explore, so long as we do so with sensitivity and responsibility.[3] But the attitude in any case seems to me to display a profound failure of imagination. We have nothing to fear from a scientific origin of life. It will not rob us of our dignity, though it may enhance our humility. It will not come even close to explaining why we laugh or cry, nor even will it explain what motivates some of us to probe into such issues in the first place. It will not strip the world of mystery or excitement or romance. It should not even bring crashing to rubble our religious beliefs, if we have indeed invested them with any spiritual content. Life is, in all probability, a chemical process; but living it is perhaps something that is not even fully accessible to scientific enquiry.

Before the nineteenth century these dilemmas did not arise. Scientists then had a much simpler outlook. They considered that there were two types of substance: inorganic, such as that which comprised rocks, and organic, which was ultimately derived from living things. It was a basic tenet that, while one might be able to render organic matter "inert" in the sense of converting it to inorganic forms, the reverse operation was not possible—organic compounds could not be formed from purely inorganic ones. According to the eminent German chemist Baron Justus von Liebig, "one may consider that the reactions of simple bodies and mineral compounds…can find no kind of application in the study of the living organism".[4] Of course, this did not address the sticky question of where organic matter came from in the first place, but in those pre-Darwinian times the hand of God was ever ready to lend itself to difficult questions of this sort.

Biology and chemistry were therefore seen as distinct disciplines. At the same time, however, it was recognized that there were clearly similarities between the two: like chemistry, much of biology was concerned with the transformation of matter from one form to another. Living organisms take in organic matter as food and incorporate part of it into the body tissues, excreting the remainder as waste. But scientists saw no reason to suppose that these biological transformations need be bound by the rules of chemistry. Rather, organic substances were considered to be imbued with a "vital force" which distinguished them from inanimate matter. Inorganic or dead materials that entered the body could acquire vital properties and become part of the living organism; and the vital properties of living matter could be "worn away," leading to death. But only living organisms had the power to bestow vital properties—they could not appear spontaneously in inert matter. Indeed, it was widely believed that chemical and vital forces acted *in opposition*: the former acted to degrade organic materials, to render them inanimate, while the latter provided an organism's drive towards growth and reproduction.

The distinction between inorganic and organic chemistry was one that, during the nineteenth century, became ever harder to sustain. Chemical analyses of organic materials showed that they contained carbon and hydrogen, and commonly oxygen and nitrogen, as well as sulfur and phosphorus in some cases. All of these elements were to be found also in inorganic matter such as minerals. Chemists began to discover that it was possible to prepare compounds generally regarded as organic from inorganic starting materials: in 1828 the German Friedrich Wohler prepared urea from ammonium cyanate, a crystalline salt, and several decades later the French chemist Marcellin Berthelot combined carbon and hydrogen to form acetylene. The advent of thermodynamics, meanwhile, brought organic chemistry still closer in line with the inorganic branch by demonstrating that there was no need to distinguish a mysterious vital force from the energy changes that drive inorganic reactions.[5] Respiration, for instance, could be seem as an energy-(or heat-) liberating process in which food is combusted by atmospheric oxygen. There were undeniably differences between biochemical reactions and those of inorganic chemistry—the latter seemed to take place in a more controlled fashion, for example, and often seemed to operate in a concerted, organized manner. But chemists and biologists were ultimately forced to accept that, at the molecular level, there are no boundaries between their disciplines. Matter can pass back and forth from oxygen to inorganic materials, and the chemistry of life is subject to the same principles as the chemistry of gases, salts, minerals and metals.

Implicit in all of this are Julius Rebek's words, and their corollary that, at some point in the past, chemistry gave birth to biology.[6] We need not invoke a mysterious "spark of life" to nucleate living organisms on the planet, nor assume that vital forces were sent from God or gods to permeate matter. Life appeared spontaneously from lifeless matter. Here I will consider what we have deduced about how that happened; Latter text will say a little more about where and when. The question "why?" is not (yet) a scientific one, although no doubt it is the most interesting of all.

From *Designing the Molecular World* by G. M. Rawlins

New Words and Expressions

granite ['grænit]   *n.* 花岗岩，花岗石
oyster ['ɔistə]   *n.* 牡蛎
incline [in'klain]   *v.* 使倾向于
metabolism [me'tæbəlizəm]   *n.* 新陈代谢（作用）
immune [i'mju:n]   *a.* 免疫的
strip [strip]   *vt.* 清除，剥去
cyanate ['saiəneit]   *n.* 氰酸盐
thermodynamics [ˌθə:məudai'næmiks]   *n.* 热力学
acetylene [ə'setili:n]   *n.* 乙炔，电石气

Notes

1. 参考译文：但是现在，经过大量研究，我们了解了 DNA 的复制机理，蛋白质的产生，光合作用的化学基础，细胞的新陈代谢，免疫系统以及其他大量生命所依赖的分子作用过程。几乎没有科学家怀疑这个问题还有更合理的答案。

2. 此处 view 为动词，意"观看，认为"。参考译文：一些人对这些尝试表示厌恶，即使他们也不强烈地倾向于神学的解释。

3. 句中的 the questions 和 the territories 并列，做介词 on 的宾语，二者均后接 that 引

导的定语从句。do so 代替前面的 ask the question 和 explore the territories。参考译文：对于我们来说，如果我们确实以理智和负责的态度去对待它的话，似乎没有什么比强加在我们询问的问题上的限制、我们可以探索的领域上的制约更能造成对人的精神伤害了。

4. that 引导的是宾语从句。参考译文：人们可能认为在单体和矿物之间的反应对生命起源的研究没有任何借鉴作用。

5. 参考译文：随着热力学的到来，通过证明无需区分神秘的生命力与促使无机化学反应的能量变化，使得有机化学仍然与无机化学学科基本保持一致。

6. 参考译文：Julius Rebek 的话已暗示了所有的内容及它们的推论，即：过去的一些观点认为化学引出了生物学。

Unit 3 Fullerene Frenzy

After 1985, buckminsterfullerene acquired something approaching cult status. Everyone had heard of the *Nature* paper but most regarded it as a rather quaint curiosity. Kroto, however, became convinced that the molecule might provide the key to a whole new facet of carbon chemistry. Maybe here was a way to wrap up toxic or radioactive metal atoms in individualized carbon coatings. Perhaps C_{60} would make an excellent lubricant, since the carbon balls might roll over each other like ball bearings. The speculations were many and colorful; but they remained speculation all the same, because the stuff had been produced only in minute quantities, mixed up with all the other products of laser ablation. And because no one had succeeded in isolating significant amounts of the pure material, the experiments that could confirm the hypothetical soccer ball structure remained beyond reach.[1] In 1990, all that changed.

Like Harry Kroto, the physicists Donald Huffman at the University of Arizona in Tucson and Wolfgong Krätschmer at the Max Planck Institute for Nuclear Physics in Heidelberg had in the early 1980s become interested in the possibility that novel carbon molecules might be formed in stellar atmospheres and interstellar space. The two physicists collaborated in 1982 on experiments in which they vaporized graphite by electrical heating and measured the properties of the black soot that was produced. Huffman and Krätschmer studied how this soot absorbed ultraviolet light so as to compare the absorption spectra with those measured by astronomers. They found that their soot behaved much like that produced in ordinary combustion except for some features in the ultraviolet spectrum that were not observed for normal soot.[2] At that time, they concluded that the extra features were due to impurities that had crept into the vaporization chamber, perhaps the oil used in the vacuum pump. It was not until three years after the 1985 *Nature* paper had been published that Huffman realized that perhaps what he and Krätscher had seen back in 1982 was the signature of C_{60}.[3]

Huffman's idea was received with some skepticism by Krätschmer, but the two agreed that the idea was worth testing further. When Krätschmer's group at Heidelberg measured the mass spectrum of the carbon soot produced by heating graphite with an electrical arc discharge, they saw immediately the prominent C_{60} peak. After some trial-and-error adjustments, the researchers were able to produce C_{60} in relatively large quantities-a few milligrams—with their simple arc-discharge technique. These amounts would certainly be sufficient for the experiments that could establish the structure beyond doubt, but the obstacle that remained was the need to extract pure C_{60} from the rest of the detritus. Early in 1990, Krätschmer, Huffman and their respective students Kostantino Fostiropoulos and Lowell Lamb tried heating the soot so that part of it sublimed; when cooled, the vapor condensed back to a solid. Part of this solid dissolved in liquid benzene to give a deep red solution, and evaporation of the benzene solvent left reddish brown crystals. Mass spectrometric analysis revealed that they contained 90 percent C_{60}, the remainder being C_{70}.[4] Here at last was the opportunity to put the soccer ball structure to the test. By bouncing X-rays off the crystals, the researchers were able to deduce that the crystals comprised stacks of spherical molecules with their centers about a nanometer (one thousand-millionth of a meter) apart-just what was expected for regular arrays of C_{60} balls. In August 1990, Krätschmer and Huffman described their new method for isolating C_{60} and their evidence for the soccer ball structure in a paper in *Nature*. To Kroto the news of this success came both as a delight and as a bitter blow.[5] It showed that he and the Rice group had guessed right after all in 1985, but

Krätschmer and Huffman's breakthrough had beaten his own efforts by a whisker. Kroto had experimented with a similar arc-discharge technique in 1986, but had been severely hampered by a lack of financial backing. He had caught wind of the advances that Krätschmer and Huffman were making in 1989 when they presented a preliminary report of their work at a conference, and had resurrected the arc-discharge apparatus.[6] But he and his colleagues at Sussex faced the same problem of extracting the C_{60} from the soot. By August of 1990 Kroto's colleague Jonathon Hare hit on the benzene separation method independently, and obtained the red solution. But by then the race was already run, since Krätschmer and Huffman had managed the crucial last step of getting crystals out of the solution. When Nature asked Kroto to act as a referee of the paper sent by Krätschmer and Huffman he realized that his group had been beaten to the finishing post.[7]

All the same, the Sussex team took advantage of the fact that, with their red solution already to hand, they were at least ahead of other rival groups at that stage. By the end of August they had performed the test that clinched the case for the predicted structure of the molecule—a test that was missing from the paper of the predicted structure of Krätschmer and Huffman, although their conclusions could scarcely be doubted for all that. The experiment involved the use of a technique called nuclear magnetic resonance (NMR) spectroscopy, which showed that every one of the sixty carbon atoms is equivalent—just as is predicted for the soccer ball structure. These NMR experiments also confirmed the rugby ball structure of C_{70}.

The jury was in: C_{60} is a molecular soccer ball. Within months of publication of Krätschmer and Huffman's recipe for mass-producing C_{60} everyone was playing the game. Soon the molecules were to be seen lined up in neat rows under a new kind of microscope called the scanning tunneling microscope. Organic chemists started to explore how C_{60} behaves in chemical reactions. Most theoretical calculations predicted that it would be a relatively stable, unreactive molecule, like benzene. But it turns out to be not so difficult to open up the double bonds in the carbon cage: hydrogen and fluorine, for example, can be attached to the carbon atoms. The balls have been attached to the backbone of long, chain-like polymer molecules, like a string of lucky charms. In an electrochemical cell, C_{60} was found to take up additional electrons to form negative ions such as C_{60}^{1-} and C_{60}^{2-}, implying that it should form "salts" with metals, just as if it were an unusually large atom resembling, say, chlorine.

This led researchers at AT&T Bell Laboratories in New Jersey to react C_{60} with the alkali metals lithium, sodium, potassium, rubidium and cesium. While ionic salts were indeed formed, these compounds proved to be far stranger than the researchers had anticipated. It will suffice to say here that these experiments showed C_{60} to be not only the most interesting molecule to have come the way of chemists for many years, but also to have some astonishing revelations in store for physicists too. Compounds of C_{60} and metals now provide one of the main focuses of C_{60} research.

A particularly intriguing variety of these compounds appear to contain metal atoms inside the cage. These so-called endohedral ("inside the polyhedron") structures are made by forming fullerenes from a composite of graphite and a metal compound. The first were synthesized by Jim Heath almost immediately after he, Kroto and the Rice team discovered the molecule itself in 1985, by applying the laser ablation method to rods of graphite mixed with lanthanum oxide. They found that individual lanthanum atoms became intimately associated with the C_{60} cage; the obvious corollary was that they were trapped inside. As many as four metal atoms have now been trapped inside a fullerene shell.

From *Designing the Molecular World* by G. M. Rawlins

New Words and Expressions

lubricant [lu:brikənt]　　n. 润滑剂
ablation [æb'leiʃən]　　n. 消融，熔损
hypothetical [ˌhaipəu'θetikəl]　　a. 假设的，假定的
interstellar ['intə(:)'stelə]　　a. 星际的，星球与星球间的
astronomer [ə'strɔnəmə(r)]　　n. 天文学家
trial-and-error ['traiəl-ænd-erə]　　n. 反复试验法
obstacle ['ɔbstəkl]　　n. 障碍（物）
detritus [di'traitəs]　　n. 残屑，沉渣
sublime [sə'blaim]　　v. （使）纯化，（使）升华
nanometer ['neinəˌmi:tə]　　n. 纳米
hamper ['hæmpə]　　v. 妨碍，牵制
resurrect [ˌrezə'rekt]　　v. 复活，重新使用
rival ['raivəl]　　n. 竞争者，对手
rugby ['rʌgbi]　　n. 橄榄球
recipe ['resipi]　　n. 处方，制法，
fluorine ['flu(:)əri:n]　　n. 氟（9号元素，符号F）
alkali ['ælkəlai]　　n. 碱　a. 碱性的
lithium ['liθiəm]　　n. 锂
sodium ['səudjəm, -diəm]　　n. 钠
potassium [pə'tæsjəm]　　n. 钾（19号元素，符号K）
rubidium [ru:'bidiəm]　　n. 铷
cesium ['si:zjəm]　　n. 铯
anticipate [æn'tisipeit]　　vt. 预期，期望
lanthanum ['lænθənəm]　　n. 镧
corollary [kə'rɔləri]　　n. 结果，推论

Notes

1. that 引导的定语从句修饰 experiments，说明是什么样的实验。参考译文：能够确定想像的足球结构的实验仍然无法实现。

2. 句子结构为：they found ＋ that 引导的宾语从句，此 that 为连词。句中第二个 that 为代词，代 soot。第三个 that 为关系代词，用以引导名词之后的限定从句，尤指表示事物，代 some features。参考译文：他们发现：除了在紫外光谱上具有普通烟灰所没有的一些特性外，这些烟灰的行为与普通燃烧中的烟灰行为非常相似。

3. signature 意为"签字，信号"，指发现 C_{60} 的征兆。参考译文：直到3年后的1985年，《自然》上的论文发表后，霍夫曼才意识到他和 Krätschmer 在1982年发现的就是 C_{60}。

4. the remainder being…为独立结构，being 前省略了 be。此种结构在句中主要做状语，此处为一种补充说明。这种结构主要有 n+to v, n+v-ing, n+v-ed, n+n 等。另外的例子如：Everywhere you see people in their holiday dresses, their faces shining with smiles.

5. 参考译文：对克罗图来说，这个成功消息的到来既是喜悦也是沉重的打击。

6. 当 Krätschmer 和霍夫曼在一次会议上呈交关于他们工作的初步报告时，他认识到他们在1989年的工作的先进性，并重新发展了电弧-放电仪器。

7. 参考译文：当《自然》杂志要克罗图做 Krätschmer 和霍夫曼的论文审稿人时，他认识到他的小组的工作已经落到了后面。

Exercises

I. Comprehension

1. We can deduce from the article that ____.
   A. the difficulties lied in the experiment stimulate the Sussex team to proceed
   B. Kroto and his colleges came across the solution to extracting the C_{60} from the soot with the hint of Huffman
   C. Harry Kroto thought that novel carbon molecules might be formed in the outer space
   D. in an experiment, Huffman and Krätschmer found that the studied soot behaved in line with what they had assumed

2. We can draw a conclusion that if Kroto had enough money ____.
   A. he could not succeed because there were other obstacles in the experiment
   B. he could not succeed because the collaborators were not so smart compared with those of other teams
   C. he could succeed because there was only one step to the end
   D. maybe he would succeed although there were other obstacles in the experiment

3. It could be inferred from the passage that the experiment performed by the Sussex team showing the structure of C_{60} ____.
   A. is a necessary supplement to the paper of Krätschmer and Huffman
   B. to compete with other groups although they fell behind the Krätschmer and Huffman
   C. had been done by the Krätschmer and Huffman but they omitted it in the paper presented to *Nature*
   D. to confirm their leading position in this domain

4. From the article we could deduce that C_{60} is a compound that ____.
   A. whose mass on chemical scale is 60
   B. whose structure could not be inferred
   C. which consists of 5 dozen of carbon atoms
   D. owing to the impurities, the spectra of C_{60} was different from that of the ordinary combustion

5. The first compound—metal atoms contained inside a cage—was synthesized ____.
   A. after Huffman and Krätschmer publicized their recipe for mass-producing C_{60} in *Nature*
   B. after the Sussex team could handle the benzene separation method
   C. not much long after Kroto and the Rice team discovered the molecule
   D. after Kroto get the news that Krätschmer and Huffman could separate the C_{60}

II. Fill in the blanks with the phrases given below. Change the forms where necessary

abide by	above all	access to	at the end of
be burst into	be familiar with	be good to	combine…with
glance at	in addition to	in spite of	

1. The precept he presented was too severe to ____.
2. Switzerland has ____ the sea via the River Rhine.
3. You should ____ this kind of classification method.
4. He ____ the front page.
5. The fruit ____ people's health.
6. The volcano ____ eruption.
7. I've been looking after four young children all day and I really am ____ my tether!
8. ____ the names on the list there are six other applicants.

9. ____ the fact that his initial experiments had failed, Prof. White persisted in his research.

10. He longs ____ (else) to see his family again.

11. It's important for us to ____ revolutionary sweep ____ practicalness.

III. Problem

(1) Predict the Lewis structure of CO_2.

(2) Predict the shape of stannous chloride ($SnCl_2$).

Reading Material

Crystals That Flow

In Langmuir-Blodgett films the amphiphiles have generally been compressed enough in the Langmuir trough, prior to being deposited on the solid surface, to represent truly two-dimensional crystals.[1] But the molecules within the bilayers of vesicles are more mobile and less orderly in their packing arrangement—more like the liquid—condensed phase of Langmuir films. These bilayers are examples of molecular structures that are said to be liquid crystalline. The term "liquid crystal" is now such a familiar one, in these days of liquid crystal displays (LCDs) in watches, clocks and hifi systems, that one can easily overlook the oxymoron it represents. Think about it: by definition a crystal is a substance in which the molecules are highly ordered over long distances, yet a liquid can *flow*, implying that the molecules must be free to move and therefore must surely be packed together in a rather haphazard fashion. How can a substance be both a liquid and a crystal?

This, indeed, was the puzzle facing the discoverers of liquid crystals-Friedrich Reinitzer, an Austrian botanist, and Otto Lehmann, a German physicist. In 1888 Reinitzer synthesized a new organic compound with a most peculiar nature. The compound, cholesteryl benzoate, was derived from the cholesterol molecule, which we encountered earlier as a component of some cell membranes. Reinitzer crystallized the benzoate derivative and duly set about characterizing it according to the standard methodology of organic chemists of the time (which is much the same today): he measured the melting point of the crystal. What perplexed him was that melting of cholesteryl benzoate appeared to be a two-stage process: the crystals became liquid at 145.5 degrees Celsius, but the cloudy liquid then turned clear at 178.5 degrees. There seemed to be two kinds of liquid state, something for which Reinitzer knew of no precedent.

In perplexity the botanist sent a sample of his compound to Lehmann, who was known to be an expert in microscopic studies of crystallization. Lehmann observed that the cloudy form of the liquid exhibited a property called birefringence, which is a characteristic of many crystals that display double refraction. Double refraction occurs when the effective speed of light in a material differs in different directions. In such materials the plane of polarized light may become rotated as the light passes through the material—this is birefringence.

Lehmann was astonished to find that the first liquid state of cholesteryl benzoate is birefringent. In crystals this property derives from the ordered structure, which means that the properties may differ in different directions. In a normal liquid, on the other hand, the molecules drift about at random, so that on average one direction should look like any other. The only possible explanation for the behavior of Reinitzer's compound seemed to be that it possessed some degree of nonrandom, orderly structure. Here, apparently, was a new, fourth state of matter: neither gas, liquid nor solid, but a " soft " or " liquid " crystal. [2] Under a polarizing microscope, in which polarized light is used to illuminate the sample, the birefringence of liquid crystals gives rise to a variety of beautiful colored patterns.

In 1924 the German Daniel Vorlander showed that liquid crystalline material are comprised of molecules with long, rod-like shapes. The realization soon followed that the molecular order in liquid crystals resides in the orientation of these rods. Materials comprised of spherical particles can possess only one kind of order.[3] a regularity in the positions of the particles. But for assemblies of rods, order can also be present in the form of a regularity in the rods' orientations. Regularity in position and in orientation is independent, in that one does not necessarily imply the other. In a crystal formed from rod-like molecules, the simplest kind of periodic array has them packed side by side and all lined up in the same direction—there will be order of both position and orientation. Above the melting point, the rods can jostle around so as to lose positional order but may retain some degree of orientational order, remaining pointed in the same direction on average. The proximity of a molecule's neighbors prevents it from tilting too far out of alignment.[4] This is a liquid crystal phase, in which there is no regularity in the positions of their molecules but there is, on average, a well-defined orientational preference.

There are several degrees of disorder through which a liquid crystalline material can pass when its crystals are melted. Just a little above the melting point, the thermal motions of molecules may be insufficient to disrupt the layered structure of the crystal, so that the rods maintain this structure even though within each layer there is no positional order. This liquid crystalline phase does retain a degree of positional order perpendicular to the layers, and is called the smectic phase. Two varieties of smectic phase are common—when the orientation of the rods is perpendicular to the layers, the phase is the smectic A, while if the average orientation is tilted relative to the layers the phase is the smectic C. Seven types of smectic phase are currently known.

More pronounced thermal motions will break down the layers of the smectic phase, removing all vestiges of positional order. Orientational order, however, may remain, in that a preferred direction of the rod-like molecules can still be identified. This phase is called nematic. At greater temperatures still, the molecules will jiggle about so vigorously that even orientational order will be lost—the rods rotate and point in all directions at random. The material is then no longer a liquid crystal but a true (isotropic) liquid. The liquid crystalline phases, occurring between the crystal and the liquid, are called mesophases—"middle phases".

The clear phase of cholesteryl benzoate observed by Reinitzer and Lehmann was the true liquid phase; but the cloudy phase had neither the smectic nor the simple nematic arrangement described above. The structure of this phase is complicated further by the fact that molecules of cholesteryl benzoate are chiral—they have a handedness. For chiral molecules, the nematic phase can lower its free energy by developing a screw-like twist of the direction in which the molecules point.[5] The origin of this twist lies with the molecules' preference to lie at a slight angle to their neighbors, rather than aligning in parallel fashion as in a regular nematic phase. The result of this preference is a helical rotation of the orientation throughout the liquid crystal. This twisted phase takes its name from the compound in which it was first observer—cholesteric.

The pitch of the helix in cholesteric phases is generally of the same order of magnitude as the wavelengths of visible light, so that these phases reflect light much as crystals scatter X-rays. This wavelength—dependent reflection gives rise to iridescent colors; the iridescence of some beetle cuticles and butterfly markings stems from the formation of cholesteric phases by the molecules that comprise the tissues.

Rod-like molecules are not alone in their ability to form orientationally ordered liquid crystalline phases. Indeed, any molecules that are not essentially spherical should in principle be able to show orientational ordering, and in crystals many molecules do.[6] In the fluid state, however, only those that have a pronounced degree of nonsphericity can retain some of this order. For example, the opposite extreme to a molecule that is stretched out into a rod is one that is flattened into a disc. Orientationally ordered arrangements of discs are very familiar — just think of a stack of dinner plates or gramophone records.

The Indian physicist Sivaramakrishna Chandrasekhar of the Raman Research Institute predicted in the 1970s that disc-like molecules might form stacked, "discotic" liquid crystalline phases. In 1977, Chandrasekhar discovered the first discotic phase. Researchers have predicted that, if these stacks are formed from molecules that can act as electron acceptors and donors, electrons might be passed down the stacks as if along "molecular wires". An increase in conductivity has indeed been observed when porphyrin molecules with metal ions at their centers form discotic phases.

From *Designing the Molecular World* by G. M. Rawlins

New Words and Expressions

amphiphile [ˌæmˈfifil] n. 两亲物，两性分子
deposit [diˈpɔzit] vt. 沉积，堆积
vesicle [ˈvesikl] n. 小囊，水泡
mobile [ˈməubail] a. 可移动的，易变的
oxymoron [ˌɔksiˈmɔːrən] n. 矛盾修饰法
haphazard [ˈhæpˈhæzəd] a. 偶然的，随便的
botanist [ˈbɔtənist] n. 植物学家
cholesteryl benzoate [kɔlˈlestəriˈbenzəuˌeit] n. 胆甾醇苯甲酸酯
cholesterol [kəˈlestərəul, -rɔl] n. 胆固醇
methodology [ˌmeθəˈdɔlədʒi] n. 方法学，方法论
perplexed [pəˈplekst] a. 困惑的，不知所措的
perplexity [pəˈpleksiti] n. 困惑，茫然
birefringence [ˌbairiˈfrindʒins] n. 双折射（现象）
refraction [riˈfrækʃən] n. 折光，折射
orientation [ˌɔ(ː)rienˈteiʃən] n. 方向，取向，倾向性
perpendicular [ˌpəːpənˈdikjulə] a. 垂直的，正交的
smectic [ˈsmektik] a. 近晶相的
vestige [ˈvestidʒ] n. 遗留物，残余
nematic [niˈmætik] a. n. 向列相（的），丝状的
chiral [ˈtʃirəl] a. 手征（性）的
helical [ˈhelikəl] a. 螺旋状的
pitch [pitʃ] n. 程度，斜度
discotic [ˈdiskəutik] a. 盘柱状的

Notes

1. Langmuir-Blodgett film：L-B 膜，即朗缪尔-布罗杰特膜；amphiphile 在化学上意为

"两亲物"，为既能溶于水又能溶于油的物质。参考译文：在朗缪尔-布罗杰特膜中，两亲物通常于沉积在固体表面之前，在朗缪尔槽中被充分压缩，它代表了真正的二维晶体。

2. …neither gas, liquid nor solid, but a "soft" or "liquid" crystal.

参考译文：不是气体、液体，也不是固体，而是一种"软"或"液态"的晶体。

3. 参考译文：由球形颗粒组成的物质可以只有一种取向。

4. 参考译文：相邻分子互相接近可以防止它们倾斜而远离中心。

5. nematic phase 向列相，是液晶的一种相态。参考译文：对于手性分子，向列相可通过分子指向类螺旋方向以降低自由能。

6. 参考译文：实际上，任何本质上不是球形的分子在原理上应能够表现出取向有序性，并且在晶体中很多分子都是这样的。

Unit 4 Drinking Water Quality and Health

The main consideration in ensuring the safety of public water supplies is the elimination of the agents of waterborne infectious disease. In the last century, major epidemics of typhoid and cholera in Britain and elsewhere in Europe were only eliminated when their bacteriological origin was recognized, the contamination of water supplies with sewage was eliminated and disinfection treatment was introduced.[1] In the UK, the Croydon typhoid epidemic of 1937 led to chlorination of all public water supplies. From then until 1986, 34 outbreaks of waterborne disease were recorded in the UK. Of these outbreaks, 21 were due to public water supplies and resulted from disinfection failure or contamination of treated water. Some new problems affecting the microbiological safety of water supplies have emerged in recent years, but the basic approach of securing the adequacy of disinfection with several lines of defence, while maintaining an efficient monitoring strategy, has resulted in the achievement of an excellent record of safety.[2]

Concern about the possibility of health effects associated with the chemical components of drinking water only really developed in the second half of the 20th century, although early drinking water standards included limits for lead and some other toxic elements.[3] The main upsurge of interest in chemical aspects of water quality stemmed from the application of gas chromatography later coupled with mass spectrometry, in the 1970s and 1980s. Originally focused on pesticides, these and subsequent developments in analytical technology revealed for the first time the presence in water of a wide range of organic compounds at trace levels. The precise significance to health of these is still uncertain, but some would undoubtedly cause concern were they present at much higher concentrations. Acute health effects of the chemical constituents of drinking water are very unlikely, but effects due to exposure to low concentrations over a lifetime are feasible, although they are likely to be small and very difficult to measure.

With a shortage of clear evidence of health effects on humans, precautionary limits for chemicals in drinking water, based on toxicological evaluations have been developed and applied by national and international organizations such as the World Health Organization, the US Environmental Protection Agency, Health and Welfare Canada, the European union and others.[4] These limits cover both inorganic and organic chemicals. In 1971, the World Health Organization proposed a total of nine limits for chemicals in drinking water, eight inorganic and one organic. By 1993, in the WHO "Guidelines for Drinking Water Quality", this number had grown to a total of 94, of which 22 were for inorganics, 72 for organics. This period has therefore been associated with a remarkable increase in the complexity of drinking water standards.

Apart from any potential effects on health, the chemical composition of drinking water is of considerable importance in relation to its acceptability to the consumer in terms of appearance, taste, smell, hardness and corrosiveness.[5]

The present quality requirements for public water supplies in England and Wales are defined in regulations made under the Water Supply (Water Quality) Regulations 1989. Essentially similar regulations have been established for Scotland and Northern Ireland. UK regulations must comply with a European Union Directive on the quality of water intended for human consumption.

The Directive lays down limits for 44 contaminants that member states are required to regulate. Thus the Directive provides the basis of national legislation on minimum drinking water quality within the European Union. There is nothing to prevent more stringent limits or limits for a wider rage of contaminants from being included in national regulations.[6] For example, drinking water quality regulations for the UK include an additional 11 standards.

The World Health Organization (WHO) published "Guidelines for Drinking Water Quality" in 1984 and in 1993. These are up-to-date reviews and recommendations by international experts and are intended to provide guidance to national organizations worldwide with responsibilities for setting drinking water standards.[7] The WHO guidelines have no legal status, but they are widely referred to as a source of reliable information on health aspects of drinking water quality.

The basis of the EU Directive on Drinking Water Quality, which came into force in 1985, has never been published, but it seemed to be based to some extent on WHO Drinking Water Standards published in 1970. The Directive has been widely criticised on scientific grounds and it is now under review with particular reference to the most recently published WHO Guidelines.

The WHO Guidelines are used as the basis of national drinking water standards worldwide, but there can be many variations to take account of local circumstances. WHO stress the need to consider guideline values in the contest of local or national environmental, social, economic and cultural conditions.

Lead levels in untreated natural waters are normally very low and lead in drinking water is almost entirely due to lead pipes in household plumbing and service connections, often but not invariably in combination with soft water.[8] Where there is "plumbosolvency" the concentration of lead increases with the period of contact with the lead pipe, maximum levels arising in morning "first draw" samples. The use of lead is avoided in modern plumbing systems, but many older properties in the United Kingdom still have lead pipes, even in soft water areas. Apart from lead pipes, lead may be a constituent of solders, alloys used in water fittings and PVC pipes, all of which may be in contact with drinking water.

Lead is a general toxicant that accumulates in the skeleton and its presence in drinking water is highly undesirable. Blood lead levels are commonly used as an index of recent exposure to lead and several studies have indicated a correlation between blood lead and water lead extending down to concentrations below $50\mu g/L$ of lead in drinking water, the current EU limit. The fact that such low levels of lead in drinking water can produce a detectable elevation of blood lead in a population is not a harmful effect in itself although it gives rise to concern about the possibility of consequential problems.[9] Of particular importance is the possibility of neuro-physiological effects influencing learning ability and general behavior in children, who with pregnant women and infants are considered to be the most sensitive group of the population.[10] On the basis of a thorough review of the evidence, a health based guideline value of $10\mu g/L$ lead in drinking water was developed by WHO in 1993.

Of the possible remedies for plumbosolvency, water treatment is the most attractive, although it may present problems in isolated areas with a large number of small unmanned sources. Careful adjustment of the pH to between 8.0 and 8.5, sometimes with the addition of orthophosphate, has proved in several cases to be effective in reducing lead levels at the tap to below $50\mu g/L$. There is no chance however, that a limit of $10\mu g/L$ will be achievable by water treatment and the only remedy will be the complete replacement of lead with a more suitable material. This is an extremely expensive option and one that WHO has recognized will take time to achieve. Where plumbosolvency is known to be a problem, everything must be done to reduce the exposure of consumers by controlling the corrosiveness of the water and by advising them to avoid "first draw" water.

The concentration of lead in water that has been through a lead pipe varies according to factors such as the contact time and flow and it is especially important to ensure that the conditions of sampling are adequately specified when water is monitored for compliance with a lead standard.

There is considerable evidence that nitrate levels in water have increased in the United Kingdom since the 1960s and although the increased use of nitrogenous fertilizers has been blamed for this situation, it has been shown that additional factors need to be taken into account. These include changes in land use, in particular the conversion of pasture into arable land, and increased recycling of sewage effluent in lowland waters.

Limits for nitrate in drinking water are based on its effect on a blood disease, methaemoglobinaemia, in bottle fed infants. The 1970 WHO European Drinking Water Standards included a desirable limit for nitrate of 50mg/L (as NO_3^-), levels between 50 and 100mg/L (as NO_3^-) being "acceptable" provided that medical authorities are warned of the possible danger of infantile methaemoglobinaemia. The EU Drinking Water Directive included a Maximum Admissible Concentration (MAC) of 50mg/L (as NO_3^-) and this was set by WHO as a Guideline Value in 1993. Water supplies containing nitrate levels exceeding 50mg/L potentially affect approximately on million people in the UK, but there is no evidence of a problem with infantile methaemoglobinaemia.

There has been considerable interest in the possibility that ingested nitrate can be reduced to nitrite in the adult stomach leading, in the presence of secondary amines, to the endogenous synthesis of *N*-nitroso compounds. The significance of *N*-nitroso compounds is that many are highly carcinogenic in laboratory animals and there has been concern that high nitrate levels in water could be associated with an increased incidence of cancer of the gastrointestinal and urinary tracts. The overall picture in the UK does not, however, support this. Not only have gastric cancer rates been decreasing while nitrate levels have been increasing, but many of the areas showing the highest rates of gastric cancer have a low level of nitrate in their water supply.[11]

A WHO Working Group reviewed the available evidence for an association between nitrate levels in water and gastric cancer. It concluded: "There is no convincing evidence of a relationship between gastric cancer and consumption of drinking water containing nitrate at or below the present Guideline Value; above this level the evidence is inconclusive".

From *Pollution by R. T. Packham*

New Words and Expressions

waterborne ['wɔːtəbɔːn] *a.* 水中的，水传播的
epidemic [ˌepiˈdemik] *n.* （风尚等的）流行，流行病
typhoid ['taifɔid] *n.* 伤寒症，伤寒的
cholera ['kɔlərə] *n.* 霍乱
sewage ['sjuː(ː)idʒ] *n.* 污水，下水道
chlorination [ˌklɔːriˈneiʃən] *n.* 氯化，用氯处理
disinfection [ˌdisinˈfekʃən] *n.* 消毒
adequacy ['ædikwəsi] *n.* 适当，足够
pesticide ['pestisaid] *n.* 杀虫剂，农药，防疫药
acute [əˈkjuːt] *a.* 急性的，剧烈的

precautionary [pri'kɔːʃənəri]   a. 预防的
plumbing ['plʌmiŋ]   n. 管道（制品）
toxicant ['tɔksikənt]   n. 有毒物，毒药
orthophosphate [ˌɔːθəu'fɔsfeit]   n. 正磷酸盐
corrosiveness [kəˌrəu'sivnes]   n. 侵蚀，腐蚀
nitrate ['naitreit]   n. 硝酸盐
nitrogenous [nai'trɔdʒinəs]   a. 氮的，含氮的
fertilizer ['fəːtiˌlaizə]   n. 肥料（尤指化学肥料）
pasture ['pɑːstʃə]   n. 草原，牧场
arable ['ærəbl]   a. 可耕的，适于耕种的
methaemoglobinaemia [meθiːməuglətubi'niːmiə]   n. 正铁血红蛋白血症
nitroso [nai'trəusəu]   a. 亚硝基的
carcinogenic [kɑːsinə'dʒənik]   a. 致癌物（质）的
gastro-intestinal [ˌgæstrəuin'testənl]   a. 肠胃的

Notes

1. 该句主句主要成分为 major epidermics…were…eliminated，从句由 when 后三个并列句子充当：…origin was recognized，the contamination…，…treatment was introduced. 参考译文：上个世纪，当人们认识到细菌的起因，消除了下水道水污染，引入了消毒处理后，英国和欧洲其他国家的主要流行病：霍乱和伤寒基本消灭了。

2. 该句主要成分为：new problems have emerged，but the basic approach…has resulted. 其中 while maintaining an efficient monitoring strategy 为插入语修饰 the basic approach. Of securing the adequacy of disinfection with several lines of defence 为后置定语。参考译文：近来出现了一些影响水系统微生物安全性的新问题。但是在保持有效监控策略的同时，通过数种合适的消毒措施保持足够的安全性却使其达到了记录史最高水平。

3. 该句主句主要成分为 concern developed. 其他成分为后置定语。参考译文：尽管早期饮用水标准中已经包含了铅及其他有毒元素的标准，但 20 世纪后半叶以来，人们对健康因素与饮用水中化学成分关系的关注却仍在不断增加。

4. with 结构为伴随状语，on toxicological evaluations 为插入语，修饰 precautionary limits. 参考译文：由于缺少影响人类健康的鲜明证据，以毒理学估计为基础，许多国家、国际组织采取对饮用水中化学成分的预防限制。例如：世界健康组织、美国环境保护署、加拿大健康及福利社、欧盟等。

5. apart from：除……外；in terms of：根据；considerable：相当（大）的。参考译文：除了考虑对健康的任何潜在影响外，饮用水的化学成分在消费者的可接受性方面也是相当重要的，它涉及外观、味道、气味、硬度和腐蚀性等。

6. prevent from：使……不做……，避免……。参考译文：对更大范围内的污染物进行更严格的限制，必须包含在自然法规中。

7. provide M with N：……向 M 提供 N。参考译文：这是世界专家所做的最新综述和建议。并且，提出这些是为了负责地给世界范围内的国家机构提供制订饮用水标准的指导。

8. be due to：由……引起。句子结构：为并列句，由第一个 and 相连接。参考译文：在未处理的自来水中铅含量通常很低，在饮用水中铅几乎是完全由家庭自来水管道和设施连接处的铅管道所带来的，它经常但不总是与软水联系在一起。

9. 句子结构：the fact 主语，后由 that 引导定语从句。参考译文：饮用水中如此低的铅

含量可以导致监测血液总量的增加,虽然它引起了对可能的结果的关注,但这一事实本身并非坏事。

10. 该句为倒装结构,正常语序为:the possibility of neuro-physiological effects influencing learning ability and general behavior in children, who with pregnant woman…of the population, is of particular importance. 参考译文:影响儿童学习能力、一般行为的神经生理学因素是最重要的,这些儿童以及孕妇、婴儿是人口中的最易感人群。

11. 句子结构:not only…but…。参考译文:当硝酸盐含量升高时胃癌发生率降低,而且胃癌发生率最高的许多地方在其水供应中硝酸盐含量也很低。

Exercises

Ⅰ. Comprehension

1. The uniqueness of the compound's structure is ____ to learning its synthesis and its application.
   A. necessary   B. fundamental   C. ubiquitous   D. important

2. The structure ____ of this molecule leads to its various usage.
   A. flexibility   B. conversation   C. change   D. difference

3. There is a wide range of compounds at trace levels that cannot be thoroughly ____ from the water.
   A. separated   B. considered   C. make out   D. eliminated

4. What's the main idea of this text? ____
   A. There are many regulations for public water supplies for different organizations.
   B. Lead is harmful to people's health.
   C. Nitrate leads to gastric cancer.
   D. Water carries many chemical components that result in various diseases.

5. What happens when people are exposed to low concentrations of chemical constituents? ____
   A. They will suffer serious disease.
   B. They will show acute health effects.
   C. They will be sick over a long time, sometimes a lifelong time.
   D. They will not be affected by the exposure.

6. What kind of evidence shows that chemicals in drinking effect human health? ____
   A. There are clear evidences for it.
   B. No evidence shows it.
   C. Though no clear evidence, there are really some precautions for it.
   D. Lead is harmful to people's health.

7. Which organization does the European Union is preferred to follow its legislation on minimum drinking water quality? ____
   A. W. H. O.
   B. Directive.
   C. The U. S. Environmental Protection Agency.
   D. Health and Welfare Canada.

8. What's the reason that led is still a danger to man's health? ____
   A. Man has no immune system against it.
   B. Man is easily suffered disease caused by lead, even in trace level.
   C. There is a great deal of things made by lead around us.
   D. Although lead is seldom used now, there still exist many older lead properties in use.

9. There is no evidence that nitrate-contained water will cause gastric cancer, because ____.
   A. the increase in nitrate level sometime result to a decrease in gastric cancer rates
   B. nitrate concentration in drinking water never exceeds 50ml/L
   C. nitrogenous fertilizer has been banded for a long time
   D. the changes in land use are stopped

II. Fill in the blanks with appropriate prepositions

1. some chemicals are accumulated in the bodies of certain organisms, concentrations ____ them reflecting environmental pollution levels over time.

2. Nonyl-phenols were suspected ____ stimulating vitellogenin production in the trout.

3. Clearly, some chemical in the effluent was behaving ____ a female hormone and the fish provided an early warning of a potential problem requiring urgent investigation.

4. This compound is normally produces in the liver of female fish in response to the hormone oestradiol and is incorporated ____ the yolk of developing eggs.

5. The amount of change in the community will be related ____ the severity of the incident.

6. the definition of pollution given ____ includes the adverse effects on living resources and ecological systems so that impacts need quantifying.

7. The measured quantities can then be compared ____ standards of allowable concentrations.

8. Water pollution can be defined ____ the introduction by man into the environment of substances or energy liable ____ cause hazards to health, harm to living resources and ecological systems, damage to structure or amenity, or interference ____ legitimate uses of the environment.

9. How people design computer games is ____ me.

10. Anyone with an annual income of ____ 5000 may be eligible to apply.

III. Translation

1. 饮水中毒的例子有时是触目惊心的。

2. 生物耗氧量（biological oxygen demand）的定义是与1L废水中的还原剂作用所需的O_2质量（mg）。

3. 人体中大部分的水是喝进去的，但是相当一部分来自食物，还有相当一部分水是人体对食物中的氢原子进行氧化时生成的。

4. 但是应该清醒地认识到即使是最先进的检测方法也有可能放过一些会产生新的意想不到的后果的有害物质。

5. 这种疾病称为正铁血红蛋白血症（methemoglobinemia），是婴儿紫绀综合征（blue-baby syndrome）的病因之一——婴儿的水分和氧气需要量很大，而由于亚硝酸盐的存在，他们的血红蛋白值却很低。

IV. Translation

One of the major sources of organic pollution is effluents from sewage treatment works. In the United Kingdom, such effluents are supposed, as a minimum requirement, to meet the Royal Commission Standard, allowing no more than 30mg/L of suspended solids and 20mg/L BOD (a 30∶20 effluent). A dilution with at least eight volumes of river water, having a BOD of no more than 2mg/L, is required to achieve this standard. Unfortunately, the design capacities of many sewage treatment works are below the population they now have to serve. This may cause chronic pollution of rivers or result in periodic flushes of poor quality water that damages the aquatic community. In the majority of poorer countries of the world there are few, or indeed often no, sewage treatment facilities and the faecal contamination of water results in many parasitic infections and waterborne diseases such as dysentery, cholera and poliomyelitis. Contaminated water supplies still cause more than two million deaths a year and countless more illnesses.

V. Problem

Calculate K_a and pK_a for water.

Reading Material

Modern CO_2 Applications

Natural sources of carbon dioxide are found in many places where there are cracks in the earth's crust due to volcanic activity. One such region is in Germany east of the Rhine. It was here that Carl Gustaf Rommenhöller bought a spring called the Victoria-Mineralbrunnen in 1881. Sales grew rapidly and concessions were taken out on several sources in competition with other newly formed companies. As early as 1889, due to the high cost of distribution, Rommenhöller began to manufacture carbon dioxide in Berlin, from coke combustion. Nowadays carbon dioxide is produced from mineral oils by fermentation or combustion.

Controlled Atmospheres

Before 1939, "gas storage" was practiced commercially only in the United Kingdom. Controlled atmosphere storage began later in the United States, with its commercial debut in 1942. In the first English "gas stores", fruit packages were made gas-tight and it was left to the fruit itself to create an atmosphere enriched in CO_2 for long storage. It was soon found that the results were better if the oxygen content of the atmosphere was reduced as the CO_2 content increased.

Carbon dioxide fertilizer was tried in greenhouses and is now in general use for increasing plant production.

Fire-Fighting Equipment

From 1870, carbon dioxide was used in what were known as "fire grenades" and in patent fire extinguishers. In these, carbonic acid was created by crushing glass ampules containing sulfuric acid onto sodium bicarbonate (Fig. 4.1). In 1875 Dick's Patent Fire Exter-

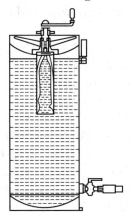

Fig. 4.1 carbon dioxide grenade and fire extinguisher, early fire-fighting equipment from the 1800s

minator was designed having a sealed glass phial of sulfuric acid suspended above a solution of sodium bicarbonate. Upon pushing in a metal pin the acid bottle was broken and the acid mixed with the sodium bicarbonate, which expelled the solution. This was the basis of the modern soda-acid extinguisher.

Other extinguishers contained a mixture of acid and alkaline chemicals which reacted with each other to produce carbon dioxide gas. The gas formed kept the contents under pressure, so they were expelled when a tap was opened. This type of extinguisher, however, could leak gas and so might fail to work when required. A further development in the 1930s of the chemical reaction principle led to the foam extinguisher, in which sodium bicarbonate, with a stabilizer to strengthen the bubbles, and a solution of aluminum sulfate are mixed when required to form fill the bubbles and force the foam out of the extinguisher. The foam blankets the flames and extinguishes them by cutting off their contact with air.

Extraction with Supercritical or Liquid CO_2
Carbon dioxide can be used as a solvent in two different physical states: as a liquified gas and under supercritical conditions. Some of the recent developments use both states.

The first observations of the solvent power of liquid carbon dioxide and of substances dissolving in supercritical gases were made over a century ago.[1] Since then various research ideas have led to practical processes and to the first commercial plants to exploit the solvent power of liquid and supercritical carbon dioxide. In 1861, G. Gore published his observations that camphor and naphthalene were soluble in liquid carbon dioxide. H. Buchner in 1906 published a major study of phase systems of carbon dioxide with many organic liquids. He found that acetone, ether, carbon disulfide, benzene, etc., were miscible with liquid carbon dioxide and that many other compounds showed some solubility. Salts were not soluble in liquid carbon dioxide.

Although much research work was done on supercritical systems, it was not until the 1930s that the first patents began to appear. A U. S. patent was issued to S. Pilat and H. Godlewicz for the use of supercritical carbon dioxide, and F. J. Horvath patented the use of liquid carbon dioxide to concentrate coffee, fruit juices, and essential oils.

In the late 1960s a semitechnical extraction plant was in use at Krasnodar in southern Russia. Their work using liquid carbon dioxide showed that many essential oils could be extracted in greater quantity and with superior quality than with steam distillation. Other experimental work showed that the aroma in tobacco could be boosted by an extract from tobacco waste. At about the same time the staff of the U. S. Department of Agriculture, Western Research Laboratory, in California was working on the extraction of flavors from many fruit and vegetable sources.

In the late 1960s work was done in the Nestlé Company's laboratories which led to the granting of a patent for the carbon dioxide extraction of freeze-dried extract from coffee.[2] Instant coffee powder was then given a richer aroma by the addition of this aroma extract. Since the 1970s supercritical fluid extraction has also been used for decaffeination of coffee (e.g., Kaffee Hag in Germany) and tea (Fig. 4.2). In the same way nicotine is removed from tobacco for low-nicotine cigarettes. Some successful attempts have also been made at extracting flavors used by the food and beverage industries. Brewers have long used this method for to extract the flavor of hops. Many new applications have appeared to extract flavor, color, and fragrance compounds from spices, herbs, fruits, and other materials. Cholesterol removal is another new market.

From the 1990s supercritical carbon dioxide has been used by Airco/BOC and Lummus

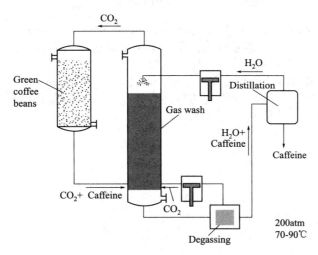

Fig. 4.2 sketch of extraction process for the decaffeination of coffee

Crest as a solvent to treat waste water.

From *History of Industrial Gades* by Almqvist, Ebbe

New Words and Expressions

gas-tight ['gæs'tait] a. 不漏气的，气密性的
greenhouse ['griːnhaus] n. 温室，花房
grenade [gri'neid] n. 消防弹，灭火弹
extinguisher [ik'stiŋgwiʃə(r)] n. 熄灭者，灭火器
ampule ['æmpuːl] n. 小型密封玻璃瓶，安瓿（装液体的密封小瓶）
sulfuric acid [sʌl'fjuərik'æsid] n. 硫酸
sodium bicarbonate ['səudjəm, bai'kɑːbənit] n. 碳酸氢钠，小苏打
exterminator [ik'stɛːmineitə(r)] n. 消防者，灭火者
soda ['səudə] n. 苏打
alkaline ['ælkəlain] a. 碱的，碱性的
aluminum [ə'ljuːminəm] n. 铝
supercritical [ˌsjuːpə'kritikəl] a. 超临界的
camphor ['kæmfə] n. 樟脑
naphthalene ['næfθəliːn] n. 萘（球），卫生球
acetone ['æsitəun] n. 丙酮
ether ['iːθə] n. 醚，乙醚
carbon disulfide ['kɑːbən, dai'sʌlfaid] n. 二硫化碳
miscible ['misibl] a. 易混合的
freeze-dry [friːz-drai] vt. （冷）冻干（燥）
aroma [ə'rəumə] n. 芳香，香气，香味
decaffeination [diˈkæfiəˈneiʃən] n. 脱咖啡因，不含咖啡因
nicotine ['nikətiːn, -tin] n. 烟碱，尼古丁
fragrance ['freigrəns] n. 芬芳，香气，香味
spice [spais] n. 香料，调味品
herb [həːb] n. 药草，香草

Notes

  1. 该句子的主干部分为：observations were made over a century ago，主语的修饰成分由 and 连接的两个部分构成。参考译文：在一个世纪以前，人们就已经观测到了液态二氧化碳的溶解力，以及物质溶解在超临界气体中现象。

  2. which 引导的名词性从句做定语，修饰 the Nestlé Company's laboratories。Extract：浓缩物。参考译文：在 20 世纪 60 年代的后期，Nestlé 公司的实验室利用二氧化碳从咖啡中提取冷冻浓缩物。为此，他们获得了专利。

PART TWO
THE FUNDAMENTALS OF CHEMISTRY

Unit 5 The Periodic Table

As our picture of the atom becomes more detailed, we find ourselves in a dilemma.[1] With more than 100 elements to deal with, how can we keep all this information straight? One way is by using the periodic table of the elements. The periodic table neatly tabulates information about atoms. It records how many protons and electrons the atoms of a particular element contain. It permits us to calculate the number of neutrons in the most common isotope for most elements. It even stores information about how electrons are arranged in the atoms of each element. The most extraordinary thing about the periodic table is that it was largely developed before anyone knew there were protons or neutrons or electrons in atoms.

Not long after Dalton presented his model for the atom (an indivisible particle whose mass determined its identity), chemists began preparing listings of elements arranged according to their atomic weights. While working out such tables of elements, these scientists observed patterns among the elements. For example, it became clear that elements that occurred at specific intervals shared a similarity in certain properties. Among the approximately 60 elements known at that time, the second and ninth showed similar properties, as did the third and tenth, the fourth and eleventh, the fifth and twelfth, and so on.[2]

In 1869, Dmitri Ivanovich Mendeleev, a Russian chemist, published his periodic table of the elements. Mendeleev prepared his table by taking into account both the atomic weights and the periodicity of certain properties of the elements. The elements were arranged primarily in order of increasing atomic weight. In a few cases, Mendeleev placed a slightly heavier element before a lighter one. He did this only when it was necessary in order to keep elements with similar chemical properties in the same row. For example, he placed tellurium (atomic weight = 128) ahead of iodine (atomic weight = 127) because tellurium resembled sulfur and selenium in its properties, whereas iodine was similar to chlorine and bromine.

Mendeleev left a number of gaps in his table. Instead of looking upon those blank spaces as defects, he boldly predicted the existence of elements as yet undiscovered.[3] Furthermore, he even predicted the properties of some of these missing elements. In succeeding years, many of the gaps were filled in by the discovery of new elements. The properties were often quite close to those Mendeleev had predicted. The predictive value of this great innovation led to the wide acceptance of Mendeleev's table.

It is now known that properties of an element depend mainly on the number of electrons in the outermost energy level of the atoms of the element. Sodium atoms have one electron in their outermost energy level (the third). Lithium atoms have a single electron in their outermost level (the second). The chemical properties of sodium and lithium are similar. The atoms of helium and neon have filled outer electron energy levels, and both elements are similar, that is, they do not undergo chemical reactions readily. Apparently, not only are similar chemical properties shared by elements whose atoms have similar electron configurations (arrangements) but also certain configurations appear to be more stable (less reactive) than others.

In Mendeleev's table, the elements were arranged by atomic weights for the most part, and this arrangement revealed the periodicity of chemical properties. Because the number of electrons determines the element's chemical properties, that number should (and now does) determine the order of the periodic table. In the modern periodic table, the elements are arranged according to atomic number. Remember, this number indicates both how many protons and how many electrons there are in a neutral atom of the element. The modern table, arranged in order of increasing atomic number, and Mendeleev's table, arranged in order of increasing atomic weight, parallels one another because an increase in atomic number is generally accompanied by an increase in atomic weight. In only a few cases (noted by Mendeleev) do the weights fall out of order. Atomic weights do not increase in precisely the same order as atomic numbers because *both protons and neutrons* contribute to the mass of an atom.[4] It is possible for an atom of lower atomic number to have more neutrons than one with a higher atomic number. Thus, it is possible for an atom with a lower atomic number to have a greater mass than an atom with a higher atomic number. Thus the atomic mass of Ar (no. 18) is more than that of K (no. 19), and Te (no. 52) has a mass greater than that of I (no. 53); see the periodic table.

The modern periodic table has vertical columns called groups or families. Each group includes elements with the same number of electrons in their outermost energy levels and, therefore, with similar chemical properties. The horizontal rows of the table are called periods.[5] Each new period indicates the opening of the next main electron energy level. For example, sodium starts row three, and the outermost electron in sodium is the first electron to be placed in the third energy level. Because each row begins a new energy level, we can predict that the size of atoms increases from top to bottom. And since electrons are easier to remove when farther from the nucleus, we can also predict that the larger the atom the lower its *ionization energy*, the energy needed to remove an electron.

In chemistry, the elements are grouped into one of two broad classifications: *metals and nonmetals*. Metals are generally hard, lustrous elements that are *ductile* (can be drawn into wires) and malleable (can be pounded into thin sheets). We also know they readily conduct electricity and heat. Many metals form the strong framework on which our modern society is built. The discovery and use of metals over 5000 years ago moved civilization beyond the Stone Age.[6] The second type of element is noted by its lack of metallic properties. These are the nonmetals. Nonmetals are generally gases or soft solids that do not conduct electricity. There are some notable exceptions to these general properties, however. There are also examples of very hard nonmetals and very soft metals. For example, a form of the nonmetal carbon (diamond) is one of the hardest substances known. Mercury, a metal, is a liquid at room temperature. Still, almost everyone has a general idea of what a metal is like. In addition to these physical properties, there are some very important chemical differences between metals and nonmetals, which we will explore in a later chapter. The division between metallic and nonmetallic properties is not sharp, so some elements have intermediate properties and are sometimes classified as a separate group.

Classifying the elements doesn't stop with the division of elements into these two groups. We find that all metals are not the same, so further classification is possible. It's like classifying the human race into two genders, men and women, but then finding that they can be further subdivided into personality types (e. g., extroverts and introverts). The first thing we note about metals is that some are chemically unreactive. That is, elements such as copper, silver, and gold are very resistant to the chemical reactions of corrosion and rust. These are the metals of coins and jewelry, not only because of their comparative rarity and beauty but also because of this chemical inertness. For this reason, they are known as the *noble metals*. Gold and silver coins on the ocean bottom, deposited from ships that foundered hundreds of years ago, can be easily polished to their original luster. Other metals are very much different. They are extremely reactive with air and water. In fact, metals such as lithium, sodium, and potassium must be stored under oil because they react violently (to the point of explosion) with water. These metals are among those known as the *active metals*. Thus, copper, silver, and gold can be placed into one family of metals and lithium, sodium, and potassium into another. Similar relationships among other elements were also noticed and appropriate grouping were made.

So far, our main emphasis concerning the periodic table has been on the vertical columns, which contain the families of elements. In fact, there are common characteristics in the horizontal rows as well. Horizontal rows of elements in the table are called periods. Each period ends with a member of the family of elements called the noble gases. These elements, like the noble metals, are chemically unreactive and are composed of individual atoms. The first period contains only two elements, hydrogen and helium. The second and third contain 8 each, the fourth and fifth contain 18 each, the sixth 32, and the seventh 26. (The seventh would also contain 32 if there were enough elements.)

Each group is designated by a number at the top of the group. The most commonly used label employs Roman numerals followed by an A or a B. Another method, which eventually may be accepted, numbers the groups 1 through 18. It is not clear at this time which method will win out, or if some alternative will yet be proposed and universally accepted.

From *Inorganic chemistry* by T. W. Swaddle

New Words and Expressions

tabulate ['tæbjuleit]   vt. 把……制成表格
isotope ['aisəutəup]   n. 同位素
atomic weight [ə'tɔmikweit]   n.. 原子量
tellurium [te'ljuəriəm]   n. 碲
iodine ['aiədain]   n. 碘,碘酒
chlorine ['klɔ:ri:n]   n. 氯
bromine ['brəumi:n]   n. 溴
helium ['hi:ljəm, -liəm]   n. 氦
neon ['ni:ən]   n. 氖
configuration [kən,figju'reiʃən]   n. 构型,结构,配置,外形
atomic number [ə'tɔmik'nʌmbə]   n. 原子序数
ionization energy [,aiənai'zeiʃən'enədʒi]   n. 电离能
ductile ['dʌktail]   a. 易拉长的,可塑的
malleable ['mæliəbl]   a. 有延展性的,可锻的
mercury ['mə:kjuri]   n. 水银,汞
corrosion [kə'rəuʒən]   n. 侵蚀,腐蚀
noble metal [nəubl'metl]   n. 贵金属,惰性金属

Notes

1. As…伴随状语从句，picture 意为描述，be in a dilemma 意为处于进退两难之地。参考译文：随着对原子的描述越来越详尽，我们发现自己处于进退两难之地。

2. Among…介词短语作状语，主要结构 the second…showed…properties，as did…从句表示下面的并列主语也具有上面的谓语部分。参考译文：当时已知的约 60 种元素中，第 2 种元素与第 9 种元素表现出相似的性质，第 3 种元素与第 10 种元素，第 4 种元素与第 11 种元素等也都具有相似的性质。

3. Instead of…：插入语，意为代替…，he…predicted…，其中 undiscovered 为后置定语。参考译文：Mendeleev 在他的周期表中留下一些空格，他非但没有将那些空格看作缺憾，反而大胆地预测还存在着仍未被发现的元素。

4. Because…原因状语从句，in…order 意为以……的顺序，the same as 意为与……一样。参考译文：因为原子质量是质子和中子质量的加和，故原子量并不完全随原子序数的增加而增加。

5. 主要结构 Each…indicates…the opening…参考译文：每一新周期预示着下一主电子能级的开始。

6. 主要结构 The discovery and use of…moved…beyond…。参考译文：五千多年前，金属的发现和使用将人类文明带出石器时代。

Exercises

Ⅰ. **Comprehension**

1. From the first paragraph, we can get information about the periodic table except ____.
   A. the periodic table is very useful in tabulating information about atoms
   B. the periodic table can tell us the number of protons and electrons of each elements contain
   C. the periodic table records how many neutrons in the atoms directly
   D. the periodic table implicated the information of the electrons' arrangement in the atoms

2. We can infer from the passage that the periodic table ____.
   A. is first presented by Dmitri Ivanovich Mendeleev
   B. is arranged the list of elements only according to their atomic weights
   C. comprises more than to elements at first time
   D. is placed two similar elements every seven elements

3. According to the passage, which is true among the following sentences? ____
   A. In Mendeleev's periodic table, the lighter element was placed before a heavier one.
   B. Mendeleev had made many valuable predictions of the undiscovered elements.
   C. The properties of an element were determined by the number of the electrons in the outer energy level of the atom.
   D. According to the periodic table, the sodium and tellurium have similar chemical properties.

4. From Mendeleev's periodic table, we can conclude that ____.
   A. the elements' arrangement brought to light the periodicity of chemical properties
   B. the number of electrons determined the element's chemical properties and the number of protons determined the order of the periodic table
   C. Mendeleev's table arranged in order of the same rules as the modern table
   D. the atomic number is also increasing with the atomic weight

5. Which sentence best states the modern periodic table? ____
  A. In modern table, each period includes elements with the same number of electrons in their outermost energy levels.
  B. In one group, elements have similar chemical properties and the same electron energy levels.
  C. The size of atoms and the activity of electrons can be predicted with the number of the element's period.
  D. In the modern table, the activity of the atoms is increasing from left to right.

6. Owing to their electron structure, the noble gases have some special character's as ____.
  A. all the noble gases exist in the atmosphere, but they are all rare
  B. because of their reactivity, the noble gases don't undergo reactions and all exist in monatomic states
  C. because of their stability, the compounds of noble gases would hardly be formed by chemical reaction
  D. because of their tiny portion of the atmosphere, the noble gases can't be concentrated by special container

7. The noble gases share a similarity in certain properties. for example ____.
  A. helium is the most useful noble gas and can take the place of hydrogen in all aspects
  B. Helium, argon and neon have the same number of electrons in their outermost energy
  C. All of the noble gases are unreactive in chemical reactions readily
  D. krypton and xenon have no important commercial applications

II. Fill in the blanks with the words given in the following

alkali metals   alkaline earth metals   chalcogens   halogens
metals   noble gases   nonmetals   transition metals

Certain groupings of elements in the periodic table are designated by special names. The heavy, stepped, diagonal line on the table divides the elements into two major classed. Those to the left of the line are called ____, and those to the right, ____. Group I A elements are known as ____; Group II A are ____; Group VII A, ____. Group VI A elements are known as the ____. The group at the extreme right of the table contains the ____. All the Group B elements are called ____.

III. Decide whether the following statements are True or False

1. The periodic table records the number of protons and how many electrons the atoms of a particular element contain.

2. The periodic even stores information about how electrons are arranged in the atoms of each element.

3. In the modern periodic table, the elements were arranged primarily in order of increasing atomic weight.

4. It is now known that properties of an element depend mainly on the number of electrons in the all energy level of the atoms.

5. The chemical properties of sodium and potassium are similar because they all have a single electron in their outermost level.

6. The number of electrons determines the elements' chemical properties and the order of the periodic table.

7. The noble gases are exceptionally resistant to chemical reaction, this lack of reactivity is a reflection of their electron structure.

8. The periodic law states that the properties of elements are periodic functions of their

atomic numbers.

9. The Mendeleev's periodic table has vertical columns called groups or families.

10. After Mendeleev presented his model for the atom, chemists began preparing listings of elements arranged according to their atomic weights.

Ⅳ. Make a sentence out of each item by rearranging the words in brackets

1. All of the gaseous elements (which do exist/except for the noble gases, /as individual atoms, /diatomic molecules/are composed of).

2. Many of the nonmetals exist (as diatomic molecules/that individual atoms/rather).

3. Room temperature, (is the standard reference temperature/exactly 25 ℃, /used to/which is defined as/describe physical state).

4. most of the familiar elements (as examples/that we will discuss and use/in this text are representative elements).

5. In the last decade of the nineteenth century (one completely unexpected/a series of elements/that made up an entirely new family, /by Mendeleev and his contemporaries/was discovered).

Ⅴ. Translation

1. 除汞外所有的金属在室温下均为固体，而且它们的原子排列的很有规则，通常彼此靠的很紧，以便占有最小的空间。

2. 直到1854年左右，铝才开始进行工业规模的生产。

3. 这两种元素不仅在常温下不起化合作用，即使在高温下也不发生明显的反应。

4. 二者都是无色气体，但像所有气体一样可以液化。

5. 这两种化合物的分离即便并非没有可能，也是十分困难的。

Ⅵ. Arrange the following aqueous acids in order of increasing acidity

HSO_4^-, H_3O^+, C_2H_5OH, H_4SiO_4, $HSeO_4^-$, CH_3GeH_3, NH_3, AsH_3, $HClO_4$, HSO_3F

Ⅶ. Problem

(a) Describe the geometry of the ammonia molecule NH_3 (an AB_3 molecule).

(b) Draw the structure of H_2O (AB_2 molecule) according to EPRT.

Reading Material

The Halogens

The chemistry of fluorine, chlorine, bromine and iodine is probably better understood than that of any other group of element except the alkali metals. This is partly because much of the chemistry of the halogens is that of singly bonded atoms or singly charged anions, and partly because of the wealth of structural and physicochemical data for most of their compounds. The fundamentals of inorganic chemistry are very often best illustrated by the discussion of the properties of these elements and of the halides, and among the topics treated earlier in this book are the bond energies in the halogens and hydrogen halides, force constants for these molecules, the electronegativities of the halogens, the structures of many metal halides, lattice energies and standard enthalpies of formation of metal halides, the properties of halide ions in solution, the ionisation of the hydrogen halides and their relative efficiencies for the protonation of weak bases, complex halide formation in solution, hydrogen fluoride and bromine trifluoride as non-aqueous solvents and hydrogen bonding in HF, NH_4F, and the HF_2^- and HCl_2^- ions. Further, each of Chapters 10~15 has included a section on halides of the elements under consideration. The pseudo-halide ions CN^- and N_3^- and their derivatives were described in Sections 13.12 and 14.3 respectively. Most of this chapter will therefore be taken up by the discussion of the halogens themselves, their oxides and oxo-acids, and interhalogen compounds and polyhalogen ions, but we shall also take the opportunity to remind the reader (often by means of cross-references) of some general aspects of the chemistry of halogen-containing compounds.

As in the last chapter, we shall confine the systematic treatment almost entirely to the stable elements. Astatine, the homologue of iodine, is known exclusively in the form of radioactive isotopes, the longest-lived of which have half-lives of only about eight hours; one of these, ^{211}At, an α-emitter, is obtained by the nuclear reaction. $^{209}_{83}Bi(\alpha,2n)$ and $^{211}_{85}At$ may be separated by vacuum distillation at 500℃. Tracer studies (which are the only sources of information about the element) show that astatine is less volatile than iodine, is soluble in organic solvents, and is reduced by sulphur dioxide to an anion which is coprecipitated with AgI or TlI, i.e. At^-.[1] Hypochlorite or peroxodisulphate oxidises astatine to an anion that is carried by IO_3^- (e.g. in precipitation of $AgIO_3$) and is therefore probably AtO_3^-; less powerful oxidising agents such as bromine also oxidise it, probably to AtO^- or AtO_2^-.

Most of the differences in inorganic chemistry between fluorine and the other halogens can be attributed to the restriction of the valence shell of fluorine to an octet of electrons, the relatively small sizes of the fluorine atom and the fluoride ion, and the low dissociation energy of the F_2 molecule; but it is sometimes also necessary (as it very often is in organic chemistry) to invoke the less rigidly defined power of attracting an electron within a stable molecule (the electronegativity) of fluorine.[2] Manifestations of the octet restriction are that fluorine forms no compounds analogous to ClF_3, $HClO_3$ or Cl_2O_7, and where it is simultaneously bonded to two atoms (e.g. in the fluorine bridges of the polymeric forms of many transition metal pentafluorides), the M—F—M bridge bonds invariably have greater M—F distances than the corresponding terminal M—F bonds, indicating that they are of order lower than unity, probably three-centre two-electron bonds. The weakness of the bond in F_2 is generally attributed to repulsion between the pairs of unshared electrons on each atom (it is noteworthy that the O—O and N—N bonds in H_2O_2 and N_2H_4 are also weak). When fluorine is bonded to other elements, the bond in the fluoride is always stronger than that in the corresponding chloride, and where there are no unshared pairs of electrons on the combined atom of the other element (or where the other element has a large atom so that repulsion is minimised) the bond in the fluoride is much stronger than that in the chloride; for example the bond energy terms in NF_3 and NCl_3 are 272kJ/mol and 193 kJ/mol, in PF_3 and PCl_3 they are 490kJ/mol and 319 kJ/mol, and in CF_4 and CCl_4 they are 485kJ/mol and 327kJ/mol respectively. The small size of the fluorine atom not only permits high coordination numbers in molecular fluorides, but it also leads to better overlap of atomic orbitals and hence to shorter and stronger bonds. The volatility of molecular fluorine compounds (e.g. of fluorocarbons, which often have boiling-points little different from those of the corresponding hydrocarbons) originates in the weakness of the van der Waals' or London dispersion forces in these compounds, which may in turn be correlated with the low polarisability and small size of the fluorine atom. Consequences of the smallness of fluoride ion include high coordination numbers in saline fluorides, high lattice energies and very negative standard enthalpies of formation of these compounds, and a large negative standard enthalpy and entropy of hydration of the ion. The high electronegativity of fluorine is involved in the strong hydrogen bonding in hydrogen fluoride, the strength of fluorine-substituted carboxylic acids, the deactivating effect of the CF_3 group in electrophilic aromatic substitution, and the non-basic character of NF_3 and $(CF_3)_3N$.

In some ways the relationship between iodine, which has the lowest ionisation energy of the elements in Table 16.1, and the other halogens is like that between tellurium and oxygen, sulphur and selenium. Although none of the halogens has yet been shown to form a stable monatomic cation, complexed or solvated I^+ is well established in species such as $I(py)_2^+$ and $I(cryptand)^+$ salts, and appears to be present in solutions obtained by the interaction of iodine and silver salts,[3] e. g.

$$I_2 + AgClO_4 \xrightarrow{Et_2O} AgI + IClO_4$$

The corresponding bromine- and chlorine-containing species are less stable, though they are probably involved in aromatic bromination and chlorination in aqueous solution. Further, iodine displays higher oxidation states in the halides ICl_3 and IF_7 than bromine or chlorine in their corresponding halides. Hydrogen iodide in solution is the strongest acid among the hydrogen halides, and solid periodic acid is not HIO_4, analogous to $HClO_4$ and $HBrO_4$, but H_5IO_6 or $OI(OH)_5$. Polyatomic cations X_2^+ and X_3^+ are known for chlorine, bromine and iodine, those of iodine being most stable; these species are discussed in Section 16.5.

The stable isotope of fluorine, ^{19}F, has a nuclear spin magnetic quantum number of 1/2, and ^{19}F nuclear magnetic resonance spectroscopy is a valuable tool in the elucidation of the structures and reaction mechanisms of fluorine compounds. There is, unfortunately, no convenient radioactive tracer for fluorine (^{18}F, the most suitable isotope, has a half-life of only 109 min), but neutron activation analysis based on the formation and estimation of ^{20}F (half-life 12s) can be used for the determination of the element, e. g. in fluorine dating of bones and teeth. These originally contain *apatite*, $Ca_5(OH)(PO_4)_3$; when they are embedded in the soil this mineral is slowly converted into the less soluble *fluorapatite*, $Ca_5F(PO_4)_3$; the fluorine content can therefore be used to estimate the age of remains, preferably in conjunction with ^{14}C dating of the organic matter present. The lower solubility of fluorapatite, incidentally, constitutes the thermodynamic basis for the argument in favour of fluoridisation of drinking water: teeth having a higher fluoride ion content are more resistant to attack and decay. Concentrations of F^- above 1 ppm ($1 ppm = 10^{-6}$), however, are harmful.

Fluorine occurs chiefly as *fluorspar* or *fluorite* (CaF_2), cryolite (Na_3AlF_6) and *fluorapatite* Cryolite is used as such in the aluminium industry, but most fluorine compounds are obtained from fluorspar via hydrogen fluoride, which is manufactured by the action of concentrated sulphuric acid on the mineral. Chlorine is made almost entirely from sodium chloride, which occurs as solid deposits in many places, by electrolysis of the aqueous solution;[4] sodium hydroxide is a by-product of the reaction. When chlorine is used for the chlorination of organic compounds, the hydrogen chloride which is also formed may be dissolved and electrolysed to regenerate further chlorine. Bromine is obtained from sea-water or from the residual liquid after the extraction of carnallite. In either case, the solution is acidified to pH 3.5 and a mixture of chlorine and air is then swept through it to liberate and remove the bromine. Iodine is obtained mostly from natural brines occurring in the USA and Japan, or from sodium iodate, present in small amount in Chile saltpetre (sodium nitrate). In the former process the iodide present is oxidised by the requisite quantity of chlorine water; in the latter, controlled reduction by sulphur dioxide produces elemental iodine, complete reduction yields sodium iodide. The most important fluorine compounds on an industrial scale are hydrogen fluoride, boron trifluoride, calcium fluoride (as a flux in metallurgy), synthetic cryolite and chlorofluorocarbons. Chlorine, in addition to its major use for the preparation of organic compounds, is employed as a bleaching and sterilising agent. Bromine and iodine are used mainly for the preparation of organic compounds; additional uses include the production of silver bromide for photography. Iodine is an essential constituent of the thyroid hormones; a deficiency in it causes goitre.

From *Inorganic chemistry* by *T. W. Swaddle*

New Words and Expressions

hydrogen halide ['haidrəudʒən'hælaid] *n.* 卤化氢
ionization [ˌaiənai'zeiʃən] *n.* 离子化，电离
trifluoride [ˌtrai'fluəraid] *n.* 三氟化物
interhalogen [ˌintə'hælədʒən] *n.* 杂卤素，杂卤化合物
polyhalogen [ˌpɔliˈhælədʒən] *n.* 多卤素
astatine ['æstəti:n] *n.* 砹（元素符号 At）
sulphur ['sʌlfə] *n.* 硫（元素符号 S），*a.* 含硫的
coprecipitate [ˌkəupri'sipiteit] *v.* 共沉淀
hypochlorite [ˌhaipəu'klɔ:rait] *n.* 次氯酸根，次氯酸盐
peroxodisulphate [pə'rɔksəudisʌlfeit] *n.* 过二硫酸盐
oxidize ['ɔksiˌdaiz] *v.* （使）氧化
dissociation energy [diˌsəuʃi'eiʃən'enədʒi] *n.* 离解能
pentafluoride [ˌpentə'fluəraid] *n.* 五氟化物
coordination [kəuˌɔ:di'neiʃən] *n.* 配位作用
hydrocarbon ['haidrəu'kɑ:bən] *n.* 烃，碳氢化合物
dispersion force [dis'pə:ʃenfɔ:s] *n.* 色散力，分散力
saline ['seilain, sə'lain] *a.* 盐的
hydration [hai'dreiʃən] *n.* 水合，水合作用
species ['spi:ʃi:z] *n.* （物）种，种类
cryptand ['kriptənd] *n.* 穴状配体
apatite ['æpətait] *n.* 磷灰石
fluorapatite [fluə'ræpətait] *n.* 氟磷灰石
fluoridisation [ˌfluərədəˈzæʃən] *n.* 氟化作用
fluorspar ['flu(:)əspɑ:] *n.* 萤石，氟石
cryolite ['kraiəlait] *n.* 冰晶石，氟铝酸钠
aluminium [ə'lju:miniəm] *n.* 铝
electrolyse [iˌlektrəlaiz] *vt.* 电解
carnallite ['kɑ:nəlait] *n.* 光卤石（$KCl \cdot MgCl_2 \cdot 6H_2O$）
brine [brain] *n.* 盐水，海水
saltpeter [sɔlt'pi:tə] *n.* 硝石，硝酸钾
boron ['bɔ:rɔn] *n.* 硼
calcium ['kælsiəm] *n.* 钙
metallurgy [me'tælədʒi] *n.* 冶金学，冶金术
thyroid ['θairɔid] *a.* 甲状腺的 *n.* 甲状腺
hormone ['hɔ:məun] *n.* 荷尔蒙，激素

Notes

1. 主要结构 tracer studies…show that… (astatine is…, is…and is…), which 为定语从句，修饰 anion。参考译文：示踪研究（元素的唯一信息源）表明砹没有碘易挥发，可溶

于有机溶剂，并能被二氧化硫还原为能与 AgI 或 TlI 形成共沉淀的阴离子 At^-。

2. 主要结构 it is…necessary to invoke…；the less rigidly defined 为 power 的前置定语；within…修饰 power；stable molecule of fluorine 中的 of 表示同位，即稳定分子氟分子；invoke 意为引用，使用，实施。参考译文：但是，有时有必要（在有机化学中常见）使用并未严格定义的稳定氟分子（电负性分子）内吸电子能力的概念来解释氟与其他卤素间的不同。

3. 主要结构 Although… 为让步状语从句。complexed or solvated 为前置定语，修饰 I^+，I^+ is…，and is…。参考译文：虽然所有卤素原子尚不能形成稳定的一价阳离子，但是，复合或溶剂化的 I^+ 可稳定存在于如 $I(py)^{2+}$，I(穴配位体)$^+$ 等盐类中，似乎也存在于由碘和银盐相互作用的溶液中。

4. 主要结构 Chloride is made…from…by…；which（定语从句）修饰 sodium chloride。参考译文：氯化钠在许多地方以沉积物形式存在，氯气几乎全部是由电解氯化钠水溶液的方法制备的。

Unit 6   Nucleophilic Substitution: The S_N2 and S_N1 Reactions

Alkyl halides are easily converted to many other functional groups. The halogen atom can leave with its bonding pair of electrons to form a stable halide ion; we say that a halide is a good *leaving group*. When another atom replaces the halide ion, the reaction is a **substitution**. When the halide ion leaves with another atom or ion (often H^+), the reaction is an **elimination**. In many eliminations, a molecule of H—X is lost from the alkyl halide to give an alkene. These eliminations are called **dehydrohalogenations** because a hydrogen halide has been removed from the alkyl halide. Substitution and elimination reactions often compete with each other.

In a **nucleophilic substitution**, a nucleophile (Nuc^-) replaces a leaving group (X^-) from a carbon atom, using its lone pair of electrons to form a new bond to the carbon atom.

Nucleophilic substitution

$$-\overset{|}{\underset{H}{C}}-\overset{|}{\underset{X}{C}}- + Nuc^- \longrightarrow -\overset{|}{\underset{H}{C}}-\overset{|}{\underset{Nuc}{C}}- + X^-$$

In an **elimination**, both the halide ion and another substituent are lost. A new π bond is formed.

Elimination

$$B^- + -\overset{|}{\underset{H}{C}}-\overset{|}{\underset{X}{C}}- \longrightarrow B-H + \overset{\diagdown}{}C=C\overset{\diagup}{} + X^-$$

In the elimination (a dehydrohalogenation), the reagent ($B:^-$) reacts as a base, abstracting a proton from the alkyl halide. Most nucleophiles are also basic and can engage in either substitution or elimination, depending on the alkyl halide and the reaction conditions.

In addition to alkyl halides, many other types of compounds undergo substitution and elimination reactions. Substitutions and eliminations are introduced in this chapter using the alkyl halides as examples. In later chapters, we encounter substitutions and eliminations of other types of compounds.

second-order nucleophilic substitution: the S_N2 reaction

A nucleophilic substitution has the general form

$$Nuc^- + -\overset{|}{\underset{|}{C}}-X \longrightarrow Nuc-\overset{|}{\underset{|}{C}}- + X^-$$

where Nuc^- is the nucleophile and $:X^-$ is the leaving halide ion. An example is the reaction of iodomethane (CH_3I) with hydroxide ion. The product is methanol.

$$HO^- + H-\overset{H}{\underset{H}{\overset{|}{C}}}-X^- \longrightarrow HO-\overset{H}{\underset{H}{\overset{|}{C}}}-H + I^-$$

    hydroxide   iodomethane   methanol   iodide

Hydroxide ion is a strong nucleophile (donor of an electron pair) because the oxygen atom has unshared pairs of electrons and a negative charge.[1] Iodomethane is called the **substrate**, meaning the compound that is attacked by the reagent. The carbon atom of iodomethane is electrophilic because it is bonded to an electronegative iodine atom. Electron density is drawn away from carbon by the halogen atom, giving the carbon atom a partial positive charge. The negative charge of hydroxide ion is attracted to this partial positive charge.

Hydroxide ion attacks the back side of the electrophilic carbon atom, donating a pair of electrons to form a new bond. (In general, nucleophiles are said to attack electrophiles, not the other way around.) Notice that arrows are used to show the movement of electron pairs, from the electron-rich nucleophile to the electron-poor carbon atom of the electrophile. Carbon can accommodate only eight electrons in its valence shell, so the carbon-iodine bond must begin to break as the carbon-oxygen bond begins to form.[2] Iodide ion is the **leaving group**; it leaves with the pair of electrons that once bonded it to the carbon atom.

The reaction of methyl iodide (iodomethane) with hydroxide ion is a **concerted reaction**, taking place in a single step with bonds breaking and forming at the same time. The middle structure is a transition state, a point of maximum energy, rather than an intermediate. In this transition state, the bond to the nucleophile (hydroxide) is partially formed, and the bond to the leaving group (iodide) is partially broken. Remember that a transition state is not a discrete molecule that can be isolated; it exists for only an instant.

The reaction-energy diagram for this substitution (Fig. 6.1) shows only one transition state and no intermediates between the reactants and the products. The reactants are shown slightly higher in energy than the products because this reaction is known to be exothermic. The transition state is much higher in energy because it involves a five-coordinate carbon atom with two partial bonds.

The one-step mechanism shown in Fig. 6.1 is supported by kinetic information. One can vary the concentrations of the reactants and observe the effects on the reaction rate (how much methanol is formed per second). The rate is found to double when the concentration of *either* reactant is doubled. The reaction is therefore first order in each of the reactants, and second order overall. The rate equation has the following form:

$$\text{rate} = k_r [\text{CH}_3\text{I}][\text{OH}^-]$$

This rate equation is consistent with the one-step mechanism shown in Fig. 6.1. This mechanism requires a collision between a molecule of methyl iodide and a hydroxide ion. Both of these species are present in the transition state, and the collision frequency is proportional to both concentrations. The rate constant k_r depends on several factors, including the energy of the transition state and the temperature.

This one-step nucleophilic substitution is an example of the **S_N2 mechanism**. The abbreviation S_N2 stands for *Substitution, Nucleophilic, bimolecular*. The term bimolecular means that the transition state of the rate-limiting step (the only step in this reaction) involves the collision of two molecules.[3] Bimolecular reactions usually have rate equations that

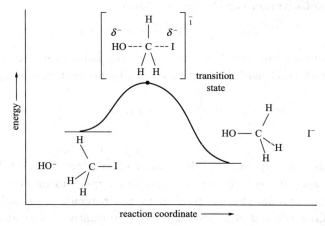

Fig. 6.1 the reaction-energy diagram for the reaction of methyl iodide with hydroxide shows only one energy maximum: the transition state, there are no intermediates

are second order overall.

First-order nucleophilic substitution: the S_N1 reaction

When *t*-butyl bromide is placed in boiling methanol, methyl *t*-butyl ether can be isolated from the reaction mixture. Because this reaction takes place with the solvent acting as the nucleophile, it is called a solvolysis (*solvo* for "solvent," plus *lysis*, meaning "cleavage").

$$(CH_3)_3C—Br + CH_3—OH \longrightarrow (CH_3)_3C—O—CH_3 + HBr$$
t-butyl bromide   methanol   methyl *t*-butyl ether

This solvolysis is a substitution because methoxide has replaced bromide on the *t*-butyl group. It does not go through the S_N2 mechanism, however. The S_N2 requires a strong nucleophile and a substrate that is not too hindered. Methanol is a weak nucleophile, and *t*-butyl bromide is a hindered tertiary halide: a poor S_N2 substrate.

An interesting characteristic of this reaction is that its rate does not depend on the concentration of methanol, the nucleophile. The rate depends only on the concentration of the substrate, *t*-butyl bromide.

$$Rate = k_r[(CH_3)_3C—Br]$$

This rate equation is first order overall: first order in the concentration of the alkyl halide and zeroth order in the concentration of the nucleophile. Because the rate does not depend on the concentration of the nucleophile, we infer that the nucleophile is not present in the transition state of the rate-limiting step. The nucleophile must react *after* the slow step.

This type of substitution is called the **S_N1 reaction**, for *Substitution, Nucleophilic, unimolecular*. The term *unimolecular* means there is only one molecule involved in the transition state of the rate-limiting step. The mechanism of the S_N1 reaction of *t*-butyl bromide with methanol is shown here. Ionization of the alkyl halide (first step) is the rate-limiting step.

Step 1: formation of carbocation (rate limiting)

$$(CH_3)_3C—Br \rightleftharpoons (CH_3)_3C^+ + Br^- \quad (slow)$$

Step 2: nucleophilic attack on the carbocation

$$(CH_3)_3C^+ \; \underset{H}{O—CH_3} \rightleftharpoons (CH_3)_3C—\underset{H}{\overset{+}{O}}—CH_3 \quad (fast)$$

Final step: loss of proton to solvent

$$(CH_3)_3C—\underset{H}{\overset{+}{O}}—CH_3 + CH_3—OH \rightleftharpoons (CH_3)_3C—O—CH_3 + CH_3—\underset{H}{\overset{+}{O}}—H \quad (fast)$$

The S_N1 mechanism is a multistep process. The first step is a slow ionization to form a carbocation. The second step is a fast attack on the carbocation by a nucleophile. The carbocation is a strong electrophile; it reacts very fast with both strong and weak nucleophiles. In the case of attack by an alcohol or water, loss of a proton gives the final uncharged product.

The reaction-energy diagram of the S_N1 reaction shows why the rate does not depend on the strength or concentration of the nucleophile. The ionization (first step) is highly endothermic, and its large activation energy determines the overall reaction rate. The nucleophilic attack (second step) is strongly exothermic, with a lower-energy transition state. In effect, a nucleophile reacts with the carbocation almost as soon as it forms.

The reaction-energy diagrams of the S_N1 mechanism and the S_N2 mechanism can be compared in Fig. 6.2. The S_N1 has a true intermediate, the carbocation. The intermediate appears as a relative minimum (a low point) in the reaction-energy diagram. Reagents and conditions that favor formation of the carbocation (the slow step) accelerate the S_N1 reaction; reagents and conditions that hinder its formation retard the reaction.[4]

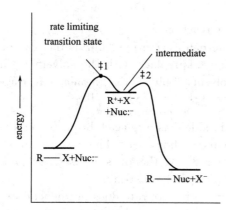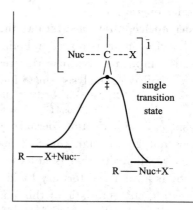

Fig. 6.2 reaction-energy diagrams of the S_N1 and S_N2 reactions, the S_N1 is a two-step mechanism with two transition states (‡1 and ‡2) and a carbocation intermediate, the S_N2 has only one transition state and no intermediate

From *Organic Chemistry by L. G. Wade, J. R.*

New Words and Expressions

alkyl ['ælkil]   *a.* 烷基的，烃基的   *n.* 烷基，烃基
substitution [ˌsʌbstiˈtjuːʃən]   *n.* 取代作用，取代反应
elimination [iˌlimiˈneiʃən]   *n.* 消除作用，消除反应
dehydrohalogenation [diːˌhaidrəuˌhælədʒəˈneiʃən]   *n.* 脱卤化氢（作用），脱去卤化氢
donor [ˈdəunə]   *n.* 给予（体），捐献者
unshared [ˌʌnˈʃead]   *a.* 非共享的，独享的
iodomethane [ˌaiədəuˈmeθein]   *n.* 碘甲烷
electronegative [iˌlektrəuˈnegətiv]   *a.* 负电的，带负电的
concerted reaction [kənˈsəːtidriː)ˈækʃən]   *n.* 协同反应
hydroxide [haiˈdrɔksaid, -sid]   *n.* 氢氧化物，羟化物
intermediate [ˌintəˈmiːdjət]   *n.* 中间体，媒介物
exothermic [ˌeksəuˈθəːmik]   *a.* 发热的，放出热量的
reactant [riːˈæktənt]   *n.* 反应物
collision [kəˈliʒən]   *n.* 碰撞，冲突
solvolysis [sɔlˈvɔlisis]   *n.* 溶剂分解（作用）
methoxide [meθˈɔksaid, -sid]   *n.* 甲醇盐，甲氧基物
zeroth [ˈziərəuð, -rəuθ, ˈziː-]   *a.* 零的
carbocation [ˌkɑːbəˈkeiʃən]   *n.* 碳阳离子

Notes

1. donor，给予体，在本句中指提供电子对的物质。substrate 译为底物，指受到试剂攻击的物质。本句为并列结构，前半句描述氢氧离子，后半句描述底物。参考译文：氢氧根离子是一个强的亲核基团（它提供了一个电子对），这是因为氧原子有未共享的电子对（即孤电子对），并呈现负价。

2. as 表示伴随，译为"当…之时"。其前后两句为并列关系。参考译文：碳原子的价层

Unit 6 Nucleophilic Substitution: The S_N2 and S_N1 Reactions

（最外层）最多只能容纳8个电子，所以当碳-氧键开始生成时，碳-碘键必须开始断裂。

3. that 后面引导宾语从句，rate-limiting step 译为"决速步骤"。参考译文："双分子"这个词表示决速步骤（在此反应中只有这一步）中的过渡态需要由两个分子进行碰撞而成。

4. 由分号分隔的并列结构，前后部分分别讲反应试剂和反应条件对 S_N1 反应的两种影响。每个句子中都包含着一个定语从句。参考译文：有利于碳正离子形成的反应试剂和条件（慢的反应步骤）会加速 S_N1 反应；阻碍碳正离子形成的反应试剂和条件则会使 S_N1 反应减速。

Exercises

I. Comprehension

1. According to the passage, which of the following statements happed in a nucleophilic substitution?

    A. Unimolecular ionization forms a carbocation and then a base abstracts a proton from the carbon atom adjacent to the C^+.

    B. A nucleophile replaces a leaving group from a carbon atom, using its lone pair of electrons to form a new bond to the carbon atom.

    C. Methoxide reacts as a base rather than as a nucleophile.

    D. A electrophile replaces a leaving group from a carbon atom, using its empty track to form a new bond to the carbon atom.

2. The difference between substitutions and eliminations is that? ____

    A. In an elimination, both the halide ion and another substituent are lost. A new π bond is formed.

    B. In an substitution, both the halide ion and another substituent are lost. A new π bond is formed.

    C. In an elimination, a nucleophile replaces a leaving group from a carbon atom, using its lone pair of electrons to form a new bond to the carbon atom.

    D. In an substitution, a nucleophile replaces a leaving group from a carbon atom, using its lone pair of electrons to form a new bond to the carbon atom.

3. The product of the reaction between iodomethane and hydroxide ion is ____.

    A. methane   B. hydromethane   C. methanol   D. ethane

4. Which of the following statements is not a feature of the transition state in S_N2 reaction? ____

    A. It reaches the point of maximum energy.

    B. It is a discrete molecule that can be isolated.

    C. The bond to the nucleophile is partially formed, and the bond to the leaving group (iodide) is partially broken.

    D. It exists for only an instant.

5. The abbreviation S_N2 stands for all of the following except ____.

    A. substitution   B. nucleophilic   C. bimolecular   D. biatomic

6. Why does the reaction of *t*-butyl bromide with methanol much more likely go though the S_N1 mechanism rather than the S_N2 mechanism? ____

    A. It is because that the reaction rate does not depend on the concentration of methanol, but depends only on the concentration of *t*-butyl bromide.

    B. It is because that *t*-butyl bromide is placed in boiling methanol and this reaction takes place with the solvent acting as the nucleophile.

    C. It is because that methanol is a weak nucleophile, and *t*-butyl bromide is a hindered tertiary halide: a pool S_N2 substrate.

D. It is because that the nucleaphile, methanol, is too strong.

7. Which of the following statements is not a character of the S_N1 mechanism? ____
A. Its rate depends on the concentration of the nucleophile.
B. The intermediate appears as a relative minimum.
C. It has a true intermediate.
D. Reagents and conditions that favor formation of the carbocation accelerate the reaction.

Ⅱ. **Fill the blank in each sentence with the appropriate form of the word or phrase from the list that correctly completes the meaning**

account for	act on	adapt to	as well as	attach to
be classified as	be known as	compare with	depend on	dry up
effect on	go out	such as	the presence of	

1. We can now easily ____ many things, which were thought to be mysterious by the ancients.
2. The acid ____ the metal and a gas is given off.
3. You should ____ yourself ____ new ways of looking at matters.
4. Electrolytes have more pronounced ____ colligative properties than do nonelectrolytes.
5. If water in these lakes evaporated at the same rate as fresh water, both would nearly ____ in a matter of years.
6. Both lakes evaporate very slowly ____ a freshwater lake or even the ocean.
7. A property that ____ only ____ the relative amounts of solute and solvent is known as a colligative property.
8. For example, both NaCl (ionic) and HCl (polar covalent) ____ electrolytes because they form ions in aqueous solution.
9. When compounds ____ NaCl and HCl are dissolved in water, the effect is obvious.
10. If the wire is cut, the light ____ because the circuit is broken.
11. When wires are ____ a charged battery and then to a light bulb, the light shines brightly.
12. Glass and wood ____ pure water are examples or nonconductors of electricity.
13. Other substances resist the flow of electricity and ____ nonconductors or insulators.
14. It has long been known that ____ a solute in water may affect its ability to conduct electricity.

Ⅲ. **Translation**

1. (a) 化学式；(b) 结构式；(c) 化学方程式；(d) 可逆反应；(e) 放热反应；(f) 复分解反应；(g) 置换反应。
2. 有时用等号代替箭头，这时我们假定反应的方向是从左到右。
3. 这些化学反应以上述方式进行是有充分理由的。
4. 参与反应的各元素原子改变了相互之间的结合方式。

Ⅳ. **Problem**

When the following compound is heated in methanol, several different products are formed. Propose mechanisms to account for the four products shown below.

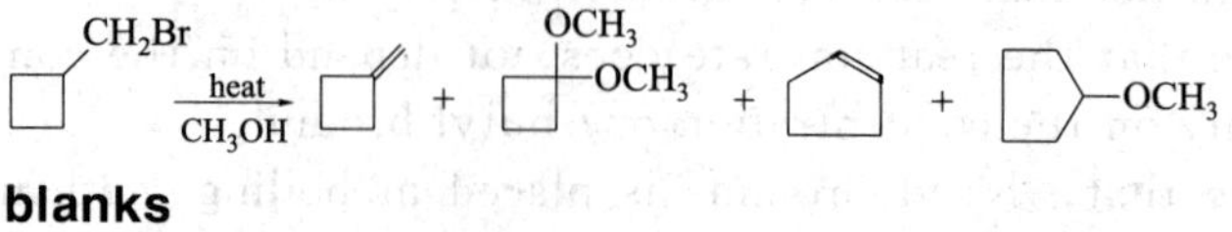

$$\square\text{-CH}_2\text{Br} \xrightarrow[\text{CH}_3\text{OH}]{\text{heat}} \square\text{=} + \square\text{-}\underset{\text{OCH}_3}{\overset{\text{OCH}_3}{|}} + \triangle + \square\text{-OCH}_3$$

Ⅴ. **Fill in the blanks**

Cooking food ____ salt water actually speeds the cooking process. The reason ____ this is that a salt solution boils ____ a higher temperature than pure water ____ the chemical reactions in the cooking process occur ____ a faster rate. A direct effect of the lowered vapor pressure ____ a solution is a higher boiling point ____ that of the solvent. Since a liquid boils at the temperature at which its vapor pressure equals the atmospheric pressure, a higher temperature is necessary ____ cause a solution to reach the same vapor pressure ____ the solvent.

Molality is a convenient concentration unit for this purpose ____ it emphasizes the relationship ____ the relative amounts of solute (expressed ____ moles) and solvent (expressed ____ kg) present ____ the volume of the solution, ____ does molarity. Also, the molality of a solution is not affected ____ the temperature. (The volume of a solution, which is used in molarity, is affected ____ the temperature.) The definition of molality is Molality $(m)=$ moles of solute/kg of solvent

Ⅵ. For each of the following compounds, draw the important resonance forms. Indicate which structures are major and minor contributors or whether they would have the same energy.

(a) $[CH_3OCH_2]^+$

(b)
$$\begin{array}{c} H \\ \diagdown \\ C^{\ominus} - C \\ \diagup \\ H \end{array} \begin{array}{c} O \\ \diagup\!\!\!\diagup \\ \diagdown \\ H \end{array}$$

(c) H_2SO_4

Reading Material

Competition with the Substitution: The E1 and E2 Reactions

Elimination involves the loss of two atoms or groups from the substrate, usually with formation of a pi bond. Depending on the reagents and conditions involved, elimination might be a first-order (E1) or second-order (E2) process.[1] In many cases, substitution and elimination reactions can take place at the same time and under the same conditions. We will consider these possibilities later, once we have discussed the E1 and E2 mechanisms.

The abbreviation E1 stands for *Elimination, unimolecular*. The mechanism is called *unimolecular* because the rate-limiting transition state involves a single molecule rather than a collision between two molecules. The slow step of an E1 reaction is the same as in the S_N1 reaction: unimolecular ionization to form a carbocation. In a fast second step, a base abstracts a proton from the carbon atom adjacent to the C^+. The electrons that once formed the carbon-hydrogen bond now form a pi bond between two carbon atoms.[2] The general mechanism for the E1 reaction is as follows.

Mechanism of the E1 Reaction

Step 1: Formation of the carbocation (rate limiting)

$$-\underset{H}{\overset{|}{C}}-\underset{X}{\overset{|}{C}}- \rightleftharpoons -\underset{H}{\overset{|}{C}}-\overset{+}{C}\!\!\diagup + X^-$$

Step 2: A base abstracts a proton (fast)

$$B^- + -\underset{H}{\overset{|}{C}}-\overset{+}{C}\!\!\diagup \rightleftharpoons B-H + \diagup\!\!\!C=C\!\!\diagup$$

The E1 reaction almost always occurs together with the S_N1. Whenever a carbocation is formed, it can undergo either substitution or elimination, and mixtures of products often result. The following reaction shows the competition between elimination and substitution in the reaction of *t*-butyl bromide with boiling ethanol.

The 2-methylpropene product results from **dehydrohalogenation**, an elimination of hydrogen and a halogen atom. Under these first-order conditions (the absence of a strong base), dehydrohalogenation takes place by the E1 mechanism: Ionization of the alkyl halide gives a carbocation intermediate, which loses a proton to give the alkene.[3] Substitution results from nucleophilic attack on the carbocation. Ethanol serves as a base in the elimination and as a nucleophile in the substitution.

Under ideal conditions, one of these first-order reactions provides a good yield of one product or the other. Often, however, carbocation intermediates react in two or more ways to give mixtures of products. For this reason, S_N1 and E1 reactions of alkyl halides are not often used for organic synthesis. They have been studied in great detail to learn about the properties of carbocations, however.

In the second step of the E1 mechanism, the carbon atom next to the C^+ must rehybridize to sp^2 as the base attacks the proton and electrons flow into the new π bond.

The potential-energy diagram for the E1 reaction is similar to that for the S_N1 reaction. The ionization step is strongly endothermic, with a rate limiting step so then state. The second step is a fast exothermic deprotonation by a base. The base is not involved in the reaction until *after* the rate-limiting step, so the rate depends only on the concentration of the alkyl halide. Weak bases are common in E1 reactions.

Like other carbocation reactions, the E1 may be accompanied by rearrangement. Compare the following E1 reaction (with rearrangement) with the S_N1 reaction of the same substrate.

Elimination can also take place under second-order conditions with a strong base present. As an example, consider the reaction of *t*-butyl bromide with methoxide ion in methanol.

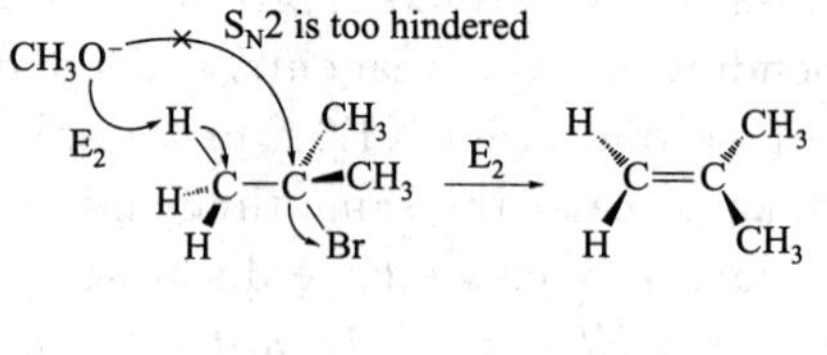

Rate=$K_r[(CH_3)_3C\text{-}Br][^-OCH_3]$

This is a second-order reaction because methoxide ion is a strong base as well as a strong nucleophile. It attacks the alkyl halide faster than the halide can ionize to give a first order reaction. No substitution product (methyl *t*-butyl ether) is observed, however. The S_N2 mechanism is blocked because the tertiary alkyl halide is too hindered. The observed product is 2-methylpropene, resulting from elimination of HBr and formation of a double bond.

In the E2 reaction, methoxide reacts as a *base* rather than as a *nucleophile*. Most strong nucleophiles are also strong bases, and elimination commonly results when a strong base/nucleophile is used with a poor S_N2 substrate. Instead of attacking the back side of the hindered electrophilic carbon, methoxide abstracts a proton front one of the methyl groups. This reaction takes place in one step, with bromide leaving as the base is abstracting a proton.

The rate of this elimination is proportional to the concentrations of both the alkyl halide and the base, giving a second-order rate equation.[4] This is a bimolecular process, with both the base and the alkyl halide participating in the transition state, so this mechanism is abbreviated E2 for *Elimination, bimolecular.*

From *Organic Chemistry* by L. G. Wade, JR.

New Words and Expressions

substrate ['sʌbstreit]   n. 底物（被试剂进攻之物）
unimolecular [ˌjuːniməuˈlekjulə]   a. 单分子的
t-butyl [ˈbjuːtil]   n. 叔丁基
2-methylpropene [tuːˈmeθilˈprəupiːn]   n. 2-甲基丙烯
rehybridize [ˌriːˈhaibridaiz]   vt. 重新杂化，再杂化
potential-energy [pəˈtenʃ(ə)lˈenədʒi]   n. 势能
deprotonation [diːˌprəutəˈneiʃən]   n. 去质子化（作用）
rearrangement [ˌriːəˈreindʒmənt]   n. 重排
tertiary [ˈtəːʃəri]   a. 第三的，三级的，叔的
methyl [ˈmeθil, ˈmiːθail]   n. 甲基

Notes

1. 该句是将定语"Depending on the reagents and conditions involved"前置，应把其放在主句后翻译。参考译文：消除反应可能是一级反应（E1），也可能是二级反应（E2），这取决于所用的反应试剂和反应条件。

2. that 后面引导的从句用来解释说明主语 the electrons。参考译文：原来形成碳-氧键的电子此时被用来形成两个碳原子间的 π 键。

3. which 后面引导定语从句，其后面的内容用来修饰宾语" a carbocation intermediate "。参考译文：卤代烃的离子化得到了一个碳正离子的中间体，其失去一个质子后生成烯烃。

4. 句中 giving a second-order rate equation 为后置定语，用来对主句进行补充说明。参考译文：消除反应的速率是与卤代烃及碱的浓度成比例的，因此对应着一个二级反应速率方程式。

Unit 7 The Nomenclature of Inorganic Substances

You will meet many compounds in this text and will learn their name as you go along. However, it is useful from the outset to know something about how to form their names. Many compounds were given common names before their compositions were known. Common names include water, salt, sugar, ammonia, and quartz. A systematic name, on the other hand, reveals which elements are present and, in some cases, how their atoms are arranged. The systematic name of table salt, for instance, is sodium chloride, which indicates at once that it is a compound of sodium and chlorine. The systematic naming of compounds, which is called chemical nomenclature, follows a set of rules, so that the name of each compound need not be memorized, only the rules.[1]

Names of Cations

The names of monatomic cations (pronounced "cat-ions") are the same as the name of the element, with the addition of the word ion, as in sodium ion for Na^+.[2] When an element can form more than one kind of cation, such as Cu^+ and Cu^{2+} from copper, we use the **Stock number**, a Roman numeral equal to the charge of the cation. Thus, Cu^+ is a copper (Ⅰ) ion and Cu^{2+} is a copper (Ⅱ) ion. Similarly, Fe^{2+} is an iron (Ⅱ) ion and Fe^{3+} is an iron (Ⅲ) ion. Most transition metals form more than one kind of ion, so it is usually necessary to include a Stock number in the names of their compounds.

An older system of nomenclature is still in use. For example, some cations were once denoted by the endings -*ous* and -*ic* for the ions with lower and higher charges, respectively. In this system, iron (Ⅱ) ions are called ferrous ions and iron (Ⅲ) ions are called ferric ions.

Names of Anions

Monatomic anions (pronounced "ann-ions") are named by adding the suffix -*ide* and the word ion to the first part of the name of the element (the "stem" of its name). There is no need to give the charge, because most elements that form monatomic anions form only one kind of ion. The ions formed by the halogens are collectively called *halide ions* and include fluoride (F^-), chloride (Cl^-), bromide (Br^-), and iodide ions (I^-).

The names of oxoanions are formed by adding the suffix -*ate* to the stem of the name of the element that is not oxygen, as in the carbonate ion, CO_3^{2-}. However, many elements can form a variety of oxoanions with different numbers of oxygen atoms; nitrogen, for example, forms both NO_2^- and NO_3^-. In such cases, the ion with the larger number of oxygen atoms is given the suffix -*ate*, and that with the smaller number of oxygen atoms is given the suffix -*ite*. Thus, NO_3^- is nitrate and NO_2^- is nitrite.

Some elements—particularly take for the halogens—form more than two oxoanions. The name of the oxoanion with the smallest number of oxygen atoms is formed by adding the prefix *hypo*- to the -*ite* form of the name, as in the hypochlorite ion, ClO^-. The oxoanion with a higher number of oxygen atoms than the -*ate* oxoanion is named with the prefix *per*- added to the -*ate* form of the name. An example is the *perchlorate* ion, ClO_4^-.

Some anions include hydrogen, such as HS^- and HCO_3^-. The names of these anions begin with "hydrogen". Thus, HCO_3^- is the hydrogen carbonate ion. In an older system of nomenclature, an anion containing a hydrogen atom was named with the prefix *bi*-, as in bicarbonate ion for HCO_3^-.

The oxoacids are molecular compounds that can be regarded as the parents of the oxoanions. The formulas of oxoacids are derived from those of the corresponding oxoanions by adding enough hydrogen ions to balance the charges. This procedure is only a formal way of building the chemical formula, because oxoacids are all *molecular* compounds.

For example, the sulfate ion, SO_4^{2-}, needs two H^+ ions to cancel its negative charge, so sulfuric acid is the molecular compound H_2SO_4. Similarly, the phosphate ion, PO_4^{3-}, needs three H^+ ions, so its parent acid is the molecular compound H_3PO_4, phosphoric acid. As these examples illustrate, the names of the parent oxoacids are derived from those of the corresponding oxoanions by replacing the *-ate* suffix with *-ic* acid. In general, *-ic* oxoacides are the parents of *-ate* oxoanions and *-ous* oxoacids are the parents of *-ite* oxoanions.

Names of Ionic Compounds

An ionic compound is named with the cation name first, followed by the name of the anion; the word ion is omitted in each case. Typical names include potassium chloride (KCl), a compound containing K^+ and Cl^- ions, and ammonium nitrate (NH_4NO_3), which contains NH_4^+ and NO_3^- ions. The copper chloride that contains Cu^+ ions (CuCl) is called copper (Ⅰ) chloride, and the chloride that contains Cu^{2+} ions ($CuCl_2$) is called copper (Ⅱ) chloride.

Some ionic compounds form crystals that incorporate a definite proportion of molecules of water as well as the ions of the compound itself. These compounds are called hydrates. For example, copper (Ⅱ) sulfate normally occurs as blue crystals of composition $CuSO_4 \cdot 5H_2O$. The raised dot in this formula is used to separate the water of hydration from the rest of the formula. This formula indicates that there are five H_2O molecules for each $CuSO_4$ formula unit. Hydrates are named by first giving the name of the compound, then adding the word hydrate with a Greek prefix[3] indicating how many molecules of water are found in each formula unit. For example, the name of $CuSO_4 \cdot 5H_2O$ is copper (Ⅱ) sulfate pentahydrate.

Names of Molecular Compounds

Many simple molecular compounds are named by using the Greek prefixes to indicate the number of each type of atom present. Usually, no prefix is used if only one atom of an element is present; an important exception to this rule is carbon monoxide, CO. Most of the common binary molecular compounds—molecular compounds built from two elements—have at least one element from Group 16 or 17. These elements are named second, with their endings changed to *-ide*.

phosphorus trichloride PCl_3 dinitrogen oxide N_2O
sulfur hexafluoride SF_6 dinitrogen pentoxide N_2O_5

Metals with Ions of Only One Charge

It is not difficult to recognize metals with only one charge because all except one are in two groups in the periodic table (There are also several transition metals that form only one cation charge, but they are not included in this discussion.). Representative element metals in Group ⅠA (alkali metals) form +1 cations exclusively. Likewise, the metals in Group ⅡA (alkaline earth metals) form +2 ions exclusively. Aluminum in Group ⅢA forms a +3 ion exclusively, but other metals in this group also form a +1 ion. When present in metal—nonmetal binary compounds, the nonmetals form -1 one type of anion. Hydrogen and Group ⅦA (halogens) form -1 ions, Group ⅥA elements form -2 ions, and N and P in Group ⅤA form -3 ions.

In both naming and writing the formula for a binary ionic compound, the metal comes first and the nonmetal second. The unchanged English name of the metal is used. (if a metal cation is named alone, the word "ion" is also included to distinguish it from the free metal.) The name of the anion includes only the English root plus *ide*. For example, *chlorine* as an anion is named chloride and oxygen as an anion is named oxide. So the names for NaCl and CaO are as follows.

Formula	Metal	Nonmetal	Compound name
NaCl	sodium	chlorine	sodium chloride
CaO	calcium	oxygen	calcium oxide

Writing formulas from names can be a somewhat more challenging task since we must then determine the number of each element present in the formula. What is important to remember is that the formulas represent neutral compounds where the positive and negative charges add to zero. In other words, the total positive charge is cancelled by the total negative charge. Thus, NaCl is neutral because one Na^+ is balanced by one Cl^- [i.e., $+1+(-1)=0$] and CaO is neutral because one Ca^{2+} is balanced by one O^{2-} [i.e., $+2+(-2)=0$]. The formula for magnesium chloride, however, requires two Cl^- ions to balance the one Mg^{2+} ion, so it is written as $MgCl_2$.

Naming Compounds with Polyatomic Ions

Most of us are somewhat familiar with names of polyatomic ions. We use bicarbonates and carbonates for indigestion, as well as sulfites and nitrites to preserve foods.

Most of the compounds containing polyatomic ions are ionic, as were the compounds discussed in the previous section. Thus we follow essentially the same rules as before. That is, the metal is written and named first. If the metal forms more than one cation, the charge on the cation is shown in parentheses. The polyatomic anion is then named or written.

In many cases, the anions are composed of oxygen and one other element. Thus these anions are called oxyanions. When there are two oxyanions of the same element (e.g., SO_4^{2-} and SO_3^{2-}), they, of course, have different names. The anion with the smaller number of oxygens uses the root of the element plus *ite*. The one with the higher number uses the root plus *ate*.

$$SO_3^{2-} \quad \text{sulfite}$$
$$SO_4^{2-} \quad \text{sulfate}$$

There are four oxyanions containing Cl. The middle two are named as before. The one with one less oxygen than the chlorite has a prefix of *hypo*. The one with one more oxygen than chlorate has a prefix of *per*.

$$ClO^- \quad \text{hypochlorite}$$
$$ClO_2^- \quad \text{chlorite}$$
$$ClO_3^- \quad \text{chlorate}$$
$$ClO_4^- \quad \text{perchlorate}$$

Certain anions are composed of more than one atom but behave similar to monatomic anions in many of their chemical reactions. Two such examples are the CN^- ion and the OH^- ion. Both of these have *ide* endings similar to the monatomic anions. Thus the CN^- anion is known as the cyanide ion and the OH^- as the hydroxide ion.

From *Inorganic chemistry by T. W. Swaddle*

New Words and Expressions

nomenclature [nəuˈmenklətʃə] n. （系统）命名法
monatomic [ˌmɔnəˈtɔmik] a. 单原子的
denote [diˈnəut] vt. 指示，表示
ferrous [ˈferəs] a. 亚铁的
ferric [ˈferik] a. （正）铁的，三价铁的
stem [stem] n. 母体词，词干
oxoanion [ɔksiˈænaiən] n. 含氧阴离子

carbonate ['kɑːbəneit]   n. 碳酸盐（或酯）
perchlorate [pə'klɔːreit]   n. 高氯酸盐（或酯）
bicarbonate [bai'kɑːbənit]   n. 碳酸氢盐，重碳酸盐
oxoacid [ɔksi'æsid]   n. 酮酸，含氧酸
sulfate ['sʌlfeit]   n. 硫酸盐，硫酸根，硫酸酯
hydrate ['haidreit]   n. 水合物
pentahydrate [ˌpentə'naidraid]   n. 五水合物
binary ['bainəri]   a. 二进位的，二元的
phosphorus ['fɔsfərəs]   n. 磷（元素符号 P）
hexafluoride ['heksəfluəraid]   a. 六氟化物
pentoxide [ˌpen'tɔksaid]   n. 五氧化物
indigestion [ˌindi'dʒestʃən]   n. 消化不良
sulfite ['sʌlfait]   n. 亚硫酸盐
oxyanion [ɔksi'ænaiən]   n. 氧离子
cyanide ['saiənaid]   n. 氰化物

Notes

1. which is called chemical nomenclature 为非限制性定语从句作插入语，so that 引导目的状语从句。only the rules 可理解为：only the rules need be memorized。参考译文：化合物的系统名称，被称作化学命名。它遵循着一套规则，以便（我们）不必去记忆每一个化合物的名称，而只需记住这个规则（即可）。

2. same 永远与 the 连用，通常 as 用在一个紧跟着的名词或代词前。e. g.：I want a shirt the same as my friend。with 用来引导伴随情况，或用来说明造成某一局面的原因，e. g.：With all this work to do, I don't know if I'll have time to go out。as in sodium ion 中的 as 等同于 like。e. g. The "h" is silent as in "hour"。在 hour 这个字中，h 不发音。参考译文：单原子阳离子的名称同元素的名称相同，后跟随离子一词，如 Na^+ 表示钠离子。

3. Greek prefix：希腊前缀。在化学专业中常用来表示化合物中相同片段（基团、原子、分子）的数目，兹举例如下：mono- 单，di- 双，tri- 3，tetra- 4，penta- 5，hexa- 6，hepta- 7，octa- 8，nona- 9，deca- 10，undeca- 11，dodeca- 12。

Exercises

Ⅰ. Comprehension

1. chemical nomenclature can indicate ____.
   A. the elements which are present in the substance
   B. the arrangement that the atoms are
   C. the common name is not necessary
   D. the common name need not be memorized

2. Which of the following sentence is not true? ____
   A. When an element can form more than one kind of cation, we should use the stock number to equal to the charge of cation.
   B. When an element can form a variety of oxoanions with different numbers of oxygen atoms, the ion with the larger number of oxygen atoms is given the suffix-ite.
   C. The metal comes first and the nonmetal second in both naming and writing the formula for a binary ionic compound.
   D. The hydrates are named by adding the hydrate with a Greek prefix behind the name of the compound.

3. The formulas of oxoacids are derived from ____.
A. the corresponding oxocations by adding enough hydrogen ions
B. the corresponding oxoanions by adding enough negative charges
C. the corresponding oxoanions by adding enough hydrogen ions
D. the corresponding oxocations by adding enough negative charges

4. Binary molecular compound ____.
A. has at least one kind of halogen
B. consists of two kinds of atoms
C. consists of two kinds of elements
D. has at least two elements from Group 16 and 17

5. in nomenclature, the prefix of *per* means ____.
A. the oxyanion has one more oxygen than corresponding ion which has the suffix *ite*
B. the oxyanion has one more oxygen than corresponding ion which has the suffix *ate*
C. the oxycation has one more oxygen than corresponding ion which has the prefix *hypo*
D. the oxycation has one more oxygen than corresponding ion which has the prefix *hypo*

II. Give the systematic name for the following

NH_4^+ Cu^{2+} Sr^{2+}
Cu^+ Fe^{2+} Zn^{2+}
H^+ Pb^{2+} Al^{3+}
Ag^+ Mg^{2+} Cr^{3+}
Ba^+ Mn^{2+} Fe^{3+}
Ca^{2+} Hg^{2+}
Cr^{2+} Sn^{2+}

CO N_2O_3 $K^+[BF_4]^-$
CO_2 P_2O_5 $[Ag(NH_3)_2]^+Cl^-$
SO_3 Cl_2O_7

AsO_4^{3-} SO_3^{2-} H^-
AsO_3^{3-} Br^- OH^-
PO_4^{3-} ClO_3^- ClO^-
PO_3^{3-} Cl^- IO_3^-
CO_3^{2-} ClO_2^- NO_3^-
CrO_4^{2-} CN^- I^-
$Cr_2O_7^{2-}$ F^- NO_3^-
O^{2-} HCO_3^- NO_2^-
S^{2-} HSO_4^- ClO_4^-
SO_4^{2-} HSO_3^- MnO_4^-

III. Complete the table

formula	Old name	Systematic name
FeO	ferrous oxide	
Fe_2O_3	ferric oxide	
$Sn(OH)_2$	stannous hydroxide	
$Sn(OH)_4$	stannic hydroxide	
Hg_2SO_4	mercurous sulfate	
$HgSO_4$	mercuric sulfate	
NaClO	sodium hypochlorite	

续表

formula	Old name	Systematic name
$K_2Cr_2O_7$	potassium dichromate	
$Cu_3(AsO_4)_2$	cupric arsenate	
$Cr(C_2H_3O_2)_3$	chromic acetate	

IV. Acid names may be obtained directly from its acid ion by changing the name of the acid ion (negative ion). Use the rule to give the name of the following acid

Formula of acid	Formula and name of Acid ion	Name of acid
H_2CO_3	CO_3^{2-}, carbonate ion	
$HClO_2$	ClO_2^-, chlorite ion	
$HClO_4$	ClO_4^-, perchlorate ion	
HCN	CN^-, cyanide ion	
HBr	Br^-, bromide ion	
H_4SiO_4	SiO_4^{4-}, silicate ion	
H_3AsO_4	AsO_4^{3-}, arsenate ion	

V. Complete the sentences with the proper form of the word given at the end of the sentence

1. Only the outermost or valence electron energy level ____ (alter) when ionic compounds are formed from atoms.

2. ____ (illustrate) these changes for sodium and chlorine we can draw modified Bohr diagrams for the atoms and ions involved.

3. The chemical formula for the compound sodium chloride is NaCl. This formula ____ (indicate) that in the compound there is one sodium ion for each chloride ion.

4. We ____ (expect) the bonds in water to be polar because oxygen is more electronegative than hydrogen.

5. If the atoms in the water molecule were in a straight row (that is, in a linear arrangement,) the two polar bonds ____ (cancel) one another out.

6. Instead of having one end of the molecule positive and the other end negative, the electrons ____ (pull) toward the right in one bond and toward the left in the other.

7. Many of the properties of compounds, like melting point, boiling point, and solubility, ____ (depend on) the polarity of the molecules of the compound.

8. Most of the ionic compounds that we have just named ____ also ____ (refer) to as salts.

9. A salt is an ionic compound ____ (form) by the combination of a cation with an anion.

10. Most of the compounds that we ____ (discuss) so far are ionic compounds, which constitute a significant portion of the "hard" part of nature.

VI. Translation

1. 物质既不能创造亦不能消灭。
2. 科学家必须知道怎样运用数字以求得对问题的准确解释。
3. 任何物质,不论是固体、液体或气体,都是由原子组成的。
4. 试验是成功,它的结果正如我们预期的一样。
5. 我们不久就会完成这个试验。

VII. Write equations for the following acid-base reactions. Use the information in inorganic textbook to predict whether the equilibrium will favor the reactants or the products

(a) $HCOOH + {}^-CN$

(b) $CH_3COO^- + CH_3OH$

(c) $CH_3OH + NaNH_2$
(d) $NaOCH_3 + HCN$
(e) $HCl + H_2O$
(f) $H_3O^+ + CH_3O^-$

VIII. Write equations for the net reactions which occur when the following materials are added to a sodium-ammonia solution
(a) methylgermane; (b) iodine; (c) diethylsulfide

Reading Material

Chemical Bonds

There are approximately 100 chemical elements. There are millions of chemical compounds, and about 600000 new compounds are prepared every year. To form these compounds, atoms of different elements must be held together in specific combinations. **Chemical bonds** are the forces that maintain these arrangements. Chemical bonding also plays a role in determining the state of matter. At room temperature, water is a liquid, carbon dioxide is a gas, and table salt is a solid because of differences in chemical bonding.

As scientists developed an understanding of the nature of chemical bonding, they gained the ability to manipulate the structure of compounds. Dynamite, birth control pills, synthetic fibers, and a thousand other products were fashioned in chemical laboratories and have dramatically changed the way we live. We are now entering an era that promises (some would say forebodes) even greater change.

Ionic Bond

Let us look at an atom of the element sodium (Na). It has 11 electrons, of which two are in the first energy level, eight in the second, and one in the third.[1] If the sodium atom could get rid of an electron, then the product, called a *sodium ion*, would have the same electron structure as an atom of the noble gas neon (Ne).

Let us immediately emphasize that the sodium ion (Na^+) and the neon atom (Ne) are not identical. The electron arrangement is the same, but the nuclei—and resulting charges—are not. As long as sodium keeps its 11 protons, it is still a form of sodium, but it is the sodium *ion*, not the sodium *atom*. **Ions** are charged particles, particles in which the number of electrons does not equal the number of protons. Positively charged ions are called **cations** (pronounced "cat-ions"). The sodium ion is a cation.

If a chlorine atom (Cl) could gain an electron, it would have the same electron structure as the noble gas argon (Ar).

The chlorine atom, having gained an electron, becomes negatively charged. It has 17 protons (17+) and 18 electrons (18−). It is written Cl^- and is called a *chloride ion*. Negatively charged ions are called **anions** (pronounced "ann-ions"). The chloride ion is an anion.

A sodium atom forms a less reactive species, a sodium ion, by *losing* an electron. A chlorine atom becomes a less reactive chloride ion by gaining an electron. A chlorine atom cannot just pluck an electron from empty space, nor can a sodium atom kick out an electron unless something else is willing to take it on.[2] What happens when sodium comes into contact with chlorine? It is obvious that a chlorine atom removes an electron from a sodium atom.

The sodium *ion* and the chloride *ion* have electron arrangements (electron configurations) like those of two noble gases (neon and argon, respectively). Not only do the ions have stable octets of electrons, they also have opposite charges. Everyone knows that opposites attract. While this rule of thumb may not always work when applied to people, it works quite well for cations and anions. The attractive force between oppositely charged ions is called an **ionic bond**, and the combination of sodium ions and chloride ions is the compound sodium chloride or table salt.

Covalent Bonds

One might expect a hydrogen atom, with its one electron, to acquire another electron and assume the helium configuration. Indeed, hydrogen atoms do just that in the presence of atoms of a reactive metal such as lithium, that is, a metal that finds it easy to give up an electron.

But what if there are no other kinds of atoms around? What if there are only hydrogen atoms (as in a sample of the pure element)? One hydrogen atom can scarcely grab an electron from another, for among hydrogen atoms all have equal attraction for electrons. (Even more important, perhaps, hydrogen atoms do not have a tendency to lose electrons at all, for the result would be a highly reactive bare proton—the hydrogen nucleus.) Still hydrogen wants a duet of electrons like helium's. If one hydrogen cannot capture another's electron, the two atoms can compromise by *sharing* their electrons.

It is as if the two hydrogen atoms, in approaching one another, get their electron clouds or orbitals so thoroughly enmeshed that they cannot easily pull them apart again.[3]

Most of time the electrons are located between the two nuclei. The electron-dot formula usually used, H : H, is therefore a fairly good picture. (If we were to attribute human qualities to hydrogen atoms, we would suggest that they are a bit nearsighted. Each one looks around, sees two electrons, and decides that these electrons are its very own and that therefore it has as arrangement like that of helium, one of the noble gases.) This combination of hydrogen atoms is called a *hydrogen molecule*. **Molecules** are discrete groups of atoms held together by shared pairs of electrons. The bond formed by a shared pair of electrons is called a **covalent bond**.

A chlorine atom will pick up an extra electron from anything willing to give one up. But, again, what if the only thing around is another chlorine atom? Chlorine atoms, too, can attain a more stable arrangement by sharing a pair of electrons.

$$:Cl\cdot + \cdot Cl: \longrightarrow :Cl:Cl:$$

Each chlorine atom in the chlorine molecule counts eight electrons around it and concludes that it has an arrangement like that of the noble gas argon. The shared pair of electrons in the chlorine molecule also creates a covalent bond.

For simplicity, the hydrogen molecule is often represented as H_2 and the chlorine molecule as Cl_2. The subscripts indicate two atoms *per* molecule. In each case, the covalent bond between the atoms is understood. Sometimes the covalent bond is indicated by a dash, H—H and Cl—Cl.

Let us be sure we understand the meaning of numbers in formulas. Take a moment to establish in your mind the difference among the following: H, H_2, 2H, $2H_2$, H_2O, $2H_2O$. Is it clear to you that although H represents a single atom of hydrogen, H_2 implies two atoms of H bonded together, whereas 2H represents two separate, free, and independent atoms of H? On the other hand, the meaning of H_2 in H_2O is totally different from that of H_2 as a molecule. In H_2O it means that two atoms of H are individually attached to O (not to themselves!) to form a molecule of water. Finally, $2H_2O$ simply refers to two individual molecules of water.

Covalent bonds are not limited to the sharing of one pair of electrons. Consider, for example, the nitrogen atom. Its electron-dot symbol is:

$$:\dot{N}\cdot$$

Now, after all we have learned about the octet rule we know that this electron arrangement is not complete. It has only five electrons in its outermost energy level. It could shared a pair of electrons with another nitrogen atom and would then look like this:

$$:\dot{N}:\dot{N}: \quad \text{(incorrect structure)}$$

The situation has not improved a great deal. Each nitrogen atom in this arrangement has only six electrons surrounding it (not eight). Each nitrogen atom has two electrons hanging out there without partners, so, to solve the dilemma, each nitrogen atom shares two additional pairs of electrons, for a total of three pairs.

$$:N:::N:$$

In drawing the nitrogen molecule (N_2), we have placed all the electrons being shared by the two atoms in the space between the two atoms. Each nitrogen atom has now satisfied the octet rule. A molecule in which *three pairs* of electrons (a total of six *individual* electrons) are being shared is said to contain a **triple bond**. Each nitrogen atom also has an unshared pair of electrons. Note that we could have drawn the *unshared* pair of electrons above or below the atomic symbol. Such a drawing would represent the same molecule.

Polar Covalent Bonds

So far we have seen that atoms combine in two different ways. Some that are quite different in electron structure (from opposite ends of the periodic table) react by the complete transfer of one or more electrons from one atom to another (ionic bond formation).[4] Atoms that are identical combine by sharing one or more pairs of electrons (covalent bond formation). Now let us look at some "in-betweeners".

Hydrogen and chlorine react to form a colorless, toxic gas called hydrogen chloride. This reaction can be represented schematically by

$$H \cdot + \cdot Cl \longrightarrow H:Cl \quad \text{or} \quad (H\text{—}Cl)$$

Both the hydrogen atom and the chlorine atom want an electron, so they compromise by sharing and form a covalent bond. Since the substances hydrogen and chlorine actually consist of diatomic molecules rather than single atoms, the reaction is more accurately represented by the scheme.

$$H:H + Cl:Cl \longrightarrow 2H:Cl$$

This can be more simply written as:

$$H_2 + Cl_2 \longrightarrow 2HCl$$

One might reasonably ask why the hydrogen molecule and the chlorine molecule react at all. Have we not just explained that they themselves were formed to provide a more stable arrangement of electrons? Yes, indeed, we did say that. But there is stable and there is more stable. The chlorine molecule represents a more stable arrangement than separate chlorine atoms, but, given the opportunity, a chlorine atom would rather bond to hydrogen than to another chlorine atom.[5]

In a molecule of hydrogen chloride, a chlorine atom shares a pair of electrons with a hydrogen atom. In this case, and in others we shall consider, sharing does not mean sharing equally. Some atoms within molecules attract electrons more strongly than do other atoms. The term **electronegativity** is used to describe the affinity of an element in a molecule for electrons. The higher the electronegativity, the more strongly the atoms of an element attract electrons to themselves. The most electronegative element is fluorine, which is located in the upper right corner of the periodic table. The electronegativity of elements decreases as one moves away from fluorine in the periodic table. Thus electronegativity decreases as one moves down a group (column) or left across a period (row).

From *Inorganic chemistry by T. W. Swaddle*

New Words and Expressions

cation ['kætaiən]   *n.* 阳离子
argon ['ɑːgɔn]   *n.* 氩
chloride ['klɔːraid]   *n.* 氯化物
anion ['ænaiən]   *n.* 阴离子
octet [ɔk'tet]   *n.* 八隅体
covalent [kəu'veilənt]   *a.* 共有原子价的，共价的
duet [djuː'et；(US) duː'et]   *n.* 二隅体
orbital ['ɔːbitl]   *n.* 轨道，轨函数
outermost ['autəməust]   *a.* 最外面的，最远的，价电子层的
nitrogen ['naitrədʒən]   *n.* 氮
triple ['tripl]   *a.* 三倍的，三重的   *n.* 三倍数
schematically [ski'mætik]   *ad.* （用图等）示意性地
electronegativity [iˌlektrɔnˌnegə'tiviti]   电负性
affinity [ə'finiti]   *n.* 亲和力

Notes

1. It 代上句的 an atom of the element sodium。which 指 11 electrons。two 是 two electrons 的省略。eight 和 one 后省略 are 和 is。参考译文：它有 11 个电子，其中两个电子在第一能级，8 个电子在第二能级，1 个电子在第三能级。

2. empty space 指"空白空间，真空空间"，这里意为"凭空，无根据"。nor 作连词，与助动词和情态动词连用，句中主语与动词倒置。e. g.：He can't see, nor could he hear until a month ago. 他现在看不见，一个月之前他还听不见。She isn't rich; nor do I imagine that she ever will be. 她现在不富，我看她将来也富不了。kick out：逐出，解雇，开除。e. g.：They kicked him out (of the club) for fighting. 他因为斗殴被开除（出俱乐部）。something else：别的东西，take on：接纳，承受。参考译文：氯原子不能凭空获得一个电子，而钠原子也不会凭空失去一个电子，除非别的东西愿接受电子。

3. In approaching one another 作插入语。as if 与 as though 用法相同，意为：宛如，仿佛，好像。as if 后面常用过去时表示现在，以说明所作的比较"不是真的"。e. g. You look as if you'd seen a ghost. 在非正式文体中，常用 like 代替 as if。e. g. He sat there smiling like it was his birthday. 参考译文：就好像两个氢原子，当它们互相靠近时，其电子云充分重叠，以至于难以再分开。

4. From opposite ends of the periodic table：周期表中相对的两端。这里指周期表中左右两端，如第一主族和第七主族等。transfer 在这里作名词。句子结构为：some…react by…。参考译文：那些电子结构截然不同的原子（周期表左右两端），通过将一个或数个电子由一个原子传递到另一个原子的方式反应（离子键形式）。

5. would rather……than…… 含有选择的意思，可译作"宁可……而不……"。e. g.：I would rather die than live in dishonour.。句中的 bond 为动词，意为"成键"，than 后省略 bond。would rather 与 than 后面为平行结构。参考译文：氯分子代表着比单独的氯原子更稳定的排列，但是，若有机会，氯原子宁可与氢成键而不愿与另一个氯成键。

Unit 8 Hard and Soft Acids and Bases

In addition to their intrinsic strength, acids and bases have other properties that determine the extent of reaction. For example, silver halides have a range of solubilities in aqueous solution. A simple series shows the trend:

$$AgF(s) + H_2O \longrightarrow Ag^+(aq) + F^-(aq) \quad K_{sp} = 205$$
$$AgCl(s) + H_2O \longrightarrow Ag^+(aq) + Cl^-(aq) \quad K_{sp} = 1.8 \times 10^{-10}$$
$$AgBr(s) + H_2O \longrightarrow Ag^+(aq) + Br^-(aq) \quad K_{sp} = 5.2 \times 10^{-13}$$
$$AgI(s) + H_2O \longrightarrow Ag^+(aq) + I^-(aq) \quad K_{sp} = 8.3 \times 10^{-17}$$

Solvation of the ions is certainly a factor in these reactions, with fluoride ion being much more strongly solvated than the other anions.[1] However, the trend is also related to changes in the degree of interaction between the halides and the silver ions. The interactions can be expressed in terms of **hard and soft acids and bases** (HSAB), in which the metal cation is the Lewis acid and the halide anion is the Lewis base. Hard acids and bases are small and nonpolarizable, whereas soft acids and bases are larger and more polarizable; interactions between two hard or two soft species are stronger than those between one hard and one soft species. In the series of silver ion-halide reactions, iodide ion is much softer (more polarizable) than the others, and interacts more strongly with silver ion, a soft cation. The result is a more covalent bond. The colors of the salts are also worth noting. Silver iodide is yellow, silver bromide is slightly yellow, and silver chloride and silver fluoride are white. Color depends on the difference in energy between occupied and unoccupied orbitals. A large difference results in absorption in the ultraviolet region of the spectrum; a smaller difference in energy levels moves the absorption into the visible region. Compounds absorbing violet appear to be yellow; as the absorption band moves toward lower energy, the color shifts and becomes more intense. Black indicates very broad and very strong absorption. Color and low solubility typically go with soft-soft interactions; colorless compounds and high solubility generally go with hard-hard interactions, although some hard-hard combinations have low solubility.

For example, the lithium halides have solubilities roughly in the reverse order: LiBr > LiCl > LiI > LiF. The solubilities show a strong hard-hard interaction in LiF that overcomes the solvation of water, but the weaker hard-soft interactions of the other halides are not strong enough to prevent solvation and these halides are more soluble than LiF. LiI is out of order, probably because of the poor solvation of the very large iodide ion, but it is still about 100 times as soluble as LiF on a molecular basis.

These reactions illustrate the general rules described by Fajans in 1923. They can be summarized in four rules, in which increased covalent character means lower solubility, increased color, and shorter interionic distances:

1. For a given cation, covalent character increases with increase in size of the anion.
2. For a given anion, covalent character increases with decrease in size of the cation.
3. Covalent character increases with increasing charge on either ion.
4. Covalent character is greater for cations with nonnoble gas electronic configurations.

These rules are helpful in predicting behavior of specific cation-anion combinations in relation to others, although they are not enough to explain all such reactions. For example, the lithium series (omitting LiI) does not fit and requires a different explanation, which is provided by HSAB arguments. The solubilities of the alkaline earth carbonates are $MgCO_3 > CaCO_3 > SrCO_3 > BaCO_3$. Rule 2 predicts the reverse of this order. The difference appears to lie in the aquation of the metal ions. Mg^{2+} (small, with higher charge density) attracts water molecules much more strongly than the others, with Ba^{2+} (large, with smaller charge density) the least strongly solvated.

Ahrland, Chatt, and Davies classified some of the same phenomena (as well as others) by dividing the metal ions into two classes:

Class(a)ions	Class(b)ions
Most metals	$Cu^{2+}, Pd^{2+}, Ag^+, Pt^{2+}, Au^+, Hg_2^{2+}, Hg^{2+}, Tl^+, Tl^{3+}, Pb^{2+}$, and heavier transition metal ions

The members of class (b) are located in a small region in the periodic table at the lower right-hand side of the transition metals. In the periodic table, the elements that are always in class (b) and those that are commonly in class (b) when they have low or zero oxidation states are identified.[2] In addition, the transition metals have class (b) character in compounds in which their oxidation state is zero (organometallic compounds). The class (b) ions form halides whose solubility is in the order $F^- > Cl^- > Br^- > I^-$. The solubility of class (a) halides is in the reverse order. The class (b) metal ions also have a larger enthalpy of reaction with phosphorus donors than with nitrogen donors, again the reverse of the class (a) metal ion reactions.

Ahrland, Chatt, and Davies explained the class (b) metals as having d electrons available for π bonding. Therefore, high oxidation states of elements to the right of the transition metals have more class (b) character than low oxidation states. For example, thallium (Ⅲ) and thallium (Ⅰ) are both class (b) in their reactions with halides, but Tl (Ⅲ) shows stronger class (b) character because Tl (Ⅰ) has two $6s$ electrons that screen the $5d$ electrons and keep them from being fully available for π bonding. Elements farther left in the table have more class (b) character in low or zero oxidation states, when more d electrons are present.

Donor molecules or ions that have the most favorable enthalpies of reaction with class (b) metals are those that are readily polarizable and have vacant d or π^* orbitals available for π bonding.[3]

Pearson designated the class (a) ions **hard acids** and class (b) ions **soft acids**. Bases are also classified as hard or soft. The halide ions range from F^-, a very hard base, through less hard Cl^- and Br^- to I^-, a soft base. Reactions are more favorable for hard-hard and soft-soft interactions than for a mix of hard and soft in the reactants. For example, in aqueous solution:

$Ag^+ + I^- \longrightarrow AgI$ (s)   is a very favorable soft-soft reaction; AgI is very insoluble.

$Li^+ + F^- \longrightarrow LiF$ (s)   is a very favorable hard-hard reaction; LiF is only slightly soluble.

$Ag^+ + F^- \longrightarrow AgF$ (s)   is a soft-hard reaction that is not favored; AgF is moderately soluble.

$Li^+ + I^- \longrightarrow LiI$ (s)   is a hard-soft reaction that is not favored; LiI is soluble. (although it is something of a special case, as mentioned earlier).

Much of the hard-soft distinction depends on polarizability, the degree to which a molecule or ion is easily distorted by interaction with other molecules or ions. Electrons in polarizable molecules can be attracted or repelled by charges on other molecules, forming slightly polar species that can then interact with the other molecules. Hard acids and bases are relatively small, compact, and nonpolarizable; soft acids and bases are larger and more polarizable (therefore " softer "). The hard acids are therefore any cations with large positive charge (3+ or larger) or those whose d electrons are relatively unavailable for π bonding (e.g., alkaline earth ions, Al^{3+}). Other hard acid cations that do not fit this description are Cr^{3+}, Mn^{3+}, Fe^{3+}, and Co^{3+}. Soft acids are those whose d electrons or orbitals are readily available for π bonding (+1 cations, heavier +2 cations). In addition, the larger and more massive the atom, the softer it is likely to be, because the large numbers of inner electrons shield the outer ones and make the atom more polarizable. This description fits the class (b) ions well because they are primarily 1+ and 2+ ions with filled or nearly filled d orbitals, and most are in the second and third rows of the transition elements, with 45 or more electrons.

The trends in bases are even easier to see, with fluoride hard and iodide soft. Again, more electrons and larger size lead to softer behavior. In another example, S^{2-} is softer than O^{2-} because it has more electrons spread over a slightly larger volume, making S^{2-} more polarizable. Within a group, such comparisons are easy; as the electronic structure and size change, comparisons become more difficult but are still possible.[4] Thus, S^{2-} is softer than Cl^{-}, which has the same electronic structure, because S^{2-} has a smaller nuclear charge and a slightly larger size. As a result, the negative charge is more available for polarization. Soft acids tend to react with soft bases and hard acids with hard bases, so the reactions produce hard-hard and soft-soft combinations.

From *Inorganic Chemistry* by Gary L. Miessler

New Words and Expressions

solubility [ˌsɔljuˈbiliti] *n.* 溶解度，溶解性
aqueous [ˈeikwiəs] *a.* 水的，水溶液的
solvation [sælˈveiʃən] *n.* 溶液，溶解
solvate [ˈsɔlveit] *n.* 溶质，被溶解物，溶剂化物
nonpolarizable [nɔnˈpəuləraizəbl] *a.* 不可极化的
polarizable [ˈpəuləraizəbl] *a.* 可极化的
iodide [ˈaiədaid] *n.* 碘化物
spectrum [ˈspektrəm] *n.* 光谱，型谱，频谱
interionic [ˌintəaiˈɔnik] *a.* 离子间的
aquation [əˈkweiʃən] *n.* 水合（作用）水化作用
transition [trænˈziʒən, -ˈsiʃən] *n.* 转变，过渡，跃迁
oxidation [ˌɔksiˈdeiʃən] *n.* 氧化（作用）
organometallic [ˌɔːgənəumiˈtælik] *a.* 有机金属的
enthalpy [ˈenθælpi, enˈθælpi] *n.* 焓，热函
thallium [ˈθæliəm] *n.* 铊［元素符号Tl］
vacant [ˈveikənt] *a.* 空的，空白的，未被占用的
polarizability [ˈpəuləˌraizəˈbiləti] *n.* 极化性，极化率，极化度
polarization [ˌpəulərai'zeiʃən; -ri'z-] *n.* 偏振（现象），极化（作用）

Notes

1. with 后面是句子的补语，是对前面主句的补充说明。solvation 意为溶解。参考译文：离子的溶解是这些反应得以进行的一个明显因素，其中，氟离子比其他的阴离子更易被溶解。

2. 包括由 that 引导的定语从句以及由 when 引导的状语从句，class 是指由文中 Ahrland，Chatt，and Davies 划分的金属的种类。参考译文：在元素周期表中，那些总是属于 b 类金属，以及那些在低价或零价氧化态时通常属于 b 类的元素是可以被确定的。

3. that 引导的为定语从句，修饰" Donor molecules or ions "，those 指代前半句的" Donor molecules or ions "，donor 意思为（电子的）施者，enthalpies 意思为焓。参考译文：能够与 b 类金属反应，过程中产生最明显焓变的给电子分子或离子，都是那些易被极化的，具有空的 d 轨道或空的反键 π 轨道用于生成 π 键的（分子和离子）。

4. 由分号将前后两句连接起来，表示并列结构，相当于" and "。as 表示"伴随，随着"之意。参考译文：在同一族中，如此的比较更加简单易懂；随着电子的结构和大小的变化，比较也变的越来越难，但是依然是可行的。

Exercises

I. Comprehension

1. When comparison hard acids and soft acids，we could find that ____.
   A. hard acids are small and nonpolarizable
   B. hard acids are larger and more polarizable
   C. soft acids are small and nonpolarizable
   D. there are completely no differences between them

2. The correct order for solubilities of the lithium halides is ____.
   A. LiF>LlCl>LiBr>LiI   B. LiCl>LlF>LiBr>LiI
   C. LiBr>LlCl>LiI>LiF   D. LiI>LlBr>LiCl>LiF

3. According to the general rules described by Fajans，which of the followings is NOT true? ____
   A. For a given cation，covalent character increases with increase in size of the anion.
   B. For a given anion，covalent character increases with decrease in size of the cation.
   C. Covalent character increases with decreasing charge on either ion.
   D. Covalent character is greater for cations with nonnoble gas electronic configurations.

4. From what we have known from the passage，which of the followings tends to gain more class (b) character? ____
   A. The transition metals with a high oxidation state
   B. High oxidation states of elements to the right of the transition metals
   C. High oxidation states of elements farther left in the table
   D. Low or zero oxidation states of elements to the right of the transition metals

5. According to the passage，the larger and more massive the atom is ____.
   A. the softer the atom is likely to be
   B. the large numbers of outer electrons shield the inner ones
   C. the atom is less polarizable
   D. the harder the atom is likely to be

6. Which of the followings does NOT describe the relationship between S^{2-} and Cl^-?
   A. S^{2-} is softer than Cl^-
   B. S^{2-} has a smaller nuclear charge and a slightly larger size than does Cl^-
   C. S^{2-} is more polarizable than Cl^-
   D. S^{2-} has different electronic structure

II. Explain each the following，using Fajan's rules

a. Ag_2S is much less soluble than Ag_2O.
b. $Fe(OH)_3$ is much less soluble than $Fe(OH)_2$.
c. FeS is much less soluble than $Fe(OH)_2$.

d. Ag_2S is much less soluble than AgCl.

e. Salts of the transition metals are usually less soluble than the corresponding salts of the alkali and alkaline earth metals.

III. Is OH^- or S^{2-} more likely to form insoluble salts with 3+ transition metal ions? Which is more likely to form insoluble salts with 2+ transition metal ions?

IV. Some of the products of the following reactions will be insoluble and some form soluble adducts. Consider only the HSAB characteristics in your answers.

(a). Will Cu^{2+} react more strongly with OH^- or NH_3? With O^{2-} or S^{2-}?

(b). Will Fe^{3+} react more strongly with OH^- or NH_3? With O^{2-} or S^{2-}?

(c). Will Ag^+ react more strongly with NH_3 or PH_3?

(d). Will Fe, Fe^{2+}, or Fe^{3+} react more strongly with CO?

V. **Translation**

An acid or a base may be either hard or soft and at the same time be either strong or weak. The strength of the acid or base may be more important than the hard-soft characteristics; both must be considered at the same time. If two soft bases are in competition for the same acid, the one with more inherent base strength may be favored unless there is considerable difference in softness. As an example, consider the following reaction. Two hard-soft combinations react to give a hard-hard and a soft-soft combination, although ZnO is composed of the strongest acid (Zn^{2+}) and the strongest base (O^{2-}):

$$ZnO\ +\ 2\ LiC_4H_9 \longrightarrow Zn(C_4H_9)_2\ +\ Li_2O$$
soft-hard   hard-soft   soft-soft   hard-hard

In this case, the HSAB parameters are more important than acid-base strength, because Zn^{2+} is considerably softer than Li^+. As a general rule, hard-hard combinations are more favorable energetically than soft-soft combinations.

Reading Material

Valence Shell Electron Pair Repulsion Theory

Valence shell electron pair repulsion theory (VSEPR) provides a method for predicting the shape of molecules, based on the electron pair electrostatic repulsion. It was described by Sidgwick and Powell in 1940 and further developed by Gillespie and Nyholm in 1957. In spite of this method's very simple approach, based on Lewis electron-dot structures, the VSEPR method predicts shapes that compare favorably with those determined experimentally.[1] However, this approach at best provides approximate shapes for molecules, not a complete picture of bonding. The most common method of determining the actual structures is X-ray diffraction, although electron diffraction, neutron diffraction, and many types of spectroscopy are also used. In Chapter 5, we will provide some of the molecular orbital arguments for the shapes of simple molecules.

Electrons repel each other because they are negatively charged. The quantum mechanical rules force some of them to be fairly close to each other in bonding pairs or lone pairs, but each pair repels all other pairs. According to the VSEPR model, therefore, molecules adopt geometries in which their valence electron pairs position themselves as far from each other as possible. A molecule can be described by the generic formula AX_mE_n, where A is the central atom, X stands for any atom or group of atoms surrounding the central atom, and E represents a lone pair of electrons. The **steric number** $(SN=m+n)$ is the number of positions occupied by atoms or lone pairs around a central atom; lone pairs and bonds are nearly equal in their influence on molecular shape.

Carbon dioxide is an example with two bonding positions $(SN=2)$ on the central atom and double bonds in each direction. The electrons in each double bond must be between C and O, and the repulsion between the electrons in the double bonds forces a linear structure on the molecule. Sulfur trioxide has three bonding positions $(SN=3)$, with partial double bond character in each. The best positions for the oxygens in this molecule are at the corners of an equilateral triangle, with O—S—O bond angles of 120°.[2] The multiple bonding does not affect the geometry because it is shared equally among the three bonds.

The same pattern of finding the Lewis structure and then matching it to a geometry that minimizes the repulsive energy of bonding electrons is followed through steric numbers four, five, six, seven, and eight.

The structures for two, three, four, and six electron pairs are completely regular, with all bond angles and distances the same. Neither 5- nor 7-coordinate structures can have uniform angles and distances, because there are no regular polyhedra with these numbers of vertices. The 5-coordinate molecules have a trigonal bipyramidal structure, with a central triangular plane of three positions plus two other positions above and below the center of the plane. The 7-coordinate molecules have a pentagonal bipyramidal structure, with a pentagonal plane of five positions and positions above and below the center of the plane. The regular square antiprism structure $(SN = 8)$ is like a cube with the top and bottom faces twisted 45° into the antiprism arrangement. It has three different bond angles for adjacent fluorines. $[TaF_8]^{3-}$ has square antiprism symmetry, but is distorted from this ideal in the solid. (A simple cube has only the 109.5° and 70.5° bond angles measured between two corners and the center of the cube, because all edges are equal and any square face can be taken as the bottom or top.)

We must keep in mind that we are always attempting to match our explanations to experimental data. The explanation that fits the data best should be the current favorite, but new theories are continually being suggested and tested. Because we are working with such a wide variety of atoms and molecular structures, it is unlikely that a single, simple approach will work for all of them. Although the fundamental ideas of atomic and molecular structures are relatively simple, their application to complex molecules is not. It is also helpful to keep in mind that for many purposes, prediction of exact bond angles is not usually required. To a first approximation, lone pairs, single bonds, double bonds, and triple bonds can all be treated similarly when predicting molecular shapes. However, better predictions of overall shapes can be made by considering some important differences between lone pairs and bonding pairs. These methods are sufficient to show the trends and explain the bonding, as in explaining why the H—N—H angle in ammonia is smaller than the tetrahedral angle in methane and larger than the H—O—H angle in water.

The isoelectronic molecules CH_4, NH_3, and H_2O illustrate the effect of lone pairs on molecular shape. Methane has four identical bonds between carbon and each of the hydrogen. When the four pairs of electrons are arranged as far from each other as possible, the result is the familiar tetrahedral shape. The tetrahedron, with all H—C—H angles measuring 109.5°, has four identical bonds.

Ammonia also has four pairs of electrons around the central atom, but three are bonding pairs between N and H and the fourth is a lone pair on the nitrogen. The nuclei form a trigonal pyramid with the three bonding pairs; with the lone pair, they make a nearly tetrahedral shape. Because each of the three bonding pairs is attracted by two positively charged nuclei (H and N), these pairs are largely confined to the regions between the H and N atoms. The lone pair, on the other hand, is concentrated near the nitrogen; it has no second nucleus to confine it to a small region of space. Consequently, the lone pair tends to spread out and to occupy more space around the nitrogen than the bonding pairs. As a result, the H—N—H angles are 106.6°, nearly 3° smaller than the angles in methane (Fig. 8.1).

Fig. 8.1 shapes of methane, ammonia, and water

The same principles apply to the water molecule, in which two lone pairs and two bonding pairs repel each other. Again, the electron pairs have a nearly tetrahedral arrangement, with the atoms arranged in a V shape.[3] The angle of largest repulsion, between the two lone pairs, is not directly measurable. However, the lone pair-bonding pair (lp-bp) repulsion is greater than the bonding pair-bonding pair (bp-bp) repulsion, and as a result the H—O—H bond angle is only 104.5°, another 2.1° decrease from the ammonia angles. The net result is that we can predict approximate molecular shapes by assigning more space to lone electron pairs; being attracted to one nucleus rather than two, the lone pairs are able to spread out and occupy more space.[4]

The VSEPR model considers double and triple bonds to have slightly greater repulsive effects than single bonds because of the repulsive effect of π electrons. For example, the H_3C—C—CH_3 angle in $(CH_3)_2C=CH_2$ is smaller and the H_3C—C=CH_2 angle is larger than the trigonal 120°.

Additional examples of the effect of multiple bonds on molecular geometry are shown in Fig. 8.3. Comparing Fig. 8.2 and Fig. 8.3 indicates that multiple bonds tend to occupy the same positions as lone pairs. For example, the double bonds to oxygen in SOF_4, ClO_2F_3, and XeO_3F_2 are all equatorial, as are the lone pairs in the matching compounds of steric number 5, SF_4, BrF_3, and XeF_2. Also, multiple bonds, like lone pairs, tend to occupy more space than single bonds and to cause distortions that in effect squeeze the rest of the molecule together. In molecules that have both lone pairs and multiple bonds, these features may compete for space; examples are shown in Fig. 8.4.

Fig. 8.2 the repulsive effect of π electrons

Fig. 8.3 the effect of multiple bonds on molecular geometry

Fig. 8.4 molecule which has both lone pairs and multiple bonds

From *Inorganic Chemistry* by Gary L. Miessler

New Words and Expressions

electrostatic [iˈlektrəuˈstætik]   *a.* 静电的，静电学的

diffraction [di'frækʃən]   n. 衍射，折射
spectroscopy [spek'trɔskəpi]   n. 光谱学，波谱学
steric ['stiərik, 'sterik]   n. 立体的，空间（排列）的
trioxide [trai'ɔksaid]   n. 三氧化物
coordinate [kəu'ɔ:dinit]   a. 配位的，同等的，并列的
polyhedron [pɔli'hedrən]   n. 多面体
bipyramidal [,bai'pirəmid]   n. 双锥（体）a. 双锥体的
antiprism ['ænti'prizəm]   n. 反棱柱体
isoelectronic [,aisəuilek'trɔnik]   a. 等电子的
tetrahedral ['tetrə'hedrəl]   a. 有四面的，四面体的
repulsive [ri'pʌlsiv]   a. 推斥的，排斥的

Notes

1. this method 指代的是 Lewis 电子点结构，VSEPR 指价层电子对互斥理论。参考译文：尽管建立在 Lewis 电子点结构基础上的这种方法简单易懂，但是通过 VSEPR 推测的分子模型与通过实验确定的模型吻合的更好。

2. with 后面的补语是对前面主句的补充说明，equilateral triangle 的意思为等边三角形。参考译文：在这个分子中，氧原子的最佳位置是等边三角形的三个顶点，这时 O—S—O 键的键角为 120°。

3. again 表示强调，与前文呼应，with 后面的补语是对前面主句的补充说明，tetrahedral 的意思为四面体的。参考译文：电子对再次以近似于四面体的方式排布，此时原子排布成 V 形。

4. 句中的；将前后两句话连接起来（；前后均是完整句子），that 引导宾语从句，by 后是名词性短语，修饰预测分子模型的方法，being attracted to one nucleus rather than two 用来修饰 lone pairs。net 表示"净的，最终的"。参考译文：最后的结果就是，我们可以指定给孤对电子更多的空间来预测分子的大概模型；孤电子对受到的是一个原子核的吸引而不是两个原子核的吸引，同时被两个原子核吸引相比，对更倾向于被一个原子核所吸引，因此他们会扩展从而占据更多的空间。

Unit 9   Chemical Kinetics: Basic Principles

Chemical kinetics (i.e., reaction rates) and equilibria are interrelated in that chemical equilibria are *dynamic* — that is, reaction continues in both the forward and reverse directions at equilibrium, but the *rates* in the opposing directions are exactly equal. It follows that the energetic factors considered above also influence reaction rates. Kinetic phenomena, however, are most in evidence far from equilibrium, and they are more difficult to treat theoretically than are equilibria. Thus, although thermodynamics can tell us whether a particular reaction should proceed from reactants to specific products under given conditions of temperature, pressure, concentration, etc., it tells us nothing about how the reaction could take place at the molecular level (the reaction mechanism) nor how *fast* equilibrium will be approached.[1] The reaction may be "infinitely slow" for lack of a favorable mechanism. Reaction kinetics and mechanism are intimately related; the rate of a reaction is largely determined by (a) how the reacting molecules organize themselves in space, ready to set up new bonds and break old ones, (b) how many of the potential reactant molecules have enough energy to get over the bond making/breaking energy barrier (activation energy), and (c) (for reactions in solution) how the solvent molecules rearrange to facilitate the activation process.

The rate of a reaction is expressed as the increase in the amount of a particular product, or the decrease in the amount of a reactant, per second at a time t. For reactions in a fluid phase, it is usual to substitute concentrations, or for gases partial pressures, for amounts. Note that the numerical value of the rate may depend on how we choose to define it. For example, in the oxidation of aqueous iodide ion by arsenic acid to give triiodide ion and arsenious acid,

$$H_3AsO_4 + 3I^- + 2H^+ \rightleftharpoons H_3AsO_3 + I_3^- + H_2O \qquad (9.1)$$

The rate may be defined as $d[I_3^-]/dt$, or $-d[H_3AsO_4]/dt$, or $-d[I^-]/dt$, etc., but the stoichiometric coefficients in reaction 9.1 tell us that the last rate is numerically three times either of the other two. Thus, we must state clearly what we mean by "reaction rate" (such as the rate of disappearance of iodide ion, or the rate of appearance of arsenious acid) wherever ambiguity may arise.

Relation of Rate Equation to Mechanism

The *rate equation*, sometimes called the "rate law," relates the rate at time t to the activities (less rigorously, the concentrations) of the reactants remaining at that instant. Unlike the equilibrium expression, however, the form of the rate equation generally cannot be obtained merely by inspection of the stoichiometric equation unless the reaction is known to proceed to completion in a single step. The rate equation must be determined experimentally, and this includes finding out whether the reaction is or is not a single-step process. The activities (in practice, concentrations or, for gases, partial pressures) and the powers to which they are raised (reaction *orders*) in the experimentally determined rate equation tell us which molecules, or fragments thereof, are actually involved in the rate-determining step of the reaction. Any reactant particles that are not involved in this bottleneck configuration or *transition state* will not affect the observed reaction rate but will be consumed relatively rapidly in subsequent steps. Thus, it is found that the rate of the forward reaction in Eq. 9.1 is *first order* with respect to each of arsenic acid, iodide ion, and hydrogen ion (and so *third order overall*).[2] We cannot determine the order with respect to water, as this is the solvent and its activity is essentially unity at all times

$$\frac{d[I_3^-]}{dt} = k_f[H_3AsO_4][I^-][H^+] \qquad (9.2)$$

In Eq. 9.2, k_f is the forward rate constant, and the composition of the transition state is $\{H_4AsO_4I\}$, although it could contain additionally (or be short of) the elements of one or more water molecules, since we cannot determine the order with respect to the solvent. Eq. 9.2 cannot be arrived at from reaction 9.1, but consideration of the concentration factors in the two equations tells us at once the rate law for the reverse reaction (Eq. 9.4, rate constant k_r), since, according to reaction 9.1, the equilibrium expression has to be

$$K = \frac{[H_3AsO_3][I_3^-]}{[H_3AsO_4][I^-]^3[H^+]^2} \tag{9.3}$$

And, at equilibrium, the forward and reverse rate must be equal:

$$-\frac{d[I_3^-]}{dt} = k_r \frac{[H_3AsO_3][I_3^-]}{[I^-]^2[H^+]} \tag{9.4}$$

It follows that the equilibrium constant K is given by k_f/k_r. The reverse reaction is inverse second order in iodide, and inverse first-order in H^+. This means that the transition state for the reverse reaction contains the elements of arsenious acid and triiodide ion less two iodides and one hydrogen ion, namely, $\{H_2AsO_3I\}$. This is the same as that for the forward reaction, except for the elements of one molecule of water, the solvent, the participation of which cannot be determined experimentally.[3] The concept of a common transition state for the forward and reverse reactions is called the principle of microscopic reversibility.

However, more than one reaction pathway may exist, in which case the rate equation will contain sums of terms representing the competing reaction pathways. For example, one of the oxidation reactions that convert the atmospheric pollutant sulfur dioxide to sulfuric acid (a component of acid rain) in water droplets in clouds involves dissolved ozone, O_3:

$$SO_2(g) + H_2O(l) \rightleftharpoons H_2SO_3(aq) = HSO_3^-(aq) + H^+(aq) \tag{9.5}$$

$$HSO_3^- + O_3 \longrightarrow H^+ + SO_4^{2-} + O_2 \tag{9.6}$$

The rate equation for Eq. 9.6 turns out to be

$$-\frac{d[HSO_3^-]}{dt} = \left(k_1 + \frac{k_2}{[H^+]}\right)[HSO_3][O_3] \tag{9.7}$$

which implies two parallel pathways: an $[H^+]$ independent one with a transition state composition $\{HSO_6\}^-$ and rate constant k_1, and an $[H^+]$ dependent one with transition state $\{SO_6\}^{2-}$ and rate constant k_2. (actually, $[H^+]$ also affects the overall aqueous ozone oxidation process through the solubility equilibrium of SO_2, reaction 9.5.)

Rate equations of considerable complexity can result from *chain reactions*, such as the reaction of bromine with hydrogen in the gas phase between 200℃ and 300℃ to form hydrogen bromide. These are reactions in which a chain carrier is created in an initiation step (here, a Br• atom from dissociation of Br_2) and goes on to create more carriers (Br• + $H_2 \longrightarrow$ HBr + H•, followed by H• + $Br_2 \longrightarrow$ HBr + Br•, and so on) until a recombination step ends the chain.[4] The rate equation for HBr formation has been shown to be:

$$\frac{d[HBr]}{dt} = \frac{k_1[H_2][Br_2]^{\frac{1}{2}}}{1 + \frac{k_2[HBr]}{[Br_2]}} \tag{9.8}$$

Chain reactions are important in certain polymerizations, organic halogenation reactions, combustion processes, and explosions. Usually they involve a *radical* (a molecule or atom with an odd valence electron, e.g., Br•), since these will create another radical each time they react with an ordinary molecule having only paired electrons. Detailed discussions are available in standard texts.

Differential rate equations such as Eq. 9.4 are often used in integrated form, so that the rate constant can be evaluated simply by measuring concentrations rather than rates at selected times t.[5] Integration of the rate equation, however, may be difficult or may give an unwieldy result. In this book, we are concerned primarily with reaction rates as such, and the reader is therefore referred to texts devoted to chemical kinetics for information on integrated rate equations.

Temperature Effects on Rates

The temperature dependence of a rate constant is usually given empirically by the Arrhenius equation:

$$K = A \exp\left(-\frac{E_a}{RT}\right) \tag{9.9}$$

In which E_a is the Arrhenius activation energy (typically on the order of 50 kJ/mol to 100 kJ/mol) and the pre-exponential factor A includes such factors as the frequency of collision between the reactant molecules and the probability of their mutual orientation being favorable for reaction.[6] Thus, ln$K$ is a linear function of the reciprocal Kelvin temperature, so that if we know K at any two temperatures, or at one temperature when E_a is known, we can use Eq. 9.9 to calculate K at any other temperature. This does not apply for reactions proceeding by two or more parallel pathways of different E_a (unless one can evaluate Eq. 9.9 for the various pathways separately, e. g., if one can solve Eq. 9.7 for k_1 and k_2 at two temperatures) or for multistep reactions if a different step becomes rate determining as the temperature changes.[7] In either case, a curved plot of ln$K$ against T^{-1} will result. Simple Arrhenius treatments work well in great many cases.

An alternative to Eq. 9.9 that is popular with modern kineticists is the Eyring equation (Eq. 9.10), which derives from the notion that the transition state is in (very unfavorable) equilibrium with the reactants but decays with a universal frequency given by $k_B T/h$, where k_B is Boltzmann's constant and h is Planck's constant. Then, by analogy with $\Delta G^\ominus = -RT\ln K^\ominus$ and $\Delta G^\ominus = -nF\Delta E^\ominus$, we have

$$K = k_B T/h \exp(-\Delta G^{\neq}/RT) = 2.083 \times 10^{10} T \exp[-(\Delta H^{\neq} - T\Delta S^{\neq})/RT] \tag{9.10}$$

Where ΔG, ΔH, and ΔS are the *free energy*, *enthalpy*, and *entropy of activation*, respectively. Thus, $\ln(K/T)$ should be a linear function of T^{-1}. This is slightly different from the Arrhenius expectation, but in practice data usually fit either Eq. 9.9 or Eq. 9.10 equally well within the inevitable experimental errors. For reactions in solution, $\Delta H^{\neq} = E_a - RT$.

Pressure Effects on Rates

Pressure effects on K can be accommodated in terms of a *volume of activation*, $\Delta V^{\neq}$, which is the pressure derivative of ΔG:

$$(\partial \ln K/\partial P)_T = -\Delta V^{\neq}/RT \tag{9.11}$$

If $\Delta V^{\neq}$ can be taken to be constant over the experimental pressure range (this approximation is often a poor one for ranges of more than 100 MPa), then ln$k$ becomes a linear function of pressure:

$$\ln k_p = \ln k_0 - P\Delta V^{\neq}/RT \tag{9.12}$$

Values of $\Delta V^{\neq}$ are frequently on the order of 10 cm^3/mol for simple reactions in solution, in which case K would be retarded or accelerated by a factor of only about 1.5 on going from ambient P and T to 100 MPa. If, however, $\Delta V^{\neq}$ is around -30 cm^3/mol for a reaction that is impracticably slow at room temperature and pressure, and a 2 GPa press is available, the reaction can in principle be accelerated by a factor of 3×10^{10} without heating. In practice, the acceleration will almost certainly be somewhat less than this, as $\Delta V^{\neq}$ is likely to become numerically smaller (less negative) as the pressure increases over this wide range.

The Eyring approach has the advantage that the pseudothermodynamic activation parameters can be readily related to the true thermodynamic quantities that govern the equilibrium of the reaction.[8] The Arrhenius equation, on the other hand, is easier to use for simple interpolations or extrapolations of rate data.

From *Chemical Kinetics and Dynamics* by Jeffrey I. Steinfeld

New Words and Expressions

kinetics [kai'netiks] $n.$ 动力学
interrelate [ˌintə(ː)ri'leit] $v.$ 使相互关联
mechanism ['mekənizəm] $n.$ 机理,进程
intimately ['intimitli] $ad.$ 亲切地,密切地
solvent ['sɔlvənt] $n.$ 溶剂
arsenic ['ɑːsənik] $n.$ 砷[元素符号 As]
triiodide [ˌtriaiədaid] $n.$ 三碘化物
arsenious [ɑː'siːniəs] $a.$ 亚砷的,三价砷的
microscopic ['maikrə'skɔpik] $a.$ 微观的,细致的
reversibility [riˌvəːsə'biliti] $n.$ 可反转性,可逆性
pollutant [pə'luːtənt] $n.$ 污染物,污染源
sulfur [sʌl'fjuːrik] $n.$ 硫[元素符号 S]
sulfuric ['sʌlfə] $a.$ 硫的,含硫的
initiation [iˌniʃi'eiʃən] $n.$ 开始,初始
polymerization ['pɔliməraizeiʃən] $n.$ 聚合(作用)
halogenation [hælədʒə'neiʃən] $n.$ 卤化(作用),卤代反应
combustion [kəm'bʌstʃən] $n.$ 燃烧,氧化
reciprocal [ri'siprəkəl] $a.$ 倒数的
pseudothermodynamic ['sjuːdəu'θəːməudai'næmik] $a.$ 假热(力)学的
extrapolation [iksˌtræpə'leiʃən] $n.$ 外推(法)

Notes

1. dynamics 意思是"动力学"。e.g.:flow (fluid) dynamics 流体动力学。gas dynamics 气体动力学。specific 在这里是"具体的,特定的"意思。参考译文:因此,尽管热力学可以告诉我们在给定的温度、压力、浓度条件下,从反应物到具体产物的特定反应是否可以进行,但我们既无法知晓在分子水平上反应如何发生(反应机理)的,也无法知晓达到平衡的速度有多快。

2. 参考译文:因此,我们发现平衡反应式 9.1 中,正反应的速率从砷酸、碘离子、氢离子的方面来看是一级反应(从整体来看是三级反应)。

3. 句中 which 是关系代词,代 solvent。参考译文:正反应也如此,除水分子外,溶剂的加入不影响实验结果。

4. 在这个句子中,which 是关系代词,代替 reactions,它引导一个状语从句。carrier 本意是"载体",此处 chain carrier 是一个专业名词,意思是"链反应活性中心"。参考译文:在这些反应中,引发步骤产生链反应活性中心(这里是 Br_2 离解产生的 Br? 原子),接下来产生更多的活性中心(Br· $+ H_2 \longrightarrow$ HBr $+$ H·,下一步是 H· $+ Br_2 \longrightarrow$ HBr $+$ Br·,如此继续下去),直到终止链反应。

5. rather than 的意思是"是……,而不是"。参考译文:微分速率方程(如方程式 9.4)通常是以积分的形式使用,这样速率常数可以通过测定浓度的简单方法来确定,而不需要确定特定时间的速率。

6. 参考译文:在这个方程中,E_a 是阿仑尼乌斯活化能(一般约 50~100kJ/mol),前指数系数 A 包含了反应物分子碰撞的频率和它们相互取向以适合反应的概率。

7. 参考译文:这个方法不适用于通过两个或两个以上的相似步骤进行反应且 E_a 不同的情况(除非可以用方程式(9.9)分别求得不同反应步骤的数值。如可用方程式(9.7)求出两种温度下的 k_1 和 k_2 值)。如果在多步反应中,各步骤在温度改变时速率也变化的话,该方法也不适用。

8. pseudo- 源自希腊文,作为构词前缀,表示"伪,假,拟"。参考译文:埃林法具有以下优点:伪热动力活化参数可以很容易地与控制反应平衡的真实的热动力学参数联系起来。

PART TWO THE FUNDAMENTALS OF CHEMISTRY

Exercises

I. Comprehension

1. On the basis of the first paragraph, we can conclude that _____.
   A. because of the dynamic chemical equilibrium, reaction rates and equilibrium are relative intimately
   B. given conditions of temperature, pressure, concentration, a molecular reaction should proceed from reactants to products
   C. the reaction mechanism can reveal how the molecular reaction will take place and how fast equilibrium will be approached
   D. reaction rates can determine the reaction mechanism by setting up new bonds and breaking old ones

2. According to the following chemical reaction, which definition of the reaction rate is not true? $H_3AsO_4 + 3I^- + 2H^+ \rightleftharpoons H_3AsO_3 + I_3^- + H_2O$ _____.
   A. $d[I_3^-]/dt$
   B. $-d[H_3AsO_3]/dt$
   C. $-d[H_3AsO_4]/dt$
   D. $-d[I^-]/dt$

3. Which is right about the statement of the rate equation? _____
   A. The rate equation reveals whether the reaction is a single-step process or not.
   B. The rate equation can be determined by the form of the stoichiometric equation.
   C. All reactants of the reaction are involved in the rate-determining step of the reaction.
   D. The solvent also take a part in determining the rate equation.

4. According to the chemical kinetics, the reverse rate law is _____ of the following reaction.
$$H_3AsO_4 + 3I^- + 2H^+ \rightleftharpoons H_3AsO_3 + I_3^- + H_2O$$
   A. $d[I_3^-]/dt = k_f[H_3AsO_4][I^-]^2[H^+]$
   B. $K = [H_3AsO_3][I_3^-]/([H_3AsO_3][I^-]^3[H^+]^2)$
   C. $-d[I_3^-]/dt = k_r[H_3AsO_4][I_3^-]/([I^-]^2[H^+])$
   D. $-d[I_3^-]/dt = k_f[H_3AsO_4][I^-][H^+]$

5. What is the most important effect of temperature on reaction rates? _____
   A. The constant K can be calculated at any two temperatures.
   B. The equation $K = A \exp(-E_a/RT)$ applies for reactions proceeding by two pathway of different E_a.
   C. It is well known the Eyring equation is more popular than the Arrhenius equation.
   D. The temperature can determined the rate constant by affecting the Arrhenius activation energy.

6. Which conclusion the authors mostly support? _____
   A. The rate equation can be calculated from the theoretic deduction.
   B. There are more than one competing reaction path ways in a reaction.
   C. Chain reaction can impossibly result from the rate equations of considerable complexity.
   D. The Eyring equation becomes more popular for is can died out the experimental errors.

II. Fill in the blanks

Another factor affecting the rate _____ a chemical reaction is the concentration of reactants. The more reactant molecules there are _____ a volume of space, _____ collisions will occur. The more collisions there are, the more reactions occur.

_____ reactions in solution, the concentration of reactants can be increased _____ greater amounts are dissolved. With gases, concentration can also be increased _____ increasing the pressure.

Materials burn (i. e., react _____ oxygen) _____ a certain rate in air, which in only 21% oxygen. The same material burn much more rapidly _____ pure oxygen. The prohibition against smoking in hospital rooms where patients are undergoing oxygen therapy acknowledges this effect of concentration _____ reaction rates.

III. Translation
1. 催化剂是一种能改变反应速率而自身不发生永久变化的物质。
2. 化学反应速率,即反应进程的快慢,受可改变有效碰撞数的因素的影响。
3. 在产物开始形成前,必须打破反应物分子的化学键。
4. 吸热反应中,反应物吸收能量并将其转化为储存于不稳定化合物中的化学键的潜能。
5. 放热反应中,反应物释放潜能形成更稳定的化合物。

IV. Translation
There are two basic questions that a chemical engineer must ask concerning a given chemical reaction:

(a) How far does it go, if it is allowed to proceed to equilibrium? (Indeed, does it go in the direction of interest at all?)

(b) How fast does it progress?

Question (b) is a matter of chemical *kinetics* and reduces to the need to know the *rate equation* and the *rate constants* (customarily designated k) for the various steps involved in the reaction mechanism. Note that the rate equation for a particular reaction is not necessarily obtainable by inspection of the stoichiometry of the reaction, unless the mechanism is a one-step process-and this is something that usually has to be determined by experiment. Chemical reaction time scales range from fractions of a nanosecond to millions of years or ore. Thus, even if the answer to question (a) is that the reaction is expected to go to essential completion, the reaction may be so slow as to be totally impractical in engineering terms.

V. Problem
Given that the partial of the in the reaction at 298K
$$CO(g) + H_2O(g) \longrightarrow H_2(g) + CO_2(g)$$
are

$CO(g) = 5$ atm $\qquad H_2(g) = 3$ atm
$H_2O(g) = 2$ atm $\qquad CO_2(g) = 3$ atm

And the fact that the reaction is not at equilibrium, using appropriate tables and equations, calculate ΔG_{reac}, $\Delta G_{reac}^\ominus$ and K_p and discuss in the reaction will proceed.

Reading Material

Chemical Thermodynamics

A rigorous treatment of chemical thermodynamics is beyond the scope of this book. However, there are several thermodynamic relationships that can provide important insights, even if we resort to a few oversimplifications of thermodynamic concepts. In an overview of inorganic chemistry and its applications, it is more important to appreciate what thermodynamics can tell us then to worry about its rigor or theoretical significance.[1]

Perhaps the most important equation relates the *thermodynamic equilibrium constant* $K^\ominus$ to the *standard free energy change* $\Delta G^\ominus$ of the reaction:
$$\Delta G^\ominus = -RT\ln K^\ominus \qquad (9.13)$$

Where R is the gas constant 8.3143J/(K·mol) and T is the temperature in Kelvin's (degrees Celsius + 273.15). The standard Gibbs free energy $G^\ominus$ represents the capacity of the system for doing external work at constant pressure; thus, the thermodynamic driving force of a chemical reaction is the tendency to minimize this free energy. When $G^\ominus$ is minimized, the reaction ceases, that is, has reached equilibrium.[2]

Activities, and hence $K^\ominus$ values, are necessarily dimensionless quantities and are defined with reference to a convenient standard state. The standard state now universally adopted in the Système International d'Unités (SI) is

(a) pressure $(p) = 100\text{kPa}(0.1\text{MPa}, 1\text{bar})$,
(b) temperature $(T) = 298.15\text{K}(25.00\text{°C})$,
(c) solute concentrations hypothetically 1 mole
(d) ideal gas behavior (i.e., as if $p \to 0$), and
(e) ideal solution behavior (i.e., as if infinitely dilute).

The last restriction explains the hypothetical standard concentration of 1 mole: obviously, 1 mol/kg is quite concentrated, and the standard state conditions are extrapolated from high dilution. Gas concentrations are conveniently expressed as partial pressures:

$$\text{Concentration} = n \text{ mol} / \text{volume } V = p/RT (\text{ideally}) \propto p, \text{ at } 25\text{°C} \qquad (9.14)$$

So the standard state for a gaseous reactant is 1 bar partial pressure with (extrapolated) ideal behavior.

Thus, if we start with our reactants and products under standard conditions and allow the reaction to proceed to equilibrium, an amount of energy $\Delta G^\ominus$ becomes available for external work. In the context of doing external electrical work, an oxidation-reduction reaction can generate a standard electromotive force $\Delta E^\ominus$ given by

$$\Delta G^\ominus = -nF\Delta E^\ominus \qquad (9.15)$$

where n is the number of moles of electrons transferred in the reaction and F is the charge of one mole of electrons (the Faraday constant, 96485C/mol). However, the change in standard heat content, or enthalpy change ($\Delta H^\ominus$), associated with the reaction is not the same as $\Delta G^\ominus$, since some of the heat content can never be extracted.[3] We speak of the standard entropy of a substance $S^\ominus$ as being its isothermally unavailable heat content per Kelvin:

$$\Delta G^\ominus = \Delta H^\ominus - T\Delta S^\ominus \qquad (9.16)$$

The enthalpy change of the reaction, $\Delta H^\ominus$, can be calculated by subtracting the heat contents of the reactants from those of the products (Hess's law):

$$\Delta H^\ominus = \Sigma H^\ominus (\text{products}) - \Sigma H^\ominus (\text{reactants}). \qquad (9.17)$$

However, the absolute heat contents of individual substances are generally not available. The arbitrary assumption is therefore made that $H^\ominus$ is zero for the chemical elements in their most stable form at 25°C and 1 bar. For the formation of liquid water,

$$H_2 + 1/2 O_2(g) \xrightarrow[\text{1 bar}]{25\text{°C}} H_2O(l) \qquad (9.18)$$

$\Delta H_f^\ominus$ is -285.830 kJ/mol; for water vapor, $\Delta H_f^\ominus$ is -241.818 kJ/mol, the difference being simply the heat of evaporation of 1 mole of water under standard conditions. For the formation of carbon monoxide,

$$C(s) + 1/2 O_2(g) = CO(g) \qquad (9.19)$$

$\Delta H_f^\ominus$ is -110.525 kJ/mol, relative to $\Delta H_f^\ominus = 0$ for graphite. (Diamond, the other familiar form of elemental carbon, is actually less stable than graphite at 25°C and 1 bar; $\Delta H_f^\ominus = 1.895$ kJ/mol.) We can therefore calculate a standard heat of reaction for the water-gas reaction,

$$C(s) + H_2O(g) = H_2(g) + CO(g) \qquad (9.20)$$

To be $(-110.525) - (-241.818) = +131.293$.

Note that reaction 9.20 is endothermic (the plus sign for $\Delta H^\ominus$ means that heat is taken into the system), whereas reaction 9.18 and reaction 9.19 are exothermic (the reactions give out heat to the surroundings). Many heats of formation or of reaction can be measured by calorimetry. (i. e. , by recording capacity when the reaction of interest is carried out in it) or can be obtained from other $\Delta H_f^\ominus$ data, as shown for the water-gas reaction. If we know $\Delta H^\ominus$ and also know the standard entropy change ($\Delta S^\ominus$) for a given reaction, we can calculate its equilibrium constant ($K^\ominus$) from a combination of Eq. 9.13 and Eq. 9.16:

$$\ln K^\ominus = \Delta S^\ominus / R - \Delta H^\ominus / (RT) \qquad (9.21)$$

Now $S^\ominus$, the standard entropy of a single substance, unlike $H^\ominus$, can be calculated absolutely if we know the standard heat capacity $C_p^\ominus$ (at constant pressure) of that substance as a function of temperature from zero kelvin[4]:

$$S^\ominus = \int_0^T (C_p^\ominus / T) dT = \int_0^T C_p^\ominus \, d(\ln T). \qquad (9.22)$$

Entropies are thus determinable from statistical mechanics or from calorimetry. They are listed along with $\Delta H_f^\ominus$ values for many substances in various reference books. Values of $S^\ominus$ for $H_2(g)$, $O_2(g)$, and $H_2O(l)$ are 130.684 J/(K·mol), 205.138 J/(K·mol), and 69.91 J/(K·mol), respectively.

It is important to note that the enteropies of gases are larger than those of liquids or solids. This is because entropy is a function of the degree of randomness or disorder at the molecular level. Customarily, $S^\ominus$ values are given joules per Kelvin per mole, whereas $\Delta G^\ominus$ and $\Delta H^\ominus$ are given in kilojoules; remember to multiply the latter by 1000 when doing calculations. The entropy of formation of liquid H_2O (reaction 9.18) is then:

$$\Delta S^\ominus_{f H_2O(l)} = S^\ominus_{H_2O(l)} - S^\ominus_{H_2} - 1/2 S^\ominus_{O_2(g)} = -163.34 [J/(K \cdot mol)] \qquad (9.23)$$

The free energy of formation of liquid water at 25℃ is:

$$\Delta G_f^\ominus = \Delta H_f^\ominus - T \Delta S_f^\ominus = -237.13 (kJ/mol) \qquad (9.24)$$

and the thermodynamic equilibrium constant for reaction 9.18 is:

$$K^\ominus = \{H_2O(l)\} / \{H_2(g)\}\{O_2(g)\}^{1/2} \qquad (9.25)$$

The activity of the pure water phase, which is separate from the gaseous reactants, can be set to unity, and the gas activities may be approximated as equal to the partial pressures in bars[5]:

$$K = 1/P_{H_2} P_{O_2}^{1/2} \, \text{bar}^{-3/2} = \exp(-\Delta G^\ominus / RT) = 3.5 \times 10^{41} (\text{bar}^{-3/2}) \qquad (9.26)$$

Thus, the equilibrium pressure of hydrogen created by dissociation of airfree liquid water would be only 2×10^{-28} bar, or one molecule in 200 m³. In effect, then, reaction 9.18 goes to total completion because it is highly exergonic, that is, because $\Delta G_f^\ominus$ is so strongly negative, and liquid water simply does not dissociate detectably at 25℃ (even if this were kinetically favored).

Usually, $\Delta H_f^\ominus$ is the dominant term in Eq. 9.21. For example, the formation of nitric oxide,

$$1/2 N_2(g) + 1/2 O_2 = NO \qquad (9.27)$$

is endothermic ($\Delta H_f^\ominus = +90.25 kJ/mol$) and also endergonic, that is $\Delta G_f^\ominus$ is positive (+86.55 kJ/mol) corresponding to $K^\ominus \ll 1$. In other words, equilibrium 9.27 lies very far to the left at 25℃. Thus, thermodynamics predicts that NO should decompose almost completely to nitrogen and oxygen at room temperature. In fast, it does not, because the reaction is so slow (unless catalyzed).

Note that reaction 9.18, reaction 9.19, and reaction 9.27 involve fractional stoichiometric coefficients on the left-hand sides. This is because we wanted to define conventional *enthalpies of formation* (etc.) of *one mole* of each of the respective products. However, if we are not concerned about the conventional thermodynamic quantities of formation, we can get rid of fractional coefficients by multiplying throughout by the appropriate factor. For example, reaction 9.18 could be doubled, whereupon $\Delta G^\ominus$ becomes $2\Delta G_f^\ominus$, $\Delta H^\ominus = 2\Delta H_f^\ominus$, and

$\Delta S = 2\Delta S_f^\ominus$, and the right-hand sides of Eq. 9.25 and Eq. 9.26 must be squared so that the new equilibrium constant $K' = K^2 = 1.23 \times 10^{83}$ bar^{-3}. Thus, whenever we give a numerical value for an equilibrium constant or an associated thermodynamic quantity, we must make clear how we chose to define the equilibrium.[6] The concentrations we calculate from an equilibrium constant will, of course, be the same, no matter how it was defined. Sometimes, as in Eq. 9.26, the units given for K will imply the definition, but in certain cases such as reaction 9.27 K is dimensionless.

From *Chemical Kinetics and Dynamics by Jeffrey I. Steinfeld*

New Words and Expressions

hypothetically [ˌhaipəu'θetikəli]　*ad.* 假设地，臆说地
molal ['məuləl]　*a.* 摩尔的
entropy ['entrəpi]　*n.* 熵
isothermally [ˌaisəu'θə:məli]　*ad.* 等温（线）地
graphite ['græfait]　*n.* 石墨
endothermic [ˌendəu'θɜ:mik]　*a.* 吸热（反应）的，内热的
calorimetry [ˌkælə'rimitri]　*n.* 热量测定
exergonic [ˌeksə'gɔnik]　*a.* 释出能量的，放热的

Notes

1. 参考译文：对无机化学及其应用的回顾，重要的是要关心热力学可以告诉我们什么，而不是去关心它的精确理论意义。

2. that is 意思是"即，也就是说"。参考译文：当 $G^\ominus$ 降到最低点时，反应就停止了。也就是说，达到了平衡。

3. 参考译文：然而，反应的标准热量的变化，或焓变（$\Delta H^\ominus$），与 $\Delta G^\ominus$ 不同，因为一些热量无法被提取出来。

4. kelvin scale 开尔文温标。参考译文：现在，与 $H^\ominus$ 不同，已知单一物质的标准热容量（$C_p^\ominus$ 恒压下）就可以完全计算出其标准熵 $S^\ominus$，$C_p^\ominus$ 为从 0 开尔文温度开始的温度函数。

5. 参考译文：纯水相的行为可以被看作一个整体（与气相反应物是分开的），而气相行为可近似等于以巴为单位的部分压力。

6. 参考译文：因此，无论何时当我们给出一个平衡常数或一个相关热力学数值时，我们必须弄清楚是如何确定平衡的。

Unit 10 Nomenclature of Hydrocarbons

Alkanes

Ideally, every organic compound should have a name that clearly describes its structure and from which a structural formula can be drawn. For this purpose, chemists throughout the world have accepted a set of rules established by the International Union of Pure and Applied Chemistry (IUPAC). This system is known as the **IUPAC system**, or alternatively, the **Geneva system** because the first meetings of the IUPAC were held in Geneva, Switzerland. The IUPAC name of an alkane with an unbranched chain of carbon atoms consists of two parts: (ⅰ) a prefix that indicates the number of carbon atoms in the chain; and (ⅱ) the ending -*ane*, to show that the compound is an alkane. Prefixes used to show the presence of from one to 20 carbon atoms are given in Table 10.1.

Table 10.1 prefixes used in the IUPAC system to indicate one to 20 carbon atoms in a chain

Prefix	number of carbon atoms	Prefix	number of carbon atoms	Prefix	number of carbon atoms
meth	1	oct	8	pentadec	15
eth	2	non	9	hexadec	16
prop	3	dec	10	heptadec	17
but	4	undec	11	octadec	18
pent	5	dodec	12	nonadec	19
hex	6	tridec	13	eicos	20
hept	7	tetradec	14		

The first four prefixes listed in Table 10.1 were chosen by the IUPAC because they were well established in the language of organic chemistry. In fact, they were established even before there were hints of the structural theory underlying the discipline, for example, the prefix but- appears in the name butyric acid, a compound of four carbon atoms present in butter fat (Latin *butyrum*: butter). Roots to show five or more carbons are derived from Greek or Latin roots.

The IUPAC name of a substituted alkane consists of a **parent name**, which indicates the longest chain of carbon atoms in the compound, and **substituent names**, which indicate the groups attached to the parent chain.[1]

$$CH_3-CH_2-CH_2-\underset{\underset{Substituent}{CH_3}}{CH}-CH_2-CH_2-CH_2-CH_3 \quad (Parent)$$

A substituent group derived from an alkane is called an **alkyl group**. The letter R— is commonly used to show the presence of an alkyl group. Alkyl groups are named by dropping the "-ane" from the name of the parent alkane and adding the suffix -*yl*. For example, the alkyl substituent CH_3CH_2- is named ethyl.

$$H_3C-CH_3 \qquad\qquad H_3C-CH_2-$$
ethane (parent hydrocarbon)   ethyl group (an alkyl group)

Following are the rules of the IUPAC system for naming alkanes.

1. The general name of a saturated hydrocarbon is **alkane**.

2. For branched-chain hydrocarbon, the hydrocarbon derived from the longest chain of carbon atoms is taken as the parent chain, and the IUPAC name is derived from that of the parent chain.

3. Groups attached to the parent chain are called **substituents**. Each substituent is given a name and a number. The number shows the carbon atom of the parent chain to which the substituent is attached.

4. If the same substituent occurs more than once, the number of each carbon of the parent chain on which the substituent occurs is given. In addition, the number of times the substituent group occurs is indicated by a prefix *di-*, *tri-*, *tetra-*, *penta-*, and so on.

5. If there is one substituent, the parent chain is numbered from the end that gives it the lower number. If there are two or more substituents, the parent chain is numbered from the end that gives the lower number to the substituent encountered first.

6. If there are two or more different substituents, they are listed in alphabetical order. When listing substituents, the prefixes **iso-** and **neo-** are considered in alphabetizing. The prefixes *sec-* and *tert-* are ignored in alphabetizing substituents. Further, the multiplying prefixes *di-*, *tri-*, *tetra-*, and so on are also ignored in alphabetizing substituents. [2]

Alkenes

Alkanes have a single bond between the carbon atoms. Alkenes have a double bond (two bonds) between two of the carbon atoms.

The general formula for alkenes is

$$C_n H_{2n}$$

Simple alkenes are named much like alkanes, using the root name of the longest chain containing the double bond. The ending is changed from *-ane* to *-ene*. For example, "ethane" becomes "ethene", "propane" becomes "propene", and "octane" becomes "octene".

Note that the names of these compounds end in *-ene*. This is true of all alkenes. Note that the names of these compounds are similar to those of the alkanes except for the ending, which is *-ene* instead of *-ane*. [3]

When the chain contains more than three carbon atoms, a number is used to give the location of the double bond. The chain is numbered starting from the end closest to the double bond, and the double bond is given the lower number of its two double bonded carbon atoms.

In 1993, the IUPAC recommended a logical change in the positions of the numbers used in names. Instead of placing the numbers before the root name (1-butene), they recommended placing them immediately before the part of the name they locate the numbers, because both are widely used. *(the reader should draw the structures in terms of the rules)*

IUPAC names:	1-butene	2-pentene
new IUPAC names:	but-1-ene	pent-2-ene

If an alkene contains two double bonds, it is called a **diene**; a **triene** contains three double bonds, and a tetraene contains four double bonds. Numbers are used to specify the locations of the double bonds.

IUPAC names:	1,3-butadiene	1,3,5-heptatriene
new IUPAC names:	buta-1,3-diene	hepta-1,3,5-triene

1-3-butadiene is used in the manufacture of automobile tires, and leukotriene is involved in the body's allergic responses.

Each alkyl group attached to the main chain is listed with a number to give its location. Note that the double bond is still given preference in numbering, however. The following compound is called 2-methyl-2-butene.

$$\overset{4}{C}H_3 - \overset{3}{C}H = \overset{2}{C} - \overset{1}{C}H_3$$
$$\underset{CH_3}{|}$$

Similarly, we can give following names according to the principle.

IUPAC names:	3-methyl-1-butene	3,6-dimethyl-2-heptene
new IUPAC names:	3-methylbut-1-ene	3,6-dimethylhept-2-ene
IUPAC names:	3-propyl-1-heptene	2-ethyl-1,3-cyclohexadiene
new IUPAC names:	3-propylhept-1-ene	2-ethylcyclohexa-1,3-diene

Alkenes named as substituents are called alkenyl groups. They can be named systematically (ethenyl, propenyl, etc.), or by common names. Common substituents are the vinyl, allyl, methylene, and phenyl groups.

The vinyl group has the structure
$$H_2C=CH-$$
Vinyl chloride ($H_2C=CHCl$) is used in the manufacture of such products as floor tile, raincoats, fabrics, and furniture coverings. However, evidence has shown that several workers exposed to vinyl chloride during their work have died from a very rare form of liver cancer.[4] In addition, exposure to vinyl chloride is suspected to be responsible for certain types of birth defects.

Vinyl chloride is used in the manufacture of polyvinyl chloride (PVC), a plastic.

IUPAC names:	3-vinyl-1,5-hexadiene
new IUPAC names:	3-vinylhexa-1,5-diene

Following are some *cis* and *trans* alkenes and some alkenes that cannot show cis-trans isomerism.

IUPAC names:	*cis*-2-pentene	*trans*-2-pentene
new IUPAC names:	*cis*-pent-2-ene	*trans*-pent-2-ene
IUPAC names:	2-methyl-2-pentene	1-pentene
new IUPAC names:	2-methylpent-2-ene	pent-1-ene
		(neither cis nor trans)

Alkynes

Consider two carbon atoms connected by a triple bond.
$$-C\equiv C-$$
How many hydrogen atoms must be connected to these two carbon atoms to satisfy all the bond requirements? The answer is two, so the molecular formula of this compound is C_2H_2. This compound is called ethyne. Its structure is:
$$H-C\equiv C-H \qquad (H:C::C:H)$$
Ethyne is commonly called acetylene. However, this name is not preferred because the ending -ene denotes a double bond, whereas this compound actually has a triple bond between the carbon atoms.
$$C\equiv C-C$$
If three carbon atoms are placed in a chain with a triple bond between two of them, only four hydrogen atoms can be placed around these carbons to satisfy all the bonds. The compound then becomes
$$H-C\equiv C-CH_3$$
With the molecular formula C_3H_4. This compound is called propyne.

These two compounds, ethyne and propyne, are **alkynes**. They have a triple bond between two of the carbon atoms. All their names end in -*yne*. The general formula for alkynes is

$$C_n H_{2n-2}$$

Thus hexyne, which has six carbon atoms, has the formula $C_6 H_{(2 \times 6)-2}$ or $C_6 H_{10}$. Likewise, octyne has the molecular formula $C_8 H_{14}$.

The IUPAC nomenclature for alkynes is similar to that for alkenes. We find the longest continuous chain of carbon atoms that includes the triple bond and change the -*ane* ending of the parent alkane to —*yne*. The chain is numbered from the end closest to the triple bond, and the position of the triple bond is designated by its lower-numbered carbon atom. substituents are given numbers to indicate their locations.

IUPAC names:	ethyne	propyne	2-butyne	4-methyl-2-hexyne
new IUPAC names:			but-2-yne	4-methylhex-2-yne

When additional functional groups are present, the suffixes are combined to produce the compound names of alkenynes (a double bond and a triple bond), alkynols (a triple bond and an alcohol), and so on. The new IUPAC system (placing the number right before the group) helps with these names. As with alkenes, alkynes are named with the triple bond having the smallest number.

$$CH_2=C-C\equiv C-CH_3 \qquad CH_3-CH-C\equiv C-H$$
$$\;\;\;\;\;\;\;\;\;\;\;\;\;|\qquad\qquad\qquad\qquad\qquad\quad|$$
$$\;\;\;\;\;\;\;\;\;\;\;\;\;CH_3\qquad\qquad\qquad\qquad\qquad\;OH$$

IUPAC names:	2-methyl-1-penten-3-yne	3-butyn-2-ol
new IUPAC names:	2-methylpent-1-en-3-yne	but-3-yn-ol

From *Organic Chemistry by Beyer and Walter*
and *Organic Chemistry by L. G. Wade, J. R.*

New Words and Expressions

alkane ['ælkein]   *n.* 烷烃
butyric acid [bju(:)'tirik'æsid]   *n.* 丁酸
substituent [sʌb'stitjuənt]   *n.* 取代（基）
ethane ['eθein] *n.* 乙烷
alphabetical [ˌælfə'betikəl]   *a.* 依字母顺序的
alphabetize ['ælfəbitaiz]   *vt.* 依字母顺序排列，用字母标示
alkene ['ælkiːn]   *n.* 烯烃
ethene ['eθiːn]   *n.* 乙烯
propene ['prəupiːn]   *n.* 丙烯
butane ['bjuːtein]   *n.* 丁烷
butene ['bjuːtiːn]   *n.* 丁烯
octene ['ɔktiːn]   *n.* 辛烯
octyne ['ɔktin]   *n.* 辛炔
vinyl ['vainil, 'vinil]   *n.* 乙烯基
diene ['daiiːn]   *n.* 二烯（烃）
triene ['traiiːn]   *n.* 三烯（烃）
leukotriene [ljuːku'triin]   *n.* 白三烯
vinyl chloride ['vainil-'klɔːraid]   *n.* 氯乙烯
fabric ['fæbrik]   *n.* 编织物，结构，组织
polyvinyl [ˌpɔli'vainil]   *a.* 聚乙烯的
alkyne ['ælkain]   *n.* 炔（烃）

ethyne [ˈeθain] n. 乙炔
propyne [ˈprəupain] n. 丙炔
hexyne [ˈhekˌsain] n. 己炔

Notes

1. which 引导非限制性定语从句，第一个 which 从句修饰 parent name，第二个 which 从句修饰 substituent name。consist of sth. 由 sth 组成或构成，一般不用于进行时态。e. g.：The committee consists of ten members. 委员会由十人组成。参考译文：含取代基的烷烃的 IUPAC 名称由母体名称和取代基名称组成，母体名称代表化合物的最长碳链，取代基名称代表连接在主链上的基团。

2. and so on：等等。放在罗列事物的末尾，用以表示列举未尽。e. g.：He talked about how much we owed to our parents, our duty to our country and so on. 他谈到我们受到父母多少恩惠、我们对国家应尽的义务等。参考译文：此外，按字母顺序排列取代基时，表示倍数的前缀 2、3、4、等也被省略。

3. 该句为祈使句，表示请求、命令等，它的主语是 you，通常不说出。祈使句的肯定结构中，谓语动词一律用动词原形，句末用惊叹号或句号。本句翻译时，可将 except for 放在前面。参考译文：注意，除结尾处用 ene 代替 ane 外，这些化合物的命名与相应烷烃的命名类似。

4. died from…死于……原因。liver cancer 肝癌，参考译文：然而，有迹象表明工作期间暴露于氯乙烯中的几位工人死于一种罕见的肝癌。

Exercises

Ⅰ. Comprehension

1. The IUPAC system is also known as Geneva system because the first meetings of IUPAC system were held in _____.
   A. Stock, Sweden
   B. Bern(e), Switzerland
   C. Geneva, Switzerland
   D. Madrid, Spain.

2. According to the second paragraph, the first four prefixes listed in Table 10.1 were _____.
   A. chosen by the IUPAC because they were well establish in
   B. established before there were the language of organic chemistry
   C. established by organic chemists
   D. both A and B

3. If there are two or more different substituents when listing them in alphabetical order, we can not ignore _____.
   A. the prefixes sec- and tert-.
   B. the prefixes iso- and neo-.
   C. multiplying prefixes di, tri, tetra.
   D. none of the above.

4. Despite the precision of IUPAC system, routine communication in organic chemistry still relies on _____.
   A. trival names
   B. semisystematic names
   C. systematic names
   D. a combination of A, B and C

5. The name assigned to any compound with a chain of carbon atoms consist of _____.
   A. one part
   B. two parts
   C. three parts
   D. four parts

6. The infix of the name of any compound tells _____.
   A. the number of carbon atoms in the parent chain

B. the nature of carbon-carbon bonds in the parent chain
C. the class of compound to which the substance belongs
D. the property of compound

II. Name the following compounds by the IUPAC system

1. $CH_3(CH_2)_nCH_3$ ($n=2, 3, 4, 6$, respectively)
2. $(CH_3)_2CH_2—CH_2—CH_2—CH_3$
3. $(CH_3)_3C—CH_2—CH(C_2H_5)—CH_2—CH_3$
4. $(CH_3)_2CH—CH_2CH_2—CH(CH_2CH_2CH_3)—CH(CH_3)_2$
5. $CH_3—CH_2—CH_2—C(CH_2CH_2CH_3)_2—CH(CH_3)_2$
6. 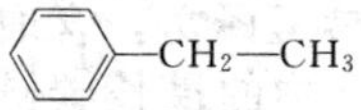 $C_6H_5—CH_2—CH_3$
7. 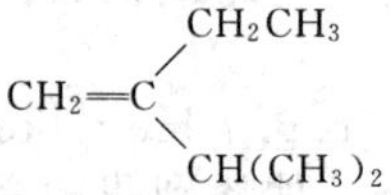 $CH_2=C(CH_2CH_3)(CH(CH_3)_2)$
8. $CH_3—CH_2—CH=CH—CHCl—CH_3$
9. $CH_3—CH(CH_3)—CH(C_2H_5)—C\equiv C—CH_3$
10. $CH_2=CH—C\equiv CH$
11. $(CH_3)_2CH—CH_2CH(OH)CH_3$
12. $CH_3CH_2CH=CHCH(OH)CH_3$
13. $(CH_3)_3C—OH$
14. $(CH_3)_3C—OCH_2H_5$
15. $(CH_3)_2CH—CH_2—O—C_2H_5$
16. $(CH_2OH)_2$
17. $CH_3—CH(OH)—CH_2(OH)$
18. $CH_2(OH)—CH(OH)—CH_2(OH)$
19. $CH_3CH_2NH_2$
20. $CH_3CH_2CH_2CH(CH_3)CH—NH—CH_3$

III. Draw structures for the following compounds

1. 3-octene
2. 3-methyl-2-heptene
3. cyclohexene
4. 2-pentyne
5. 3,3-dimethylhexyne
6. 3-bromotoluene
7. vinyl chloride
8. acetylene
9. *para*-dichlorobenzene
10. m-chlorobromobenzene
11. toluene
12. chlorobenzene
13. 1,2-dibromobenzene
14. naphthalene
15. anthracene
16. phenanthrene
17. 2-methyl-1-propanol
18. cyclohexanol
19. methoxyethene
20. trans-2-ethoxycyclohexanol

IV. Decide which item best completes each unfinished sentence

1. Alkynes react primarily by _____.
A. addition B. substitution C. polymerization D. hydrogenation
2. The structure △ represents: _____.
A. cyclopropane B. cyclopropene C. propane D. propene
3. Which of the following is an alkene? _____
A. C_2H_2 B. C_6H_{12} C. $C_{12}H_{22}$ D. none of these
4. How many disubstitution products are possible for benzene? _____
A. 1 B. 2 C. 3 D. 4

V. Problem

Each of the following names is incorrect. Draw the structure represented by the incorrect name (or a consistent structure if the name is ambiguous), and give your drawing the correct name.

(a) *cis*-2,3-dimethyl-2-pentene
(b) 3-vinylhex-4-ene
(c) 2-methylcyclopentene
(d) 6-chlorocyclohexadiene
(e) 3,4-dimethylcyclohexene
(f) *cis*-2,5-dibromo-3-ethylpent-2-ene

Reading Material

Nomenclature of Derivative

Alcohols

In the IUPAC system, the longest chain of carbon atoms containing the —OH group is selected as the parent compound. To show that the compound is an alcohol, the suffix *-e* is changed to *-ol* and a number is added to show the location of the —OH group.[1] The parent chain must be numbered to give the —OH group the smallest possible number.

Common names for alcohols are derived by naming the alkyl group attached to —OH and then adding the word "alcohol".

In the IUPAC system, compounds containing two hydroxyl groups are called diols, those containing three hydroxyl groups are called triols, and so on.[2] Note that in IUPAC names for these compounds, the final *-e* (the suffix) of the parent name is retained.

$$\begin{array}{ccc}
CH_2-CH_2 & CH_3-CH-CH_2 & CH_2-CH-CH_2 \\
| \quad | & | \quad | & | \quad | \quad | \\
OH \quad OH & OH \quad OH & OH \quad OH \quad OH
\end{array}$$

1,2-ethanediol   1,2-propanediol   1,2,3-propanetriol
(ethylene glycol)   (propylene glycol)   (glycerol, glycerine)

Common names for compounds containing two hydroxyl groups on adjacent carbons are often referred to as **glycols**. Ethylene glycol and propylene glycol are synthesized from ethylene and propylene respectively, hence their common names.

Compounds containing —OH and C=C groups are called **unsaturated alcohols**, because of the presence of the carbon-carbon double bond. In the IUPAC system, they are named as alcohols and the parent chain is numbered to give the —OH group the lowest possible number. That the carbon chain contains a double bond is shown by changing the infix from *-an-* to *-en-*. Numbers must be used to show the location of both the carbon-carbon double bond and the hydroxyl group.

Ethers

In the IUPAC system, ethers are named by selecting the longest carbon chain as the parent compound and naming the —OR group as an alkoxy substituent. Following are IUPAC names for three low-molecular-weight ethers.

$$\overset{8}{C}H_3\overset{7}{C}H_2\overset{6}{C}H_2\overset{5}{C}H_2\overset{4}{C}H\overset{3}{C}H_2\overset{2}{C}H_2\overset{1}{C}H_3$$
$$\quad\quad\quad\quad\quad\quad\quad |$$
$$\quad\quad\quad\quad\quad\quad OCH_3$$

$C_2H_5-O-C_2H_5$

4-methoxyoctane   *trans*-2-ethoxycyclohexanol   ethoxyethane
                                                          (diethyl ether)

Common names for ethers are derived by specifying the alkyl groups attached to oxygen in alphabetical order and adding the word "ether".

CH_3-O-CH_3 $(CH_3)_2CH-O-CH(CH_3)_2$ $CH_3-O-C(CH_3)_3$
Dimethyl ether   diisopropyl ether   *tert*-butyl methyl ether

Chemists almost invariably use common names for low-molecular-weight ether. For example, although ethoxyethane is the IUPAC name for $CH_3CH_2OCH_2CH_3$, it is rarely used; rather, chemists use the names diethyl ether, ethyl ether, or, even more common, simply ether.[3]

Amines

In IUPAC nomenclature, the longest chain of carbon atoms that contains the amino group is taken as the parent and —NH_2 is considered a substituent, like —Cl, —NO_2, and so on. Its presence is indicated by the prefix amino-, and a number is used to show its location. If more than one alkyl group is attached to nitrogen, the alkyl group containing the longest chain of carbon atoms is taken as the parent; other substituents on nitrogen are named as alkyl groups and are preceded by N- to show that they are bonded to the nitrogen atom of the amine.

In these and the following examples, IUPAC names are given first. Instead of showing the same structural formulas again under "common names," we have listed common names, where they exist, in parentheses under IUPAC names. As you will discover in your reading, common names for most amines are more widely used than are IUPAC names[4].

$CH_3CH_2NH_2$ aminoethane (ethylamine)

$(CH_3)_2CHCH_2CH_2NH_2$ 1-amino-3-methylbutane (isopentylamine)

$CH_3CH_2CH_2CH(CH_3)CH_2NHCH_3$ N-methyl-1-amino-2-methylpentane

Compounds containing two or more amino groups are named by prefixes di-, tri-, and so on to show multiple substitution and by numbers to show the location of each substituent. Following are three diamines. The first, 1,6-diaminohexane, is one of two starting materials for the synthesis of Nylon 66. The second two amines are products of the decomposition of animal matter, as their alternative common names surely suggest.

1,6-diaminohexane (hexamethylenediamine)

1,5-diaminopentane (pentamethylenediamine; cadaverine)

1,4-diaminobutane (tetramethylenediamine; putrescine)

If the —NH_2 group is one of two or more substituent, it is shown by the prefix amino-, as in the following examples:

2-aminoethanol (ethanolamine)

4-aminophenol (*p*-aminophenol)

The compound $C_6H_5NH_2$ is named aniline, which becomes the parent name for its derivatives. Several simple derivatives of aniline are known almost exclusively by their common names; as, for example, is toluidine (the *ortho* isomer is shown).

aniline   4-chloroaniline   2-methylaniline
                       (*p*-chloroaniline)   (*o*-methylaniline or *o*-toluidine)

When a nitrogen atom has four organic groups attached to it (any combination of aliphatic or aromatic), the compound is named as an **ammonium salt**, as in the following examples:

Tetramethylammonium hydroxide

Trimethylphenylammonium iodide

Aldehydes and Ketones

The IUPAC nomenclature for aldehydes and ketones follows the familiar pattern of selecting as the parent compound the longest chain of carbon atoms that contains the functional group.[5] The aldehyde group is shown by changing the suffix -*e* of the parent name to -*al*.

Because the aldehyde group can appear only at the end of a hydrocarbon chain and because numbering must start with it as carbon 1, its position is unambiguous and therefore there is no need to use a number to locate it. Following are IUPAC names for several low-molecular-weight aldehydes.

CH_3CH_2CHO $(CH_3)_2CHCH_2CHO$ $CH_3CH_2CH(CH_3)CHO$
propanal   3-methylbutanal   2-methylbutanal

For unsaturated aldehydes (that is, those also containing an alkene), the presence of the carbon-carbon double bond is indicated by the infix -en-, as shown in the following examples. As with other molecules with both an infix and a suffix, the location of the suffix determines the numbering pattern.

2-propenal   3,7-dimethyl-2,6-octadienal

(the reader should draw the structures in terms of the rules)

Among aldehydes for which the IUPAC system retains common names are benzaldehyde and cinnamaldehyde.

benzaldehyde   cinnamaldehyde

In the IUPAC system, ketones are named by selecting as the parent compound the longest chain that contains the carbonyl group and then indicating its presence by changing the suffix from -e to -one. The parent chain is numbered from the direction that gives the carbonyl group the lowest number. The IUPAC system retains the common names acetone and acetophenone. The followings are some examples:

2-propanone   acetone   2-butanone   4-methyl-3-hexanone

2-methylcyclohexanone   acetophenone   *p*-chloroacetophenone

(the reader should draw the structures in terms of the rules)

For naming compounds that contain more than one functional group — that is, more than one that might be indicated by a suffix — the IUPAC system has established what is known as an **order of precedence** of functions.[6] The order of precedence for the functional groups we will deal with most often is given in Table 10.2. There you will find how to indicate a given functional group if it has a higher precedence, and also how to show it if it has a lower precedence rules.

Table 10.2   order of precedence of several functional groups

Functional group	suffix if higher precedence	prefix if lower precedence
—COOH	-oic acid	
—CHO	-al	oxo-
—CO—	-one	oxo-
—OH	-ol	hydroxy-
—NH$_2$	-amine	amino-
—SH	-thiol	mercapto-

Note: Arrow shows decreasing precedence

CH_3COCH_2CHO $CH_3CH(OH)CH_2CH_2CHO$ CH_3COCH_2COOH
3-oxobutanal   4-hydroxypentanal   3-oxobutanoic acid

Carboxylic acids

The IUPAC system of nomenclature for carboxylic acids selects as the parent compound the longest chain of carbon atoms that contains the carboxyl group. The carboxyl group is indicated by changing the suffix *-e* of the parent compound to *-oic acid*. Because the carbon of the carboxyl group is always carbon 1 of parent compound, there is no need to give it a number. Following are structural formulas and IUPAC names for several carboxylic acids. Note that the IUPAC system retains the common names formic acid and acetic acid.

    methanoic acid   ethanoic acid   propanoic acid   3-methylbutanoic
     (formic acid)   (acetic acid)

(*the reader can draw the structures in terms of the rules*)

If the carboxylic acid contains a carbon—carbon double bond, the infix is changed from *-an-* to *-en-* to indicate a double bond. The position of the double bond is shown by a number, just as for simple alkenes. Following are two carboxylic acids, each also containing a carbon-carbon double bond. In parentheses is the common name of each acid.

          2-propenoic acid   3-phenyl-2-propenoic acid
           (acrylic acid)   (cinnamic acid)

(*the reader can draw the structures in terms of the rules*)

In the IUPAC system, a carboxyl group takes precedence over most other functional groups, including the hydroxyl group and also the carbonyl group of aldehydes and ketones (Table 10.2). In a substituted carboxylic acid, the presence of an —OH group is indicated by the prefix hydroxy-; the presence of a carbonyl group of an aldehyde or ketone is indicated by the prefix *oxo-*, as illustrated in the following examples.

          5-hydroxyhexanoic acid   5-oxohexanoic acid

(*the reader can draw the structures in terms of the rules*)

Dicarboxylic acids are named by adding the suffix *-dioic acid* to the name of the parent compound that contains both carboxyl groups. The IUPAC system retains certain common names including *oxalic*, *malonic*, *succinic*, and *tartaric acids*. The name of *oxalic acid* is derived from one of its sources in the biological world, namely plants of the genus *Oxalis*, one of which is rhubarb.[7] Oxalic acid is used as a cleansing agent for automobile radiators, as a laundry bleach, and in textile finishing and cleaning. Tartaric acid is a byproduct of fermentation of grape juice to wine. It is collected as the potassium salt and sold under the name cream of tartar. Adipic acid is one of the two monomers required for the synthesis of the polymer Nylon 66. In 1985, the U.S. chemical industry produced 1.63 billion pounds of adipic acid, solely for the synthesis of Nylon 66.

Tri- and higher carboxylic acids are named by using the suffixes *-tricarboxylic acid*, *-tetracarboxylic acid*, and so on. An example of tricarboxylic acid is 2-hydroxy-1,2,3-propanetricarboxylic acid, whose common name, *citric acid*, is also retained by the IUPAC system. Citric acid is important in a metabolic pathway known as the tricarboxylic acid (TCA) cycle, or Krebs cycle.[8]

        2-hydroxy-1,2,3-propanetricarboxylic acid (citric acid)

From *Organic Chemistry by Beyer and Walter*

New Words and Expressions

diol ['daiəul] *n.* 二醇

triol ['traiɔːl] n. 三元醇
1,2-ethanediol ['eθeindaioul] n. 1,2-乙二醇
1,2-propanediol [prə'pænədiəul] n. 1,2-丙二醇
glycol ['glaikɔl] n. 乙二醇,甘醇
glycerol ['glisəˌrɔl] n. 丙三醇,甘油
glycerine ['glisəriːn] n. 甘油
alkoxy [æl'kɔksi] n. 烷氧基,烃氧基
4-methoxyoctane ['meθɔksi'ɔktein] n. 4-甲氧基辛烷
ethoxyethane [eθɔksi'eθein] n. 乙氧基乙烷,乙醚
diisopropyl ether [daiˌaisə'prəupil'estə] n. 二异丙基醚
aminoethane ['æminəu'eθein] n. 氨基乙烷,乙胺
isopentylamine [aisuəˌpentil'æmiːn] n. 异戊胺
1,6-diaminohexane [dai'æminəu, heksein] n. 1,6-己二胺
hexamethylenediamine [heksein'meθiliːn, daiəmiːn] n. 1,6-己二胺,亚己基二胺
1,5-diaminopentane [dai'əminiəupentein] n. 1,5-戊二胺
cadaverine [kə'dævəriːn] n. 尸胺,1,5-戊二胺
1,4-diaminobutane ['daiəmin, əbjutein] n. 1,4-二氨基丁烷
tetramethylenediamine [, tetrimeθiliːndaimiːn] n. 丁二胺,腐胺,四亚甲基二胺
putrescine [pjuː'tresiːn, -in] n. 腐胺,丁二胺
ethanolamine [ˌeθə'nɔləmiːn] n. 乙醇胺,氨基乙醇,胆胺
toluidine [tə'ljuːidin] n. 邻甲苯胺
propanal ['prəupəˌnæl] n. 丙醛
2-methylbutanal [meθilbjuːtinəl] n. 2-甲基丁醛
benzaldehyde [ben'zældiˌhaid] n. 苯甲醛,安息香醛
cinnamaldehyde [sini'məldihaid] n. 肉桂醛
chloroacetophenone [ˌklɔːrəuˌæsətəufə'nəun] n. 氯苯乙酮
carboxyl [kɑː'bɔksil] n. 羧基
formic ['fɔːmik] a. 蚁的,蚁酸的
acrylic acid [ə'krilik] n. 丙烯酸
cinnamic [si'næmik] n. 肉桂酸的,苯乙烯的
dicarboxylic [daiˌkɑːbɔk'silik] a. 二(元)羧基的
oxalic [ɔk'sælik] a. 醋浆草的
malonic ['mælənik] a. 丙二酸的
succinic [sək'sinik] a. 丁二酸的,琥珀酸的
tartaric [tɑː'tærik] a. 酒石(酸)的
oxalis ['ɔksəlis] a. 酢浆草
rhubarb ['ruːbɑːb] n. (植物)大黄
tartar ['tɑːtə] n. 酒石(酿造葡萄酒时酒桶底的沉淀物质,为酒石酸的原料)
adipic [ə'dipik] a. 己二酸的
tricarboxylic [traiˌkɑːbɔk'silik] a. 三羧酸的
tetracarboxylic [te'tri, kæːbɔksilik] a. 四羧基的,四羧酸的
Krebs cycle 克雷布斯循环

Notes

1. 参考译文:为表明该化合物为醇,将相应烷烃名称的后缀 -e 变为 -ol,并加上数字

来表示羟基的位置。

2. 化合物命名时，常用 di-，tri- 来表示相同的基团或取代基，如：diethyl 二乙基，di-amino 二氨基，trimethyl 三甲基，tetrahydro 四氢基。在 IUPAC 系统中，因用 -ol 作为醇的后缀，故 diol 为二醇，triol 为三醇，tetraol 为四醇。

3. rather：most certainly 用于对某些问题的肯定回答，有"确实如此，一定"之意。参考译文：例如，$CH_3CH_2OCH_2CH_3$ 的 IUPAC 命名为乙氧基乙烷，但却很少被使用。相反，化学家使用二乙基醚、乙醚，甚至更普通些，使用简单醚这样的名称。

4. than are IUPAC names 倒装结构，正常语序为 than IUPAC names (are used)。参考译文：正如在阅读中将发现的一样，对大多数胺来说，普通命名比 IUPAC 命名的应用更为广泛。

5. select sb/sth (as sth) 选择……作……，选拔（尤指最好的或最合适的）。句子结构可调整为 …of selecting the longest chain…as the parent compound. 参考译文：对醛酮的 IUPAC 命名遵循熟悉的模式，即选择含官能团的最长碳链作母体化合物。

6. 参考译文：对那些含有多于一个官能团的化合物，即有不止一个官能团需用词缀表示的化合物的命名，IUPAC 系统建立了一个被称作官能团优先顺序的规则。

7. be derived from 源自于……，namely 即，也就是。参考译文：草酸的名称源自于它的生物来源，即酢浆草类植物，其中之一叫大黄。

8. known as 意为"通常所说的，以……著称，通称"。Krebs cycle 克雷布氏循环，也称作柠檬酸循环或三羧酸循环（TCA）。是主要营养品（碳水化合物、蛋白质、脂肪）彻底氧化的主要途径。糖被氧化生成中间产物丙酮酸，丙酮酸经氧化生成乙酰辅酶 A，乙酰辅酶 A 与草酰乙酸缩合生成柠檬酸，再经一系列氧化和脱羧作用重新生成草酰乙酸而形成一个循环（克雷布氏循环）。每一次循环，一分子的丙酮便被氧化生成二氧化碳和水。参考译文：柠檬酸在代谢过程，即通常所说的三羧酸循环或克雷布氏循环中起重要作用。

Unit 11 Carboxylic Acids and Their Derivatives

Acid halides, acid anhydrides, esters, and **amides** are all functional derivatives of carboxylic acids. A general formula for the characteristic structural feature of each of these derivatives is

$$\underset{\text{(acid halide)}}{R-\overset{\overset{O}{\|}}{C}-X} \quad \underset{\text{(acid anhydride)}}{R-\overset{\overset{O}{\|}}{C}-O-\overset{\overset{O}{\|}}{C}-R} \quad \underset{\text{(ester)}}{R-\overset{\overset{O}{\|}}{C}-O-R} \quad \underset{\text{(amide)}}{R-\overset{\overset{O}{\|}}{C}-NH_2}$$

One way to relate the structural formulas of these functional groups to the structural formula of a carboxylic acid is to imagine a reaction in which $-OH$ from the carboxyl and $-H$ from a mineral acid, a carboxylic acid, an alcohol, or an amine is removed as water and the remaining atoms are joined in the following ways[1]:

$$\underset{\text{(a carboxylic acid)}}{CH_3COOH} + \underset{\text{(a mineral acid)}}{HCl} \longrightarrow \underset{\text{(an acid chloride)}}{CH_3COCl} + \underset{\text{(water)}}{H_2O}$$

$$\underset{\text{(a carboxylic acid)}}{CH_3COOH} + \underset{\text{(a carboxylic acid)}}{HO-COCH_3} \longrightarrow \underset{\text{(an anhydride)}}{CH_3COOCOCH_3} + \underset{\text{(water)}}{H_2O}$$

$$\underset{\text{(a carboxylic acid)}}{CH_3COOH} + \underset{\text{(an alcohol)}}{HO-CH_3} \longrightarrow \underset{\text{(an ester)}}{CH_3COOCH_3} + \underset{\text{(water)}}{H_2O}$$

$$\underset{\text{(a carboxylic acid)}}{CH_3COOH} + \underset{\text{(ammonia)}}{H-NH_2} \longrightarrow \underset{\text{(an amide)}}{CH_3-CO-NH_2} + \underset{\text{(water)}}{H_2O}$$

These equations are shown only to illustrate the relationship between a carboxylic acid and the four functional derivatives of it that we will study. They are not meant to illustrate methods for the synthesis of these functional groups.

Acid Halides

The characteristic structural feature of an acid halide is the presence of an $-CO-X$ group, where $-X$ is a halogen, F, Cl, Br, or I. Acid halides are named as derivatives of carboxylic acids by replacing the suffix *-ic acid* by *-yl*, and adding the name of the halide. Following are names and structural formulas for two acid halides.

$$\underset{\text{ethanoyl chloride (acetyl chloride)}}{CH_3-COCl} \qquad \underset{\text{benzoyl bromide}}{\underset{}{\text{C}_6\text{H}_5-\overset{\overset{O}{\|}}{C}-Br}}$$

Of the acid halides, acid chlorides are the more commonly prepared and used in both the laboratory and in industrial organic chemistry. Acid chlorides are most often prepared by the reaction of a carboxylic acid with either thionyl chloride or phosphorus pentachloride in much the same way that alkyl chlorides are prepared from alcohols.[2]

$$\underset{\text{(acetic acid)}}{CH_3-COOH} + \underset{\text{(thionyl chloride)}}{\overset{\overset{O}{\|}}{\underset{Cl\;\;Cl}{S}}} \longrightarrow \underset{\text{(acetyl chloride)}}{CH_3-COCl} + \underset{\text{(sulfur dioxide)}}{SO_2} + HCl$$

$$\underset{\text{(benzoic acid)}}{C_6H_5-\overset{\overset{O}{\|}}{C}-OH} + \underset{\substack{\text{(phosphorus}\\\text{pentachloride)}}}{PCl_5} \longrightarrow \underset{\substack{\text{(benzoyl}\\\text{chloride)}}}{C_6H_5-\overset{\overset{O}{\|}}{C}-Cl} + \underset{\substack{\text{(phosphorus}\\\text{oxychiloride)}}}{POCl_3} + HCl$$

Of the four functional derivatives of carboxylic acids we will discuss, acid halides are the most reactive. They react readily with water to form carboxylic acids, with alcohols and phenols to form esters, and with ammonia and primary and secondary amines to form amides.

1. *Reaction with Water*

Reaction of an acid chloride with water regenerates the parent carboxylic acid.

$$CH_3COCl + H_2O \longrightarrow CH_3COOH + HCl$$

Acetyl chloride and other low-molecular-weight acid halides react so readily with water that they must be protected from atmospheric moisture during storage.[3]

2. *Reaction with Alcohols*

Acid chlorides react with alcohols and phenols to give esters. Such reactions are most often carried out in the presence of an organic base such as pyridine, which both catalyzes the reaction and neutralizes the HCl formed as a byproduct.

$$CH_3COCl + (CH_3)_3COH \xrightarrow{\text{pyridine}} CH_3COOC(CH_3)_3$$

3. *Reaction with Ammonia and Primary and Secondary Amines*

Acid chlorides react with ammonia and primary and secondary amines to give amides. In these reactions, it is necessary to use 2 moles of ammonia or amine for each mole of acid chloride, the first to form an amide and the second to neutralize the HCl produced in the reaction.

$$\underset{\text{acetyl chloride}}{CH_3COCl} + \underset{\text{ammonia}}{2NH_3} \longrightarrow \underset{\text{acetamide}}{CH_3CONH_2} + \underset{\text{ammonium chloride}}{NH_4^+Cl^-}$$

Acid Anhydrides

The characteristic structural feature of an acid anhydride is the presence of a —CO—O—CO— group. Two examples of symmetrical anhydrides — that is, anhydrides derived from a single carboxylic acid — are acetic anhydride and benzoic anhydride.

In the IUPAC system, anhydrides are named by adding the word "anhydride" to the name of the parent acid. The anhydride derived from two molecules of acetic acid is named acetic anhydride; that derived from two molecules of benzoic acid is named benzoic anhydride.

Of the four classes of functional derivatives of carboxylic acid discussed in this chapter, acid anhydrides are very close in relative reactivity to acid halides. Acid anhydrides react with water to form carboxylic acids, with alcohols to form esters, and with ammonia and primary and secondary amines to form amides.[4] Thus, they too are valuable starting materials for preparing these functional groups.

The most commonly used acid anhydride is acetic anhydride, and this compound is commercially available. Other anhydrides can be prepared by reaction of an acid halide with the sodium or potassium salt of a carboxylic acid. In this reaction, the carboxylate anion is the nucleophile that reacts with the carbonyl carbon of the acid chloride to form a tetrahedral carbonyl addition intermediate that then collapses to give the acid anhydride. An example of this reaction is formation of the mixed anhydride between benzoic acid and acetic acid.

1. *Reaction with Water*: *Hydrolysis*

In hydrolysis, an anhydride is cleaved to form two molecules of carboxylic acid, as illustrated by the hydrolysis of acetic anhydride:

$$\underset{\text{acetic anhydride}}{CH_3COOCOCH_3} + H_2O \longrightarrow \underset{\text{acetic acid}}{CH_3COOH} + \underset{\text{acetic acid}}{CH_3COOH}$$

As with acid halides, acetic anhydride and other low-molecular-weight anhydrides react so readily with water that they too must be protected from moisture during storage.[5]

2. *Reaction with Alcohols*: *Formation of Esters*

Anhydrides react with alcohols to give one molecule of ester and one molecule of a carboxylic acid. Thus, reaction of an alcohol with an anhydride is a useful method for the synthesis of esters.

$$\underset{\text{acetic anhydride}}{CH_3COOCOCH_3} + \underset{\text{}}{HOCH_2CH_3} \longrightarrow \underset{\text{ethyl acetate}}{CH_3COOC_2H_5} + CH_3COOH$$

Aspirin is prepared by reaction of acetic anhydride with the phenolic —OH group of salicylic acid. The CH_3CO- group is commonly called an acetyl group, a name derived from acetic acid by dropping the *-ic* from the name of the acid and adding *-yl*. Therefore, the chemical name of the product formed by reaction of acetic anhydride and salicylic acid is acetyl salicylic acid.

$$HO-C_6H_4-COOH + (CH_3CO)_2O \longrightarrow CH_3-CO-O-C_6H_4-COOH + CH_3COOH$$

salicylic acid   acetyl salicylic acid (aspirin)

Aspirin is one of the few drugs produced on an industrial scale. In 1977, the United States produced 35 million pounds of it. Aspirin has been used since the turn of the century for relief of minor pain and headaches and for the reduction of fever. Compared with other commonly used drugs, aspirin is safe and well tolerated. However, it does have side effects. Because of its relative insolubility and acidity, it can irritate the stomach wall. These effects can be partially overcome by using its more soluble sodium salt instead. Because of these side effects, there has been increasing use of newer nonprescription analgesics, such as acetaminophen and ibuprofen.

$$H_3C-CO-NH-C_6H_4-OH \qquad CH_3CHCH_2-C_6H_4-CH(CH_3)COOH$$

N-acetyl-4-aminophenol (acetaminophen)   2-(4-isobutylphenyl)-propanoid acid (ibuprofen)

Ibuprofen was introduced in the United Kingdom in 1969 by the Boots Company as an anti-inflammatory agent for the treatment of rheumatoid arthritis and allied conditions.[6] The Upjohn Company introduced it in the United States in 1974 and it is now marketed in over 120 countries. As an analgesic, it is approximately 28 times more potent than aspirin, and as a fever-reducing agent it is approximately 20 times more potent.[7] Recently, it became available in this country as an over-the-counter (nonprescription) drug.

3. *Reaction with Ammonia and Amines: Formation of Amides*

Acid anhydrides react with ammonia, as well as with primary and secondary amines, to form amides. For complete conversion of an acid anhydride to an amide, 2 moles of amine are required, the first to form the amide and the second to neutralize the carboxylic acid by-product. Reaction of an acid anhydride with an amine is one of the most common laboratory methods for synthesizing amides.

$$CH_3COOCOCH_3 + 2NH_3 \longrightarrow CH_3CONH_2 + CH_3COO^- NH_4^+$$
acetic anhydride   acetamide   ammonium acetate

$$CH_3COCCH_3 + HN(CH_3)_2 \longrightarrow CH_3CN(CH_3)_2 + CH_3CO^- H_2N^+(CH_3)_2$$
acetic anhydride   dimethylamine   N,N-dimethylacetamide   dimethylammonium acetate

From *Organic Chemistry by Beyer and Walter*

New Words and Expressions

carboxylic acid [ˌkɑːbɔkˈsilikˈæsid] *n.* 羧酸
halide [ˈhælaid] *n.* 卤化物 *a.* 卤化物的
anhydride [ænˈhaidraid] *n.* 酐，脱水物

ester [ˈestə]　　n. 酯，酯类
amide [ˈæmaid]　　n. 酰胺
ammonia [ˈæməunjə]　　n. 氨，氨水
ethanoyl [ˈeθənouil]　　n. 乙酰基
acetyl [ˈæsitil]　　a. 乙酰基，醋酸的
thionyl [ˈθaiənil]　　n. 亚硫酰（基）
thionyl chloride [ˈθaiənilˈklɔːraid]　　n. 二氯亚砜
pentachloride [ˈpentəˈklɔːraid]　　n. 五氯化物
acetamide [æsiˈtæmaid]　　n. 乙酰胺
ammonium [ˈməunjəm]　　n. 铵，铵盐
symmetrical [siˈmetrikəl]　　a. 对称的，匀称的
benzoic [benˈzəuik]　　a. 安息香的，苯甲酸的
carboxylate [kɑːˈbɔksileit]　　n. 羧酸盐，羧酸酯
nucleophile [ˈnjuːkliəfail]　　a. 亲核试剂
aspirin [ˈæspərin]　　n. 阿司匹林，乙酰水杨酸
phenolic [fiˈnɔlik]　　a. 酚的，石炭酸的
salicylic [ˌsæliˈsilik]　　a. 水杨酸的
nonprescription [ˌnɔnpriˈskripʃən]　　a. 非处方的，无医生处方也可买到的（药）
analgesic [ˌænælˈdʒiːsik]　　n. 止疼剂
acetaminophen [ˌæsiˈtæminəfən]　　n. 退热净，对乙酰氨基酚
ibuprofen [ˌaibjuˈprəufin]　　n. 布洛芬（一种镇痛药）
rheumatoid [ˈruːmətɔid]　　a. 风湿症的，患风湿症的

Notes

1. 该句为主从复合句，主句结构为 One way is to imagine a reaction。which 引导表方式的状语从句，此状语从句是一个由 and 连接的并列结构。—OH from 之间、—H from 之间均省略 coming。参考译文：将这些衍生物官能团的结构式与羧酸的结构式联系起来的一种方法是设想一种反应，该反应中来自于羧基的—OH 与来自于无机酸、羧酸、醇或氨中的—H 以水的形式离去，其他原子以下列形式结合在一起。

2. by the reaction of…with…，通过……与……反应。in much the same way，如……方法一样，与……类似。参考译文：酰氯大多由二氯亚砜或五氯化磷与羧酸反应制得，类似于由醇制备卤代烷的方法。

3. 该句主要成分为 acetyl…react …with water，含有 so…that 从句。参考译文：酰氯以及其他低分子量的酰基卤化物容易与水发生反应，因此储存此类化合物时应避免与空气中的水分接触。

4. 该句主要成分为 Acid anhydrides react with…，三个 with 为并列结构。译文：酸酐与水反应生成羧酸，与醇反应生成酯，与氨气、伯胺、仲胺反应生成酰胺。

5. as with 结构表示比较，该句主要成分为 acetic anhydride…react …with water，含有 so…that 从句。译文：与酰氯一样，乙酸酐及其他低分子量酸酐易与水发生反应，储存时也应避免与空气中的水分接触。

6. introduce sth in/into sth，初次投入使用或运作；引进；推行；采用。如 introduce a ban on smoking in public places. 推行在公共场所禁止吸烟的规则。参考译文：作为治疗风湿性关节炎和类似症状的消炎药剂，布洛芬首次由 Boots 公司于 1969 年引入英国。

7. As 为插入语，and 并列从句，more…than 表示比较。参考译文：作为止痛药，它的药效大约是阿司匹林的 28 倍；作为退烧药，其药效大约是阿斯匹林强的 20 倍。

Unit 11 Carboxylic Acids and Their Derivatives

Exercises

I. Comprehension

1. In the reaction of the carboxylic acid with the alcohol, _____.
   A. —H from the carboxylic acid and —OH from the alcohol forms water
   B. —OH from the carboxylic acid and —H from the alcohol forms water
   C. water and halide are formed
   D. water and ether are formed

2. The author believes that the acid halide can be formed _____.
   A. by the reaction of the carboxylic acid with a mineral acid
   B. by the reaction of the carboxylic acid with thionyl chloride
   C. by the reacting with the carboxylic acid with thionyl chloride
   D. between the thionyl chloride and phosphorus pentachloride

3. The anhydride derived from two molecules of phosphoric is a strong acid, _____.
   A. because it has a net charge of —4
   B. because it is completely hydrolysis at pH 7.0
   C. because it is completely ionized at pH 7.0
   D. because it is easily ionized with a net charge of —4

4. Halides react readily with water to form _____ with phenols to form _____ and with ammonia to form _____.
   A. carboxylic acids/ ethers/ amines
   B. Carboxylic acids/ esters/ amines
   C. Carboxylic acids/ ethers/ imines
   D. Carboxylic acids/ esters/ amides

5. In _____, an anhydride is cut into two molecules of carboxylic acid.
   A. hydrolysis reaction   B. electrolysis reaction
   C. reducing reaction   D. ionization reaction

6. Ibuprofen has been used widely as newer nonprescription analgesics, _____.
   A. because Aspirin can irritate the stomach wall
   B. because Aspirin is more soluble than its salt
   C. because Ibuprofen was marked in over 120 countries in 1974
   D. because Ibuprofen is approximately 28 times more potent than Aspirin as a fever-reducing agent

II. Fill in the blanks with the phrases given below

be dependent on	in general
be different from	on the contrary
be made up of	put together
break down into	stand for
bring out	such as
consist of	sum up
divide by	
dozen or so	

1. When the collection of papers was first _____, it was well received by the reviewers.

2. In the same way the _____ most common kinds of atoms can be _____ in many millions of different ways to make molecules.

3. Elements _____ tiny fundamental particles called atoms. Fundamental, as it is

used here, means that they cannot be further _____ any chemical methods.

4. Each element has atoms that _____ the atoms of other elements.

5. It would not be quite round; _____ it would _____ three parts represented by spheres.

6. It is not to be _____ in a single product or word, but in an idea or basic concept.

7. The chemical symbol of an element may _____ the element _____.

8. The rate of a chemical reaction is influenced by several factors _____ temperature, concentration of reagents, particle size, light, and catalyst.

9. All forms of life on Earth _____ very _____ chemical reactions or chemical changes.

10. A chemical reaction occurs when elements and compounds react together to produce different compounds, or when compounds _____ simpler compounds or elements.

Ⅲ. Put in proper prepositions or adverbs into the blanks

1. Any suitable material to prevent the metal remaining in close contact _____ air and water may be used _____ a rust preventative.

2. The modern theory of burning is attributed _____ Antoine Lavoisier, a Frenchman.

3. One way to begin to organize our thinking about chemical reactions in general is to see what we know and can learn _____ a familiar kind of chemical reaction—burning.

4. What is there about the chemical makeup or properties of combustible things that makes them different _____ noncombustible things?

5. Rather than plunging _____ an attack on this problem we can do what the scientist often does: make an indirect attack by asking another common sense question.

Ⅳ. Translation

1. 同样，溶剂也可以不是液态物质，而是其他物质。
2. 以溶解度作为一个坐标，以温度作为另一个坐标所作的曲线图称为溶解度曲线。
3. 空气是混合物气体，含量最多的是以 N_2 形式存在的氮。
4. 反应的方向和平衡的位置也受温度、压力、和其他条件的影响。
5. 氢对氧有着很强的亲和力，很容易与氧化合形成水。

Ⅴ. Translation

Soon after Bohr's model was presented, it was discovered that the electron in an atom was much more complex than Bohr had suggested. Experiments confirmed that the electron has properties of both a particle (mass) and of light (wave nature). Because of its dual nature, the electron could not be viewed as a simple particle circling the nucleus at a definite distance. Also, if the electron moved with a high velocity, as Bohr had claimed, one could not know its location with much certainty.

Reading Material

Esters

In the IUPAC system, an ester is named as a derivative of the carboxylic acid from which it is derived. The alkyl or aryl group attached to oxygen is named first. Then the acid is named by dropping the suffix *-ic acid* and adding the suffix *-ate*. In Table 11.1, names of esters are derived in a stepwise manner. First is given the name of the alkyl or aryl group attached to oxygen, then IUPAC and common names of the acid from which the ester is derived, and finally the name of the ester.

Table 11.1 examples of derivation of names of esters

structural formula	alkyl group attached to oxygen	name of carboxylic acid	name of ester
$CH_3COOC_2H_5$	ethyl	ethanoic acid(acetic acid)	ethyl ethanoate(ethyl acetate)
$C_6H_5COOCH(CH_3)_2$	isopropyl	benzoic acid	isopropyl benzoate
$(CH_2COOC_2H_5)_2$	diethyl	butanedioic acid (succinic acid)	diethyl butanedioate (diethyl succinate)

Fischer Esterification

As we explained in the previous sections, esters can be prepared by reaction of an alcohol or phenol with either an acid halide or an acid anhydride. Esters can also be prepared by reacting a carboxylic acid with an alcohol in the presence of an acid catalyst, usually concentrated sulfuric acid, dry hydrogen chloride, or an ionexchange resin in the acid form. Conversion of a carboxylic acid and an alcohol to an ester in the presence of an acid catalyst is called Fischer esterification. As an example of Fischer esterification, reaction of acetic acid and ethanol in the presence of concentrated sulfuric acid gives ethyl acetate and water:

$$CH_3COOH + HOC_2H_5 \xrightleftharpoons{H^+} CH_3COOC_2H_5 + H_2O$$

ethanoic acid (acetic acid)   ethanol (ethyl alcohol)   ethyl ethanoate (ethyl acetate)

Acid-catalyzed esterification is an equilibrium reaction, and generally at equilibrium the quantities of both ester and alcohol are appreciable. If, for example, 60.1 g (1.0 mole) of acetic acid and 60.1g (1.0 mole) of 1-propanol are heated under reflux in the presence of a few drops of concentrated sulfuric acid until equilibrium is reached, the reaction mixture will contain about 0.67 mole each of propyl acetate and water, and about 0.33 mole each of acetic acid and 1-propanol. At equilibrium, about 67 percent of the acid and alcohol has been converted to the desired ester.

$$CH_3COOH + HO(CH_2)_2CH_3 \xrightleftharpoons{H^+} CH_3COOC_3H_7 + H_2O$$

ethanoic acid (acetic acid)   1-propanol (propyl alcohol)   propyl ethanoate (propyl acetate)   water

Initial: 1.00 mole   1.00 mole   0.00 mole   0.00 mole
Equilibrium: 0.33 mole   0.33 mole   0.67 mole   0.67 mole

By controlling reaction conditions, chemists can use direct esterification to prepare esters in high yields. For example, if the alcohol is inexpensive compared with the acid, a large excess of it can be used to drive the reaction to the right and achieve a high conversion of carboxylic acid to its ester.[1] Or it may be possible to take advantage of a situation in which the boiling points of the reactants and ester are higher than the boiling point of water. In this case, heating the reaction mixture somewhat above 100℃ removes water as it is formed and shifts the position of equilibrium toward the production of a higher yield of ester.

Of the three methods we have presented for preparation of esters, the use of acid chlorides is often the most convenient primarily because both the preparation of the acid chlorides and their reaction with alcohols are rapid and irreversible reactions. In contrast, Fischer esterification is a slow, reversible reaction, and yields of ester depend on the position of equilibrium.[2]

Following is a mechanism for acid-catalyzed esterification. Protonation of the carbonyl oxygen in step 1 gives a resonance-stabilized cation. Reaction of this cation in step 2 with a pair of electrons on the oxygen atom of the alcohol gives an oxonium ion that loses H^+ in step 3 to give a tetrahedral carbonyl addition intermediate. Reaction of an —OH of this intermediate with H^+ in step 4 followed by loss of a molecule of water in step 5 gives a new carbocation that then loses H^+ in step 6 to give the ester.[3]

step 1: Reaction of the carbonyl oxygen with H^+ to give a resonance-stabilized cation.
step 2: Reaction with oxygen of the alcohol to form an oxonium ion.
step 3: Loss of H^+ to form a tetradhedral carbonyl addition intermediate.
step 4: Reaction of an —OH of the tetrahedral carbonyl addition intermediate with H^+ to give a new oxonium ion.
step 5: Loss of H_2O to form a carbocation.
step 6: Loss of H^+ from the carbocation to give the ester.

This mechanism is a specific example of the more general mechanism we proposed in Section 10.3. for nucleophilic substitution at a carbonyl carbon. A key step in Fischer esterification is formation of a tetrahedral carbonyl addition intermediate:

$$CH_3COOH + HO-CH_3 \rightleftharpoons [CH_3-C(OH)_2(OCH_3)] \rightleftharpoons CH_3COOCH_3 + H_2O$$
tetrahedral carbonyl addition intermediate

The six-step mechanism we have proposed for Fischer esterification predicts that the oxygen atom of the alcohol is incorporated into the ester and that the oxygen atom appearing in the water molecule is derived from one of the two oxygen atoms of the carboxyl group.[4] This prediction has been tested in the following way. Oxygen in nature is a mixture of three isotopes.

isotope	natural abundance/%	isotope	natural abundance/%
oxygen-16	99.76	oxygen-18	0.204
oxygen-17	0.037		

Through the use of modern techniques for separating isotopes, it is possible to prepare compounds significantly enriched in oxygen-18. Such compounds are said to be isotopically enriched, or **isotopically labeled**. One easily prepared compound now commercially available is isotopically labeled methanol. When methanol enriched with oxygen-18 is reacted with benzoic acid containing only naturally occurring amounts of oxygen-18, all the isotope enrichment (the isotope label) is found in the ester.[5]

$$C_6H_4\text{-}COOH + H^{18}OCH_3 \longrightarrow C_6H_4\text{-}COOCH_3 + H_2O$$
labeled methanol   labeled ester

Hydrolysis

Esters are normally unreactive with water. However, in the presence of either aqueous acid (most commonly HCl or H_2SO_4) or aqueous base (most commonly NaOH or KOH), they are split into a carboxylic acid and an alcohol. Following is an equation for acid-catalyzed hydrolysis of ethyl acetate to give acetic acid and ethanol:

$$CH_3COOCH_2CH_3 + H_2O \underset{}{\overset{H^+}{\rightleftharpoons}} CH_3COOH + CH_3CH_2OH$$

Because the mechanism we proposed in Section 10.7A for acid-catalyzed esterification is reversible, formation of the same tetrahedral carbonyl addition intermediate accounts equally well for acid-catalyzed hydrolysis.

$$\underset{}{CH_3\overset{O}{\overset{\|}{C}}OCH_2CH_3} + HOH \rightleftharpoons \left[CH_3\underset{OH}{\overset{OH}{\underset{|}{\overset{|}{C}}}}OCH_2CH_3 \right] \rightleftharpoons CH_3\overset{O}{\overset{\|}{C}}OH + CH_3CH_2OH$$

hydrolysis →
← esterification

If acid-catalyzed hydrolysis is carried out in a large excess of water, the position of equilibrium is shifted in favor of formation of a carboxylic acid and alcohol.

Esters are hydrolyzed in aqueous base to a carboxylate anion and an alcohol. Alkaline hydrolysis of esters is often referred to as saponification, a name derived from the Latin root *sapo, saponis*: soap. For saponfication, 1 mole of base is required for each mole of ester, as illustrated in the equation:

$$CH_3COOC_2H_5 + NaOH \xrightarrow[\text{saponification}]{H_2O} CH_3COO^-Na^+ + CH_3CH_2OH$$

For all practical purposes, hydrolysis of an ester in aqueous base is irreversible because the carboxylate anion, once formed, has no tendency to react with an alcohol.

From *Organic Chemistry by Beyer and Walter*

New Words and Expressions

aryl [ˈæril]   *n.* 芳基
esterification [esˌterifiˈkeiʃən]   *n.* 酯化
phenol [ˈfiːnəl]   *n.* （苯）酚，石炭酸
propanol [ˈprəupənɔl]   *n.* 丙醇
reflux [ˈriːflʌks]   *n.* 回流
protonation [ˌprəutəˈneiʃən]   *n.* 质子化（作用）
oxonium [ɔkˈsəunjəm]   *n.* 氧鎓（离子）
saponification [səpɔnifiˈkeiʃən]   *n.* 皂化（作用）
soap [səup]   *n.* 肥皂，脂肪酸盐

Notes

1. For…插入语，if…条件状语从句，主结构 a large excess…can be used to…drive…and achieve…参考译文：例如，如果醇比酸便宜，可用过量的醇以使反应（平衡）向右进行，使羧酸生成酯的转化率提高。

2. In contrast 插入语，主要结构 Fischer…is…reaction and yields…depend on…。参考译文：相反，费歇尔酯化反应是一反应速度较慢的可逆反应，酯的收率取决于酯化反应的平衡位置。

3. 主要结构 Reaction…followed by…and then…。参考译文：第四步，中间体上的—OH 与 H^+ 反应；第五步，失去一分子水形成一新的碳阳离子；最后，在第六步反应中失去 H^+ 而生成酯。

4. 主要结构 The six-step mechanism（we…esterification 为其定语从句）predicts that（宾语从句 the…is…ester）and that [宾语从句 the…atom（appearing…为其定语从句）is…]。参考译文：我们为费歇尔酯化反应提出的六步反应机理表明醇中的氧原子结合到酯中，而水分子中的氧原子则来自羧基中两个氧原子的其中一个。

5. 主要结构 When…[methanol…enriched…（定语）is…acid（定语）] 条件状语从句，all…is…。参考译文：当富含氧-18 的甲醇与苯甲酸（仅含有以天然含量存在的氧-18）反应时，发现所有的浓集同位素（同位素标记）都存在于酯中。

PART THREE
ANALYTICAL TECHNOLOGY FOR SAMPLE

Unit 12 What Is Analytical Chemistry

Perhaps the most functional definition of analytical chemistry is that it is "the qualitative and quantitative characterization of matter".[1] The word "characterization" is used in a very broad sense. It may mean the identification of the chemical compounds or elements present in a sample to answer questions such as "Is there any vitamin E in this shampoo as indicated on the label?" or "Is this white tablet an aspirin tablet?" or "Is this piece of metal iron or nickel?"[2] This type of characterization, to tell us what is present is called qualitative analysis. Qualitative analysis is the identification of one or more chemical species present in a material. Characterization may also mean the determination of how much of a particular compound or element is present in a sample, to answer questions such as "How much acetylsalicylic acid is in this aspirin tablet?" or "How much nickel is in this steel?" This determination of how much of a species is present in a sample is called quantitative analysis. Quantitative analysis is the determination of the exact amount of a chemical species present in a sample. The chemical species may be an element, compound, or ion. The compound may be organic or inorganic. Characterization can refer to the entire sample (bulk analysis), such as the elemental composition of a piece of steel, or to the surface of a sample (surface analysis), such as the identification of the composition and thickness of the oxide layer that forms on the surface of most metals exposed to air and water. The characterization of a material may go beyond chemical analysis to include structural determination of materials, the measurement of physical properties of a material, and the measurement of physical chemistry parameters like reaction kinetics. Examples of such measurements are the degree to which a polymer is crystalline as opposed to amorphous, the temperature at which a material loses its water of hydration, how long it takes for antacid "Brand A" to neutralize stomach acid, and how fast a pesticide degrades in sunlight.[3] These diverse applications make analytical chemistry one of the broadest in scope of all scientific disciplines. Analytical chemistry is critical to our understanding of biochemistry, medicinal chemistry, geochemistry, environmental science, atmospheric chemistry, the behavior of materials such as polymers, metal alloys, and ceramics, and many other scientific disciplines.

For many years, analytical chemistry relied on chemical reactions to identify and determine the components present in a sample. These types of classical methods, often called "wet chemical methods", usually required that a part of the sample be taken, dissolved in a suitable solvent if necessary and the desired reaction carried out. The most important analytical fields based on this approach were volumetric and gravimetric analysis. Acid-base titrations, oxidation-reduction titrations, and gravimetric determinations, such as the determination of silver by precipitation as silver chloride are all examples of wet chemical analyses.

These types of analyses require a high degree of skill and attention to detail on the part of the analyst if accurate and precise results are to be obtained[4]. They are also time consuming and the demands of today's high-throughput pharmaceutical development labs and industrial quality control labs often do not permit the use of such time-consuming methods for routine analysis. In addition, it may be necessary to analyze samples without destroying them[5]. Examples include evaluation of valuable artwork to determine if a painting is really by a famous "Old Master" or is a modern forgery, as well as in forensic analysis, where the evidence may need to be preserved. For these types of analyses, nondestructive analysis methods are needed, and wet chemical analysis will not do the job. Wet chemical analysis is still used in specialized areas of analysis, but many of the volumetric methods have been transferred to automated instruments. Classical analysis and instrumental analysis are similar in many respects, such as in the need for proper sampling, sample preparation, assessment of accuracy and precision, and proper record keeping.[6]

Most analyses today are carried out with specially designed electronic instruments controlled by computers. These instruments make use of the interaction of electromagnetic radiation and matter, or of some physical property of matter, to characterize the sample being analyzed. Often these instruments have automated sample introduction, automated data processing, and even automated sample preparation. To understand how the instrumentation operates and what information it can provide requires knowledge of chemistry, physics, mathematics, and engineering. The fundamentals of common analytical instruments and how measurements are performed with these instruments are the subjects of the following chapters on specific instrumental techniques. The analytical chemist must not only know and understand analytical chemistry and instrumentation, but must also be able to serve as a problem solver to colleagues in other scientific areas. This means that the analytical chemist may need to understand materials science, metallurgy, biology, pharmacology, agricultural science, food science, geology, and other fields. The field of analytical chemistry is advancing rapidly. To keep up with the advances, the analytical chemist must understand the fundamentals of common analytical techniques, their capabilities, and their shortcomings. The analytical chemist must understand the problem to be solved, select the appropriate technique or techniques to use, design the analytical experiment to provide relevant data, and ensure that the data obtained are valid. [7] Merely providing data to other scientists is not enough; the analytical chemist must be able to interpret the data, and communicate the meaning of the results, together with the accuracy and precision (the reliability) of the data, to scientists who will use the data[8]. In addition to understanding the scientific problem, the modern analytical chemist often must also consider factors such as time limitations and cost limitations in providing an analysis. Whether one is working for a government regulatory agency, a hospital, a private company, or a university, analytical data must be legally defensible. It must be of known, documented quality. Record keeping, especially computer record keeping, assessing accuracy and precision, statistical handling of data, documenting, and ensuring that the data meet the applicable technical standards are especially critical aspects of the job of modern analytical chemists.

Many analytical results are expressed as the concentration of the measured substance in a certain amount of sample. The measured substance is called the analyte. Commonly used concentration units include molarity (moles of substance per liter of solution), weight percent (grams of substance per gram of sample $\times 100\%$), and units for trace levels of substances. One part per million (ppm) by weight is one microgram of analyte in a gram of sample, that is, 1×10^{-6} g analyte/g sample. One part per billion (ppb) by weight is one nanogram of element in a gram of sample or 1×10^{-9} g analyte/g sample. For many elements, the technique known as inductively coupled plasma mass spectrometry (ICP-MS), can detect parts per trillion of the element, that is, picograms of element per gram of sample (1×10^{-12} g analyte/g sample).[9] To give you a feeling for these quantities, a million seconds is 12 days (11.57 days, to be exact). One part per million in units of seconds would be one second in 12 days. A part per billion in units of seconds would be 1s in 32 years, and one part per trillion is one second in 32000 years. Today, lawmakers set environmental levels of allowed chemicals in air and water based on measurements of compounds and elements at part per trillion levels because instrumental methods can detect part per trillion levels of analytes. It is the analytical chemist who is responsible for generating the data that these lawmakers rely on.

From *Undergraduate Instrumental Analysis By James W. Robinson*

New Words and Expressions

qualitative [ˈkwɔlitətiv] *a.* 定性的，性质上的
quantitative [ˈkwɔntitətiv] *a.* 定量的，数量的
determination [diˌtəːmiˈneiʃən] *n.* 测定，确定
acetylsalicylic [əˌsitilˌsæliˈsilik] *n.* 乙酰水杨酸，阿司匹林
bulk analysis   全分析
surface analysis   表面分析
volumetric analysis   容量分析
crystalline [ˈkristəlain] *a.* 晶体的，晶体状的；水晶的   *n.* 结晶体（质），晶态
amorphous [əˈmɔːfəs] *a.* 无定形的，；非结晶质的；没有明确晶体结构的
antacid [æntˈæsid] *n.* 抗酸剂；*a.* 中和酸性的，抗酸性的
neutralize [ˈnjuːtrəlaiz] *v.* 使中性，使（溶液）呈中性；中和
alloy [ˈælɔi] *n.* 合金   *vt.* 使成合金，减低成色
ceramic [siˈræmik] *a.* 陶器的   *n.* 陶瓷制品
discipline [ˈdisiplin] *n.* 纪律，学科   *v.* 训练
gravimetric analysis   重量分析
titration [taiˈtreiʃən] *n.* 滴定
throughput [ˈθruːput] *n.* 生产量，生产能力，吞吐量
pharmaceutical [ˌfɑːməˈsjuːtikəl] *n.* 药物；*a.* 制药（学）上的
forgery [ˈfɔːdʒəri] *n.* 伪造物，伪造罪，伪造
forensic [fəˈrensik] *a.* 法院的，公开辩论的；*n.* 辩论术
do the job   发挥作用
electromagnetic radiation   电磁辐射
sample introduction   进样
pharmacology [ˌfɑːməˈkɔlədʒi] *n.* 药理学
regulatory agency   管理机构
defensible [diˈfensəbl] *a.* 可防御的；可辩护的
concentration [ˌkɔnsenˈtreiʃən] *n.* 集中，集合，专心，浓缩，浓度
molarity [məuˈlæriti] *n.* 摩尔浓度
microgram [ˈmaikrəugræm] *n.* 微观图，显微照片
nanogram [ˈneinəgræm] *n.* 毫微克，纳克
pictogram [ˈpikəgræm] *n.* 皮（可）克，微微克（10^{-12}g）
trillion [ˈtriljən] *num.* 万亿，等于10^{12}

Notes

1. 该句宾语从句，句子结构是…definition…is that…参考译文：也许对分析化学最实用的定义是：对物质进行定性及定量表征。

2. this piece of metal 这块金属。参考译文：它可能意味着在回答诸如"在洗发香波中是否如标签所示有维生素 E？""这是一个白色阿司匹林片？"或"这块金属是铁或镍？"等问题时，对样本中的化合物或元素进行的鉴定。

3. as opposed to 与……相对；与……成对比。参考译文：这些测量的实例有：聚合物的结晶度（与非晶态相比）？物质失去结晶水的温度？"A 牌"抗酸剂中和胃酸所需时间？农药在阳光下降解的速度？

4. be to 形式用于条件从句；the part 指 skill。参考译文：要想获得准确、精密的结果，这类分析需要高度技巧及分析工作者对技巧细节的关注。

5. 结构：it may be necessary to…对……可能是必要的。参考译文：另外，可能有必要不通过损坏它们来分析样品。

6. 参考译文：经典分析和仪器分析在许多方面都有相似之处，例如都需要适当的采样、样品制备、评估准确度和精确度以及正确记录数据。

7. technique or techniques 指各种分析技术及联用技术。参考译文：分析化学家必须了解要解决的问题，选择恰当的分离技术及联用技术，设计分析实验以提供相关数据，并确保数据有效。

8. communicate to 传递关于……的信息给……，使……知道；传达，传送。参考译文：仅仅提供数据给其他科学家是不够的；分析化学家必须能够解读数据，并能将结果的意义和数据的精度（可靠性），传达给使用这些数据的科学家们。

9. 此句为同位语从句，…element, that is…。inductively coupled plasma mass spectrometry (ICP-MS) 电感耦合等离子体质谱。参考译文：对多组分体系，电感耦合等离子体质谱技术（质谱分析），可以检测出含量为万亿分之一的成分，即每克样品中含量为皮克的成分（1×10^{-12} g 被检测物/每克样品）。

Exercises

Ⅰ. Comprehension

1. According to the first paragraph, the most functional definition of analytical chemistry is _____.
   A. identification of the chemical compounds or elements present in a sample
   B. determination of how much of a particular compound or element is present in a sample
   C. the qualitative and quantitative characterization of matter
   D. the qualitative analysis and quantitative analysis

2. The characterization of material can refer to _____.
   A. bulk analysis and surface analysis   B. structure analysis
   C. property analysis   D. all of above

3. Which is not the example of volumetric analysis? _____
   A. Determination of the amount of HAc in vinegar
   B. Determination of total amount of Ca^{2+}, Mg^{2+} in tap water
   C. Determination of sulfur by precipitation
   D. Determination of Fe^{2+} in $Fe(NH_4)_2(SO_4)_2$ by $KMnO_4$

4. Following are the similarities between classical analysis and instrumental analysis with the exception of _____.
   A. proper sampling and sample preparation   B. assessment of accuracy and precision

  C. proper record keeping   D. time consuming
5. What is the second last paragraph mainly talking about? _____
  A. The analytical chemist must ensure that the data obtained are valid.
  B. The analytical chemist must use techniques to solve problems.
  C. The analytical chemist must need to understand materials science, metallurgy, biology, pharmacology, agricultural science, food science, geology, and other fields.
  D. The analytical chemist must interpret the data to scientist who will use them.

II. Complete the sentences with the proper form of the word given at the end of the sentence.

1. Almost every use of electricity suffers from _____, an unavoidable phenomenon inside conventional wires and other conductors that turns part of any flow of electrical energy into useless heat. (resist)

2. Dozens of labs are working on wires and films thin enough to _____ on computer chips. (deposit)

3. Robots are manipulator s designed to perform useful work _____ without human assistance. (automate)

4. To most people electronics _____ to be a mysterious art veiled in strange practices. (appearance)

5. In the past forty years, weather forecasting has become almost entirely _____. (computer)

6. Accidents at work usually occur either because equipment is dangerous or workers are not trained to do their jobs _____. (proper)

7. Although the moon has not held great prominence in the history of religion, the _____ of the moon by some societies has been practiced since early times. (venerate)

8. All living things have certain _____ that are passed on form one generation to the next. (attribution)

9. Matters can _____ in three possible states: gas, liquid, and solid. (existent)

10. The _____ of a substance in water is usually given in terms of the number of grams of the substance that will produce a saturated solution in 100 g of water. (soluble)

III. Translation

1. 分析化学是研究物质及其变化的重要化学方法之一。
2. 几乎任何科学研究,只要涉及化学现象,都需要分析化学提供各种信息,以解决科学研究中的问题。
3. 以物质化学反应为基础的分析方法称为化学分析法。
4. 经典的分析方法无论在教育价值上和实用价值上都是不可忽视的。
5. 分析化学在工农业生产中起着重要的作用。

IV. Translation

  A gravimetric method is one in which the analysis is completed by a weighing operation. A volumetric method is one in which the analysis is completed by measuring the volume of a solution of established concentration needed to react completely with the substance being determined. Ordinarily, volumetric methods are equivalent in accuracy to gravimetric procedures and are more rapid and convenient; their use is widespread.

V. Problem

(1) What is the pH of a solution that is made up to be 1.00mol/L in HOAC (K_a for HOAC is 1.8×10^{-5})

(2) The pH of an 0.0100mol/L solution of formic acid (HCOOH) in H_2O is 2.90 Calculate K_a for this acid (note hat formic acid gives up only one proton)

Reading Material

Sample Preparation

Few samples in the real world can be analyzed without some chemical or physical preparation. The aim of all sample preparation is to provide the analyte of interest in the physical form required by the instrument, free of interfering substances, and in the concentration range required by the instrument.[1] For many instruments, a solution of analyte in organic solvent or water is required. We have already discussed some of the sample preparation steps that may be needed. Solid samples may need to be crushed or ground, or they may need to be washed with water, acid, or solvent to remove surface contamination. Liquid samples with more than one phase may need to be extracted or separated. Filtration or centrifugation may be required.

If the physical form of the sample is different from the physical form required by the analytical instrument, more elaborate sample preparation is required. Samples may need to be dissolved to form a solution or pressed into pellets or cast into thin films or cut and polished smooth.[2] The type of sample preparation needed depends on the nature of the sample, the analytical technique chosen, the analyte to be measured, and the problem to be solved. Most samples are not homogeneous. Many samples contain components that interfere with the determination of the analyte. A wide variety of approaches to sample preparation has been developed to deal with these problems in real samples.[3]

Notes that none of the sample preparation methods described here should be attempted without approval, written instructions, and close supervision by your professor or laboratory instructor. The methods described present many potential hazards. Many methods use concentrated acids, flammable solvents, and/or high temperatures and high pressures. Reactions can generate harmful gases. The potential for "runaway reactions" and even explosions exists with preparation of real samples. Sample preparation should be performed in a laboratory fume hood for safety. Goggles, lab coats or aprons, and gloves resistant to the chemicals in use should be worn at all times in the laboratory.

1. Acid Dissolution and Digestion

Metals, alloys, ores, geological samples, ceramics, and glass react with concentrated acids and this approach is commonly used for dissolving such samples. Organic materials can be decomposed (digested or "wet ashed") using concentrated acids to remove the carbonaceous material and solubilize the trace elements in samples such as biological tissues, foods, and plastics. A sample is generally weighed into an open beaker, concentrated acid is added, and the beaker heated on a hot plate until the solid material dissolves. Dissolution often is much faster if the sample can be heated at pressures greater than atmospheric pressure. The boiling point of the solvent is raised at elevated pressure, allowing the sample and solvent to be heated to higher temperatures than can be attained at atmospheric pressure. This can be done in a sealed vessel, which also has the advantage of not allowing volatile elements to escape from the sample. Special stainless steel high-pressure vessels, called "bombs", are available for acid dissolution and for the combustion of organic samples under oxygen. While these vessels do speed up the dissolution, they operate at pressures of hundreds of atmospheres and can be very dangerous if not operated properly. Another sealed vessel digestion technique uses microwave digestion. This technique uses sealed sample vessels made of polymer, which are heated in a specially designed laboratory microwave oven. (NEVER use a kitchen-type microwave oven for sample preparations. The electronics in kitchen-type units are not protected from corrosive fumes, arcing can occur, and the microwave source, the magnetron, can easily overheat and burn out.) The sealed vessel microwave digestion approach keeps volatile elements in solution, prevents external contaminants from falling into the sample, and is much faster than digestion on a hot plate in an open beaker. Microwave energy efficiently heats solutions of polar molecules (such as water) and ions (aqueous mineral acids) and samples that contain polar molecules and/or ions.[4] In addition, the sealed vessel results in increased pressure and increased boiling point.

2. Fusions

Heating a finely powdered solid sample with a finely powdered salt at high temperatures until the mixture melts is called a fusion or molten salt fusion. The reacted and cooled melt is leached with water or dilute acid to dissolve the analytes for determination of elements by atomic spectroscopy or ICP-MS. Often, the molten fusion mixture is poured into a flat bottomed mold and allowed to cool. The resulting glassy disk is used for quantitative XRF measurements. Molten salt fusions are useful for the dissolution of silica-containing minerals, glass, ceramics, ores, human bone, and many difficultly soluble materials like carbides and borides. The salts used (called "fluxes") include sodium carbonate, borax (sodium tetraborate), lithium metaborate, and sodium peroxide. The fusions are carried out over a burner or in a muffle furnace in crucibles of the appropriate material. Depending on the flux used and the analytes to be measured, crucibles may be made of platinum, nickel, zirconium, porcelain, quartz, or glassy carbon. Automated "fluxers" are available that will fuse up to six samples at once and pour the melts into XRF molds or into beakers, for laboratories that perform large numbers of fusions. The drawback of fusion is that the salts used as fluxes can introduce many trace element contaminants into the sample, the crucible material itself may contaminate the sample, and the elements present in the flux itself cannot be analytes in the sample. Fusion cannot be used for boron determinations if the flux is borax or lithium metaborate, for example. Platinum crucibles cannot be used if trace levels of platinum catalyst are to be determined.

3. Dry Ashing and Combustion

To analyze organic compounds or substances for the inorganic elements present, it is often necessary to remove the organic material.[5] Wet ashing with concentrated acids has been mentioned as one way of doing this. The other approach is "dry ashing", that is, ignition of the organic material in air or oxygen. The organic components react to form gaseous carbon dioxide and water vapor, leaving the inorganic components behind as solid oxides. Ashing is often done in a crucible or evaporating dish of platinum or fused silica in a muffle furnace. Volatile elements will be lost even at relatively low temperatures; dry ashing cannot be used for the determination of mercury, arsenic, cadmium, and a number of other metals of environmental and biological interest for this reason. Oxygen bomb combustions can be performed in a high-pressure steel vessel very similar to a bomb calorimeter. One gram or less of organic material is ignited electrically in a pure oxygen atmosphere with a small amount of absorbing solution such as water or dilute acid. The organic components form carbon dioxide and water and the elements of interest dissolve in the absorbing solution. Combustion in oxygen at atmospheric pressure can be done in a glass apparatus called a Schöniger flask. The limitation to this technique is sample size; no more than 10 mg sample can be burned. However, the technique is used to obtain aqueous solutions of sulfur, phosphorus, and the halogens from organic compounds containing these heteroatoms. These elements can then be determined by ion selective potentiometry, ion chromatography, or other methods.[6]

4. Extraction

The sample preparation techniques earlier discussed are used for inorganic samples or for the determination of inorganic components in organic materials by removing the organic matrix. Obviously, they cannot be used if we want to determine organic analytes. The most common approach for organic analytes is to extract the analytes out of the sample matrix using a suitable solvent. Solvents are chosen with the polarity of the analyte in mind, since "like dissolves like".[7] That is, polar solvents dissolve polar compounds, while nonpolar solvents dissolve nonpolar compounds. Common extraction solvents include hexane, methylene chloride, methylisobutyl ketone (MIBK), and xylene.

From *Undergraduate Instrumental Analysis By James W. Robinson*

New Words and Expressions

interfering substance　干扰物质
filtration [fil'treiʃən]　*n.* 过滤，筛选
centrifugation [ˌsenˌtrifjuˈgeiʃən]　*n.* 离心法，离心过滤
homogeneous [ˌhɔməuˈdʒi:njəs]　*a.* 均匀的，均相的
runaway ['rʌnəwei]　*a.* 不受控制的，摆脱控制、限制或局限的
runaway reaction　失控反应
fume hood　烟橱，通风橱
carbonaceous [ˌkɑ:bəˈneiʃəs]　*a.* 碳的，碳质的，含碳的
solubilize ['sɔljubilaiz]　*v.* （使）溶解，（使）增溶
bomb [bɔm]　*n.* 高压气体储罐
magnetron ['mægnitrɔn]　*n.* 磁电管
fusion ['fju:ʒən]　*n.* 熔化，熔解，熔融
leach [li:tʃ]　*v.* 沥滤；浸提
XRF ＝X-ray fluorescence　X射线荧光
carbide ['kɑ:baid]　*n.* 碳化物
boride ['bɔ:raid]　*n.* 硼化物
flux [flʌks]　*n.* 助熔剂　流量　*vi.* 熔化，流出　*vt.* 使熔融
borax ['bɔ:ræks]　*n.* 硼砂，$Na_2B_4O_7 \cdot 10H_2O$
tetraborate [ˌtetrəˈbɔ:reit]　*n.* 四硼酸盐
metaborate [ˌmetəˈbɔ:reit]　*n.* 偏硼酸盐 MBO_2
peroxide [pəˈrɔksaid]　*n.* 过氧化物，过氧化氢
muffle furnace　马弗炉，套炉，回热炉，膛式炉，隔焰炉
crucible ['kru:sibl]　*n.* 坩埚
porcelain ['pɔ:slin, -lein]　*n.* 瓷器，瓷；*a.* 瓷制的，精美的，脆的
glassy carbon　玻璃化炭黑
dry ashing　干法灰化
calorimeter [ˌkæləˈrimitə]　*n.* 热量计
heteroatom ['hetərəuˌætəm]　*n.* 杂原子，杂环原子
potentiometry [pəˌtenʃiˈɔmitri]　*n.* 电势［位］测定法
extraction [iksˈtrækʃən]　*n.* 抽出，提取（法），萃取法，抽出物
xylene ['zaili:n]　*n.* 二甲苯

Notes

1. physical form 外形，外观，实物形态。参考译文：实际操作中，几乎没有不经过化学或物理方法预处理就可以分析的样品。所有样品制备的目的就是按照仪器所要求的实物形态提供被分析物，不含干扰物质，浓度范围符合仪器的要求。

2. pressed into pellets 压片；cast into thin films 铸膜。参考译文：样品可能要被液化形成溶液，或压制成颗粒，或铸造成薄或切割和打磨光滑。

3. deal with 处理，解决。参考译文：大量样品制备的方法已发展到在实际样本中处理这些问题。

4. 参考译文：微波能量能有效地加热由极性分子（如水）、离子（无机酸水溶液）和含有极性分子或离子样品所组成的溶液。

5. 该句的结构为：It is necessary to…做…是必要的。参考译文：在分析有机化合物或有机物质中的无机元素时，除去其中的有机成分是必要的。

6. ion selective potentiometry 离子选择电位法；ion chromatography 离子色谱。参考译文：灼烧法的局限是对样品量的限制，只有不超过10mg的样品才能被充分燃烧。然而这种方法可用来从含硫、磷和卤素杂原子的有机化合物中得到这些元素的水溶液。进而用离子选择电位法和离子色谱法，或者其他方法测定这些元素。

7. "like dissolves like" 相似相溶。参考译文：根据"相似相容原理"，选择溶剂时要考虑被分析物的极性。

Unit 13 Ultraviolet and Visible Molecular Spectroscopy

Probably the first physical method used in analytical chemistry was based on the quality of the color in colored solution. The first things we observe regarding colored solutions are their hue, or color, and the color's depth, or intensity. These observations led to the technique historically called colorimetry; the color of the solution could identify species (qualitative analysis) while the intensity of the color could identify the concentration of the species present (quantitative analysis). This technique was the first use of what we now understand to be absorption spectroscopy for chemical analysis[1]. When white light passes through a solution and emerges as red light, we say that the solution is red. What has actually happened is that the solution has allowed the red component of white light to pass through, whereas it has absorbed the complementary color, yellow and blue. The more concentrated the sample solution, the more yellow and blue light is absorbed and the more intensely red the solution appears to the eye. For a long time, experimental work made use of the human eye as the detector to measure the hue and intensity of colors in solutions. However, even the best analyst can have difficulty comparing the intensity of two colors with slightly different hues, and there are of course people who are color-blind and cannot see certain colors. Instruments have been developed to perform the measurements more accurately and reliably than the human eye. While the human eye can only detect visible light, this chapter will focus on both the ultraviolet (UV) and the visible (Vis) portions of the spectrum.

The wavelength range of UV radiation starts at the blue end of visible light (about 400 nm) and ends at approximately 200 nm for spectrometers operated in air. The radiation has sufficient energy to excite valence electrons in many atoms and molecules; consequently, UV radiation is involved with electronic excitation. Visible light, considered to be light with wavelengths from 800 to 400 nm, acts in the same way as UV light. It is also considered part of the electronic excitation region.[2] For this reason we find commercial spectroscopic instrumentation often operates with wavelengths between 800 and 200 nm. Spectrometers of this type are called UV/Visible (or UV/Vis) spectrometers. The vacuum UV region of the spectrum extends below 200 nm to the X-ray region of the spectrum, at $\sim$ 100 Å. It has called the vacuum UV region because oxygen, water vapor, and other molecules in air absorb UV radiation below 200 nm, so the spectrometer light path[3] must be free of air to observe wavelengths<200 nm. The instrument must be evacuated (kept under vacuum) or purged with an appropriate non-UV absorbing gas such as helium for this region to be used. Vacuum UV radiation is also involved in electronic excitation but the spectrometers are specialized and not commonly found in undergraduate or routine analytical laboratories. For our purposes the term UV will mean radiation between 200nm and 400 nm, unless stated otherwise.

The interaction of UV and visible radiation with matter can provide qualitative identification of molecules and polyatomic species, including ions and complexes. Structural information about molecules and polyatomic species, especially organic molecules, can be acquired. This qualitative information is usually obtained by observing the UV/Vis spectrum, the absorption of UV and visible radiation as a function of wavelength by molecules.

The shape and intensity of UV/Vis absorption bands are related to the electronic structure of the absorbing species. The molecule is often dissolved in a solvent to acquire the spectrum. We will look at how we can use the absorption maximum of a chromophore and a set of guidelines to predict the position of the absorption maximum in a specific molecule.

We will also consider how the solvent affects the spectrum of some molecules. As a reminder, the transitions that give rise to UV/Vis absorption by organic molecules are the $n \rightarrow \delta^*$, $\pi \rightarrow \pi^*$, and $n \rightarrow \pi^*$ transitions.

Some terms need to be defined. A chromophore is a group of atoms (part of a molecule) that gives rise to an electronic absorption. An auxochrome is a substituent that contains unshared (nonbonding) electron pairs, such as OH, NH, and halogens. An auxochrome attached to a chromophore with π electrons shifts the absorption maximum to longer wavelengths. A shift to longer wavelengths is called a bathochromic shift or red shift. A shift to shorter wavelengths is called a hypsochromic shift or blue shift. An increase in the intensity of absorption band (that is, an increase in ε_{max}) is called hyperchromism; a decrease in intensity is called hypochromism. These shifts in wavelength and intensity come about as a result of the structure of the entire molecule or as a result of interaction between the solute molecules and the solvent molecules.

As described at the beginning of the chapter, the types of compounds that absorb UV radiation are those with nonbonded electrons (n electrons) and conjugated double bond systems (π electrons) such as aromatic compounds and conjugated olefins. Unfortunately, such compounds absorb over similar wavelength ranges, and the absorption spectra overlap considerably. As a first step in qualitative analysis, it is necessary to purify the sample to eliminate absorption bands due to impurities. Even when pure, however, the spectra are often broad and frequently without fine structure. For these reasons, UV absorption is much less useful for the qualitative identification of functional groups or particular molecules than analytical methods such as MS, IR, and NMR. UV absorption is rarely used for organic structural elucidation today in modern laboratories because of the ease of use and power of NMR, IR, and MS.

UV and visible absorption spectrometry is a powerful tool for quantitative analysis. It is used in chemical research, biochemistry, chemical analysis, and industrial processing. Quantitative analysis is based on the relationship between the degree of absorption and the concentration of the absorbing material. Mathematically, it is described for many chemical systems by Beer's Law, $A=abc$. The term applied to quantitative absorption spectrometry by measuring intensity ratios is spectrophotometry. The use of spectrophotometry in the visible region of the spectrum used to be referred to as colorimetry.[4] UV/Vis spectrophotometry is a widely used spectroscopic technique. It has found use everywhere in the world for research, clinical analysis, environmental analysis, and many other applications. Some typical applications of UV absorption spectroscopy include the determination of (i) the concentrations of phenol, nonionic surfactants, sulfate, sulfide, phosphates, fluoride, nitrate, a variety of metal ions, and other chemicals in drinking water in environmental testing; (ii) natural products, such an steroids or chlorophyll; (iii) dyestuff materials; (iv) vitamins, proteins, DNA, and enzymes in biochemisty.

Spectrophotometry in the UV region of the spectrum is used for the direct measurement of many organic compounds, especially those with aromatic rings and conjugated multiple bonds. There are also colorless inorganic species that absorb in the UV. A good example is the nitrate ion, NO_3^-. A rapid screening method for nitrate in drinking water is performed by measuring the absorbance of the water at 220 nm and at 275 nm. Nitrate ion absorbs at 220 nm but not at 275 nm; the measurement at 275 nm is to check for interfering organic compounds that may be present.[5] Spectrophotometic analysis in the visible region can be used whenever the sample is colored. Many materials are inherently colored without chemical reaction (e. g., inorganic ions such as dichromate, permanganate, cupric ion, and ferric ion) and need no further chemical reaction to form colored compounds. Colored organic compounds, such as dyestuffs, are also naturally colored. Solution of such materials can be analyzed directly. The majority of metal and nonmetal ions, however, are colorless. The presence of these ions in a sample solution can be determined by first reacting the ion with an organic reagent to form a strongly absorbing species. If the product of the reaction is colored, absorbance can be measured in the visible region; alternatively, the product formed may be colorless but absorb in the UV. The majority of spectrophotometric determinations result in an increase in absorbance (darker color if visible) as the concentration of the analyte increases.[6]

Quantitative analysis by absorption spectrophotometry requires that the samples be free from particulates, that is, free from turbidity. The reason for this is that particles can scatter light. If light is scattered by the sample away from the detector, it is interpreted as an absorbance.[7] The absorbance will be erroneously high if the sample is turbid. We can make use of the scattering of light to characterize samples as discussed in Section 5.7, but particulates must be avoided for accurate absorbance measurements.

Quantitative analysis by absorption spectrophotometry generally requires the preparation of a calibration curve, using the same conditions of pH, reagents added, and so on for all of the standards, samples, and blanks. It is critical to have a reagent blank that contains everything that has been added to the samples (except the analyte). The absorbance is measured for all blanks, standards, and samples. The absorbance of the blank is subtracted from all other absorbances and a calibration curve is constructed from the standards. The highest accuracy results from working in the linear region of the calibration curve. These quantitative methods can be quite complicated in the chemistry involved, the number of steps required (extraction, back-extraction, pH-adjustment, precipitation, masking, and many other types of operations may be involved in a method), and the analyst must pay attention all the details to achieve accurate and precise results. There is both science and art involved in performing many of these analyses. Many standard or regulatory methods have published precision and accuracies data in the methods. These are the precisions and accuracies that can be achieved by an experienced analyst.

From *Undergraduate Instrumental Analysis By James W. Robinson*

New Words and Expressions

hue [hjuː]　*n.* 色彩，色调，颜色
colorimetry [ˌkʌləˈrimitri]　*n.* 比色法
spectroscopic [ˌspektrəˈskɔpik]　*a.* 分光镜的，借助分光镜的；光谱（学）的
polyatomic [ˌpɔliəˈtɔmik]　*a.* 多原子的
chromophore [ˈkrəuməfɔː]　*n.* 发色团，生色团
auxochrome [ˈɔːksəkrəum]　*n.* 助色团
bathochromic [ˌbæθəˈkrɔmik]　shift　化合物的吸收光谱向光谱带的红端移动，红移
hypsochromic [ˌhipsəˈkrɔmik]　shift　蓝移
hyperchromism [ˌhaipəˈkrəumizəm]　*n.* 增色
hypochromism [ˌhaipəuˈkrəumizəm]　*n.* 减色
spectrophotometry [ˌspektrəufəuˈtɔmitri]　*n.* 分光光度测定法，分光光度技术
nonionic [ˈnɔnaiˈɔnik]　*a.* 在溶液中不分解成离子的；非离子的
surfactant [səˈfæktənt]　*n. & a.* 表面活性剂（的）
steroid [ˈstiərɔid]　*n.* 类固醇，甾族化合物
chlorophyll [ˈklɔːrəfil]　*n.* 叶绿素
dyestuff [ˈdaistʌf]　*n.* 染料

dichromate [daiˈkrəumeit]   n. 重铬酸盐
absorbance [bˈsɔːbəns]   n. 吸光率，吸光度
particulate [pəˈtikjulit, -leit]   n. 微粒 a. 微粒的
turbidity [təːˈbiditi]   n. 混浊，混乱；混浊度，含砂量
erroneously [iˈrəunjəsli]   adv. 错误，不正确地
calibration curve   校准（定标，标定）曲线
back-extraction   反萃取，逆萃取

Notes

1. 其中 what = the thing(s) that。参考译文：这项技术是首次使用人们所了解的吸收光谱进行化学分析。

2. the same…as… 和……一样。参考译文：可见光被认为是波长从 800nm 到 400nm 的光，与物质的作用方式跟紫外光相同，也是电子激发光谱的一部分。

3. light path 光路，光程。参考译文：它被称为真空紫外区是由于氧，水蒸气和空气中的其他分子吸收紫外线辐射低于 200nm，分光计光路也一样。

4. be referred to as 叫做……，被称之为……参考译文：人们过去将分光光度测定法在可见光区的应用称为比色法。

5. to check for 检查……，验证……。参考译文：硝酸根离子在 220nm 处吸收，而不是 275nm；在 275 nm 处测量是检查可能出现的干扰有机物。

6. 该句的结构为：…result in…as… 由于……导致……参考译文：在大多数分光光度测定中，吸光度随着分析物浓度的增加而增加。

7. be interpreted as 被认为是……，被看作……。参考译文：如果入射光被样品散射而不能被检测器检测到的话，那么这部分散射光就被认为是吸收了。

Exercises

Ⅰ. Comprehension

1. According to the first paragraph, which of the following statement is true? _____
   A. Human eyes can be used as a type of highly sensitive detector.
   B. The best analyst can compare the intensity of two colors with slightly different hues without the aid of other instrumental methods.
   C. Even the best analyst can have difficulty comparing the intensity of two colors with slightly different hues.
   D. Human eyes can detect visible light, as well as ultraviolet light.

2. It must be free of air to observe vacuum UV spectrum because _____.
   A. oxygen in air absorb UV radiation below 200 nm
   B. water vapor in air absorb UV radiation below 200 nm
   C. helium absorb UV radiation below 200 nm
   D. both A and B

3. An increase in the intensity of absorption band (that is, an increase in ε_{max}) is called _____.
   A. hypochromism   B. bathochromic shift
   C. hypsochromic shift   D. hyperchromism

4. UV absorption is rarely used for organic structural elucidation today in modern laboratories because of _____.
   A. the ease of use and power of NMR, IR, and MS

B. compounds with nonbonded electrons and conjugated double bond systems having similar UV absorption wavelength ranges

C. the UV spectra of most compounds often with broad bands and frequently without fine structure

D. all of the above

5. According to the last paragraph, calibration curve is constructed from _____.
A. a reagent blank   B. the standards   C. samples   D. none of the above

II. Fill in the blanks

A particular type _____ precipitation system used in the metal plating industry is known _____ the Integrated Method of Treatment. The principal feature of this system is that the rinsing stage immediately after the metal plating stages a chemical rinse which precipitates the metal _____ the liquid around the article being plated. A further water rinse is then required to wash _____ the treatment chemical. _____ the case of nickel plating the chemical rinse would contain sodium carbonate _____ precipitate nickel carbonate, whilst _____ chromium, a prior stage _____ effect reduction from hexavalent to trivalent form would be required. The integrated system has the advantages that water reuse can be readily practised and that the metals are not precipitated _____ a mixture and _____ can also be recovered. However, it is sometimes difficult _____ adapt the system _____ existing plating lines, _____ it necessitates the placement _____ and extra tank in the line.

III. Fill the blank in each sentence with an appropriate phrase in its proper form

account for	as against	as compared to	as in the case of
be attached to	except for	in contrast to	on the contrary
owing to	take part in	think of…as	

1. Atomic structure _____ the difference in ductility and malleability between metals and nonmetals.

2. In a metal, the electrons in the outer shell of the atom are loosely held and can _____ the electron flow that we call electric current.

3. We may _____ a metal _____ made up of atoms fixed in the crystalline structure of the metal.

4. _____ the electrons in metals, the clectrons in nonmetals, in the solid state, are firmly fixed.

5. A particular atom _____ often _____ its neighbors by sharing valence electrons in what is called a covalent bond.

6. A nonmental, _____, because of the fixity of its electrons, cannot re-emit the light waves so readily.

7. _____ diamond, the atoms are firmly attached to one another and great force is required to displace them.

8. The luster of metals _____ the lack of luster of nonmetals can also be explained on the basis on loose electrons _____ fixed electrons.

9. Some metals, _____ their structure and the forces between their atoms, are hard and brittle.

10. _____ noble metals like gold and platinum, metals readily combine with other substances, including the oxygen of the air.

IV. Problem

Can you rationalize the shift in peak wavelength with a charge in alkali metal in the absorption spectra of the M^- species?

Reading Material

Structural Analysis (IR)

This chapter describes how the structure of an unknown compound can be deduced from its infrared spectrum with the help of other spectroscopic information and physical data. It is assumed in what follows that the student is able to obtain low resolution (~ 4 cm^{-1}) infrared spectra and, when necessary, to obtain Raman spectra to help in the reasonably pure, since even 5% of an impurity could give rise to spurious peaks in the spectra. Gas chromatography usually gives an indication of the purity of a compound.

A preliminary infrared spectrum of a solid is recorded using a hydrocarbon mull (Nujol) or a KBr pellet, whereas that of a liquid is recorded as a film between two NaCl or KBr plates. When hydrogen bonding is evident from very broad bands, especially between 3500cm^{-1} and 2500 cm^{-1}, spectra also should be obtained from dilute solutions in CCl$_4$ or from some other suitable solvent. For a detailed study, several spectra may be needed from solutions of various concentrations, from mulls or pellets containing various relative amounts of sample, or from liquid films of various thicknesses. The variation of concentrations, and so forth should cover at least an order of magnitude, so that the weak features are brought out as well as the very strong absorptions.[1]

When Raman spectra of pure liquids or solids are recorded, the problems of pathlength or concentration do not arise. However, when Raman spectra of solutions are recorded, the highest concentrations possible should be used because the spectra are inherently weak and one does not have the option of increasing the pathlength.

An examination of the infrared spectrum indicates the various X-H bonds present in the molecule and the presence or absence of triple or double bonds, carbonyl groups, aromatic rings, and other functional groups. This information, together with other data such as elemental analysis, molecular weights, Raman, UV, mass and NMR spectra will suggest various possible structures. The infrared and Raman spectra can then be searched in detail for bands due to the various groups in the postulated structures. Comparison with published infrared spectra of compounds having the suggested or a similar structure should be made. Also, the computer attached to a modern FT-IR spectrometer often has a search routine and a library of infrared spectra, which may be searched for spectra that most closely match the spectrum of the unknown compound.

The infrared spectrum can be arbitrarily divided into the regions. The presence of bands in these regions gives immediate information. The absence of bands in these regions also is important information, since many groups can be excluded from further analysis, provided the factors discussed in Section 8.2 has been considered.[2]

Certain types of compounds give strong, broad absorptions, which are very prominent in the infrared spectrum. The hydrogen-bonded OH stretching bands of alcohols, phenols, and carboxylic acids are easily recognized at the high-frequency end of the spectrum. The stretching of the NH$_3^+$ group in amino acids gives a very broad, asymmetric band, which extends over several hundred wavenumbers. Broad bands associated with bending of NH$_2$ or NH groups of primary or secondary amines are found at the low-frequency end of the spectrum. Amides also give a broad band in this region. Examples of these characteristic absorptions are illustrated. It is well worth looking through one of the published collections of infrared spectra to familiarize oneself with these bands. *The Aldrich Library of FT-IR Spectra* is particularly valuable for this purpose, since the spectra are arranged by class of compound.

In the infrared spectra of certain compounds there are weak but characteristic bands that are known to be due to overtones or combinations.

In the following three sections, suggestions are given for the preliminary analysis of the infrared spectra of hydrocarbons or the hydrocarbon parts of molecules; of compounds containing carbon, hydrogen, and oxygen; and of compounds containing nitrogen.[3] After this preliminary study of the spectrum, the analyst should have some idea of the kind of compound under investigation. The spectrum is then examined in more detail. In later sections, some of the detailed structural information that can be obtained from such an examination is discussed. In many cases, Raman spectra provide important additional information.

The nature of a hydrocarbon or the hydrocarbon part of a molecule can be identified by first looking in the region between 3100 cm^{-1} and 2800 cm^{-1}. If there is no absorption between 3000 cm^{-1} and 3100 cm^{-1}, the compound contains no aromatic or unsaturated aliphatic CH groups. Cyclopropanes, which absorb above 3000 cm^{-1}, are an exception. If the absorption is entirely above 3000 cm^{-1}, the compound is probably aromatic or contains =CH or =CH_2 groups only. Absorption both above and below 3000 cm^{-1} indicates both saturated and unsaturated or cyclic hydrocarbon moieties.

The region between 1000 cm^{-1} and 650 cm^{-1} should be examined to confirm the conclusions. Strong bands in this region suggest alkenes or aromatic structures. A small, sharp band near 725 cm^{-1} is indicative of a linear chain containing four or more CH_2 groups. The presence of CH_2 groups is also indicated by a strong band near 1440 cm^{-1} in the infrared and Raman spectra.

If it is known from an elemental analysis that there is an oxygen atom present in the molecule, one should look in three regions for bands due to the oxygen-containing functional group.[4] A strong, broad band between 3500 cm^{-1} and 3200 cm^{-1} is likely due to the hydrogen-bonded OH stretching mode of an alcohol or a phenol. Be aware that water also absorbs in this region. When hydrogen bonding is absent the OH stretching band is sharp and at higher frequencies (3650~3600 cm^{-1}). Carboxylic acids give very broad OH stretching bands between 3200 cm^{-1} and 2700 cm^{-1}. Several sharp peaks may be seen on this broad band near 3000 cm^{-1} due to CH stretching vibrations.

One should next look for a very strong band between 1850 cm^{-1} and 1650 cm^{-1} due to the C=O stretching of a carbonyl group. The third region is between 1300 cm^{-1} and 1000 cm^{-1}, where bands due to C—OH stretching of alcohols and carboxylic acids and C—O—C stretching modes of ethers and esters are observed.[5] The presence or absence of the bands due to OH, C=O, and C—O stretching gives a good indication of the type of oxygen-containing compound. Infrared spectra of aldehydes and ketones show only the C=O band, whereas spectra of ethers have only the C—O—C band. Esters have bands due to both C=O and C—O—C groups, but none due to the OH group. Alcohols have bands due to both OH and C—O groups, but no C=O stretching band. Spectra of carboxylic acids contain bands in all three regions mentioned above.

In a preliminary examination of the infrared spectrum of a compound known to contain nitrogen, one or two bands in the region 3500~3300 cm^{-1} indicate primary or secondary amines or amides. These bands may be confused with OH stretching bands in the infrared, but are more easily identified in the Raman spectrum, where the OH stretching band is very weak. Amides may be identified by a strong doublet in the infrared spectrum centered near 1640 cm^{-1}. The Raman spectrum of an amide has bands near 1650 cm^{-1} and 1400 cm^{-1}. These bands are associated with the stretching of the C=O group and bending of the NH_2 group of the amide. A sharp band near 2200 cm^{-1} in either infrared or Raman spectra is characteristic of a *nitrile*.

When both nitrogen and oxygen are present, but no NH groups are indicated, two very strong bands near 1560 cm^{-1} and 1370 cm^{-1} provide evidence of the presence of nitro groups.[6] An extremely broad band with some structure centered near 3000 cm^{-1} and extending as low as 2200 cm^{-1} is indicative of an amino acid or an amine hydrohalide, whereas a broad band below 1000 cm^{-1} suggests an amine or an amide.

From *Organic Structural Spectroscopy By Joseph B. Lambert*

New Words and Expressions

impurity [imˈpjuəriti] *n.* 杂质，混杂物，不纯
chromatography [ˌkrəuməˈtɔgrəfi] *n.* 色谱
dilute [daiˈljuːt] *v. a.* 冲淡（的），稀释（的）
magnitude [ˈmæɡnitjuːd] *n.* 大小，数量，巨大，广大
inherently [inˈhiərəntli] *ad.* 天生地，本质上
postulate [ˈpɔstjuleit] *n.* 假定，基本条件，公理 *vt.* 要求，假设
spectrometer [spekˈtrɔmitə] *n.* 分光计
asymmetric [ˌæsiˈmetrik] *a.* 不匀称的，不对称的，不均匀的
hydrohalide [ˌhaidriˈhelaid] *n.* 氢卤化物

Notes

1. ring out：显示出，the order of magnitude：数量级，so that 引导让步状语从句。参考译文：浓度等变化应该涉及至少一个数量级，这样弱吸收以及强吸收就可以被显示出来。

2. 参考译文：在这些区域不存在谱带是重要的信息，因为如果考虑章节 8.2 所讨论的因素，许多官能团是可以通过进一步的分析而被排除掉的。

3. 参考译文：在下面的三部分中给出了碳氢化合物或分子中的碳氢部分，含碳、氢、氧化合物以及含氮化合物的红外谱图初步分析。

4. due to：由于，因为，归因于。参考译文：如果通过元素分析知道分子中含氧原子，那么由于有含氧官能团就应该观察三个区域的谱带。

5. 句子结构：从句中 bands 为主语，are observed 为谓语。参考译文：第三个区域界于 1300～1000cm^{-1} 之间，在这里可观察到由乙醇和羧酸的 C—OH 伸缩振动，以及由醚和酯的 C—O—C 伸缩振动所产生的谱带。

6. 参考译文：当氮和氧存在，但无 NH 基团存在时，在 1560cm^{-1} 和 1370cm^{-1} 附近的两个很强的谱带，为硝基的存在提供了证据。

Unit 14 The Chemical Shift

NMR is a valuable structural tool because the observed resonance frequency ν_0 depends on the molecular environment as well as on γ and B_0.[1] The electron cloud that surrounds the nucleus also has charge, motion, and hence a magnetic moment. The magnetic field that electrons generate alters the B_0 field in the microenvironment around the nucleus.

The actual field experienced by a given nucleus thus depends on the nature of the surrounding electrons. This electronic modulation of the B_0 field is termed *shielding*, which is represented by the Greek letter σ. The actual field experienced by the nucleus becomes B_{local} and may be expressed as $B_0(1-\sigma)$, in which electronic shielding σ normally is positive. Variation of the resonance frequency with shielding has been termed the *chemical shift*.

The expression for the resonance frequency in terms of shielding is given by Eq. 14.2, by substituting B_{local} into Eq. 14.1.

$$\nu_0 = B_{local}/2\pi \tag{14.1}$$
$$\nu_0 = \gamma B_0(1-\sigma)/2\pi \tag{14.2}$$

Decreased shielding results in a higher resonance frequency ν_0 at constant B_0, since σ enters the equation with a negative sign. For example, the presence of an electron-withdrawing group in a molecule reduces the electron density around a proton, so that there is less shielding and a higher resonance frequency than in the case of a molecule that lacks the electron-withdrawing group. Thus protons in fluoromethane (CH_3F) resonate at a higher frequency than those in methane (CH_4) because the fluorine atom withdraws electrons from around the hydrogen nuclei.

Fig. 14.1 shows the NMR spectra separately of the protons and the carbons of methyl acetate ($CH_3CO_2CH_3$). Although 98.9% of naturally occurring carbon is the nonmagnetic ^{12}C, the carbon NMR experiment is carried out in the 1.1% of ^{13}C, which has an I of ½. Because of differential electronic shielding, the ^1H spectrum contains separate resonances for the two types of protons (O—CH_3 and C—CH_3), and the ^{13}C spectrum contains separate resonances for the three types of carbon (O—CH_3, C—CH_3, and carbonyl) (Fig. 14.2)

The proton resonances may be assigned on the basis of the electron-withdrawing abilities (electronegativity) of the neighboring atoms. The ester oxygen is more electron withdrawing than the carbonyl group, so the O—CH_3 resonance occurs at higher frequency than (and to the left of) the C—CH_3 resonance. By convention, frequency in the spectrum increases from right to left for consistency with other forms of spectroscopy. Therefore shielding increases from left to right.

The system of units depicted in Fig. 14.1 and used throughout this book has been developed to overcome the fact that chemical information is found in small differences between large numbers.[2] An intuitive system might be absolute frequency, for example in Hz. At the common field of 7.05T, for example, all protons resonate in the vicinity of 300 MHz. A scale involving numbers like 300.000764, however, is cumbersome and the frequencies would vary from one B_0 field to another.[3] For each element or isotope, a reference material has been chosen and assigned a relative frequency of zero. For both protons and carbons, the substance is tetramethylsilane [$(CH_3)_4Si$, usually called TMS], which is soluble in most organic solvents, unreactive, and volatile. In addition, the low electronegativity of silicon means that the protons and carbons are surrounded by a relatively high density of electrons. Hence they are highly shielded and resonate at low frequency. Shielding by silicon in fact is so strong that the proton and carbon resonances of TMS are placed at the right extreme of

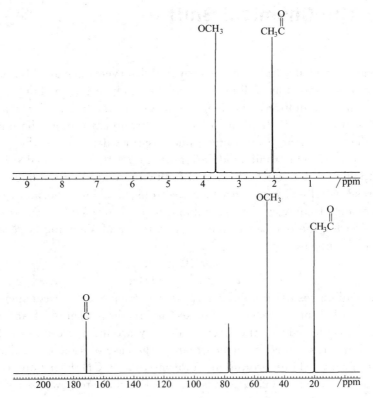

Fig. 14.1 the 300 MHz ^{1}H spectrum (upper) and the 75.45 MHz ^{13}C spectrum (lower) of methyl acetate in CDCl$_3$ (the triplet at δ77 is from solvent), the ^{13}C spectrum has been decoupled from the protons

Fig. 14.2 resonance types of ^{1}H and the ^{13}C for methyl acetate

the spectrum, thus providing a convenient spectral zero. In Fig. 14.1 the position marked "0 ppm" (1ppm=10^{-6}) is the hypothetical position of TMS.

To have a common unit that applies to any B_0 field, the chemical shift δ of a given nucleus i is calculated from that of the reference TMS by the equation $\delta = (\nu_i - \nu_{TMS})/\nu_{TMS}$. Because the difference between chemical shifts $\nu_i - \nu_{TMS}$ is generally on the order of Hz and the absolute frequency for TMS (ν_{TMS}) is in MHz, values of δ are in parts per million (ppm). As seen in the ^{1}H spectrum of methyl acetate (see Fig. 14.1), the δ value for the C—CH$_3$ protons is 2.17 ppm and that for the O—CH$_3$ protons is 3.67 ppm. These values remain the same in spectra taken at a field of either 1.41T (60 MHz) or 18.8T (800MHz), which represent the extremes of spectrometers currently in use. Chemical shifts in Hz, however, vary from field to field. Thus a resonance that is 90 Hz from TMS at 60 MHz is 450 Hz from TMS at 300 MHz but always has a δ value of 1.50 ppm ($\delta = 90/60 = 450/300 = 1.50$).[4] Note that a resonance to the right of TMS has a negative value of δ. Since TMS is insoluble in water, other internal standards are used for this solvent, such as 3-(trimethylsilyl)-1-propanesulfonic acid [(CH$_3$)$_3$Si(CH$_2$)$_3$SO$_3$Na] or 3-(trimethylsilyl) propionic acid

$[(CH_3)_3SiCH_2CH_2CO_2Na]$ (sodium salts).

In the first generation of spectrometers, the range of chemical shifts, such as those in the scale at the bottom of Fig. 14.1, was generated by varying the B_0 field while holding the B_1 field and hence the resonance frequency constant. Consideration of Eq. 14.2 [$\nu_0 = \gamma B_0 (1-\sigma) 2\pi$] indicates that an increase in shielding (σ) requires B_0 to be raised to keep ν_0 constant. Since more shielded nuclei resonate at the right side of the spectrum, the B_0 field in this experiment increases from left to right. Consequently, the right end came to be known as the high field or upfield end, and the left end as the low field or downfield end.[5] This method was termed *continuous wave, field sweep*.

Modern spectrometers allow the frequency to be varied while the B_0 field is kept constant. An increase in shielding (σ) lowers the right side of eq. 14.2, so that ν_0 must decrease to maintain a constant B_0. Thus the right end of the spectrum, as noted before, corresponds to lower frequencies for more shielded nuclei. The general result is that frequency increases from right to left and field increases from left to right. The right end of the spectrum is still often referred to as the high field or upfield end in deference to the old field sweep experiment, although it is more appropriate to call it the low frequency or more shielded end.

From *Organic Structural Spectroscopy By Joseph B. Lambert*

New Words and Expressions

microenvironment ['maikrəuin'vaiərənmənt] n. 小环境
modulation [ˌmɔdju'leiʃən] n. 调整
shield ['ʃi:ld] n. 护罩，盾，盾状物 v. 保护，防护
electron-withdrawing a. 吸电子的
withdraw [wið'drɔ:] vt. 收回，撤回 vi. 撤退
fluoromethane ['flu:ərəu'meθein] n. 氟代甲烷
decouple [di'kʌpl] n. 分离，断开，吸收（核子爆炸）的震力
nonmagnetic [ˌmɔdju'leiʃən] a. 非磁性的 n. 非磁性物
consistency [kən'sistənsi] n. 坚固，浓度，密度，一贯
depict [di'pikt] v. 描出，描写，描述
intuitive [in'tju(:)itiv] a. 直观的，直觉的
vicinity [vi'siniti] n. 附近，接近，邻近，附近地区
cumbersome ['kʌmbəsəm] a. 讨厌的，笨重的
volatile ['vɔlətail] a. 挥发性的，反复无常的
silicon ['silikən] n. 硅
resonate ['rezəˌneit] vt. vi. （使）共鸣，（使）共振
insoluble [in'sɔljubl] a. 不能溶解的
upfield [ʌpfi:ld] n. 高磁场
downfield ['daun'fi:ld] n. 低磁场
sweep [swi:p] n. 扫除，掠过 v. 打扫，吹走

Notes

1. resonance frequency 意为"谐振频率"或"共振频率"，也可表示为 resonant frequency。depend on 本意是"依靠"，在这里可理解为"与……有关"。参考译文：NMR 是一个极有价值

的结构测定工具，因为观察到的共振频率 ν_0 与分子环境有关，ν 和 B_0 有关。

2. 这个句子的主体结构是 The system has been developed to overcome the fact，to 后带动词不定式表示目的。that 是关系代词，它所引导的从句用来解释 the fact。参考译文：图 14.1 所描述的和贯穿本书所使用的系统单位已经解决了这样一个问题：大数值中有关化学信息的细微差异。

3. however 意为"然而，但是"，作副词。参考译文：然而，一个具有像 300.00076 这样的数字标度是很不方便的，并且频率会在 B_0 场和其他场之间发生变化。

4. 在此句中，that 引导的是定语从句，说明主语 a resonance。参考译文：在 60 MHz 磁场中响应频率为 90 Hz TMS，在 300 MHz 磁场中响应频率为 450 Hz。但是其 δ 值却均为 1.5 ppm($\delta = 90/60 = 450/300 = 1.50$)。

5. Consequently 意为"因而，所以"。参考译文：因此，可知右端是高场或强场，左端是低场或弱场。

Exercises

I. Comprehension

1. Which of the following is the best title for the passage? _____
   A. NMR-shift
   B. What's the shielding
   C. How to use TMS
   D. A magnetic field

2. Which of the following is not true? _____
   A. The resonance frequency ν_0 relies on the molecular circumstances γ and B_0.
   B. The electronic shielding always is positive.
   C. The resonance frequency ν_0 will increase at constant B_0 when decrease shielding.
   D. —F is an electron-withdrawing group.

3. According to the passage, TMS _____.
   A. is tetramethylsilane
   B. can be dissolved in most organic solvents
   C. can provide the hypothetical position called "0 ppm"
   D. A, B and C

4. It can be inferred from the passage that _____.
   A. an increase in σ requires B_0 to e raised to keep ν_0 constant
   B. an decrease in ν_0 requires s to become less to hold B_0 constant
   C. in order to keep B_0 constant, when ν_0 is decreased, σ must be increased
   D. the frequency increases from right to left and field increases from left to right

5. "In terms of" in line 10 is closest in meaning to _____.
   A. according to
   B. in time of
   C. because of
   D. in excess of

II. Fill in the blanks

Exciting new discoveries sometimes are not verified _____ further study. In 1988 a pair of respected chemists reported that they had observed "cold fusion," the merging of nuclei of one kind _____ hydrogen to form helium nuclei _____ room temperature. Because this was an immense departure _____ the predictions of theory and a potential source of unlimited, inexpensive energy, the entire world took immediate notice. Although cold fusion experiments are not difficult _____ perform, their results are quite difficult _____ interpret. Many laboratories tried to duplicate the first reports, _____ ambiguous and sometimes conflicting results. Several years _____ detailed studies failed to provide definite confirmation of the original reports. Research _____ cold fusion continues, but most scientists now think that the original interpretation ignored unsuspected errors _____ the way the data were collected. Cold fusion _____ a scale that would have practical applications has been verified.

III. Make a sentence out of each item by rearranging the words in brackets

1. There is a plausible chemical explanation (for the formation / in the Earth's early atmosphere / of biochemical substances).

2. To understand why an ecosystem (a biologist / responds to changes the way / must be aware of / both thermodynamic limits and kinetic constraints / it does,).

3. Thermodynamics describes (and / what is possible / what is impossible / where changes occur / in any system).

4. Any disruption of the dynamic balance in an ecosystem (consequences / far-reaching / may have / biological).

5. Chemistry (of matter of science that studies / is the branch / the properties and interactions).

IV. Fill in the blanks with the phrase given in the following

a great deal of   according to   at the beginning of   be familiar with
by means of   depend on   for example   give off
in addition to   on the basis of   set free

1. _____ the atomic theory, all matter is composed of tiny particles called atoms.

2. The atomic theory was developed _____ the nineteenth century to explain the observations of early chemists.

3. The sample is placed in the most homogeneous region of the magnetic field _____ an adjustable probe.

4. It is important to _____ the natural sensitivity of a nucleus before designing a NMR experiment.

5. _____ these factors, the table also contains the NMR resonance frequency at 7.05T.

6. The actual field experienced by a given nucleus thus _____ the nature of the surrounding electrons.

7. The proton resonances may be assigned _____ the electron-withdrawing abilities of the neighboring atoms.

8. The reaction is exothermic; that is, it _____ energy.

9. Once the burning of magnesium is started in the oxygen of the air, _____ energy is _____.

10. The human body, _____, is about three per cent nitrogen.

V. Problem

A 300-MHz spectrometer records a proton that absorbs at a frequency 2130 Hz downfield from TMS.

(a) Determine its chemical shift.

(b) Predict this proton's chemical shift at 60 MHz. In a 60 MHz spectrometer, how far downfield (in hertz) from TMS would this proton absorb?

VI. Translation

Sometimes experiments give surprising results. An event may occur that a current theory claims is impossible. It can be exciting when experimental observations contradict theoretical predictions, but chemists proceed cautiously when this happens. They repeat the experiments to be sure that the original observations are reproducible. If the disagreement between prediction and experiment is verified, the theories must be modified. When theory and experiment disagree, the theory must be wrong. To give you some sense of the excitement that accompanies the ever-expanding field of chemistry, here are three recent developments that have affected how chemists view their subject.

Reading Material

Experimental Methods (NMR)

Although there is a wide variety of NMR instrumentation available, certain components are common to all, including a magnet to supply the B_0 field, devices to generate the B_1 pulse and to receive the NMR signal, a probe for positioning the sample in the magnet, hardware for stabilizing the B_0 field and optimizing the signal, and computers for controlling much of the operation and processing the signal.[1]

Early NMR machines relied on electromagnets. Although a generation of chemists used them, the magnets had low sensitivity and poor stability. Less popular permanent magnets were simpler to maintain but still had low sensitivity. Most research grade instruments today use a superconducting magnet and operate at 3.5~18.8T (150~800 MHz for protons). These magnets provide high sensitivity and stability. Possibly most important, the very high fields produced by superconducting magnets result in better separation of resonances, because chemical shifts and hence chemical shift differences increase with field strength.[2] The superconducting magnet resembles a solid cylinder with a central axial hole. The direction of the B_0 field (z) is aligned with the axis of the cylinder.

Separate from the magnet is a console that contains, among other components, the transmitter and receiver of the NMR signal. The B_1 field of the transmitter in the pulse experiment is 1~40 mT. In spectrometers designed to record the resonances of several nuclides (multinuclear spectrometers), the B_1 field must be tunable over a range of frequencies. The console in addition contains a recorder to display the signal.

The sample is placed in the most homogeneous region of the magnetic field by means of an adjustable probe. The probe contains a holder for the sample, mechanical means for adjusting its position in the field, electronic leads for supplying the B_1 and B_2 (double resonance) fields and for receiving the signal, and devices for improving magnetic homogeneity.

Liquid samples are examined in a cylindrical tube, usually 5mm in outer diameter for protons. The axis of the tube is placed parallel to the (z) axis of the superconducting cylinder. Usually a volume of 300~400μL is used, but, if sample is in short supply, microtubes are available that require a much smaller volume. Wider diameter tubes are available for samples in low concentration or for low sensitivity nuclei. In practice, ^{1}H spectra may be obtained on less than 1 μg of material, although the result depends on the molecular weight.

The sample must have good solubility in a solvent, which must have no resonances in the regions of interest. For protons, $CDCl_3$, D_2O, and acetone-d_6 are traditional NMR solvents. If the spectrum is to be recorded above or below room temperature, the solvent chosen must not boil or freeze during the experiment.

The NMR experiment is plagued by the dual problems of sensitivity and resolution. Peak separations of <0.5 Hz may need to be resolved, so the B_0 field must be uniform to a very high degree (for a separation of 0.3 Hz at 300 MHz, field homogeneity must be better than 1 part in 10^9). Corrections to field inhomogeneity may be made for small gradients in B_0 by the use of *shim coils*.[3] For example, the field along the z direction might be slightly higher at one point than at another. Such a gradient may be compensated for by applying a small current through a shim coil built into the probe. Shim coils are available for correcting gradients in all three cartesian coordinates as well as higher order gradients (x^2, xy, and so on).

The sample is spun along the axis of its cylinder at a rate of 20~50 Hz by an air flow to improve homogeneity within the tube. Spinning improves resolution because a nucleus at a particular location in the tube experiences a field that is averaged over a circular path. In the superconducting magnet, the axis of the tube is in the z direction (in electromagnets it is spun along the y direction). Spinning does not average gradients along the axis of the cylinder, so shimming is required primarily for z gradients for a superconducting magnet or y gradients for an elctromagnet. [4]

All magnet are subject to field drift, which can be minimized by electronically locking the field to the resonance of a substance contained in the sample. Because deuterated solvents are used quite commonly for this purpose, an *internal lock* normally is at the deuterium frequency for both ^1H and ^{13}C spectra. In some instruments, the field is locked to a sample contained in a separate tube located permanently elsewhere in the probe. This *external lock* is usually found only in spectrometers designed for a highly specific use, such as taking only ^1H spectra.

Since there in an excess of only some 50 spin 1/2 nuclei per million, the NMR experiment is inherently insensitive. [5] The sensitivity of a given experiment depends on the natural abundance and the natural sensitivity of the observed nucleus (related to the magnetic moment and gyromagnetic ratio). The experimentalist has no control over these factors. The sample size may be increased by using a larger diameter container, and the field strength may be increased (sensitivity increases with the 3/2 power of B_0). Decoupling also can bring about sensitivity enhancement through the nuclear Overhauser effect. Complex manipulation of pulses can raise sensitivity.

Finally, routine improvement of signal to noise is achieved through multiple scanning or signal averaging. In this procedure, the digitized NMR spectrum is stored in computer memory. The spectrum is recorded multiple times and is stored in the same locations. Any signal present is reinforced, but noise tends to be canceled out. If n such scans are carried out and added digitally, the theory of random processes states that the signal amplitude is proportional to n and the noise is proportional to $\sqrt{n}$. The signal to noise ratio (S/N) therefore increases by $n/\sqrt{n}$ or $\sqrt{n}$. [6] Thus 100 scans added together theoretically enhance S/N by a factor of about 10. Multiple scanning is routine for most nuclei and necessary for many, such as ^{13}C and ^{15}N.

In the pulsed experiment, resolution is controlled directly by the amount of time taken to acquire the signal. To distinguish two signals separated by $\Delta\nu$ (in Hz), acquisition of data must continue for at least $1/\nu$ seconds. For example, a desired resolution of 0.5 Hz in a ^{13}C spectrum requires an *acquisition time* (t_a) of $1/0.5$ or 2.0s. Sample for a longer time would improve resolution; for example, acquisition for 4.0s could yield a resolution of 0.25 Hz. Thus longer acquisition times are necessary to produce narrow lines. The tail of the FID contains mostly noise mixed with signals from narrow lines. If sensitivity is the primary concern, either shorter acquisition times should be used or the later portions of the FID may be reduced artificially by a weighting function. [7] In this way noise is reduced, but at the possible expense of lower resolution. Decreased weighting of the data from longer times (from the bottom to the top of the figure) results in lower resolution and broader peaks.

After acquisition is complete, a *delay time* is necessary to allow the nuclei to relax before they can be examined again for the purpose of signal averaging. For optimal results, the delay time is on the order of 3~5 times the spin-lattice relaxation time. For a typical ^{13}C relaxation time of 10s, a total cycle thus might take up to 50s. Such cycle times are excessive and can be reduced by using a pulse angle θ that is less than 90°. When fewer spins are flipped, T_1 relaxation can occur more rapidly and the delay time can be shortened. In practice, proper balance between θ and t_a (to optimize resolution) can result in essentially no delay time, and the next pulse cycle can be initiated immediately after acquisition.

The detected range of frequencies (the *spectral width*) is determined by how often the detector samples the value of the FID: the *sampling rate*. The FID is made up of a collection of sinusoidal signals. A single, specific signal must be sampled at least twice within one sinusoidal cycle to determine its frequency. For a collection of signals up to a frequency of N, the FID thus must be sampled at a rate of 2N Hz. For example, for a ^{13}C spectral width of 15000 (200 ppm at 75 MHz), the signal must be sampled 30000 times per second. Fig. 14.3 illustrates this situation. The top signal (a) be sampled exactly twice per cycle (each dot is a sampling). The higher frequency signal in (b) is sampled at the same rate, but not often enough to determine its frequency. In fact, the lower frequency signal in (c) gives exactly the same collection of points as in (b). A real signal from the points in (b) is indistinguishable from a *foldover signal* with the frequency in (c). For example, if the ^{13}C spectrum is sampled only 15000 times per second, for a spectral width of 7500 Hz (100 ppm at 75 MHz), a signal with a frequency of 150 ppm (11250 Hz) appears as a foldover peak in the 0~100 ppm region.

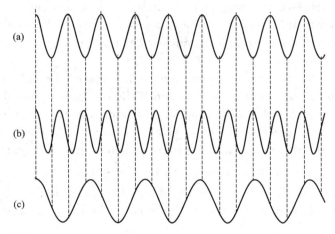

Fig. 14.3 the FID is made up of a collection of sinusoidal signals

If a signal is sampled 20000 times per second, the detector spends 50 μs on each point. The reciprocal of the sampling rate is called the dwell time, which signifies the amount of time between sampling.[8] Reducing the dwell time means that more data points are collected in the same period of time, so that a larger computer memory is required. If the acquisition time is 4.0s (for a resolution of 0.25 Hz) and the sampling rate is 20000 times per second (for a spectral width of 10000 Hz), the computer must store 80000 data points. Making do with fewer points because of computer limitations would require either lowering the resolution of decreasing the spectral width.

From *Exploring Chemical Analysis by Daniel C. Harris*

New Words and Expressions

probe [prəub]   n. 探针，探测品 v. 探查，穿刺
optimizing ['ɔptimaiziŋ]   n. 充分利用，有效利用

axial [ˈæksiəl]   *a.* 轴的，轴向的
align [əˈlain]   *v.* 使成一线，结盟，调节
console [kənˈsəul]   *n.* 悬臂，肘托，控制台 *v.* 安慰，抚慰
tunable [ˈtju:nəbl]   *a.* 悦耳的
homogeneity [ˌhɔməudʒeˈni:iti]   *n.* 同种，同质，同次性
cylindrical [siˈlindrikl]   *a.* 圆柱的
microtube [maikrəutju:b]   *n.* 微管
plague [pleig]   *n.* 瘟疫，灾祸 *vt.* 使染瘟疫，烦扰
dual [ˈdju:əl]   *a.* 双的，二重的，二元的
inhomogeneity [ˈinˌhəumədʒiˈni:iti]   *n.* 不同类，不同族，不同质
gyromagnetic ratio   回转磁比率
decoupling [diˈkʌpliŋ]   *n.* 去耦合，去耦合装置，退耦
Overhauser [ˈəuvəhed]   奥佛豪塞（人名）
random [ˈrændəm]   *a.* 随机的，随意的 *n.* 随机，随意
amplitude [ˈæmplitju:d]   *n.* 广大，充足，振幅
acquisition [ˌækwiˈziʃən]   *n.* 获得，获得物
flip [flip]   *v.* 轻击，掷，弹，抽打，迅速翻动
spectral [ˈspektrəl]   *a.* 幽灵的，鬼魂的
sinusoidal [sainəsɔeidəl]   *a.* 正弦波的 *n.* 正弦
foldover [fɔ:dˈəuvə]   *n.* 重叠，叠影，摺过

Notes

1. 句子的基本结构是："Although…available"是状语从句，说明情况或条件，谓语是are，"including…processing the signals"是较复杂的分词短语，用来说明certain components。句子可变换为certain components including…processing the signals are common to all。including＋名词组成的短语中，名词有magnet，devices（由不定式to＋动词修饰说明用途），probe，hardware，computers（由for＋分词短语修饰说明用途）。参考译文：尽管可供使用的NMR各种各样，但它们某些特定部件却是共同的，包括提供B_0场的磁体，产生B_1脉冲和接收NMR信号的装置，给磁场中样品定位的探针，稳定B_0场和使信号最优化的硬件，以及控制大部分操作和处理信号的计算机。

2. 参考译文：可能最重要的是超导磁体产生的很高的场会使共振更好地分离，因为化学位移和化学位移差会随场的加强而增加。

3. 参考译文：使用垫片线圈可以对不均匀B_0场进行小梯度的修正。

4. 参考译文：旋转不能使圆柱体轴线上的梯度均一，所以对于超导磁体的z梯度和电磁体的y梯度，填以薄垫片是很重要的。

5. Some 在此处是副词，意为"大约"，nuclei 是 nucleus 的复数形式，意思是"原子核"。参考译文：由于每一百万中只有约50个1/2自旋原子核过量，核磁共振实验具有固有的不敏感性。

6. 在此处to是介词，表示比较。e. g.：The some was 6 to 2. 参考译文：因此，信噪比（S/N）增加了$n/\sqrt{n}$或$\sqrt{n}$。

7. 参考译文：如果敏感性是首要的考虑因素，那就要么使用较短的检测时间，要么通过（加）权函数人为减少FID的后一部分的份额。

8. 参考译文：取样检测速率的倒数称作驻留时间，它表示取样检测的间隔时间。

Unit 15 Mass Spectrometry

Although nominally a spectroscopic method, mass spectrometry is unlike other forms of spectroscopy because it does not involve electromagnetic radiation. Instead it involves chemical manipulations (such as ionization and fragmentation), and the relative intensity of each peak is a measure of the quantity of the corresponding ionic species.[1] Mass spectrometry is an analytical tool used for measuring the molecular mass and elucidating molecular structure of a sample. For large samples such as biomolecules, molecular masses can be measured to within an accuracy of 0.01% of the total molecular mass of the sample i. e. within a 4 Daltons (Da) or atomic mass units (amu) error for a sample of 40000 Da. This is sufficient to allow minor mass changes to be detected, e. g. the substitution of one amino acid for another, or a post-translational modification. For small organic molecules the molecular mass can be measured to within an accuracy of 5 ppm or less, which is often sufficient to confirm the molecular formula of a compound, and is also a standard requirement for publication in a chemical journal. Structural information can be generated using certain types of mass spectrometers, usually those with multiple analysers which are known as tandem mass spectrometers. This is achieved by fragmenting the sample inside the instrument and analyzing the products generated. This procedure is useful for the structural elucidation of organic compounds and for peptide or oligonucleotide sequencing.

Mass spectrometers are used in industry and academia for both routine and research purposes. The following list is just a brief summary of the major mass spectrometric applications:

Biotechnology: *the analysis of proteins, peptides, oligonucleotides*

Pharmaceutical: *drug discovery, combinatorial chemistry, pharmacokinetics, drug metabolism*

Clinical: *neonatal screening, haemoglobin analysis, drug testing*

Environmental: *PAHs, PCBs, water quality, food contamination*

Geological: *oil composition*

All mass spectrometers require a sample input system, an ionization source, a mass analyzer, and a detector. The sample has to be introduced into the ionization source of the instrument. Once inside the ionization source, the sample molecules are ionized, because ions are easier to manipulate than neutral molecules. These ions are extracted into the analyser region of the mass spectrometer where they are separated according to their mass (m) -to-charge (z) ratios (m/z). The separated ions are detected and this signal sent to a data system where the m/z ratios are stored together with their relative abundance for presentation in the format of a m/z spectrum. All of the components with the exception of some sample input systems or ion source volumes are under vacuum ($10^{-6} \sim 10^{-8}$ torr for that portion where ions are separated by mass, i. e., the analyzer, or $10^{-4} \sim 10^{-5}$ torr in some ion sources, where the ions are initially formed), so vacuum pumps of various types are required.[2] Modern mass spectrometers have all of the components under computer control, with a computer-based data acquisition and processing system.

Sample introduction

The method of sample introduction to the ionization source often depends on the ionization method being used, as well as the type and complexity of the sample. The sample can be inserted directly into the ionization source, or can undergo some type of chromatography *en route* to the ionization source. This latter method of sample introduction usually involves the mass spectrometer being coupled directly to a high pressure liquid chromatography (HPLC), gas chromatography (GC) or capillary electrophoresis (CE) separation column, and hence the sample is separated into a series of components which then enter the mass spectrometer sequentially for individual analysis.

Methods of sample ionization

Many ionization methods are available and each has its own advantages and disadvantages. The ionization method to be used should depend on the type of sample under investigation and the mass spectrometer available.

Ionization methods include the following:
Atmospheric Pressure Chemical Ionization (APCI)
Chemical Ionization (CI)
Electron Impact (EI)
Electrospray Ionisation (ESI)
Fast Atom Bombardment (FAB)
Field Desorption / Field Ionisation (FD/FI)
Matrix Assisted Laser Desorption Ionisation (MALDI)
Thermospray Ionisation (TSP)

A chemical ionization (CI) source is considered a soft ionization source; it results in less fragmentation of analyte molecules and a simpler mass spectrum than that resulting from EI. Most importantly, the molecular ion is much more abundant using CI, allowing the determination of the molecular weight. If the CI process is "soft" enough the spectrum may consist almost entirely of only the molecular ion. Such a lack of fragmentation provides less structural information than an EI spectrum. If a fragmented EI spectrum is absent a molecular ion, then combining data from a CI spectrum containing a strong molecular ion will greatly assist interpretation of an unknown compound's spectra.[3] The two modes complement one another for identification and quantitation of unknowns.

During standard electrospray ionization (ESI), the sample is dissolved in a polar, volatile solvent and pumped through a narrow, stainless steel capillary (75~150 micrometers i.d.) at a flow rate of between 1 μL/min and 1 mL/min. A high voltage of 3kV or 4 kV is applied to the tip of the capillary, which is situated within the ionization source of the mass spectrometer, and as a consequence of this strong electric field, the sample emerging from the tip is dispersed into an aerosol of highly charged droplets, a process that is aided by a coaxially introduced nebulizing gas flowing around the outside of the capillary.[4] This gas, usually nitrogen, helps to direct the spray emerging from the capillary tip towards the mass spectrometer. The charged droplets diminish in size by solvent evaporation, assisted by a warm flow of nitrogen known as the drying gas which passes across the front of the ionization source. Eventually charged sample ions, free from solvent, are released from the droplets, some of which pass through a sampling cone or orifice into an intermediate vacuum region, and from there through a small aperture into the analyser of the mass spectrometer, which is held under high vacuum. The lens voltages are optimised individually for each sample.

The ionization methods used for the majority of biochemical analyses are Electrospray Ionization (ESI) and Matrix Assisted Laser Desorption Ionization (MALDI), and these are described in more detail in Sections 5 and 6 respectively.

Analysis and Separation of Sample Ions

The main function of the mass analyser is to separate, or resolve, the ions formed in the ionization source of the mass spectrometer according to their mass-to-charge (m/z) ratios. There are a number of mass analysers currently available, the better known of which include quadrupoles, time-of-flight (TOF) analysers, magnetic sectors, and both Fourier transform and quadrupole ion traps.

These mass analysers have different features, including the m/z range that can be covered, the mass accuracy, and the achievable resolution. The compatibility of different analysers with different ionization methods varies. For example, all of the analysers listed above can be used in conjunction with electrospray ionization, whereas MALDI is not usually coupled to a quadrupole analyser.

Tandem (MS-MS) mass spectrometers are instruments that have more than one analyser and so can be used for structural and sequencing studies. Two, three and four analysers have all been incorporated into commercially available tandem instruments, and the analysers do not necessarily have to be of the same type, in which case the instrument is a hybrid one[5]. More popular tandem mass spectrometers include those of the quadrupole-quadrupole, magnetic sector-quadrupole, and more recently, the quadrupole-time-of-flight geometries.

Detection and recording of sample ions

The detector monitors the ion current, amplifies it and the signal is then transmitted to the data system where it is recorded in the form of mass spectra. The m/z values of the ions are plotted against their intensities to show the number of components in the sample, the molecular mass of each component, and the relative abundance of the various components in the sample. The type of detector is supplied to suit the type of analyser; the more common ones are the photomultiplier, the electron multiplier, Faraday cup and the micro-channel plate detectors.

The electron multiplier is very similar in concept to the photomultiplier tube for optical detection. It is very sensitive and has fast response. The EM is based on the dynode, which has a surface that emits electrons when struck by fast-moving electrons, positive ions, negative ions, or neutrals. A discrete-dynode EM uses a series of $12 \sim 24$ dynodes, each biased more positively than the preceding dynode. A collision releases several electrons from the dynode surface. These electrons are then accelerated to a second such surface, which, in turn, generates several electrons for each electron that bombards it. This process is continued until a cascade of electrons (an amplified current) arrives at the collector. Typically, one ion can produce 10^5 electrons or more; this ratio of electrons measured per ion is referred to as the gain. The gain of the detector can be adjusted, with operating gains of $10^4 \sim 10^8$ used, depending on the application. A disadvantage to dynode-based detectors is that the number of secondary electrons released depends on the type of incident primary particle, its angle and energy. Therefore, they can exhibit mass discrimination due to differences in ion velocity. Heavy ions from quadrupole mass analyzers and from QIT mass analyzers impact the dynode surface at lower velocities than light ions. EM detectors for these instruments must be designed to overcome the difference in velocities, often by accelerating the ions prior to them striking the first electron-emitting dynode.

The least-expensive ion detector is the Faraday cup, a metal or carbon cup that serves to capture ions and store the charge. The resulting current of a few microamperes is measured and amplified. The cup shape decreases the loss of electrons from the metal due to ion impact. The Faraday cup is an absolute detector and can be used to calibrate other detectors. Unlike dynode-based detectors, the Faraday cup does not exhibit mass discrimination. The detector does have a long response time, which limits its utility. The Faraday cup detector is used for making very accurate measurements in isotope-ratio MS, where the ion currents do not change rapidly. Faraday cup detector has no gain associated with it, unlike dynode-based detectors. This limits the sensitivity of the measurement.

From *Undergraduate Instrumental Analysis By James W. Robinson*

New Words and Expressions

nominally ['nɒminəli] adv. 有名无实地，名义上地
Dalton (Da) ['dɔ:ltən] n. 道尔顿（质量单位，等于一氧原子质量的 1/16，约为 1.65×10^{-24} g）
atomic mass unit (amu) n. 原子质量单位，1 u = 1 Da
post-translational modification n. 遗传转译模式
tandem ['tændəm] mass spectrometers n. 串联质谱计
peptide ['peptaid] n. 缩氨酸
oligonucleotide [ˌɔligəʊ'nju:kliəʊtaid] n. 低（聚）核苷酸，寡核苷酸
pharmacokinetics [ˌfɑ:məkəʊkai'netiks] n. 药物（代谢）动力学
neonatal [ˌni:əʊ'neitəl] a. 新生的，初生的；新生儿的
neonatal screening n. 新生儿筛选
haemoglobin [ˌhi:məʊ'gləʊbin] n. 血色素，血红蛋白
haemoglobin analysis n. 血红蛋白分析
PAHs = polycyclic aromatic hydrocarbons 多环芳烃，稠环芳烃
PCBs = polychlorinated biphenyls 多氯化联（二）苯
mass-to-charge ratios (m/z) 质荷比
en route [ɒn'ru:t] adv. & a. 在途中或在沿途
capillary [kə'piləri] n. 毛细管；a. 毛状的，毛细作用的
electrophoresis [iˌlektrəfə'ri:sis] n. 电泳，电泳分离法
CE = capillary electrophoresis 毛细管电泳
electrospray n. 电喷雾
bombardment [bɒm'bɑ:dmənt] n. 轰击，炮击
MALDI = Matrix Assisted Laser Desorption Ionization 基体辅助激光解吸离子化
droplets ['drɒplit] n. 小（微，液，熔）滴；水珠
nebulize ['nebjulaiz] vt. 雾化，使（液体）化为细的喷雾；喷为雾状
orifice ['ɔrifis] n. 锐孔；喷嘴（管，口）
aperture ['æpətjuə] n. 孔；缝隙；孔径
quadrupoles ['kwɒdrəˌpəʊl] n. [物] 四极
dynode ['dainəʊd] n. [电子] 倍增器电极
cascade [kæs'keid] n. 小瀑布，喷流；一连串的阶段、过程、运作或单位

Notes

1. 参考译文：相反，质谱涉及许多化学处理，如，离子化、裂分；且每个峰的相对强度是对相应种类离子多少的测量。

2. 括号中内容可译为：质量分析器中真空度达 $10^{-6} \sim 10^{-8}$ Torr，不同质量的离子在这里得以分离，而初始形成离子的某些离子源中的真空度则只需 $10^{-4} \sim 10^{-5}$ Torr。

3. 其中 a molecular ion, a strong molecular ion 后面均省略了"peak"一词。参考译文：如果由电子轰击离子源离子化所得的质谱中缺分子离子峰，那么就要结合由化学离子源离子化所得的、出现强的分子离子峰的质谱数据，这样非常有助于解析未知化合物的质谱。

4. a process that is aided by a co-axially introduced nebulizing gas flowing around the outside of the capillary. 同位语从句，解释前面的整个过程是通过绕毛细管外围、同轴引入的雾化气流的辅助下完成的。参考译文：3kV 或者 4kV 的高压应用于毛细管的顶端，这个毛细管被安装在质谱仪的电离源里，并且是强电场的结果，来自顶端的样品被分散在气溶胶高电荷液滴里，整个过程是通过绕毛细管外围、同轴引入的雾化气流的辅助下完成的。

5. a hybrid one 混合型质谱计，one 指代 instrument。参考译文：二，三和四分析器均已成为商业上可获得的连用工具，并且分析器不需要是同一型号，在这种情况下仪器是混合型质谱计。

Exercises

I. Comprehension

1. What is the main topic of the passage? _____.
   A. Sample introduction
   B. Ionization
   C. Mass analysis
   D. Introduction to mass spectrometers

2. According to the author, mass spectrometry in different from other spectrometry. The reason is that _____.
   A. mass spectrometry is often used to determine the molecular weight of compounds
   B. mass spectrometry is out of relation to electromagnetic radiation
   C. mass spectrometry usually gives different signals for isotopic forms of an ion
   D. mass spectrometry an separate samples of complex mixtures

3. From the third paragraph, we can say _____.
   A. all components of mass spectrometer must be situated in vacuumed system
   B. all components of mass spectrometer with the exception of some sample input systems must be situated in vacuumed system
   C. the analyzer must be under vacuum of $10^{-4} \sim 10^{-5}$ torr petrol pumps
   D. the ionization source must be under vacuum of $10^{-6} \sim 10^{-8}$ torr

4. If you want to complement the identification and quantitation of unknown organic compounds made by CI mass spectrometer, which ionization source will you choose? _____
   A. APCI   B. FAB   C. EI   D. MALDI

5. According to the text, Faraday cup detectors _____.
   A. have mass discrimination
   B. have high sensitivity of the measurement
   C. are absolute detector and can be used to calibrate other detectors
   D. are used for making very accurate measurements in organic compounds MS

II. Fill in the blanks

Exact mass measurements are performed _____ mass spectrometers capable _____ high mass resolution, namely double-focusing sector _____ Fourier transform instruments. High-resolution measurements can be made after ionization _____ any of the common methods. The resolution required to separate ions that differ _____ the units CH_4/O (both nominally 16 Da) (mass difference 32×10^{-3} Da) is approximately _____ 10^5 at 3300 Da. This value illustrates the need _____ supplementary data to assign molecular formulas confidently. Frequently, only the composition _____ the molecular ion and several of the more abundant fragment ions are measured _____ solving structural problems.

III. Write the original words for the abbreviation

IR	CD	ORD	HPLC
NMR	GC	HOMO	TG
MS	LC	LUMO	SFC
UV-Vis	GC-MS	TMS	DSC

IV. Make a sentence out of each item by rearranging the words in brackets

1. Structure assignments (can be made / by de novo interpretation or / by comparison of the mass spectrum / with a library of spectra).

2. Determination of molecular structure (is based on interpretation / by mass spectrometry / of fragmentation patterns).

3. The effectiveness of molecular weight determination (the choice of / ionizing agent / often depends on).

4. The variety of experiments (is illustrated by / used to determine molecular weight /

the case of / the amino acid arginine).

5. Among the many possibilities, (a selection / the nature of the sample / can be made / based on /).

V. Translation

1. 质谱可用来获取所有有机物的信息，包括分子量、分子式、分子结构、同位素丰度及混合物中成分的浓度。

2. 我们已经讨论了与钢有关的铁的化学，但铁的许多化合物具有有用的特性。

3. 混合样品一般通过气相色谱或液相色谱将其引入质谱仪中。

4. 这一发现首次证明：某些原子具有相同的化学性质但原子量不同。

5. 每当我们写一个有机物结构式时，都必须进行核对，以保证每一个碳原子都有四个共价键。

VI. Translation

A molecular formula is normally derived from an exact mass measurement. Exact mass measurements frequently can be made to an accuracy of better than 10^{-3} Da using an internal standard of known exact mass. Even with this accuracy, however, a unique fit is seldom obtained when all possible elemental compositions at any nominal mass are considered. The number of possibilities increases with the number of elements that may be present, with the number of atoms of each element possible, and with the molecular weight. For organic compounds that have only the common heteroatoms (O, N, F, Cl, Br, I, S, and Si) and molecular weights less than 500 Da, only a few possibilities need be considered. Thus, while exact mass measurement seldom gives a single formula, it often gives a singly reasonable formula, especially when other information on the sample is considered. Some of this ancillary information may come from the mass spectrum itself including isotopic abundance distributions, which are considered in the next section.

VII. Problem

A graduate student was following a procedure to make 3-propyl-1, 4-cyclohexadiene. During the workup procedure, he was called away to the telephone. By the time the student returned to his bench, the product had warmed to a higher temperature than recommended. He isolated the product, which gave the appropriate =C—H stretch in the IR, but the C=C stretch appeared around 1630 cm^{-1} as opposed to the literature value of 1650 cm^{-1} for the desired product. The mass spectrum showed the correct molecular weight, but the base peak was at M-29 rather than at M-43 as expected.

(a) Should he have his IR recalibrated or should he repeat the experiment, watching the temperature more carefully? What does the 1630 cm^{-1} absorption suggest?

(b) Draw the structure of the desired product, and propose a structure for the actual product.

(c) Show why he expected the MS base peak to be at M-43, and show how your proposed structure would give an intense peak at M-29.

Reading Material

Introduction to Chromatography

Many of the techniques of spectroscopy are selective for certain atoms or functional groups and structural elements of molecules. Often this selectivity is insufficient to distinguish compounds of closely related structure from each other. It may be insufficient for measurement of low levels of a compound in a mixture of others which produce an interfering spectral signal[1]. Conversely, when we wish to measure the presence and amounts of a large number of different compounds in a mixture, even the availability of unique spectral signatures for each analyte may require laborious repeated measurements with different spectral techniques to characterize the mixture fully. Living systems have evolved large protein molecules (e. g. , receptors, enzymes, immune system antibodies) with unique 3D structures which can bind strongly only to very specific organic compounds. Analytical procedures such as immunoassay, enzyme mediated assays, and competitive binding assays, employ the extreme selectivity of such protein macromolecules to measure particular biomolecules in very complex mixtures. Microarrays of thousands of these, each with unique selectivity, can rapidly screen complex mixtures for a list of expected components. However, precise quantitation of each detected component is difficult to achieve this way.

Analysis of complex mixtures often requires separation and isolation of components, or classes of components. [2] Examples in noninstrumental analysis include extraction, precipitation, and distillation. These procedures partition components between two phases based on differences in the components' physical properties. In liquid-liquid extraction components are distributed between two immiscible liquids based on their similarity in polarity to the two liquids (i. e. , "like dissolves like"). In precipitation, the separation between solid and liquid phases depends on relative solubility in the liquid phase. In distillation the partition between the mixture liquid phase and its vapor (prior to recondensation of the separated vapor) is primarily governed by the relative vapor pressures of the components at different temperatures (i. e. , differences in boiling points). When the relevant physical properties of the two components are very similar, their distribution between the phases at equilibrium will result in slight enrichment of each in one of the phases, rather than complete separation.[3] To attain nearly complete separation the partition process must be repeated multiple times, and the partially separated fractions recombined and repartitioned multiple times in a carefully organized fashion. This is achieved in the laborious batch processes of countercurrent liquid-liquid extraction, fractional crystallization, and fractional distillation. The latter appears to operate continuously, as the vapors from a single equilibration chamber are drawn off and recondensed, but the equilibration in each of the chambers or "plates" of a fractional distillation tower represents a discrete equilibration at a characteristic temperature.

A procedure called chromatography automatically and simply applies the principles of these "fractional" separation procedures. Chromatography can separate very complex mixtures composed of many very similar components. The various types of chromatographic instrumentation which have been developed and made commercially available over the past half century now comprise a majority of the analytical instruments for measuring a wide variety of analytes in mixtures. They are indispensable for detecting and quantitating trace contaminants in complex matrices. A single chromatographic analysis can isolate, identify, and quantitate dozens or even hundreds of components of mixtures. Without their ability to efficiently characterize complex mixtures of organic bio-chemicals at trace levels from microscale samples, research in molecular biology as we know it today would be impossible. We will be discussing another powerful separation technology, electrophoresis, together with chromatography, because much of the way electrophoresis operates, and the appearance of its separations, is analogous to chromatography, even though the underlying separation principle is different.[4] Chromatographic-type separation is at the heart of the instrumentation used to separate fragmented DNA molecules and to sequence the order of the "bases" which form the genomes of all living creatures on earth.[5] The heroic sequencing of around 3 billion DNA bases in the human genome, completed in the year 2001, could never have been envisioned, let alone completed, without chromatographic-type instrumentation. This forms the basis of the new field of genomics. Even more extensive analytical separation, identification, and quantitation problems arise in the next new field of molecular biological research, coming in the so-called "post-genomic" era; namely, proteomics. This requires separation, identification, and quantitation of the thousands of proteins that may be produced ("expressed") by the genome of each type of living cell. The contents and proportions of this mix will depend on what the cell is doing, and whether it is in a healthy or diseased state. The amounts of analytes may be at the nanomolar scale or less, and unlike DNA analyses, there is no handy polymerase chain reaction (PCR) procedure to amplify the amounts of analytes. If genomics provides a complete parts list for an organism, then proteomics will be necessary to understand the assembly and operating manual. Billions of dollars of chromatography-based instrumentation, and hundreds of thousands of jobs using it, will be required for research in these fields. Environmental monitoring and regulation has the potential of becoming another multimillion dollar market which can benefit from chromatography's ability to isolate, identify, and measure trace pollutants in complex environmental mixtures.

The Russian botanist Mikhail Tswett invented the technique and coined the name chromatography. Early in the 20th century he placed extracts containing a mixture of plant pigments on the top of glass columns filled with particles of calcium carbonate. Continued washing (elution) of the mixtures through the columns with additional solvent (called the eluent) resulted in the separation of the pigments, which appeared as colored bands adsorbed on the solid particles, moving along the column at different rates, thus appearing at different distances down the column. He named this technique "chromatography", from the Greek for "color writing". By collecting separated components as they exit the bottom of the column, one could isolate pure material. If a detector in the exiting fluid stream (called the effluent) can respond to some property of a separated component other than color, then neither a transparent column nor colored analytes are necessary to separate and measure materials by "chromatography".

When there is a great difference in the retention of different components on the material filling the column, a short column can be used to separate and isolate a rapidly moving component from highly retained material. This is the basis of a useful sample preparation technique called solid phase extraction (SPE).

Real instrumental chromatography employs highly engineered materials for the stationary phase past which the mobile phase fluid carrying the mixture of analytes passes, with continuous partitioning of the analytes between the two phases. The column needs to be sufficiently long and the eluent flow sufficiently slow for the process to approach equilibrium conditions. Then partitioning will be repeated a large number of times. Even very slight differences among mixture components in the ratio of the amounts which would exist in each phase at equilibrium will result in their separation into bands along the column. These bands can be separately detected or collected as they elute off the column.

The critical defining properties of a chromatographic process are:

1. immiscible stationary and mobile phases;

2. an arrangement whereby a mixture is deposited at one end of the stationary phase;

3. flow of the mobile phase toward the other end of the stationary phase;

4. different rates or ratios of partitioning for each component of the mixture, and many cycles of this process during elution;

5. a means of either visualizing bands of separated components on or adjacent to the stationary phase, or of detecting the eluting bands as peaks in the mobile phase of fluent.

(Note that in some applications the bands are also referred to as zones.)

The first major implementation of instrumental chromatography was based on partition between a liquid, nonvolatile, stationary phase supported on inert solid particles packed in metal columns, and an inert, gaseous mobile phase flowing through the column from a pressurized tank. The various partition ratios between the phases, which affected separation, were primarily related to the components' different volatilities (i. e., boiling points). The initial application of this procedure, gas chromatography (GC), to petroleum hydrocarbon samples, led to facile separation of many more components than could be achieved by the fractional distillation process used in petroleum refining. Instead of just petroleum "fractions", individual specific hydrocarbons could be resolved and isolated, if the GC column was long enough. The analogy to the theoretically well-studied multiple plate fractional distillation columns used in refining processes led to the initial plate theory of the chromatographic process. This assumed that the separation of the bands as they migrated down the column proceeded as a series of sequential, discrete equilibrium partitions, instead of the actual situation, which is a continuous, not-quite-in-equilibrium process. Nevertheless, this plate theory proved fairly accurate for most cases. It contained useful terms [e. g., N = the number of plates in a column as a descriptor of its separation efficiency, and the "height equivalent to a theoretical plate" (HETP)]. These remain central to the simplified theoretical characterization of the chromatographic process, despite the fact that continuous, non-equilibrium kinetic (or rate) theory is more accurate, and there exist no actual plates in a chromatographic column. GC was not suitable for separation and measurement of more polar, and less volatile or less thermally stable large biomolecules. Optimized chromatographic separations of these molecules at ambient temperatures were achieved later using more polar, water miscible liquid mobile phases. The instruments and stationary phases which enabled this improvement on the traditional vertical gravity column LC apparatus, form the basis of the even more widely used HPLC.

From *Undergraduate Instrumental Analysis* by James W. Robinson

New Words and Expressions

signature ['signitʃə]   n. 签名，署名，信号
spectral signature   光谱信号
receptor [ri'septə]   n. 接受器，感受器，受体
immunoassay [ˌimjunəu'æsei]   n. 免疫测定，免疫分析
assay [ə'sei]   n. & v. 化验，分析，评估
enzyme mediated assays   酶仲裁分析
macromolecule [ˌmækrəu'mɔlikju:l]   n. 巨大分子，高分子
precipitation [priˌsipi'teiʃən]   n. 沉淀，沉淀作用
distillation [ˌdisti'leiʃən]   n. 蒸馏，蒸馏法，蒸馏物，精华，精髓
immiscible [i'misəbl]   a. 不能混合的，不互溶的
recondensation [ˌri:kɔnden'seiʃən]   n. 浓缩，凝结
enrichment [in'ritʃmənt]   n. 富集，浓缩，发财致富，丰富，肥沃
batch [bætʃ]   n. 一批；一组；大量，vt. 分批处理
countercurrent ['kauntəˌkʌrənt]   n. 逆流，反向电流 adv. 相反地
recondense [ˌri:kən'dens]   v. 再浓缩，再凝结
quantitate ['kwɔntiteit]   v. 测定（估计）的数量，用数量来表示
at trace level   在痕量水平上
chromatographic [ˌkrəumætə'græfik]   a. 色析法的，层离法的
genome ['dʒi:nəum]   n. 基因组，染色体组

heroic [hi'rəuik] *a.* 英雄的，英勇的；大小或范围很大的，宏大的
polymerase ['pɔliməˌreis] *n.* 聚合酶
pigment ['pigmənt] *n.* 色素，颜料
eluent [eljuent] *n.* 洗脱液，洗脱剂
retention [ri'tenʃən] *n.* 保持，保留，保持力
stationary phase　固定相
mobile phase　流动相
gas chromatography　气相色谱
plate theory　塔板理论

Notes

1. be selective for 对……有选择性。distinguish…from 与……区别。参考译文：许多光谱技术对于特定原子或者分子中的官能团以及结构部分具有选择性。通常这种选择性不足以区分结构极其相似的化合物；当混合物中其他组分产生干扰光谱信号时，这种选择性也不足以测定其中低含量的化合物。

2. 参考译文：复杂混合物的分析经常需要将组分分离离析，即对组分进行筛分。

3. 该句的结构为：…result in…，rather than… 导致……，而不是……。参考译文：当两种组分相应的物理性质十分相近时，它们在两相中的分配平衡会使某一组分在其中一相中轻微富集，而不是完全分离。

4. 该句的结构为：…be analogous to 类似于……，与……相似。参考译文：在介绍色谱时，我们还要讨论另一种有效的分离技术—电泳，电泳的许多运作方式及分离细节类似于色谱，尽管两者根本的分离原理不同。

5. fragmented DNA molecules，DNA 分子片断。参考译文：色谱型分离仪器是用来分离 DNA 分子片断并对碱基行序列进行分析的核心设备，其中，碱基是在地球上形成的所有生物体的基因组。

PART FOUR
UNIT OPERATION

Unit 16 Techniques of Thin-Layer Chromatography in Food and Agricultural Analysis

Thin-layer chromatography (TLC) is widely used in laboratories throughout the world for food analysis and quality control. Numerous applications of TLC have been reported in the areas of food composition, intentional additives, adulterants, contaminants, and decomposition involving determinations of compound classes such as amino acids (protein quality), lipids and fatty acids (quality and adulteration of fat), sugars (beverage quality), biogenic amines (storage stability), vitamins (added as nutrients, colorants, and antioxidants), and organic acids (preservatives). TLC has also been widely used to analyze agricultural products and plants.

Sample preparation and application

Procedures for obtaining, storing, and preparing samples are generally similar to those for GC and HPLC, except sample preparation can often be simplified because the layer is used only once.[1] Some samples can be directly spotted or require only dilution prior to TLC. Solvent extraction (separatory funnel, Soxhlet, and extraction under reflux), macro and micro steam distillation, liquid-liquid partitioning with controlled pH, and liquid-solid column chromatography continue to be used widely for recovery, concentration, and cleanup of samples. However, these traditional approaches are increasingly being replaced by methods such as supercritical fluid extraction (SFE) and solid-phase extraction (SPE) with a cartridge, minicolumn, or disk.[2] The ability to reduce required extract purification in many TLC analyses enables high sample throughput, e. g., in the qualitative and quantitative evaluation of Passiflora coerulea flavonoids by HPTLC with detection using two fluorescence reagents for 'finger-printing' of different representatives of this genera.

In general, samples seldom require derivatization prior to TLC analysis, as is often the case with HPLC and, especially, GC. Hydrolysis of the sample by acid, base, or enzymes may be required for specific analyses, such as amino acids in proteins or sugars in starch.

Layers and mobile phases

Many types of adsorption, partition, and ion-exchange layers have been used for food analysis, but the great majority of all separations are carried out currently on normal or straight phase (NP) precoated silica gel TLC or HPTLC layers. Plates containing a preabsorbent or concentrating zone facilitate rapid sample application and formation of compact, band-shaped zones after development.[3] Other NP layers that are used for some food analyses include alumina and cellulose. Reversed phase (RP) TLC is performed mostly on chemically bonded C-18, C-2, C-8, and diphenyl layers.

The use of corn starch, rice starch, talc, and impregnated corn starch layers was reported for densitometric quantification of organic acids, carbohydrates, fat-soluble vitamins, amino acids, and anthocyanins in foods. Hydrophilic diol-bonded layers were used for identification (preparative TLC) and densitometry of 2-hydroxycinnamaldehyde in commercial cinnamons and for densitometry of sugars in foods after automated multiple development (AMD).

The mobile phase for TLC is usually chosen by trial and error guided by literature descriptions of earlier similar separations or by use of systematic mobile phase design and optimization models.[4] The most widely used of these is the "Prisma" model, which was used to select the optimum mobile phase for the overpressured layer chromatography (OPLC) analysis of food antioxidants. Mobile phases for a variety of analyte classes are specified in many of the TLC applications.

Development of the layer

TLC is usually performed in one-dimension by gravity-flow ascending development with a single mobile phase in a solvent vapor-saturated, paper-lined glass N-chamber. Multiple developments in one direction with the one or more mobile phases can improve resolution in some cases. Multistep, manual gradient elution in a sandwich chamber was used for the separation and densitometry of the colored pigments in red wine on reversed-phase paraffin-impregnated silica gel plates.

AMD is becoming widely used for high-efficiency automated HPTLC separations prior to quantification by densitometry. In AMD, an automated instrument produces a $20 \sim 25$ step mobile phase gradient ranging from stronger to weaker elution power, with successive developments occurring over a longer incremental distance (typically 3 mm or less). Large spot capacities result because of the reconcentration effect caused by the multiple development, as well as separation of complex mixtures with a wide range of polarities because of gradient development.

Two-dimensional (2D) development improves resolution of a complex mixture by development with two mobile phases at right angles. As an example, the effect of soybean pretreatment on the phospholipids content in crude and degummed oils was studied by qualitative 2D TLC on silica gel with chloroform-methanol-28% ammonia (13 : 5 : 1) in the first direction and chloroform-methanol-acetic acid-water (170 : 25 : 25 : 6) in the second.

Forced flow development by OPLC involves pumping the mobile phase through a layer that is sandwiched between a rigid plate and a flexible membrane under pressure. OPLC results in large spot capacities and short development times, and gradient elution can be used. OPLC with dichloromethane-ethyl acetate (93 : 7) mobile phase and densitometry at 313nm has been used to determine biogenic amines in cheese and to study the formaldehyde cycle in budding and apoptosis of trees.

Detection of zones

Many hundreds of chromogenic and fluorogenic reagents are described in the literature for detection on layers of analytes that cannot be visualized by natural color in daylight or by natural fluorescence or fluorescence quenching under 254nm or 366nm UV light. Fluorescence detection is preferred when possible because of its specificity and sensitivity. An example is the detection of nitroimidazoles from poultry on silica gel HPTLC plates by reduction of the nitro group followed by reaction with fluorescamine fluorogenic reagent (detection limit $15 \sim 20$ng) or by spraying with pyridine ($3 \sim 25$ng) and viewing under 366nm UV light. Although generally less sensitive, chromogenic reagents are widely used, e. g., for detection of monosodium glutamate in foods prior to quantification by densitometry at 520nm.

New detection methods are reported regularly in the TLC literature and are reviewed biennially by Sherma. As an example, a new method for wavelengths for detection of animal neutral lipids prior to quantification by densitometry at 430nm involved spraying with three different reagents: (ⅰ) 3% cupric acetate in 6% aq. phosphoric acid solution, followed by heating at 100℃ for 10 min; (ⅱ) 35% aq. sulfuric acid, followed by heating at 140℃ for 10 min; (ⅲ) procedure (ⅰ) followed by procedure (ⅱ). The specific detection of phosphorothionate and phosphorothiolothionate pesticides extracted from mushrooms as deep magenta zones by reaction with 4-amino-N,N-diethylaniline is a second new method; limit of detection is 0.05~0.5 mg/zone.

Documentation of chromatograms

Photography of chromatograms is an important method for recording and preserving the results of a TLC analysis; such documentation is becoming increasingly important to meet GLP (good laboratory practice) and GMP (good manufacturing practice) requirements. Photographic documentation is currently being replaced at an increasing rate by video camera and computer scanning technology.

Quantification by densitometry

Quantitative analysis is carried out in situ by measurement of sample and standard zones on layers with a slit-scanning densitometer or video or CCD camera (image processing). Slit-scanning instruments have a number of advantages and were used in most of the densitometry papers cited in this review. However, more papers are being published each year with quantification based on image analysis. For example, plant phenolics were quantified on normal and reversed-phase layers using video-densitometry, and results were compared with those from a dualwavelength, flying spot UV densitometer. Densitometry is best performed at the wavelength of maximum absorption for visible/UV absorption scanning and the maximum excitation/emission wavelengths for fluorescence scanning.

Special techniques

Preparative layer chromatography (PLC) is carried out on thicker layers with application of larger weights and volumes of samples in order to separate and recover 10~1000 mg of compound for further analysis. As an example, new colored compounds from the Maillard reaction between xylose and lysine were isolated by PLC on silica gel layers with a concentrating zone using chloroform-ethyl acetate-ethanol (15:2:2) and methyl acetate-water (8:1) mobile phases, detection in daylight and under 366 nm UV light, and quantification by HPLC with a diode array detector after elution from the layer.

The separation and measurement of radio-labelled compounds on TLC plates is a widely used method for following metabolism reactions of compounds such as drugs and pesticides. Radio-TLC with scintillation counter was used to study inhibition of aggregation and alteration of eicosanoid metabolism in human blood platelets caused by curcumin, a major component of food spice tumeric. On-line coupling of reversed-phase HPLC and normal-phase TLC provides a multi-mechanism analytical system with high peak capacity. An on-line system consisting of a microbore HPLC syringe pump and a modified TLC personal computer autosampler enabling effluent to be sprayed from the column in fractions onto the plate at defined locations was applied to the densitometric determination of multiple pesticide residues and iprodion residues with AMD in foods.

From *Thin-layer chromatography in food and agricultural analysis by Joseph Sherma*

New Words and Expressions

adulterant [əˈdʌltərənt]   *a.* 掺杂用的；*n.* 掺杂物
amino acid [ˈæminəuˈæsid]   *n.* 氨基酸
lipids [ˈlipid, ˈlaipid]   *n.* 脂质，油脂
biogenic [ˌbaiəuˈdʒenik]   *a.* 源于生物的，生物所造成的

antioxidant [ˌænti'ɔksidənt] n. 抗氧化剂，硬化防止剂，防老剂
cartridge ['kɑːtridʒ] n.（萃取柱）柱体
minicolumn ['mini'kɔləm] n. 小型柱
fluorescence [fluə'resns] n. 荧光，荧光性
starch [stɑːtʃ] n. 淀粉 vt. 给……上浆
precoat ['priːkəut] vt. 预涂（预敷，预浇）n. 预涂层（预敷层）
anthocyanin [ˌænθə'saiənin] n. 花青素，花青苷，花青苷，花色素苷
densitometry [ˌdensi'tɔmitri] n. 密度测定法（显像测密术，测光密度术）
cinnamon ['sinəmən] n. 肉桂，肉桂树，肉桂色
analyte ['ænəlait] n. 分析物；被分析物
sandwich ['sænwidʒ, -tʃ] v. 插入，夹入
reconcentration ['riːkɔnsen'treiʃən] n. 再浓缩
dimensional [di'menʃənəl] a. ……维的
soybean ['sɔibiːn] n. 大豆，黄豆
phospholipid [ˌfɔsfəu'lipid] n. 磷脂
degumm [diː'gʌm] vt. 使……脱胶（使……去胶）
membrane ['membrein] n. 薄膜，隔膜
dichloromethane [daiˌklɔːrə'meθein] n. 二氯甲烷
formaldehyde [fɔː'mældiˌhaid] n. 甲醛，蚁醛
chromogenic [ˌkrəumə'dʒenik] a. 发色的，发色体的
fluorogenic ['fluːərədʒən] a. 荧光团的
quenching ['kwentʃiŋ] n. 淬火，猝灭
nitroimidazole ['naitrəuˌimi'dæzəul, -də'zəul] n. 硝基咪唑
fluorescamine [ˌfluːə'reskəmiːn] n. 荧光胺
pyridine [ˌpirə'dainə] n. 嘧啶
wavelength ['weivleŋθ] n. 波长
scintillation [ˌsinti'leiʃən] n. 闪烁（现象）
platelet ['pleitlit] n. 血小板
curcumin ['kəːkjumin] n. 姜黄色素，酸性黄

Notes

1. 句中，"GC"为"gas chromatography"的缩写；"HPLC"为"high performance liquid chromatograpgy"的缩写。参考译文：样品的获取、储存、制备程序与气谱、高性能液相色谱一样，除了简化样品制备，因为纸层只用一次。

2. "approaches"可译为处理方法。参考译文：然而，这些传统的方法愈来愈被用卡盘、小型柱或圆盘进行的超临界流体萃取和固相萃取的方法所取代。

3. "preabsorbent"为预吸附剂，"application"意为贴合作用。参考译文：含有预吸附剂或浓缩区域的板促使样品的快速贴合和在展开后紧凑、有形带的形成。

4. "trial and error"意为试差试验。

Exercises

Ⅰ. Comprehension

1. Numerous applications of TLC have been reported in the areas of the followings except for _____.
  A. food composition and intentional additives
  B. adulterants and contaminants
  C. decomposition involving determinations of compound classes

D. determinations of chemical groups

2. The mobile phase for TLC is usually chosen by _____ test (s) guided by literature descriptions of earlier similar separations or by use of systematic mobile phase design and optimization models.

    A. one time   B. trial and error   C. no   D. calculation

3. Two-dimensional development improves resolution of a complex mixture by development with two mobile phases _____ .

    A. at the same angles   B. at 180 degree   C. with parallel   D. at right angles

4. A new method for wavelengths for detection of animal neutral lipids prior to quantification by densitometry at 430 nm involved spraying with three different reagents: _____ .

    A. 3% cupric acetate + 6% aq. phosphoric acid solution +35% aq. sulfuric acid
    B. 3% cupric acetate + 3% aq. phosphoric acid solution +3% aq. sulfuric acid
    C. 6% cupric acetate + 3% aq. phosphoric acid solution +35% aq. sulfuric acid
    D. 3% cupric acetate + 6% aq. phosphoric acid solution +3% aq. sulfuric acid

II. Fill in the blanks with the phrases given below

in the presence of	examples of	composed of	in general
carried out	prior to	according to	a variety of
in the presence of	impregnated with	in studies of	compared to
were identified by	at a level of	followed by	for this purpose

1. References describing advances in techniques and applications to important analyte and sample classes that were published in this period are presented, _____ brief descriptions of selected analyses as _____ typical protocols for food and agricultural TLC analysis.

2. Modern high-performance TLC (HPTLC) is an efficient, instrumentalized, quantitative method that is _____ on layers _____ particles with a smaller particle diameter, 5 μm _____ 12~20 μm for conventional TLC.

3. _____ samples seldom require derivatization prior to TLC analysis, as is often the case with HPLC and, especially, GC.

4. Sample preparation methods _____ TLC analysis are specified in the applications described in Section 4 and a few of those in Section 3.

5. Ascending development with dichloro-methanol (1 : 1) has been widely used _____ .

6. Complete validation of an HPTLC method for determination of caffeine in cola _____ ICH guidelines for selectivity, analyte stability, linearity, precision, and robustness was demonstrated for quantification with a slit-scanning densitometer and an image-analyzing system.

7. Oryzalin (3, 5-dinitro-N^4, N^4-dipropylsulfanilamide) and degradation products were separated on silica gel with _____ mobile phases and detected and quantified by densitometry _____ sorption and degradation in agricultural products.

8. Similar methods were used to quantify erythromycin and tylosine in animal feeds _____ two tetracycline antibiotics and the other drugs listed above.

9. Milk fat triglycerides _____ TLC on silica gel _____ silver nitrate and developed with chloroform.

10. Pentachlorophenol (PCP) was determined on wood _____ 100 ppm/100 mg sample by silica gel HPTLC with toluene mobile phase and detection after nitric acid-mediated oxidation of PCP to tetrachloro-1, 4-benzoquinone by spraying with acid reagent.

III. Complete the sentences with the proper form of the word given at the end of the sentence.

1. The following are brief summaries of selected applications of TLC for the _____ of important compounds in food and agricultural samples. (determine)

2. This rather straightforward example indicates that modern TLC should not be neglected as either a selective _____ method or for quantitative assays. (separate)

3. The characteristic features that _____ between the two techniques is set out below. (distinguish)

4. The elution mode is commonly used for separations in column chromatography _____ all solutes to migrate the same distance corresponding to the length of the sorbent bed. (require)

5. In this case all solutes have the same _____ time during which separated zones _____ different distances. (migrate)

6. Several detection techniques can be employed sequentially, _____ that they are nondestructive, and detection techniques employing chemical reactions can be optimized free of time constraints. (provide)

7. Since the total sample occupies the chromatogram and not just the portion which elutes from the column, the integrity of the analysis is guaranteed in planar chromatography but can only _____ in column chromatography. (imply)

8. It is important to emphasize the complementary rather than _____ aspects of the two separation techniques. (compete)

9. Both approaches to liquid chromatography are no more than separation tools for which the job at hand is responsible for selecting the _____ technique. (prefer)

10. The determination of the flavor potential and _____ of vanilla is based in part on the concentration ratios of the principal polar aromatic flavor compounds determined by reversed-phase liquid chromatography. (authentic)

Ⅳ. Problem

1. The Langmuir isotherm is a moderately good representation of the adsorption behaviour of gases on a variety of surfaces, and it has the virtue of considerable simplicity. Quite a few of the kind of the problems in this chapter will be based on it and they will give familiarity with the kind of calculations that can be done. As a first step, show that if a diatomic gas adsorbs as atoms the Langmuir isotherm becomes

$$\theta = \sqrt{K_p}/(1+\sqrt{K_p})$$

2. How do we test the non-dissociative Langmuir isotherm? One way is to plot p/θ against p, but θ might not always be known. Show that a plot of p/V_a, where V_a is the volume of gas adsorbed against p should give a straight line from which both V_a^o, the volume corresponding to complete coverage, and the constant K may be determined. Also show that for small surface coverages another test is to plot $\ln(\theta/p)$ against θ, when a line of gradient -1 should be obtained. What should the slope be when $\ln V_a/p$ is plotted against V_a at small coverages?

Ⅴ. Translation the following words and expressions into English

薄层色谱 离子交换 定量分析 定性分析 密度测试法 浸渍 液-液分配
试差试验 溶剂萃取 分液漏斗 选择性 紫外/可见吸收 浓度

Reading Material

Development of Thin-layer Chromatography

Thin-layer chromatography (TLC) can trace its origins to the introduction of drop chromatography by Izmailov and Shraiber in the late 1930s as a fast, convenient and more powerful separation tool for analytical applications than conventional column liquid chromatography. Thin-layer chromatography as we know it today was established in the 1950s, due in part to the efforts of Stahl and Kirchner, who devised standardized procedures to improve separation performance and reproducibility and contributed to the development of many new applications. At about the same time commercialization of materials and devices commenced making the technique accessible to all laboratories. This heralded in a golden age in the evolution of TLC which quickly displaced paper chromatography as the main liquid chromatographic separation method in laboratory investigations. The 1970s saw a declining interest in TLC as modern column liquid chromatography was developed into an automated and fully instrumentalized separation method. Further optimized conditions for TLC, more generally known as high-performance TLC or modern TLC, failed to sustain the previous interest in the technique.

By the 1980s modern TLC had become fully instrumentalized but at the same time detached from the main stream of chromatographic research. In its conventional form TLC continued to provide a quick, inexpensive, flexible, and portable method for monitoring synthetic reaction mixtures and similar applications. On the other hand, modern TLC was becoming increasingly marginalized and virtually invisible at major symposia on chromatography. At the turn of the century modern TLC faces an uncertain future, while conventional TLC is likely to survive as a general laboratory tool in the same mold as precipitation, crystallization and distillation, having survived as indispensable, low cost and low technology operations. The general invisibility of modern TLC, more so on the American continent than Europe, is its main enemy today.[1] Training in modern TLC is virtually nonexistent within industry and academia, and the loss of institutional knowledge means that many contemporary scientists are unaware of when TLC could be the method of choice for solving certain problems. Modern TLC survives because of strong support from a few enthusiastic individuals who continue to develop and nurture the technique, and because its world wide user base is still large enough to support its commercialization. The last decade has seen strong growth in the use of TLC in the technically less advanced countries where the latest technology for column chromatography is often not cost efficient for solving local problems.

Two 15 minute developments with the mobile phase hexane-chloroform-carbon tetrachloride-ethanol (7 : 18 : 22 : 1) on a silica gel 60 HPTLC plate. Chromatogram was recorded by scanning densitometry at 220 nm.

If modern TLC had no role to play in the future of separation sciences, then further comment would not be required. The disappearance of paper chromatography as a common laboratory tool was compensated for by the evolution of other techniques, ironically, including TLC. In my opinion modern TLC still has a role to play in separation science as a complement to other, column-based liquid chromatographic techniques. It is this case that will be presented in this article, together with an appraisal of the current state-of-the-art in TLC, and identification of those areas in need of further development.

The main characteristic features of modern TLC are the use of fine particle layers for fast and efficient separations; sorbents with a wide range of sorption properties to optimize selectivity; the use of instrumentation for convenient (automated) sample application, development and detection; and the accurate and precise in situ recording and quantitation of chromatograms. These features are the exact opposite of conventional TLC, which thrives because it does not require instrumentation and has low operating costs.

Expectations in terms of performance, ease of use, and quantitative information from the two approaches to TLC are truly opposite. As an example of expectations for a separation by modern TLC we show the chromatogram in Fig. 16.1. The ethynyl steroids are the

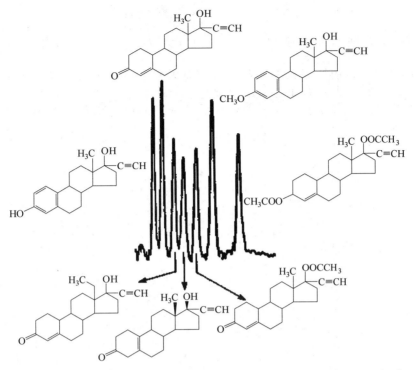

Fig. 16.1 separation of ethynyl steroids by modern thin-layer chromatography

main components of the birth control pill. Since they have a similar biological function, their structures are similar, and high selectivity is required for their separation. Typical tablet formulations contain two steroids only but the method illustrated was designed for universal application requiring the baseline separation of all possible active ingredients. Baseline separation is obtained with a short migration distance typical of fine particle layers and scanning densitometry provides a conventional record of the separation in the form of a chromatogram, as well as quantitation of individual components in the mixture after calibration.[2] By way of example, for a typical tablet formulation stated to contain norgestrel at 0.5mg and ethynodiol diacetate at 2.0 mg per tablet the measured quantities were $0.509mg \pm 0.008mg$ ($n=10$) and $2.00mg \pm 0.03mg$ ($n=10$). Sample preparation involved dissolution and filtration only. The quantitative results are similar in accuracy and precision to other chromatographic techniques and the method is suitable for routine analytical assays. This rather straightforward example indicates that modern TLC should not be neglected as either a selective separation method or for quantitative assays.

From *Planar chromatography at the turn of the century* by Colin F. Poole

New Words and Expressions

herald ['herəld]　　*n.* 使者，先驱，预兆；*vt.* 预报，宣布
marginalize ['mɑːdʒinəlaiz]　　*vt.* 忽视，排斥
academia [ˌækə'diːmjə]　　*n.* 学术界，学术环境
ethynyl [e'θainil]　　*n.* 乙炔基
steroid ['stiərɔid]　　*n.* 类固醇
norgestrel [nɔː'dʒestrəl]　　*n.* 甲基炔诺酮，18-甲炔诺酮
diacetate [dai'æsiteit]　　*n.* 双乙酸盐（酯）

Notes

1. 参考译文：当前 TLC 总体上的不可见性，在美洲大陆比欧洲更是这样，是当前它的主要敌人。

2. 参考译文：典型的片剂配方仅含有两种类固醇，但说明的方法为普遍适用于要求所有可能活性组分的基线分离而设计，用细小颗粒层典型的短的迁移距离来获得基线分离和扫描密度测定法提供传统的以色谱形式记录的分离以及校核后可对混合物中各组分进行定量。

Unit 17 Crystallisation

Crystallisation ranks high in the list of industrial processes devoted to the production of pure chemicals. Apart from the fact that its final product has an attractive appearance, crystallisation frequently proves to be the cheapest and sometimes the easiest way in which a pure substance can be produced from an impure solution. Conventional distillation techniques cannot separate efficiently close-boiling liquids or those that from azeotropes, yet crystallisation may often lead to their complete separation. There is evidence that the petroleum industry is now turning its attention to crystallisation techniques to deal with difficult separations.

The methods available for crystallisation are many and varied. Crystals can be grown from the liquid or the vapor phase, but in all cases the state of supersaturation has first to be achieved. The way in which supersaturation is produced depends on the characteristics of the crystallising system; some solutes are readily deposited from their solutions merely by cooling, while others have to be evaporated to a more concentrated form. In cases of very high solubility, or for heat-labile solutions, another substance may have to be added to the system to reduce the solubility of the solute in the solvent. Again, supersaturation of the liquid or gaseous phase may be caused by the chemical reaction of two substances; one of the reaction products is then precipitated.

Methods for Achieving Supersaturation

1) Cooling and Evaporation

One of the most common ways in which the supersaturation of a liquid can be achieved is by means of a cooling process. If the solubility of the solute in the solvent decreases with a decrease in temperature, some of the solute will be deposited on cooling; a slow controlled rate of cooling in an agitated system can result in the production of crystals of regular size. The crystal yield may be slightly increased if some of the solvent evaporates during the cooling process.

If the solubility characteristics of the solute in the solvent are such that there is little change with a reduction in temperature, some of the solvent may have to be deliberately evaporated from the system in order to effect the necessary supersaturation and crystal deposition. Cooling and evaporative techniques are widely used in industrial crystallisation; the majority of the solute solvent systems of commercial importance can be processed by one or other of these methods. Descriptions of many of the cooling and evaporating crystallisers commonly encountered are given later.

The yield from a cooler or evaporator can be calculated from the general equation:

$$Y = \frac{WR\,[c_1 - c_2\,(1-V)]}{1 - c_2\,(R-1)} \tag{17.1}$$

where $Y=$ crystal yield (kg); $W=$ weight of solvent present initially (kg); $V=$ weight of solvent lost, either deliberately or unavoidably, by evaporation (kg per kg of original solvent); $R=$ ratio of the molecular weights of solvate (e. g. hydrate) and unsolvated (e. g. anhydrous) solute; and c_1, $c_2 =$ initial and final solution concentrations, respectively (kg of unsolvated solute per kg of solvent). The yield calculated from the above equation is the theoretical maximum on the assumptions (a) that c_2 refers to the equilibrium saturation at the final temperature, and (b) that no solute is lost when the crystals are washed after being separated from the mother liquor.

2) Controlled Seeding

During a crystallisation operation the accidental production of nuclei (false grain) must be avoided at all costs; the solution must never be allowed to become labile. The deliberate addition of carefully selected seeds, however, is permitted so long as the deposition of crystalline matter takes place on these nuclei only. The seeds should be dispersed uniformly throughout the solution by means of gentle agitation; and if the temperature is carefully regulated, considerable control is possible over the final product size.[1] Deliberate seeding is frequently employed in industrial crystallisations; the actual weight of seed material to be added depends on the solute deposition, the size of the seeds and the product:

$$W_s = W_p \ (L_S^3/L_P^3) \qquad (17.2)$$

where W_s and W_p are the weights and L_S and L_P are the mean particle sizes of the seed and product, respectively. The product weight, W_p, is the crystal yield, Y, e. g. as calculated from solubility data using equation (17.1), plus the weight of added seeds, i. e. $W_p = Y + W_s$, and

$$W_s = Y \frac{L_S^3}{L_P^3 - L_S^3} \qquad (17.2a)$$

Seeds as small as $5\mu m$ have been used in sugar boiling practice; these tiny particles are produced by prolonged ball-milling in an inert medium, e. g. isopropyl alcohol or mineral oil, and 500g of such seeds may be quite sufficient for $50m^3$ of massecuite.

The seeds do not necessarily have to consist of the material being crystallised, unless absolute purity of the final product is required. A few tiny crystals of some isomorphous substance may be used to induce crystallisation. For example, phosphates will often nucleate solutions of arsenates. Small quantities of sodium tetraborate decahydrate can induce the crystallisation of sodium sulphate decahydrate. Crystalline organic homologues, derivatives and isomers are frequently used for inducing crystallisation; phenol can nucleate m-cresol, and ethyl acetanilide can nucleate methyl acetanilide.

During the operation if the temperature is curbed, then the crystallisation could be called "controlled crystallisation". The temperature is controlled so that the system is kept in the metastable state throughout the operation, and the rate of growth of the small crystal is governed solely by the rate of cooling. There is no sudden deposition of fine crystals, because the system does not enter the labile zone, then crystals of a regular and predetermined size can be grown. Many large-scale crystallisation operations are carried out in this manner.

The mass of crystal seeds accidentally produced in large crystallisers may be very small indeed, yet on account of their minute size the number of seeds can be exceptionally large. If, for simplicity, spheres of diameter d and density ρ are considered, the mass of one seed is $\pi/(6\rho d^3)$. Thus 100g of 0.1mm (~150 mesh) seeds of a substance of density $2g/cm^3$ will contain about 100 million separate particles, and every seed is a potential crystal. For controlled growth, the liquor in the crystalliser must not be allowed to nucleate. Vigorous agitation and mechanical and thermal shock should be avoided, and the supersaturation should be kept to the absolute working minimum; high magma densities, up to 20~30 percent suspended solids, help in this respect. If, despite these precautions, unwanted nucleation still occurs, some system of false grain removal must be operated; continuous circulation of the spent liquor through a fines trap is one such method.

3) Salting-out Crystallisation

Another way in which the supersaturation of a solution can be effected is by the addition to the system of some substance that reduces the solubility of the solute in the solvent. The added substance which may be a liquid, solid, or gas, is often referred to as a diluent or precipitant. Liquid diluents are most frequently used. Such a process is known as salting-out, precipitation or crystallisation by dilution. The properties required of the diluent are that it be miscible with the solvent of the original solution, at least over the ranges of concentration encountered, that the solute be relatively insoluble in it, and also that the final solvent-diluent mixture be capable of easy separation, e. g. by distillation.

Although salting-out is widely employed industrially, relatively few published data are available regarding its use in crystallisation operations. The process is commonly encountered, for instance, in the crystallisation of organic substances from water-miscible organic solvents by the controlled addition of water to the solution; the term 'watering-out' is used in this connection. Some of the advantages of salting-out or dilution crystallisation are as follows. Very concentrated initial solutions can be prepared, often with great ease, by dissolving the impure crystalline mass in a suitable solvent. A high solute recovery can be made by cooling the solution as well as salting it out. If the solute is very soluble in the initial solvent, high dissolution temperatures are not necessary, and the temperature of the batch during the crystallisation operation can be kept low; this is advantageous when heat-labile substances are being processed. Purification is sometimes greatly simplified when the mother liquor retains undesirable impurities owing to their greater solubility in the solvent—diluent mixture. Probably the biggest disadvantage of dilution crystallisation is the need for a recovery unit to handle fairly large quantities of the mother liquor in order to separate solvent and diluent, one or both of which may be valuable.[2]

From *Unit Operation of Chemical Engineering 4 th edition*, by Warren L. Mccabe, et. al

New Words and Expressions

supersaturate [sju:pə'sætʃəreit]　*vt.* 使过饱和
supersaturation ['sju:pəˌsætʃə'reiʃən]　*n.* 过饱和（现象）
deposition [ˌdepə'ziʃən, di:-]　*n.* 沉淀，沉淀物
evaporator [i'væpəreitə]　*n.* （食物干燥）蒸发器
homologue (homolog) ['hɔməlɔg]　*n.* 同系物，同源染色体，相应物
acetanilide [ˌæsi'tænilid]　*n.* 乙酰苯胺，退热冰
methyl acetanilide　甲基乙酰苯胺
metastable [ˌmetə'steibl]　*a.* 亚稳的，准稳的
mesh [meʃ]　*n.* 筛眼，每平方英寸的网孔（筛眼）数
mother liquor　母液

Notes

1. 句中"be dispersed uniformly throughout the solution"为"在溶液中均匀分散晶种"；"considerable"为"值得考虑的，大量的，相当大的"，此为：对最终产品尺寸进行相当程度上控制是可能的。参考译文：晶种应该通过缓慢的搅拌均匀地分散在整个溶液中。如果温度小心调节的话，对于成品大小能够控制得相当好。

2. 句中"dilution crystallisation"为盐析结晶。从常理来看结晶需要浓缩，此时为"dilution crystallisation"，即字面上是"稀释结晶"，实际意为通过加入某种促进结晶的溶剂，即盐析效应来使结晶过程更易进行。参考译文：稀结晶最大的缺点就是需要一个回收单元来处理相当大量的母液，这是为了分离溶剂和稀释剂，其中一个或者两个也许是有价值的。

Exercises

Ⅰ. Comprehension

1. Crystallisation ranks high in the list of industrial processes devoted to the production

of pure chemicals, because of _____.
   A. that its final product has an attractive appearance
   B. crystallisation frequently proves to be the cheapest
   C. the easiest way in which a pure substance can be produced from an impure solution
   D. All of the above
2. A slow controlled rate of cooling in an agitated system can result in _____.
   A. the production of crystals of regular size   B. high purity of product
   C. small energy consumption   D. continuous process
3. The seeds do not necessarily have to consist of the material being crystallised, unless _____.
   A. the absolute purity of the final product is required
   B. the regular size of the final product is required
   C. the crystallisation process is difficult
   D. both A and B
4. The mass of crystal seeds accidentally produced in large crystallisers may be _____.
   A. very small   B. very large
   C. depending on the kind of crystal   D. both A and C
5. Although salting-out is widely employed industrially, _____ published data are available regarding its use in crystallisation operations.
   A. relatively few   B. relatively many   C. no   D. almost no

II. Fill in the blanks with the proper word given below

interna	responsible	reasonable	symmetrical
Furthermore	composed	stage	physical
basis	overall		

At an early _____ it was suggested that the regular external form of crystals implied _____ regularity. That crystals are regular _____ bodies suggests that the techniques described in this chapter should be a _____ both for their classification and for a rapid assessment of their _____ properties. _____ since crystals are _____ of ions, atoms, or molecules stacked together in a manner that is _____ for the external appearance or morphology (morphos is the Greek for 'form') of the crystal, it is also _____ to expect group theory to provide a way of discussing how the local symmetry of molecules in the crystal can account for their _____ symmetry.

III. Choose the item from (1) ~ (6) that best matches the item in (a) ~ (f) to make a correct sentence.

(1) The theories of overall crystallization kinetics are being applied
(2) A crystal is composed
(3) The regular external morphology suggests that the crystal is formed
(4) The crystallization analysis is frequently based on
(5) Similar remarks also concern the efforts to predict
(6) The most frequently used analysis of experimental data concerning isothermal crystallization is based on

(a) in numerous papers to analyze the crystallization, especially the nucleation.
(b) of an array of ions, atoms, or molecules.
(c) from small units which are themselves symmetrical.
(d) the simplest equations neglecting the possible complexity of the phenomenon, even in quiescent state.
(e) the overall crystallization kinetics during processing.

(f) the classic Evans-Avrami (E-A) equation, while for nonisothermal crystallization data the Ozawa equation is used.

IV. Please fill in the blanks with the proper preposition

(1) Polymer crystallization from the melt _____ quiescent state occurs usually in the form of polycrystalline aggregates-the _____ spherulites.

(2) The first attempts to describe the conversion of the amorphous material _____ crystalline domains were focused on the growth from nuclei randomly distributed in a sample.

(3) Later development of the theory was focused on the description of nonisothermal crystallization, crystallization _____ a temperature gradient and crystallization in a confined volume.

(4) These theories are also widely used to predict crystallization _____ processing.

(5) In fact, people generally use the well-established equations _____ a means to fit experimental data _____ real insight into the basic assumptions or further simplifications, which have led to the equations.

(6) The Avrami plot of isothermal experimental data makes it possible _____ determine the exponent value.

V. Answer the following questions

(1) Copper (Ⅰ) chloride (cuprous chloride) forms cubic crystals with four molecules per unit cell. The only reflections present in a powder photograph are those either with all even indices or with all odd. What is the nature of the unit cell? Note that this type of question about the form of the radiation: it is determined by symmetry, not size.

(2) Show that the maximum proportion of the available volume that may be filled by hard spheres is (a) 0.52 for a simple cubic lattice, (b) 0.68 for a b.c.c. lattice, (c) 0.74 for an f.c.c. lattice. These numbers are the packing fractions of the lattices. What method of packing is most economical for shipping (hard) oranges?

VI. Translate the following into Chinese

azeotrope	isomorphous	supersaturation	arsenate	nuclei
isopropyl	alcohol	sodium	sulphate	m-cresol
massecuite	decahydrate	crystalline	homologues	derivative
crystallisation	tetraborate	salting-out	ethyl acetanilide	mineral oil

---

Reading Material

Crystallisation Equipment

Commercial crystallizers (crystallisers) may operate either continuously or batchwise. Except for special applications, continuous operation is preferred. The first requirement of any crystallizer is to create a supersaturated solution, as crystallization cannot occur without supersaturation. The means used to produce supersaturation depend primarily on the solubility curve of the solute.[1] Solutes like common salt have solubilities nearly independent of temperature, and others, such as anhydrous sodium sulfate and sodium carbonate monohydrate, have inverted solubility curves and become more soluble as the temperature is lowered. To crystallize these materials, supersaturation must be developed by evaporation. Other materials, such as glauber's salt, epsom salt, copperas, and sodium thiosulfate, are much less soluble at low temperatures than at high, and cooling without evaporation produces supersaturation. In intermediate cases, a combination of evaporation and cooling is effective. Sodium nitrate, for example, may be satisfactorily crystallized by cooling without evaporation, evaporation without cooling, or a combination of cooling and evaporation.

Variations in Crystallizers

Commercial crystallizers may also be differentiated in several other ways. One important difference is in how the crystals are brought into contact with the supersaturated liquid. In the first technique, called the *circulating-liquid method*, a stream of supersaturated solution is passed through a fluidized bed of growing crystals, within which supersaturation is released by nucleation and growth.[2] The saturated liquid then is pumped through a cooling or evaporating zone, in which supersaturation is generated, and finally the supersaturated solution is recycled through the crystallizing zone. In the second technique, called the *circulating-magma method*, the entire magma is circulated through both crystallization and supersaturation steps without separating the liquid from the solid. Supersaturation as well as crystallization occurs in the presence of crystals. In both methods feed solution added to the circulating stream between the crystallizing and supersaturating zones.

One type of crystallizer uses size-classification devices designed to retain small crystals in the growth zone for further growth and to allow only crystals of a specified minimum size to leave the unit as product. Ideally, such a crystallizer would produce a classified product of a single uniform size. Other crystallizers are designed to maintain a thoroughly mixed suspension in the crystallizing zone, in which crystals of all sizes from nuclei to large crystals are uniformly distributed throughout the magma. Ideally, the size distribution in the product from a mixed suspension unit is identical to that in the crystallizing magma itself.

Again, some crystallizers are equipped with devices to segregate fine crystals as soon as possible after nucleation and to remove the bulk of them from the crystallizing zone. The objective of this is to reduce sharply the number of nuclei present in order that the remaining ones can grow. The presence of too many nuclei means that the mass of precipitating solute available for each particle is too small to permit adequate growth. The nuclei withdrawn, which actually have a very small mass, are redissolved and returned to the crystallizer. In situations where the size specification for the product is not so severe, removal of nuclei is unnecessary.

Most crystallizers utilize some form of agitation to improve growth rate, to prevent segregation of supersaturated solution that causes excessive nucleation, and to keep crystals in suspension throughout the crystallizing zone.[3] Internal propeller agitators may be used, often equipped with draft tubes and baffles, and external pumps also are common for circulating liquid or magma through the supersaturating or crystallizing zones. The latter method is called *forced circulation*. One advantage of forced-circulation units with external heaters is that several identical units can be connected in multiple effect by using the vapor from one unit to heat the next in line. Systems of this kind are *evaporator-crystallizers*.

Vacuum Crystallizers

Most modern crystallizers fall in the category of vacuum units in which adiabatic evaporative cooling is used to create supersaturation. In its original and simplest form, such a crystallizer is a closed vessel in which a vacuum is maintained by a condenser, usually with the help of a steam-jet vacuum pump, or booster, placed between the crystallizer and the condenser. A warm saturated solution at a temperature well above the boiling point at the pressure in the crystallizer is fed to the vessel. A magma volume is maintained by controlling the level of the liquid and crystallizing solid in the vessel and the space above the magma used for release of vapor and elimination of entrainment. The feed solution cools spontaneously to the equilibrium temperature; since both the enthalpy of cooling and the enthalpy of crystallization appear as latent enthalpy of vaporization, a portion of the solvent evaporates. The supersaturation generated by both cooling and evaporation causes nucleation and growth. Product magma is drawn from the bottom of the crystallizer. The theoretical yield of crystals is proportional to the difference between the concentration of the feed and the solubility of the solute at equilibrium temperature.

The fig. 17.1 shows a modern continuous vacuum crystallizer with the conventional auxiliary units for feeding the unit and processing the product magma. The essential action of a single body is much like that of a single-effect evaporator, and in fact these units can be operated in multiple effect. The magma circulates from the cone bottom of the crystallizer body through a downpipe to a low-speed low- head circulating pump, passes upward through a vertical tubular heater with condensing steam in the shell, and thence into the body. The heated stream enters through a tangential inlet just below the level of the magma surface. This impacts a swirling motion to the magma, which facilitates flash evaporation and equilibrates the magam with the vapor through the action of an adiabatic flash.[4] The supersaturation thus generated provides the driving potential for nucleation and growth. The volume of the magma divided by the volumetric flow rate of magma through the system gives the time for growth.

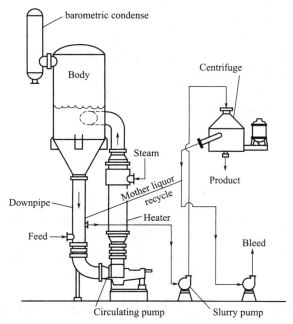

Fig. 17.1 continuous crystallizer

Feed solution enters the downpipe before the suction of the circulating pump. Mother liquor and crystals are drawn off through a discharge pipe positioned above the feed inlet in the downpipe. Mother liquor is separated from the crystals in a continuous centrifuge; the crystals are taken off as a product or for further processing and the mother liquor is recycled to the downpipe. Some of the mother liquor is bled from the system by a pump to prevent accumulation of impurities.

The simple form of vacuum crystallizer also has serious limitations from the standpoint of crystallization. Under the low pressure existing in the unit, the effect of static head on the boiling point is important; e.g., water at 45 °F has a vapor pressure of 0.30 in. Hg, which is a pressure easily obtainable by steam-jet boosters. A static head of 1ft increases the absolute pressure to 1.18 in. Hg, where the boiling point of water is 84 °F. Feed at this temperature would not flash if admitted at any level more than 1ft below the surface of the magma. Admission of the feed at a point where it does not flash is advantageous in controlling nucleation, but the feed has a tendency to short-circuit to the discharge without releasing its supersaturation.[5]

Because of the effect of static head, evaporation and cooling occur only in the liquid layer near the magma surface, and concentration and temperature gradients near the surface are formed. Also crystals tend to settle to the bottom of the crystallizer, where there may be little or no supersaturation. The crystallizer will not operate satisfactorily unless the magma is well agitated, to equalize concentration and temperature gradients and suspend the crystals. The simple vacuum crystallizer provides no good method for nucleation control, for classification, or for removal of excess nuclei and very small crystals.

From *Unit Operation of Chemical Engineering 4th edition*, by Warren L. Mccabe, et. al

New Words and Expressions

batchwise [bætʃwaiz]   *a.* 成批的
differentia [ˌdifəˈrenʃiə]   *n.* 差异，特异，种差，特殊性
differentiate [ˌdifəˈrenʃieit]   *vt.* 区分，区别，使分化，求……微分
supersaturation zone   过饱和区
segregate [ˈsegrigeit]   *vt.* 分凝，分异，成熟分裂时等位基因分离
category [ˈkætigəri]   *n.* 种类，部属，范畴
circulating pump   往复泵
swirl [swəːl]   *vt.* 旋动，使打旋，涡动，旋涡
volumetric [ˌvɔljuˈmetrik]   *a.* 测容量的，容量的
standpoint [ˈstændpɔint]   *n.* 立场观点

Notes

1. 句中 solubility curve of the solute 为溶解曲线，是物质溶解能力（溶解度）与温度的关系曲线。参考译文：产生过饱和的方法要视溶质的溶解曲线而行。

2. 其中 release 本意为"释放"，在这里为"解除"。参考译文：第一种技术中，我们称为循环液方法，让过饱和溶液通过正在生长的晶体的流化床，在流化床中因晶核形成和生长而解除了过饱和。

3. 参考译文：大多数结晶器利用搅拌促进晶体生长速度，防止过饱和溶液离析（这将引起过度成核），保持晶体在结晶区悬浮。句中三个动词不定式并列作为目的状语，并按过程的程序排列。

4. 参考译文：加热的流体进入糊状物中，引起糊状物产生旋涡，而这旋涡促进闪蒸作用。并且使糊状物在绝热闪蒸作用下达到蒸汽平衡。翻译时要搞清 this 指代的内容并将之译出。

5. 参考译文：在原料不会闪蒸处引入原料有利于控制成核，但这样的话，原料在未破解除过饱和时就会短路回到出口处。

Unit 18 Distillation

In practice, distillation may be carried out by either of two principal methods. The first method is based on the production of a vapor by boiling the liquid mixture to be separated and condensing the vapors without allowing any liquid to return to the still. There is then no reflux. The second method is based on the return of part of the condensate to the still under such conditions that this returning liquid is brought into intimate contact with the vapors on their way to the condenser. Either of these methods may be conducted as a continuous process or as a batch process.

Flash Distillation

Flash distillation consists of vaporizing a definite fraction of the liquid in such a way that the evolved vapor is in equilibrium with the residual liquid, separating the vapor from the liquid, and condensing the vapor.[1] Fig. 18.1 shows the elements of a flash-distillation plant. Feed is pumped by pump a through heater b, and the pressure is reduced through valve c. An intimate mixture of vapor and liquid enters the vapor separator d, in which sufficient time is allowed for the vapor and liquid portions to separate.[2] Because of the intimacy of contact of liquid and vapor before separation, the separated streams are in equilibrium. Vapor leaves through the line e and liquid through line g.

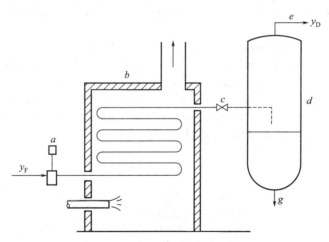

Fig. 18.1 Plant for flash distillation

Flash Distillation of Binary Mixtures

consider 1 mol of a two-component mixture fed to the equipment shown in Fig. 18.1. Let the concentration of the feed be x_f, in mole fraction of the more volatile component. Let f be the molal fraction of the feed that is vaporized and withdrawn continuously as vapor.[3] Then $1-f$ is the molal fraction of the feed that leaves continuously as liquid. Let y_D and x_B be the concentrations of the vapor and liquid, respectively. By a material balance for the more volatile component, based on 1 mol of feed, all of that component in the feed must leave in the two exit streams, or

$$x_F = f y_D + (1-f) x_B \qquad (18.1)$$

There are two unknowns in Eq (18.1), x_B and y_D. To use the equation a second relationship between the unknowns must be available. Such a relationship is provided by the equilibrium curve, as y_D and x_B are coordinates of a point on this curve. If x_B and y_D are replaced by x and y, respectively, Eq (18.1) can be written

$$y=-\frac{1-f}{f}x+\frac{x_F}{f} \qquad (18.2)$$

The fraction f is not fixed directly but depends on the enthalpy of the hot incoming liquid and the enthalpies of the vapor and liquid leaving the flash chamber. For a given feed condition, the fraction f can be increased by flashing to a lower pressure.

Eq(18.2) is the equation of a straight line with a slope of $-(1-f)/f$ and can be plotted on the equilibrium diagram. The coordinates of the intersection of the line and the equilibrium curve are $x=x_B$, and $y=y_D$. The intersection of this material-balance line and the diagonal $x=y$ can be used conveniently as a point on the line. letting $x=x_F$ in Eq. (18.2) gives:

$$y=-\frac{(1-f)}{f}x_F+\frac{x_F}{f}$$

from which $y = x_F = x$. The material-balance line crosses the diagonal at $x=x_F$ for all values of f.

Continuous Distillation with Reflux (Rectification)

Flash distillation is used most for separating components which boil at widely different temperatures. It is not effective in separating components of comparatble volativity, since then both the condensed vapor and residual liquid are far from pure. By many successive redistillations small amounts of some nearly pure components may finally be obtained, but this method is too inefficient for industrial distillations when nearly pure components are wanted. Modern methods used in both laboratory and plant apply the principle of rectification, which is described in this section.

Rectification on an Ideal Plate

Consider a single plate in a column or caseade of ideal plates. Assume that the plates are numbered serially from the top down and that the plate under consideration is the nth plate from the top.[4] It is shown diagrammatically in Fig. 18.2. Then the plate immediately above this plate is plate $n-1$, and that immediately below it is plate $n+1$. Subscripts are used on all quantities showing the point of origin of the quantity.

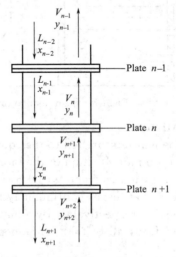

Fig. 18.2　material-balance diagram for plate n

Two fluid streams enter plate n, and two leave it. A stream of liquid, L_{n-1} mol/h, from plate $n-1$, and a stream of vapor, V_{n+1} mol/h, from plate $n+1$, are brought into intimate contact. A stream of vapor, V_n mol/h, rises to plate $n-1$, and a stream of liquid, L_n mol/h, descends to plate $n+1$. Since the vapor streams are the V phase, their concentrations are denoted by y, and since the liquid streams are the L phase, their concentrations are denoted by x. Then the concentrations of the streams entering and leaving the nth plate are

Vapor leaving plate, y_n
Liquid leaving plate, x_n
Vapor entering the plate, y_{n+1}
Liquid entering the plate, x_{n-1}

Fig. 18.3 shows the boiling-point diagram for the mixture being treated. The four concentrations given above are shown in this figure. By definition of an ideal plate, the vapor and liquid leaving plate n are in equilibrium, so x_n and y_n represent equilibrium concentrations. This is shown in Fig. 18.3. Since concentrations in both phases increase with the height of the column, x_{n-1} is greater than x_n and y_n is greater than y_{n+1}. Although the streams leaving the plate are in equilibrium, those entering it are not. This can be seen from Fig. 18.3. When the vapor from plate $n+1$ and the liquid from plate $n-1$ are brought into intimate contact, their concentrations tend to move toward an equilibrium state, as shown by the arrows in Fig. 18.3. Some of the more volatile component A is vaporized from the liquid, decreasing the liquid concentration from x_{n-1} to x_n; and some of the less volatile component B is condensed from the vapor, increasing the vapor concentration from y_{n+1} to y_n. Since the liquid streams are at their bubble points and the vapor streams at their dew points, the heat necessary to vaporize component A must be supplied by the heat released in the condensation of component B. Each plate in the cascade acts as an interchange apparatus in which component A is transferred to the vapor stream and component B to the liquid stream. Also, since the concentration of A in both liquid and vapor increases with column height, the temperature decreases, and the temperature of plate n is greater than that of plate $n-1$ and less than that of plate $n+1$.

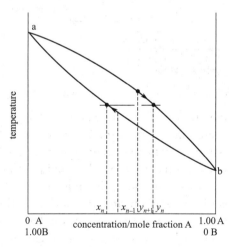

Fig. 18.3　boiling-point diagram showing rectification on ideal plate

Combination Rectification and Stripping

In distillation, the common distillation equipment cannot produce a nearly pure bottom product because the liquid in the still is not subjected to rectification. This limitation is removed by admitting the feed to a plate in the central portion of the column. Then the liquid feed flows down the column to the still, which in this type of plant is called the *reboiler*, and is subjected to rectification by the vapor rising from the reboiler. Since the liquid reaching the reboiler is stripped of component A, the bottom product can be nearly pure B.

A typical continuous fractionating column equipped with the necessary auxiliaries and containing rectifying and stripping sections is shown in Fig. 18.4. The column A is fed near its center with a definite flow of feed of definite concentration. Assume that the feed is a liquid at its boiling point. The action in the column is not dependent on this assumption, and other conditions of the feed will be discussed later. The plate on which the feed enters is called the feed plate. All plates above the feed plate constitute the rectifying section, and all plates below the feed, including the feed plate itself, constitute the stripping section. The feed flows down the stripping section to the bottom of the column, in which a definite level of liquid is maintained. Liquid flows by gravity to reboiler B. This is a steam-heated vaporizer which generates vapor and returns it to the bottom of the column. The vapor passes up the entire column. At one end of the reboiler is a weir. The bottom product is withdrawn from the pool of liquid on the downstream side of the weir, and flows through the cooler G. This cooler also preheats the feed by heat exchange with the hot bottoms.

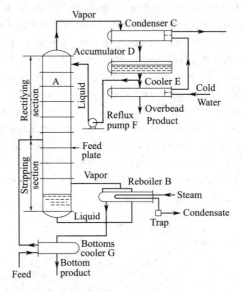

Fig. 18.4 continuous fractionating column with rectifying and stripping

The vapors rising through the rectifying section are completely condensed in condenser C, and the condensate is collected in accumulator D, in which a definite liquid level is maintained. Reflux pump F takes liquid from the accumulator and delivers it to the top plate of the tower. This liquid stream is called *reflux*. It provides the downflowing liquid in the rectifying section that is needed to act on the upflowing vapor. Without the reflux no rectification would occur in the rectifying section and the concentration of the overhead product would be no greater than that of the vapor rising from the feed plate. Condensate not picked up by the reflux pump is cooled in heat exchanger E, called the *product cooler*, and withdrawn as the overhead product.[5] If no azeotropes are encountered, both overhead and bottom products may be obtained in any desired purity if enough plates and adequate reflux are provided.

The plant shown in Fig. 18.4 is often simplified for small installations. In place of the reboiler, a heating coil may be placed in the bottom of the column and generate vapor from the pool of liquid there. The condenser is often placed above the top of the column and the reflux pump and accumulator omitted. Reflux then returns to the top plate by gravity. A special valve, called a *reflux splitter*, may be used to control the rate of reflux return. The remainder of the condensate forms the overhead product.

From *Distillation Operation*, by Henry Z. Kister

New Words and Expressions

distill [dis'til]　　*vt.* 用蒸馏法提取，蒸馏
still [stil]　　*n.* 蒸馏室，蒸馏器　*v.* 蒸馏
flash distillation　闪蒸
fraction ['frækʃən]　　*n.* 小部分，片段，馏分，级分
valved [vælvd]　　*a.* 有阀的
intimacy ['intiməsi]　　*n.* 密切，熟悉
vaporize ['veipəraiz]　　*vt/vi.* （使）蒸发，（使）汽化
slope [sləup]　　*n.* 倾斜　*v.* 倾斜
diagonal [dai'ægənl]　　*a.* 对角线的，对顶的，斜的　*n.* 对角线，对顶线
rectification [ˌrektifi'keiʃən]　　*n.* 精馏，矫正，纠正
condensation [ˌkɔnden'seiʃən]　　*n.* 冷凝
interchange [ˌintə'tʃeindʒ]　　*vt.* 内部交换，交替发生　*n.* 交换，交替
strip [strip]　　*vt.* 剥去，剥夺，使去色（化），通过蒸馏去除挥发组分
reboiler [ri'bɔilə]　　*n.* 再沸器
fractionating column　分馏柱
rectify ['rektifai]　　*vt.* 精馏，矫正，纠正
accumulator [ə'kju:mjuleitə]　　*n.* 收集器，蓄电器，存储器
overhead ['əuvəhed]　　*n.* 塔顶馏出物的　*a.* 高出地面的
azeotrope [ə'zi:ətrəup]　　*n.* 共沸混合物

Notes

1. 本句中 vaporizing, separating, condensing 均为 consist of 的并列宾语，参考译文：闪蒸包括下列步骤：蒸发液体中特定的馏分，使蒸气同残液平衡；从液相中分离气相；冷凝气相。

2. 译文中将被动改为主动态，intimate 是"亲密的，熟悉的"的意思，此处为"混合充分均匀"。参考译文：气相液相混合气充分均匀的混合物进入到气体分离器中，并在那里停留足够时间使气液两相分离。

3. 此为定义的又一方式，适用于阐述公式时字母的含义。参考译文：用 f 代表被蒸发并被以气体形式连续带走的原料的摩尔分数。

4. 科技英语中给出假定多用 assume, suppose, with the assumption of, if 等。参考译文：假定塔板都按照顺序由上而下用数字标号，也假定我们研究的板是上数第 n 块板。

5. 参考译文：未被回流泵带走的冷凝液在热交换器 E 中冷却，并作为塔顶产物被带走。其中热交换器又称为产品冷凝器。也可译为：未被回流泵带走的冷凝液在热交换器 E（又称为产品冷凝器）中冷却，并作为塔顶产物被带走。用括号来补充说明交换器的情况，或在句尾解释一下。

Exercises

Ⅰ. Comprehension

1. In practice, distillation may be carried out by either of two principal methods. The following which method is not involved.
　A. the production of a vapor without allowing any liquid to return to the still
　B. the return of part of the condensate to the still
　C. boiling the liquid mixture to be separated and condensing the vapors
　D. A and C

2. The elements of a flash-distillation plant consist of the following except _____.
A. a pump   B. a heater   C. a vapor separator   D. reflux divider

3. By definition of an ideal plate, the vapor and liquid leaving plate n are in equilibrium, so x_n and y_n represent equilibrium concentrations.
A. x_n and y_n represent liquid and vapor leaving plate concentrations, respectively.
B. x_n and y_n represent liquid and vapor entering plate concentrations, respectively.
C. x_n and y_n represent liquid leaving plate and vapor entering plate concentrations, respectively.
D. x_n and y_n represent liquid entering plate and vapor leaving plate concentrations, respectively.

4. In distillation, the common distillation equipment cannot produce a nearly pure bottom product because _____.
A. the liquid in the still is not subjected to rectification
B. the common distillation equipment can not provide enough energy
C. the common distillation equipment can not control the rate of vaporization
D. the common distillation equipment can not be cleared

II. Fill in the blanks with the phrases given below

in relation to   in a number of   in the end   a messy way
in the case of   lead to   in order to

(1) _____ discuss this process we require a temperature-composition diagram.

(2) The principal one is that, because the vapour phase is stable at high temperatures, the new diagram is upside-down _____ the pressure diagram.

(3) Using the diagram involves the same kind of thinking as _____ the vapour pressure diagram.

(4) Repeating the process leads to a condensate which _____ will be virtually pure volatile component.

(5) Nevertheless, _____ very important cases the deviations from ideality are marked and sometimes completely upset the distillation process.

(6) The deviation from ideality are not always so strong as to _____ a hump or a trough in the boiling point curves, but when they do there are important consequences for distillation.

(7) Steam distillation also provides _____ of determining relative molar masses.

III. Fill in the blanks with the proper form of the word given at the end of the sentence

(1) In a distillation experiment the vapour is withdrawn and _____. (condense)

(2) If the vapour in the last example is _____ off and completely condensed, then the first drop gives a sample of liquid of composition a_3 which is richer in the more volatile component than the original mixture. (draw)

(3) Furthermore, the liquid _____ is richer in the less volatile component, and so the boiling point shifts to higher values. (remain)

(4) Fractional distillation repeats the _____ and condensation cycle several times. (boil)

(5) The discussion above applies to many real _____. (mix)

(6) For such mixtures, the excess Gibbs function is negative (more _____ to mixing than ideal). (favour)

(7) Boiling point curves showing minima indicate that the mixture is _____ relative to the ideal, and so the molecular interactions are unfavorable. (destabilize)

IV. Answer following questions

An industrial process led to the production of mixture of toluene (T) and n-octane (O), and the vapour pressure of the mixture was investigated with a view to designing a separation plant. The following temperature-composition data were obtained at 760 mmHg: x is the mole fraction in the liquid and y the mole fraction in the vapour at equilibrium.

V. Questions for discussion
(1) Give a general account of the distillation operation.
(2) Is there any difference between flash distillation and rectification?

VI. Translate the following into Chinese:

Primary design is an extremely wide topic, encompassing vapor-liquid equilibrium, reflux-stages relationship, stage-to-stage calculations, unique features of multicomponent distillation, tray and packing efficiencies, scale-up, column diameter determination, flow patterns, type of tray, and size and material of packing. This topic occupies the bulk of most distillation arts and perhaps represents the bulk of our present distillation know-how.

Reading Material

Typical Distillation Equipment

A plant for continuous distillation is shown in Fig. 18.5 Reboiler A is fed continuously with the liquid mixture to be distilled. The liquid is converted partially into vapor by heat transferred from the heating surface B. The vapor formed in the reboiler is richer in low boiler than the unvaporized liquid, but unless the two components differ greatly in volatility, the vapor contains substantial quantities of both components, and if it were condensed, the condensate would be far from pure.[1] To increase the concentration of low boiler in the vapor, the vapor stream from the still is brought into intimate countercurrent contact with a descending stream of boiling liquid in the column, or tower, C. This liquid must be rich enough in low boiler so that there is mass transfer of the low boiler from the liquid to the vapor at each stage of the column. Such a liquid can be obtained simply by condensing the overhead vapors and returning some of the liquid to the top of the column. This return liquid is called *reflux*. The use of reflux increases the purity of the overhead product, but not without some cost, since the vapor generated in the reboiler must provide both reflux and overhead product, and this energy cost is a large part of the total cost of separation by distillation.

The reflux entering the top of the column is often at the boiling point; but if it is cold, it is almost immediately heated to its boiling point by the vapor. Throughout the rest of the column, the liquid and vapor are at their boiling and condensing temperatures, respectively, and the temperatures increase on going down the column because of the increase in high boiler concentration, and in some cases, because of increase in pressure.

Enrichment of the vapor occurs at each stage because the vapor coming to a stage has a lower concentration of the low boiler than the vapor that would be in equilibrium with the liquid fed to that stage. For example, considering the top stage, the vapor coming to this stage is less rich than the overhead product, and the reflux, which has the same composition as the product, has an *equilibrium vapor composition* which is even richer than the product. Therefore, vapor passing through the top stage will be enriched in low boiler at the expense of the reflux liquid. This makes the reflux poorer in low boiler, but if the flow rates have been adjusted correctly, the liquid passing down to the second stage will be still able to enrich the lower quality vapor coming up to the second stage. Then at all stages in the column, some low boiler diffuses from the liquid into the vapor phase, and there is a corresponding diffusion of high boiler from the vapor to the liquid. The heat of vaporization of the low boiler is supplied by the heat of condensation of the high boiler, and the total flow rate of vapor up the column is nearly constant.

The enrichment of the vapor stream as it passes through the column in contact with reflux is called *rectification*. It is immaterial where the reflux originates, provided its concentration in low boiler is sufficiently great to give the desired product.[2] The usual source of reflux is the condensate leaving condenser D. Part of the condensate is withdrawn as the product, and the remainder returned to the top of the column. Reflux is sometimes provided by partial condensation of the overhead vapor; the reflux then differs in composition from the vapor leaving as overhead product. Provided an azeotrope is not formed, the vapor reaching the condenser can be brought as close to complete purity as desired by using a tall tower and a large reflux.

From the reboiler, liquid is withdrawn which contains most of the high boiling component, because little of this component escapes with the overhead product unless that product is an azeotrope. The liquid from the reboiler, which is called the *bottom product* or *bottoms*, is not nearly pure, however, because there is no provision in the equipment of Fig. 18.5 for rectifying this stream. A method for obtaining nearly pure bottom product by rectification is described later.

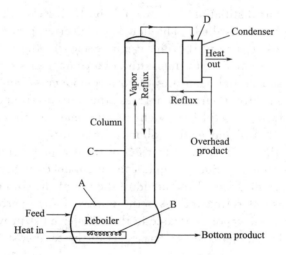

Fig. 18.5 reboiler with fractionating column
A: reboiler; B: heating surface; C: column; D: condenser

The column shown in Fig 18.5 often contains a number of perforated plates or trays, stacked one above the other. A cascade of such trays is called a *sieve-plate column*. It consists of a horizontal tray A carrying a downpipe, or downcomer C, the top of which acts as a weir, and a number of holes B. The holes are all of the same size, usually 0.25~0.5 in. in diameter. The downcomer D from the tray above reaches nearly to the tray A. This construction leads to the following flow of liquid and vapor. Liquid flows from plate to plate down the column, passing through downcomer D and across the plates. The weir maintains a minimum depth of liquid on the tray, nearly independent of the rate of flow of liquid. Vapor flows upward from tray to tray through the perforations. Except at very low vapor rates, well below the normal operating range, the vapor velocity through the perforations is sufficient to prevent leakage or "weeping" of the liquid through the holes. The vapor is subdivided by the holes into many small bubbles and passes in intimate contact through the pool of liquid on the tray.[3] Because of the action of the vapor bubbles, the liquid is actually a boiling, frothy mass. Above the froth and below the next tray is fog from collapsing bubbles. This fog for the most part settles back into the liquid, but some is entrained by the vapor and carried to the plate above. Sieve-plate columns are representative of an entire class of equipment called *plate columns*.

From *Distillation Operation by Henry Z. Kister*

New Words and Expressions

boiling point　沸点
enrich [in'ritʃ]　*vt.* 使浓缩，加浓，富集
immaterial [ˌiməˈtiəriəl]　*a.* 非物质的，无形的，不重要的
withdrawal [wiðˈdrɔːəl]　*n.* 收回，取回，提款，撤销
cascade [kæsˈkeid]　*n.* 阶式蒸发器
sieve-plate column　筛板柱
weep [wiːp]　*vt.* 渗出液体，（水珠的）渗出滴下
subdivide [ˈsʌbdiˈvaid]　*vt.* 区分，把……细分，把……分成几份
frothy [ˈfrɔθi]　*a.* 起泡沫的，多泡沫的
froth [frɔθ, frɔːθ]　*n.* 泡沫，起泡，使（啤酒）起泡沫

Notes

1. 参考译文：再沸器中形成的蒸气中低沸物的浓度比未蒸发的液体大，但是蒸气中两种组分的含量都很大，除非两组分挥发性相差很大，否则蒸气冷凝后，产物一点也不纯。

2. 参考译文：如果回流中低沸物的浓度足够大到能给出符合要求的产物时，那么回流来自于何处就不重要了。

3. 参考译文：蒸气被筛板眼细分成很多小泡泡，以紧密接触的方式通过塔板上的液体层。

Unit 19 Solvent Extraction

General Discussion

Liquid-liquid extraction is a technique in which a solution (usually aqueous) is brought into contact with a second solvent (usually organic), essentially immiscible with the first, in order to bring about a transfer of one or more solutes into the second solvent.[1] The separations that can be performed are simple, clean, rapid, and convenient. In many cases separation may be effected by shaking in a separatory funnel for a few minutes. The technique is equally applicable to trace level and large amounts of materials.

In the case of inorganic solutes we are concerned largely with samples in aqueous solution so that it is necessary to produce substances, such as neutral metal chelates and ion-association complexes, which are capable of extraction into organic solvents. For organic solutes, however, the extraction system may sometimes involve two immiscible organic solvents rather than the aqueous-organic type of extraction.

The technique of liquid-liquid extraction has, of course, been widely used to separate the components of organic systems; in particular, solvent extraction may be employed to effect a "clean-up" and to achieve concentration of the solutes of interest prior to analysis. This is illustrated by the clean-up steps which have been used for the analysis of organochlorine pesticides, at the 0.1μg/g level, in animal fats, and dairy products. In one such procedure the solution of animal fat in hexane (25mL) is extracted with three successive portions (10mL) of dimethylformamide (DMF) saturated with hexane. The combined DMF extracts are washed with hexane (10mL) saturated with DMF to remove any remaining trace of fat; after separation of the hexane it is equilibrated with further DMF (10mL) to reduce loss of pesticide residue. The pesticide compounds are finally partitioned back into clean hexane after adding water to the combined DMF extracts. The hexane layer is used for the quantitative analysis of the extracted pesticide residues using gas chromatography with an electron-capture detector. It is of interest to note that the extraction procedure involves two organic phases (i.e. no aqueous phase is involved) and that miscibility is minimised by the saturating each solvent with the other. Extraction procedures for organic species, however, do not in general possess the same degree of selectivity as may be achieved for metal-containing systems, and the chief analytical application of solvent extraction is for the determination of metals as minor and trace constituents in various inorganic and organic materials.

Although solvent extraction has been used predominantly for the isolation and pre-concentration of a single chemical species prior to its determination, it may also be applied to the extraction of groups of metals or classes of organic compounds, prior to their determination by techniques such as atomic absorption or chromatography.[2]

To understand the fundamental principles of extraction, the various terms used for expressing the effectiveness of a separation must first be considered. For a solute A distributed between two immiscible phases a and b, the Nernst Distribution (or Partition) Law states that, provided its molecular state is the same in both liquids and that the temperature is constant:

$$\frac{\text{concentration of solute in solvent a}}{\text{concentration of solute in solvent b}} = \frac{[A]_a}{[B]_b} = K_D$$

where K_D is a constant known as the **distribution** (or **partition**) **coefficient**. The law, as stated, is not themodynamically rigorous (e.g. it takes no account of the activities of the various species, and for this reason would be expected to apply only in very dilute solutions, where the ratio of the activities approaches unity), but is a useful approximation. The law in its simple form does not apply when distributing species undergoes dissociation or association in either phase. In the practical applications of solvent extraction we are interested in primarily in the fraction of the total solute in one or other phase, quite regardless of its mode of dissociation, association, or interaction with other dissolved species. It is convenient to introduce the term distribution ratio D (or extraction coefficient E):

$$D=(C_A)_a/(C_A)_b$$

where the symbol C_A denotes the concentration of A in all its forms as determined analytically.

A problem often encountered in practice is to determine what is the most efficient method for removing a substance quantitatively from solution. It can be shown that if VmL of, say, an aqueous solution containing x_0 g of a solute be extracted n times with vmL portions of a given solvent, then the weight of solute x_n remaining in the water layer is given by the expression:

$$X_n = X_0 \left(\frac{DV}{DV+v}\right)^n$$

where D is the distribution ratio between water and the given solvent. It follows therefore, that the best method of extraction with a given volume of extracting liquid is to employ the liquid in several portions rather than to utilise the whole quantity in a single extraction.

This may be illustrated by the following example. Suppose that 50mL of water containing 0.1g of iodine are shaken with 25mL of carbon tetrachoride. The distribution coefficient of iodine between water and carbon tetrachloride at the ordinary laboratory temperature is 1/85, i.e. at equilibrium the iodine concentration in the aqueous layer is 1/85 of that in the carbon tetrachloride layer. The weight of iodine remaining in the aqueous layer after one extraction with 25mL, and also after three extractions with 8.33mL of the solvent, can be calculated by application of the above formula. In the first case, if x_1 g of iodine remains in the 50mL of water, its concentration is $x_1/50$ g/mL; the concentration in the carbon tetrachloride layer will be $(0.1-x_1)/25$ g/mL.

Hence:

$$\frac{x_1/50}{(0.1-x_1)/25} = \frac{1}{85} \text{ or } x_1 = 0.00230 \text{ (g)}$$

The concentration in the aqueous layer after three extractions with 8.33mL of carbon tetrachloride is given by:

$$x_3 = 0.1 \left[\frac{(1/85) \times 50}{(50/85)+8.33}\right]^3 = 0.0000287 \text{ (g)}$$

The extraction may, therefore, be regarded as virtually complete.

If we confine our attention to the distribution of a solute A between water and an organic solvent, we may write the percentage extraction $E_\%$ as:

$$E_\% = \frac{100[A]_0 V_0}{[A]_0 V_0 + [A]_w V_w} = \frac{100D}{D+(V_w/V_0)}$$

where V_0 and V_w represent the volumes of the organic and aqueous phases respectively. Thus, the percentage of extraction varies with the volume ratio of the two phases and the distribution coefficient.

If the solution contains two solutes A and B, it often happens that under the conditions favoring the complete extraction of A, some B is extracted as well. The effectiveness of separation increases with the magnitude of the **separation coefficient** or **factor** β, which is related to the individual distribution ratios as follows:

$$\beta = \frac{[A]_0/[B]_0}{[A]_w/[B]_w} = \frac{[A]_0/[A]_w}{[B]_0/[B]_w} = \frac{D_A}{D_B}$$

If $D_A=10$ and $D_B=0.1$, a single extraction will remove 90.9 percent of A and 9.1 percent of

B, (ratio 10 : 1); a second extraction of the same aqueous phase will bring the total amount of A extracted up to 99.2 percent, but increases that of B to 17.4 percent (ratio 5.7 : 1). More complete extraction of A thus involves an increased contamination by B. Clearly, when one of the distribution ratios is relatively large and the other very small, almost complete separation can be quickly and easily achieved. If the separation factor is large but the smaller distribution ratio is of sufficient magnitude that extraction of both components occurs, it is necessary to resort to special technique to suppress the extraction of the unwanted component.

Factors Favoring Solvent Extraction

It is well known that hydrated inorganic salts tend to be more soluble in water than in organic solvents such as benzene, chloroform, etc., whereas organic substances tend to be more soluble in organic solvents than in water unless they incorporate a sufficient number of hydroxyl, sulphonic, or other hydrophilic groupings. In solvent extraction analysis of metals we are concerned with methods by which the water solubility of inorganic cations may be masked by interaction with appropriate (largely organic) reagents; this will in effect remove some or all of the water molecules associated with the metal ion to which the water solubility is due.

Ionic compounds would not be expected to extract into organic solvents from aqueous solution because of the large loss in electrostatic solvation energy which would occur. The most obvious way to make an aqueous ionic species extractable is to neutralize its charge. This can be done by formation of a neutral metal chelate complex or by ion association; the larger and more hydrophobic the resulting molecular species the better will be its extraction.

In chelation complexes (sometimes called inner complexes when uncharged) the central metal ion coordinates with a polyfunctional organic base to form a stable ring compound; e.g. copper (II) "acetylacetonate" or iron (III) "cupferrate":

The factors which influence the extraction method, especially those have significant importance on chelate effect should be listed here:

1. *the basic strength of the chelating group*. The stability of the chelate complexes formed by a given metal ion generally increase with increasing basic strength of the chelating agent, as measured by the pK_a values.

2. *The nature of the donor atoms in the chelating agent*. Ligands which contain donor atoms of the soft-base type form their most stable complexes with the relatively small group of class B metal ions (i.e. soft acids) and are thus more selective reagents. This is illustrated by the reagent diphenylthiocarbazone (dithizone) used for the solvent extraction of metal ions such as Pd^{2+}, Ag^+, Hg^{2+}, Cu^{2+}, Bi^{3+}, Pb^{2+}, and Zn^{2+}.

3. *Ring size*. Five or six-membered conjugated chelate rings are most stable since these have minimum strain. The functional groups of the ligand must be so situated that they per-

mit the formation of a stable ring.

4. *Reasonance and steric effects*. The stability of chelate structures is enhanced by contributions of resonance structures of the chelate ring; thus copper acetylacetonate has greater stability than the copper chelate of salicylaldoxime. A good example of steric hindrance is given by 2, 9-dimethylpheanthroline (neocuproin), which does not form a complex with iron (Ⅱ) as does the unsubstituted phenanthroline; this hindrance is at a minimum in the tetrahedral grouping of the reagent molecules about a univalent tetracoordinated ion such as that of copper (Ⅰ). A nearly specific reagent for copper is thus available.

The choice of a satisfactory chelating agent for a particular separation should, of course, take all the above factors into account. The critical influence of pH on the solvent extractions of metal chelates will be discussed later.

From *Quantitative Chemical Analysis* 5th by G. H. Jeffery et. al

New Words and Expressions

extraction [iks'trækʃən] n. 萃取，提取，摘要
chelate ['ki:leit] a. 螯合的，螯形的
ion-association   离子缔和络合物
dimethylformamide [ˌdaiˌmeθilˌfɔː'mæmid] n. 二甲基甲酰胺
residue ['rezidjuː] n. 残余，剩余，渣滓
chromatography [ˌkrəumə'tɔgrəfi] n. 层析，色谱法
electron-capture detector   电子捕获检测器
miscibility [ˌmisi'biliti] n. 溶混性
predominant [pri'dɔminənt] ad. 占优势的
approximation [əˌprɔksi'meiʃən] n. 近似
distribution coefficient   分配系数
carbon tetrachloride   四氯化碳
separation coefficient   分离系数
chloroform ['klɔ(ː)rəfɔːm] n. 氯仿
hydrophilic [ˌhaidrəu'filik] a. 亲水的
extract [iks'trækt] vt. 萃取，提取，摘选
neutralize ['njuːtrəlaiz; (US) nuː-] vt. 使中立，使中和
hydrophobic [ˌhaidrəu'fəubik] a. 恐水的，狂犬病的
chelation [kiː'leiʃən] n. 螯合，螯合物
polyfunctional [ˌpɔli'fʌŋkʃənəl] a. 多功能的
acetylacetonate [ˌæsiti'læsitəuˌneit]   乙酰丙酮盐
steric ['stiərik, 'sterik] a. 空间的，位的

Notes

1. 参考译文：在液液萃取技术中，溶液（通常为水溶液）同另一种溶剂混合（通常为有机溶剂），此溶剂本质上与前一种溶液中的溶剂不混溶，然后用此溶剂将一种或多种溶质转移到这种溶剂中去。翻译时，可将主句"liquid-liquid extraction is a technique"转化为介词短语。

2. 参考译文：尽管溶剂萃取一直主要用于分析单一化学物质之前此物质的分离和预富集，它也应用在使用诸如原子吸收法、色谱法等技术来分析金属或有机化合物类别之前对这些物质的萃取。

Exercises

I. Comprehension

1. The following is ture for liquid-liquid extraction separations except ____.
   A. rapid   B. convenient   C. cheap   D. expensive

2. Ionic compounds would not be expected to extract into organic solvents from aqueous solution because of ____.
   A. the large loss in electrostatic solvation energy
   B. the insolubility of ionic compounds
   C. the hydrophilicity of ionic compounds
   D. the electricity of ionic compounds

3. The factors which influence the extraction method, especially those have significant importance on chelate effect should be listed as below except ____.
   A. the basic strength of the chelating group   B. ring size
   C. the nature of the donor atoms in the chelating agent   D. the polarisability

4. The Nernst Distribution law, as stated, is not themodynamically rigorous, due to the following causes except ____.
   A. it takes no account of the activities of the various species
   B. it is a useful approximation   C. it is too simple
   D. its simple form does not apply when distributing species undergoes dissociation or association in either phase

II. Translate the following words into Chinese.

1. solvent extraction
2. liquid-liquid extraction
3. aqueous solution
4. atomic absorption
5. concentration
6. hydrated inorganic salt

III. Fill in the blanks with the phrases given below.

available for	applied to	such as	variety of
with respect to	in spite of	compete with	close to
more efficient			

(1) Although PLE uses the same aqueous and organic solvents as traditional extraction methods, it makes ____ use of them.

(2) In this review, it will be discussed experimental data on supercritical fluid extraction (SFE) from solid substratum ____ natural products, using CO_2 as solvent.

(3) Natural extracts do not ____ synthetic products with respect to cost.

(4) Therefore, it is only meaningful to compare SFE extracts, which can get very ____ the natural resource they came from, with extracts prepared by other extractive techniques, such as hydrodistillation (HD) for volatile oils, or any other low pressure solvent extraction (LPSE) process, ____ enfleurage, leaching, decoction, elutriation, elution, etc.

(5) ____ the importance of particle size on the SFE kinetics, as can be appreciated from the works of, and of the ____ sizes employed, as shown in Table 1, large extraction vessels will not operate properly with very fine particles.

(6) Therefore, little room is ____ optimizing the process ____ the particle size diameter, giving us few choices for this parameter.

IV. Fill in the blanks with the proper form of the word given at the end of the sentence.

(1) After the size and the geometry of the ____ are established, the solvent to feed ratio and the mass transfer rate must be estimated. (extract)

(2) It is mandatory to recognize that this is an extremely ____ assumption, because it neglects raw material agglomeration and fluid channelling, pressure drop increase. (simple)

(3) Two very important information for process design can be obtained from ____ scale SFE extractors: the process temperature and pressure. (analyse)

(4) Nonetheless, any other inference ____ to kinetics should be avoided, because they will not be reproducible in larger vessels. (relate)

(5) ____ experimental data obtained in screening SFE units are listed in Table 2. (addition)

V. Translate the following into English

(1) *Paragraph*

液液萃取是工业和实验室中常用的一种分离方法。某种金属离子和有机溶剂形成螯合物。此螯合物溶于有机溶剂而不溶于水。事实上它在有机溶剂和水中存在一个分配系数。在两种溶液中溶解能力的差异可使此种金属离子从一相转移到另一相起到了分离或富集的作用。常用操作是：将溶液及有机相在分液漏斗中充分混合，剧烈摇动，然后静置分层，即可萃取。当然萃取前提是待萃取技术的对象在不同的两相中有合适的分配系数。

(2) *Words*

电子捕获检测器　　　螯合络合物　　　分配系数　　　螯合试剂
离子缔和络合物　　　共轭螯合环　　　动物脂肪　　　气相色谱
有机氯杀虫剂　　　共振结构　　　2,9-二乙基甲酰胺位阻

VI. Calculation

(1) If you have a 0.1mol/L solution of Cd^{2+}, which should you add, NH_3 or CN^-, to reduce the Cd^{2+} ion concentration to the smallest possible value? Formation constants for complex ions of Cd^{2+} are as follows: 1.0×10^7 for $[Cd(NH_3)_4]^{2+}$; 1.3×10^{17} for $[Cd(CN)_4]^{2-}$.

(2) Copper (I) is best isolated in the form of complex ions. If you have a 0.015mol/L solution of $[CuCl_2]^-$, what is the concentration of Cu^+ (aq) and Cl^- (aq)?

(3) It is known that solution A and B are immiscible and the partition coefficient of A in B is 420. There is a solution with A's concentration 0.1mol/L 100mL. If B 100mL extracts A solute from the solution of A three times, how much A will be left in the solution?

Reading Material

The Application of Extraction

This section provides a brief review of a number of chelating and other extraction reagents, as well as some organic solvents, with special interest as to their selective extraction properties. The handbook of Cheng *et, al.* should be consulted for a more detailed account of organic analytical reagents.

Acetylacetone (pentane-2,4-dione), $CH_3COCH_2COCH_3$ Acetylacetone is a colourless mobile liquid, b. p. 139℃, which is sparingly soluble in water (0.17g/mL at 25℃) and miscible with many organic solvents. It is useful both as a solution (in carbon tetrachloride, choroform, benzene, xylene, etc) and as the pure liquid. The compound is a β-diketone and forms well-defined chelates with over 60 metals. Many of the chelates (acetylacetonates) are soluble in organic solvents, and the solubility is of the order of grams per litre, unlike that of most analytically used chelates, so that macro- as well as micro-scale separations are possible.[1] The selectivity can be increased by using EDTA as a masking agent. The use of acetylacetone as both solvent and extractant [e. g. for Al, Be, Ce, Co (III), Ga, Fe, In, U (VI), etc.] offers several advantages over its use in solution in carbon tetrachloride, etc.: extraction may be carried out at a lower pH than otherwise feasible because of the higher reagent concentration; and often the solubility of the chelate is greater in acetylacetone than in many organic solvents. The solvent generally used is carbon tetrachloride; the organic layer is heavier than water.

An interesting application is the separation of cobalt and nickel: neither Co (II) nor Ni (II) forms extractable chelates, but Co (III) chelate is extractable; extraction is therefore possible following oxidation.

Thenoyltrifluoroacetone (TTA), $C_4H_3SCOCH_2COCF_3$. This is a crystalline solid. m. p. 43°C. It is, of course, a β-diketone, and the trifluoromethyl group increases the acidity of the enol form so that extractions at low pH values are feasible. The reactivity of TTA is similar to that of acetylacetone: it is generally used as a 0.1~0.5mol/L solution in benzene or toluene. The difference in extraction behaviour of hafnium and zirconium, and also among lanthanides and actinides, is especially noteworthy.

Other fluorinated derivatives of acetylacetone are trifluoroacetylacetone ($CF_3COCH_2COCH_3$) and hexafluoroacetylacetone ($CF_3COCH_2COCF_3$), which form stable volatile chelates with aluminium, beryllium, chromium (III) and a number of other metal ions. These reagents have consequently been used for the solvent extraction of such metal ions, with subsequent separation and analysis by gas chromatography.[2]

8- Hydroxylquinoline (oxine). Oxine is a versatile organic reagent and forms chelates with many metallic ions. The chelates of doubly and triply charged metal ions have the general formulae M $(C_9H_6ON)_2$ and M $(C_9H_6ON)_3$; the oxinates of the metals of higher charge may differ somewhat in composition, e. g. Ce $(C_9H_6ON)_4$; Th $(C_9H_6ON)_4 \cdot (C_9H_7ON)$; $WO_2(C_9H_6ON)_2$; $MoO_2(C_9H_6ON)_2$; $U_3O_6(C_9H_6ON)_6 \cdot (C_9H_7ON)$. Oxine is generally used as a 1 percent (0.07mol/L) solution in chloroform, but concentrations as high as 10 percent are advantageous in some cases (e. g. for strontium).

Some Practical Considerations

Solvent extraction is generally employed in analysis to separate a solute (or solutes) of interest from substances which interfere in the ultimate quantitative analysis of the material; sometimes the interfering solutes are extracted selectively. Solvent extraction is also used to concentrate a species which in aqueous solution is too dilute to be analyzed.

The choice of solvent for extraction is governed by the following considerations:

1. A high distribution ratio for the solute and a low distribution ratio for undesirable impurities.

2. Low solubility in the aqueous phase.

3. Sufficiently low viscosity and sufficient density difference from the aqueous phase to avoid the formation of emulsions.

4. Low toxicity and flammability.

5. Ease of recovery of solute from the solvent for subsequent analytical processing. Thus the b. p. of the solvent and the ease of stripping by chemical reagents merit attention when a choice is possible.

Sometimes mixed solvents may be used to improve the above properties. Salting-out agents may also improve extractability.

Extraction Extraction may be accomplished in either a batch operation or a continuous operation. Batch extraction, the simplest and most widely used method, is employed where a large distribution ratio for the desired separation is readily obtainable. A small number of batch extractions readily remove the desired component completely and may be carried out in a simple separatory funnel. The two layers are shaken in the separatory funnel until equilibrium is attained, after which they are allowed to settle completely before separating. The extraction and separation should be performed at constant temperature, since the distribution ratio as well as the volumes of the solvent are influenced by temperature changes. It must be born in mind that too violent agitation of the extraction mixture often serves no useful purpose: simple repeated inversions of the vessel suffice to give equilibrium in a relatively few inversions.[3] If droplets of aqueous phase are entrained in the organic extract it is possible to remove them by filtering the extract through a dry filter paper: the filter paper should be washed several times with fresh organic solvent.

When the distribution ratio is low, continuous methods of extraction are used. This procedure makes use of a continuous flow of immiscible solvent through the solution; if the solvent is volatile, it is recycled by distillation and condensation and is dispersed in the aqueous phase by means of a sintered glass disc or equivalent device.[4] Apparatus is a available for effecting such continuous extraction with automatic return of the volatilised solvent.

Determination of Boron Using Ferroin

Discussion: The method is based upon the complexation of boron as the bis (salicylato) borate (III) anion (A), (borodisalicylate), and the solvent extraction into chloroform of the ion-association complex formed with the ferroin.

$$(A) \left[\left(\begin{array}{c} \text{salicylato structure} \end{array} \right)_2 B \right]^-$$

The intensity of the colour of the extract due to ferroin is observed spectrophotometrically and may be related by calibration to the boron content of the sample.

The method has been applied to the determination of boron in river water and sewage, the chief sources of interference being copper (II) and zinc ions, and anionic detergents. The latter interfere by forming ion-association complexes with ferroin which are extracted by chloroform: this property may, however, be utilized for the joint determination of boron and anionic detergents by the one procedure. The basis of this joint determination is that the ferroin-anionic detergent complex may be immediately extracted into chloroform, whereas the formation of the borodisalicylate anion from boric acid and salicylate requires a reaction time of one hour prior to extraction using ferroin. The absorbance of the chloroform extract obtained after zero minutes thus gives a measure of the anionic detergent concentration, whereas the absorbance of the extract after a one-hour reaction period corresponds to the amount of boron plus anionic detergent present. Interference due to copper (II) ions may be eliminated by masking with EDTA.

Reagents *Sulphuric acid solution.* 0.05 mol/L.

Sodium hudroxide solution, 0.1 mol/L.

Sodium salicylate solution, 10 percent (w/v)

EDTA solution 1 percent (w/v). Use the disodium salt of EDTA.

Ferroin solution, 2.5×10^{-2} mol/L. Dissolve 0.695g of iron (II) sulphate heptahydrate and 1.485g of 1, 10-phenanthroline hydrate in 100mL of distilled water.

Boric acid solution. 2.5×10^{-4} mol/L. Dissolve 61.8 mg of boric acid in 1 L of distilled water; dilute 250mL of this solution to 1L to give the standard boric acid solution.

Use analytical reagent grade materials whenever possible and store the solutions in polythene bottles.

Procedure (a) ***Zero-minutes Reaction Time*** Neutralise a measured volume of the sample containing 1~2mg/L of boron with sodium hydroxide or sulphuric acid (0.05mol/L) to a pH of 5.5 (use a pH meter). Note the change in volume and hence calculate the volume correction factor to be applied to the final result. Measure 100mL of the neutralized sample solution into a flask, add 10mL of 10 percent sodium salicylate solution and 17.5mL of 0.05mol/L sulphuric acid, and mix the solutions thoroughly. Adjust the pH of the solution to pH 6 to 7 with 0.1mol/L sodium hydroxide and transfer the solution immediately to a separatory funnel; wash the flask with 20mL of distilled water and add the washings to the rest of the solution. Add by pipette 1mL of 1 percent EDTA solution and 1mL of 2.5×10^{-2} mol/L ferroin solution and again throughly mix the solution. Add 50mL of chloroform and shake the funnel for 30 seconds to mix the phases thoroughly. Allow the layers to separate and transfer the chloroform layer to another separatory funnel. Wash the chloroform by shaking it vigorously for 30 seconds with 100mL of water and repeat this process with a second 100mL of water. Filter the chloroform phase through cotton-wool and measure the absorbance, A_0, against pure chloroform at 516nm in a 1cm cell [this 1 cell reading is used to calculate the boron concentration on the basis of equation (19.1) (see below), but if the zero-minutes reading is to be used for determination of anionic detergent concentration a 2 cm cell reading is more suitable].

(b) ***One-hour Reaction Time*** Measure a second 100mL of neutralised sample solution into a flask, add 10mL of 10 percent sodium salicylate solution and 17.5mL of 0.05mol/L sulphuric acid solution. Mix the solutions thoroughly, allow the mixture to stand for one hour and adjust the pH of the solution to 6~7 with 0.1mol/L sodium hydroxide. Now proceed as previously described, under (a), to obtain the absorbance, A_{1h}. The absorbance. A, to be used in the calculation of the boron concentration is obtained from the following equation:

$$A = A_{1h} - [A_o - A_{(blank)o}] \tag{19.1}$$

$A_{(blank)o}$ is determined by repeating procedure (a), i.e. zero-minutes, using 100mL of distilled water in place of the sample solution.

Calculate the amount of boron present by reference to a calibration graph of absorbance against boron concentration (mg/L). Multiply the result obtained by the appropriate volume correction factor arising from neutralisation of the sample.

Calibration: take 5mL, 10mL, 25mL, 50mL, 75mL and 100mL of the standard boric acid solution (2.5×10^{-4} mol/L) and make each up to 100mL with distilled water; this yields a boron concentration range up to 2.70mg/L. Continue with each solution as described under procedure (b), i.e. one-hour reaction time, except that the initial neutralisation of the boron solution to pH 5.5 is not necessary. Construct a calibration graph of absorbance at 516nm against boron concentration, mg/L. For maximum accuracy, the calibration should be carried out immediately prior to the analysis of samples.

From *Quantitative Chemical Analysis* 5th by G. H. Jeffery

New Words and Expressions

masking agent　掩蔽剂
hafnium ['hæfniəm]　*n.* 铪
zirconium [zəˈkəuniəm]　*n.* 锆
hexafluoroacetylacetone [ˈheksəfluərəuæsitilæsitəun]　*n.* 六氟化乙酰基丙酮
viscosity [visˈkɔsiti]　*n.* 黏性
flammability [ˌflæməˈbiləti]　*n.* 可燃性

separatory funnel　分液漏斗
borate ['bɔːreit]　n. 硼酸酯
anionic detergent　阴离子清洁剂
boric acid　硼酸

Notes

1. 句中 of the order of grams per litre，指的是乙酰丙酮盐溶解能力是每升数克的数量级。参考译文：大多数螯合物在有机溶剂中可溶，溶解能力为每升数克，这不同于分析中用的螯合物。所以这种螯合物可以进行大量和微量分离。

2. 句中 subsequent 表明了先用溶液萃取，后气相色谱分离分析的先后顺序。参考译文：这些试剂用来对金属离子进行溶液萃取，接下来就可以用气相色谱来分离和分析了。

3. 参考译文：必须记住，对萃取混合物进行太剧烈的搅拌不会起到什么好处，简单地重复倒转容器几次就足以使它达到平衡了。

4. 本句讲的是萃取中溶剂循环问题。参考译文：这个过程利用不相溶的溶剂连续流过溶液的方法，当溶剂可挥发时，可用蒸馏和冷凝循环，并借助于烧结玻璃制成的圆盘或平衡装置使之在水相中分散。

Unit 20 Supercritical Fluid Technology

Environmental acceptable manufacturing processes, including chemical synthesis, have been the recent focus of a wave of new technology commonly called "green chemistry and engineering". Among the technologies addressing this problem is supercritical fluid technology and its many variants, namely supercritical fluid extraction (SFE), supercritical fluid fractionation (SFF), supercritical fluid chromatography (SFC) and supercritical fluid reactions (SFR). In addition it is important to note that the nature of critical fluid processing has also changed in the last 30 years.

No longer is supercritical fluid extraction (SFE) the only method used for the isolation of specific components from natural matrices. As shown in Fig. 20.1, fractionation and reaction modes utilizing supercritical fluids are becoming more common, and can be coupled with SFE to produce a customized end product or fraction. Whereas the traditional first step in Fig. 20.1 was usually extraction-based (i.e., the removal of caffeine from coffee to produce a decaffeinated product, or isolation of a hops extract for flavoring), today's processes can utilize a supercritical fluid fractionation (SFF) process, either initially or coupled with SFE, to produce value-enhanced products. Recently, the recognition that critical fluids offer a unique processing media in which to conduct reactions opens but yet another option to the food and agro-product processor.

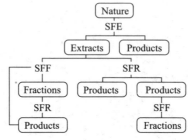

Fig. 20.1 process sequences utilizing supercritical fluid media for isolating or synthesizing desired end products

1. Fractionation with critical fluids

Prior to the mid-1980s, critical fluid-processed products were largely derived using SFE; either by selecting a given fluid density that would yield the desired product, altering the extraction fluid density as a function of processing time, or in some cases selectively decreasing the pressure after the extraction stage to achieve the desired extract. Useful separations have been attained using the above techniques, but largely between compounds differing significant in their physicochemical properties, e.g., molecular weight, vapor pressure, polarity. [1]

Recently, fractionation processes utilizing critical fluid media has been improved by combining principles utilized in supercritical extraction with other separation techniques. These improved methods often make use of fractionating columns or chromatography to yield improvements in the resolution of molecular species. The fractionating column or tower approach is somewhat analogous to operating a distillation column, but there are differences when using critical fluid media.

Fig. 20.2 illustrates the components and principles involved in fractionating using a very simple column. In this case, SC-CO_2 is brought to the desired pressure and then directed to flow upward inside the fractionating column, which usually contains a packing to encourage contact between the SC-CO_2 and the components being separated. [2] The components to be

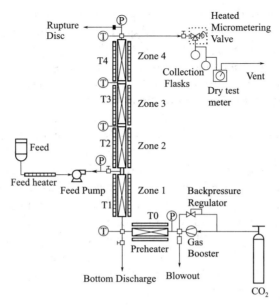

Fig. 20.2 schematic of the packed column thermal gradient fractionation system

separated are injected with a pump into the flowing SC-CO_2, prior to its entry into the column. This fluid-solute mixture then enters the first heated zone in the vertical fractionating column and the separation process is initiated. The SC-CO_2-solute mixture then ascends the column, usually encountering zones of increasing temperature, which facilitate the separation of solutes based on their relative solubilities in SC-CO_2 and their respective vapor pressures. In effect, the column is operating under a density gradient since the fluid is kept isobaric. The described fractionating column can be operated in either the batch or semi-continuous mode with co-current flow of the solute and supercritical fluid streams. The use of a packed tower fractionation scheme does not necessarily require prohibitively high processing pressures to obtain significant enrichment of the monoglyceride component in these feed mixtures.

Another SFF option is to employ chromatography in the preparative or production mode, in its own right, or coupled with a preliminary SFE enrichment stage. Our research has shown that it is possible to enrich target compounds (e.g., tocopherols) to levels that were not possible by using SFE alone. Fig. 20.3 illustrates the principle involved in this form of fractionation when using SC-CO_2, both with and without an organic cosolvent, in either the SFE or supercritical fluid chromatography (SFC) stages. Here a preliminary optimized SFE step is utilized to achieve the best possible enrichment of solutes prior to introduction of the extract to the chromatographic column. Then, using inexpensive commodity ad-

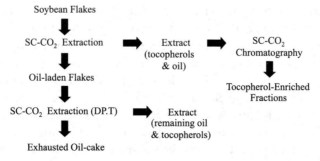

Fig. 20.3 process for the enrichment of tocopherols by SFE/SFC

sorbents whenever possible, the extract from the extraction stage is diverted onto the top of the chromatographic column, where it is further fractionated using either neat SC-CO_2, or SC-CO_2 with ethanol and water as eluents.[3] Using this approach, we have been able to enrich moieties such as tocopherols, phospholipids, or sterol esters from vegetable oils, seeds, and by-products of the milling or vegetable oil refining processes.

2. Applied reaction chemistry in critical fluids

There is a historical precedent for conducting specific reactions under supercritical conditions, such as the polymerization of ethylene or isomerization of olefins. In these reactions, it is often just the application of pressure as a thermodynamic variable that permits the reaction equilibria to be shifted, yielding the desired end products. However since the early 1990s, there has been an increasing awareness that by conducting reactions in critical fluid media, one can control not only the equilibrium position of a reaction, but the product distribution and end properties (i. e. , color or morphology).

It is also possible in some specific cases to conduct reactions at low temperatures in a non- oxidative environment (CO_2), thereby protecting compounds that would be altered in more severe thermal environments. Reaction catalysts can also be regenerated with the aid of supercritical fluids after completion of a SFR.

Two types of reactions that we have studied and have implications in the oleo chemical industry are enzymatic-catalyzed and hydrogenation reactions. The coupling of enzyme catalysis with critical fluids as CO_2 is particularly attractive, since both are "natural" agents, allowing lipid food components to be manufactured without introducing a solvent or catalyst residues into the final product. In some cases, SC-CO_2 can act as a reactant in a process or alternatively as a catalyst. An example of the latter case is the effect of SC-CO_2 on conversion of vegetable oils to yield mixed glyceride compositions enriched in monoglyceride content. However, absence of the metal catalysts in the SC-CO_2-initiated process eliminates the troublesome filtration step associated with the currently used industrial processes. Further, the produced mixed glyceride compositions are much lighter in color then those synthesized using metal catalysts. These end products represent the lower cost products for the glyceridebased emulsifier market.

3. Sub-critical and pressurized water processing

The success in applying both SC-CO_2 and liquid CO_2 (L-CO_2) as benign solvents for the extraction of naturally derived products has catalyzed the search for additional extraction media that can be used in food or nutraceutical processing. Initially, one may question the use of this hot medium to extract biological or organic materials, due to concerns of its reactivity, resulting in the subsequent degradation of solutes under elevated temperatures (note that this is not the technique of supercritical water oxidation which is usually conducted above the critical temperature of water, 375℃, for the expressed purpose of degrading organic wastes, etc.). However, recently this medium has been applied successfully, over a restricted temperature range, to the extraction of food materials and natural products.

The solvent power of subcritical water is largely varied by changing temperature and applying enough external pressure to eliminate vaporizing the water when used above its normal boiling point. Hence, by varying the temperature of water over a range of 25～250℃, its dielectric constant can be changed from 78 to less than 30, thereby attaining solvent polarities normally associated with polar organic solvents. Thus in theory, subcritical water is a perfect compliment to SC-CO_2 for processing natural products, thereby avoiding the use of organic solvents such as ethanol. The potential reactivity of solutes under subcritical water conditions, i. e. , conditions slightly above the boiling point of water, suggests that temperatures between 100～175℃ are optimal for most food and natural product applications.

The use of critical fluid media from various regions of the phase diagram is becoming more prevalent as illustrated by the use of SC-CO_2, LCO_2, subcritical water and selected co-solvents that are compatible with the environment and end use in functional foods. Although simplistic, the author has reason to believe that many natural product extractions and separation problems can be solved by the combination of carbon dioxide, ethanol, and water; an all-green trio of solvents. Supercritical processing is also beginning to merge with high pressure hydrostatic processing as the prophylactic benefits of a residual CO_2 atmosphere in SFE-derived products has been documented. Undoubtedly the coupling of membrane technologies with critical fluid media will see application in the near future.

From *Critical fluid technology for the processing of lipid-related natural products by JerryW. King*

New Words and Expressions

supercritical [ˌsjuːpəˈkritikəl] *a.* 超临界的
physicochemical [ˌfizikəuˈkemikəl] *a.* 物理化学的
isobaric [ˌaisəuˈbærik] *a.* 表示等压的；同（原子）量异序的
semi-continuous [ˌsemikənˈtinjuəs] *a.* 半连续的，断断续续的
glyceride [ˈglisəˌraid] *n.* 甘油酯，脂肪酸丙酯
tocopherol [təuˈkɔfərəul] *n.* 生育酚，维生素 E
isomerization [aiˌsɔmərai'zeiʃən] *n.* 异构化（作用）
monoglyceride [ˌmɔnəuˈglisəˌraid] *n.* 单酸甘油酯
subcritical [sʌbˈkritikl] *a.* 次临界
compliment [ˈkɔmplimənt] *n.* 称赞，致意；*vt.* 称赞，恭维
prophylactic [ˌprɔfiˈlæktik] *a.* 预防疾病的；*n.* 预防药，避孕药

Notes

1. 句中，在 but 后省略了与主句相同的主语与谓语。参考译文：有用的分离可以通过使用上述技术来获得，但是它主要运用于理化性质比如分子量、蒸汽压、极性等差异比较大的物质。

2. 句中"and then"来连接两个先后发生的动作。参考译文：在这种情况下，SC-CO_2 气体升到所需要的压力，然后在分馏柱内部向上流动。分馏柱通常装有填料，以促使 SC-CO_2 和正被分离组分的接触。

3. 句中，"eluent"在精馏分离技术中可翻译成流出物或洗出物。本句中的分词短语作状语，参考译文：只要有可能就使用廉价的日用商品吸附剂，由萃取段得到的萃取物传送到色谱柱的顶部，用纯的 SC-CO_2 或含有乙醇和水的 SC-CO_2 作为洗出物进一步进行分馏。

Exercises

Ⅰ. Comprehension

1. Critical fluid-processed products were largely derived using SFE; either by selecting a given fluid density that would yield the desired product, altering the extraction fluid density as a function of processing time, or in some cases selectively ____ after the extraction stage to achieve the desired extract.
   A. decreasing the pressure   B. increasing the pressure
   C. decreasing the temperature   D. increasing the temperature

2. In effect, the column is operating under a density gradient since the fluid is kept isobaric.
  A. A density gradient can be changed by decreasing the pressure.
  B. A density gradient can be changed by increasing the pressure.
  C. A density gradient can be changed by decreasing temperature.
  D. A density gradient can be changed by increasing temperature.
3. The most common critical fluid is ____.
  A. CO_2 B. O_2 C. N_2 D. CO
4. The solvent power of subcritical water is largely varied by ____ to eliminate vaporizing the water when used above its normal boiling point.
  A. changing temperature and applying enough external pressure
  B. changing temperature and applying enough internal pressure
  C. changing pressure and temperature   D. changing pressure

II. Fill in the blanks with the phrases given below

ranges from	in the presence of	be operated in	focused on
improved by	involved in	based on	the use of
make use of	relative to	addition of	

(1) This development was followed by the advent of conducting reactions (SFR) ____ SFs as documented in the literature.

(2) The application of supercritical fluids (SF) and similar media for the processing of agricultural or natural products has traditionally ____ the extraction mode utilizing carbon dioxide in its supercritical (SC-CO_2) or liquid (LCO_2) state.

(3) Recently, fractionation processes utilizing critical fluid media has been ____ by combining principles utilized in supercritical extraction with other separation techniques.

(4) These improved methods often ____ fractionating columns or chromatography to yield improvements in the resolution of molecular species.

(5) For an understanding of the fundamentals ____ using this technique, one should consult the books by Clifford and Brunner.

(6) The described fractionating column can ____ either the batch or semi-continuous mode with co-current flow of the solute and supercritical fluid streams.

(7) This is a considerable enrichment ____ the concentration of the phospholipids in the starting oil or seed matrix.

(8) The monoglyceride component ____ 49.2 wt% for the glycerides derived from glycerolysis of soybean oil to 41.1 wt% in the case of cottonseed oil.

(9) Classical techniques for the solvent extraction of nutraceuticals from plant matrices are ____ the choice of solvent coupled with ____ heat and/or agitation.

(10) ____ polar co-solvents (modifiers) to the supercritical CO_2 is known to significantly increase the solubility of polar compounds.

III. Put in proper prepositions or adverbs into the blanks

(1) Many nutraceuticals ____ phenolics, alkaloids and glycosidic compounds are poorly soluble in carbon dioxide and hence not extractable.

(2) Techniques aimed ____ overcoming the limited solubility of polar substances in supercritical CO_2 have been sought.

(3) ____ all the modifiers including methanol, ethanol, acetonitrile, acetone, water, ethyl ether and dichloromethane, methanol is the most commonly used.

(4) The use of methanol ____ a modifier requires a slightly higher temperature to reach the supercritical state and this could be disadvantageous ____ thermolabile compounds.

(5) They found that the decrease of particle size had a small decrease ____ the total

yield of the extracted oil.

(6) The extraction time has been proven ____ be another parameter that determines extract composition.

(7) The solubility of a solid ____ a supercritical fluid increases ____ the density of the fluid, which can be achieved ____ high pressures.

(8) Turner, King, and Mathiasson gave a review ____ supercritical fluids in the extraction and chromatographic separation of fat-soluble vitamins.

(9) However, the SFE-extracted oil was more protected ____ oxidation of the unstable polyunsaturated fatty acids than the n-hexane-extracted oil.

(10) Comparison of different extraction methods for the extraction of oleoresin ____ dried onion showed that the yield ____ supercritical CO_2 extraction was 22 times higher than that after steam distillation.

IV. Answer following questions

(1) What proportions of n-hexane and n-heptane (a) by mole fraction, (b) by weight should be mixed in order to achieve the greatest change in entropy?

(2) Henry' Law is useful for several things, and provides a simple way of finding the solubility of gases in liquids. For instance, what is the solubility of carbon dioxide in water at 25℃ when its partial pressure is (a) 0.1atm, (b) 1.0atm?

(3) An industrial process led to the production of mixture of toluene (T) and n-octane (O), and the vapour pressure of the mixture was investigated with a view to designing a separation plant. The following temperature-composition data were obtained at 760mmHg: x is the mole fraction in the liquid and y the mole fraction in the vapour at equilibrium.

$t/℃$	110.9	112.0	114.0	115.8	117.3	119.0	120.0	123.0
x_T	0.908	0.795	0.615	0.527	0.408	0.300	0.203	0.097
y_T	0.923	0.836	0.698	0.624	0.527	0.410	0.297	0.164

The boiling points are T: 110.6℃, O: 125.6℃. Plot the temperature-composition diagram for T and O. What is the composition of the vapour in equilibrium with liquid of composition (a) $x_T = 0.250$, (b) $x_O = 0.250$?

V. Translation the following words and expressions into English

超临界流体　超临界色谱　分馏　　流体-溶质混合物　　平衡位置　精馏柱
超临界介质　超临界萃取　相图　亚临界水　蒸气压　　产物分布

VI. Translation the following sentences into English

(1) 采用改进的方法往往是利用分馏柱或色谱柱来改善分子物种的分辨率。

(2) SFF 就是以预制性或制备的方式、或与初级的 SFE 富集步骤连用来使用色谱技术。

(3) 当在水的正常沸点时，改变温度和应用足够的外界压力来消除水的蒸发而极大的影响水的溶剂力。

(4) 相图的各个区域中得出的临界流体介质的使用变得越来越普遍，正如由 SC-CO_2、LCO_2、亚临界水和选择的多溶剂共存体系所表明那样。

Reading Material

Supercritical Fluid Extraction of Nutraceuticals from Plants

Principles and mechanisms

Supercritical state is achieved when the temperature and the pressure of a substance are raised over its critical value. The supercritical fluid has characteristics of both gases and liquids. Compared with liquid solvents, supercritical fluids have several major advantages: (i) the dissolving power of a supercritical fluid solvent depends on its density, which is highly adjustable by changing the pressure or/and temperature[1]; (ii) the supercritical fluid has a higher diffusion coefficient and lower viscosity and surface tension than a liquid solvent, leading to more favorable mass transfer.

A supercritical fluid extraction (SFE) system is shown in Fig. 20.4 During SFE, raw plant material is loaded into an extraction vessel, which is equipped with temperature controllers and pressure valves at both inlet and outlet to keep desired extraction conditions. The extraction vessel is pressurized with the fluid by a pump. The fluid and the dissolved compounds are transported to separators, where the salvation power of the fluid is decreased by decreasing the pressure or increasing the temperature of the fluid. The product is then collected via a valve located in the lower part of the separators. The fluid is further regenerated and cycled.

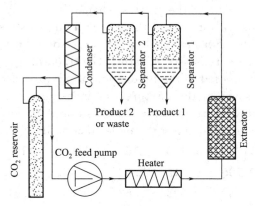

Fig. 20.4 schematic diagram of a process-scale supercritical fluid extraction system

Practical issues for supercritical fluid extraction

To develop a successful SFE, several factors must be taken into consideration. These factors include the selection of supercritical fluids, plant material preparation, modifiers and extraction conditions.

Solvent choice

Selection of supercritical fluids is critical for the development of a SFE process. With a reduction in the price of carbon dioxide and restrictions in the use of other organic solvents, carbon dioxide has begun to move from some marginal applications to being the major solvent for supercritical fluid extraction[2]. The critical state of carbon dioxide fluid is at a temperature of only 304 K and pressure of 7.3MPa. Also, carbon dioxide is non-flammable and non-toxic. Supercritical CO_2 is a good solvent for the extraction of non-polar compounds such as hydrocarbons. To extract polar compounds, some polar supercritical fluids such as Freon-22, nitrous oxide and hexane have been considered. However, their applications are limited due to their unfavorable properties with respect to safety and environmental considerations. Although supercritical water and superheated water have certain advantages such as higher extraction ability for polar compounds, it is not suitable for thermally labile compounds.

Preparation of plant materials

Preparation of plant materials is another critical factor for SFE of nutraceuticals. Fresh plant materials are frequently used in the SFE of nutraceuticals. When fresh plant materials are extracted, the high moisture content can cause mechanical difficulties such as restrictor clogging due to ice formation. Although water is only about 0.3% soluble in supercritical CO_2, highly water-soluble solutes would prefer to partition into the aqueous phase, resulting in low efficiency of SFE. Some chemicals such as Na_2SO_4, and silica gel are thus mixed with the plant materials to retain the moisture for SFE of fresh materials.

Plant particle size is an also important for a good SFE process. Large particles may result in a long extraction process because the process may be controlled by internal diffusion. However, fine powder can speed up the extraction but may also cause difficulty in maintaining a proper flow rate.

Operating conditions

The solubility of a target compound in a supercritical fluid is a major factor in determining its extraction efficiency. The temperature and density of the fluid control the solubility. The choice of a proper density of a supercritical fluid such as CO_2 is the crucial point influencing solvent power and selectivity, and the main factor determining the extract composition. It is often desirable to extract the compound right above the point where the desired compounds become soluble in the fluid so that the extraction of other compounds can be minimized.

The extraction time has been proven to be another parameter that determines extract composition. Lower molecular weight and less polar compounds are more readily extracted during supercritical CO_2 extraction since the extraction mechanism is usually controlled by internal diffusion. Therefore, the extract composition varies with the extraction time. However, the increase of CO_2 flow rate did not seem to influence the composition for the supercritical CO_2 extraction of Foeniculum vulgare volatile oil, although it increased the extraction rate.

Advantages of supercritical fluid extraction

SFE offers unusual possibilities for selective extractions and fractionations because the solubility of a chemical in a supercritical fluid can be manipulated by changing the pressure and/or temperature of the fluid. Furthermore, supercritical fluids have a density of a liquid and can solubilize a solid like a liquid solvent. The solubility of a solid in a supercritical fluid increases with the density of the fluid, which can be achieved at high pressures. The dissolved nutraceutical compounds can be recovered from the fluid by the reduction of the density of the supercritical fluid, which can usually be reduced by decreasing pressure. Therefore, SFE can eliminate the concentration process, which usually is time-consuming. Furthermore, the solutes can be separated from a supercritical solvent without a loss of volatiles due to the extreme volatility of the supercritical fluid.

Additionally, the diffusivity of a supercritical fluid is one to two orders of magnitude higher than that of other liquids, which permits rapid mass transfer, resulting in a larger extraction rate than that obtained by conventional solvent extractions[3]. Supercritical CO_2 extraction uses a moderate extraction temperature as low as 30 ℃. The low supercritical temperature of CO_2 makes it attractive for the extraction of heat sensible compounds. As SFE uses no or only minimal organic solvent (organic modifiers) in extraction, it is a more environmentally friendly extraction process than conventional solvent-solid extraction. SFE can be directly coupled with a chromatographic method for simultaneously extracting and quantifying highly volatile extracted compounds.

However, the economics and onerous operating conditions of the SFE processes has restricted the applications to some very specialized fields such as coffee decaffeination and to university research.

Potential applications of supercritical fluid extractions

SFE is a potential alternative to conventional extraction methods using organic solvents for extracting biologically active components from plants. It has been used to extract plant materials, especially lipids, essential oils and flavors. SFE can achieve higher yield and quality of essential oils, flavors and natural aromas than conventional steam distillation. The mean percentage yields of cedarwood oil for supercritical CO_2 extraction and steam distillation were 4.4% and 1.3%. The yield of supercritical CO_2 extraction of essential oil from juniper wood at 50℃ and 10MPa was 14.7% (w/w), while hydrodistillation gave a yield of 11% (w/w).[4]

The number of industrial-scale applications of SFE in plant extraction has remained very small due to the lipophilic nature of supercritical CO_2. Comparison of different extraction methods for the extraction of oleoresin from dried onion showed that the yield after supercritical CO_2 extraction was 22 times higher than that after steam distillation, but it was only 7% of the yield achieved by the extraction using a polar solvent of alcohol at 25℃. However, the flavor and biological activity of onion are attributed mainly to its sulphurcontaining compounds. The concentration of sulphur was the highest in steam distilled onion oil while it was the lowest in the extract of alcohol at 25℃. The oleoresin produced by supercritical CO_2 extraction had the best sensory quality. Many active substances in plants such as phenolics, alkaloids and glycosidic compounds are poorly soluble in CO_2 and hence not extractable.

Modifiers such as methanol and ethanol are widely used in the supercritical CO_2 extraction of polar substances. Supercritical CO_2 modified with 15% ethanol gave higher yields than pure supercritical CO_2 to extract naringin (a glycosylated flavonoid) from Citrus paradise at 9.5MPa and 58.6℃. The use of a 10% ethanol co-solvent resulted in a much higher yield of epicatechin (13mg/100g seed coat) than that with pure CO_2 (22 mg/100 g seed coat) from sweet Thai tamarind seed coat. Supercritical CO_2 extraction with methanol in the range of 3%～7% as modifier was proven to be a very efficient and fast method to recover higher than 98% of colchicines and colchicoside, and 97% of 3-demethylcolchicine from seeds of colchicum autumnale.

From *Recent advances in extraction of nutraceuticals from plants by Lijun Wang*

New Words and Expressions

efficiency [iˈfiʃənsi]　*n.*　效率
parameter [pəˈræmitə]　*n.*　参数
cedar [ˈsiːdə]　*n.*　雪松
hydrodistillation [ˌhaidrəuˌdistiˈleiʃən]　*n.*　水蒸馏法
lipophilic [ˌlipəˈfilik]　*a.*　亲油的；亲脂的
oleoresin [ˌəuliəuˈrezin]　*n.*　含油树脂；精油树脂；松脂
onion [ˈʌnjən]　*n.*　洋葱
glycosidic [ˌglaikəuˈsidik]　*a.*　糖苷的
glycosylate [ˈglaikəsileit]　*vt.*　使（蛋白质）糖基化
epicatechin [ˌepiˈkætitʃin]　*n.*　表儿茶素
colchicum [ˈkɔltʃikəm]　*n.*　秋水仙，秋水仙制成的麻药

Notes

1. 其中"or/and"在科技英语中表示或者/和的意思。
2. 句中的分词短语作介词 to 的宾语，参考译文：随着二氧化碳价格的降低和其他有机

溶剂的限制使用，二氧化碳已从某种边缘使用变成了超临界流体萃取中的主要溶剂。

3. 句中"orders of magnitude"表示数量级，"which"代主句，参考译文：另外，超临界流体的扩散性比其他液体大一至二数量级，这促使更快的传质和比传统溶剂更大的萃取速率。

4. 句中，温度和压力都用介词"at"来表示。科技英语中压力还有另一种表示方法，常见用介词"under"表示。句中的"w/w"表示质量/质量。参考译文：对于超临界CO_2萃取和蒸汽蒸馏来说，雪松木料油的平均百分收率分别为4.4%和1.3%，在50℃和10MPa条件下，用超临界CO_2萃取从桧属植物木料中获得精油的得率为14.7%（质量/质量），而水精馏得率为11%（质量/质量）。

PART FIVE
FINE CHEMICALS AND PROCESS

Unit 21　Catalysis

　　Most of the chemical reactions in industry and biology are catalytic, and many chemists and chemical engineers work to understand and apply catalysis. Catalysis is involved at some stage of the processing of a large fraction of the goods manufactured in the United States; the value of these products approaches a trillion dollars annually, more than the gross national products of all but a few countries in the world. Catalysis is the key to the efficiency of chemical conversions. In an age of increasingly limited energy and raw materials and concern for the environment, it is needed more and more. The technological needs are matched by the scientific opportunities; new techniques are bringing rapid progress in the understanding of molecular details of the workings of catalysts.

　　Nitrogen and hydrogen flow through a tube at high temperature and pressure, but they do not react to give ammonia, although the chemical equilibrium is favorable. When particles of iron are placed in the tube, however, the gases coming in contact with them are converted rapidly into ammonia.[1] Millions of kilograms of this chemical are synthesized every year in such tubular reactors at a cost of a few cents per kilogram. Ammonia is a raw material for nitrate fertilizers needed to feed the world's population. Fertilizers are assimilated by the cells of plants in complex sequences of biological reactions. Further metabolic reactions take place as animals consume the plants, reconstructing their contents to provide energy and molecular building blocks for growth. All these biological reactions proceed under the direction of naturally occurring macromolecules called enzymes; without them, the processes of life could not take place.

　　What is an enzyme, and what does it have in common with the iron in the ammonia synthesis reactor? Each is a catalyst—a substance that accelerates a chemical reaction but is not consumed in the reaction and does not affect its equilibrium.[2] Catalysts cause reactions to proceed faster than they would otherwise, and they can be used over and over again. Catalysts are the keys to the efficiency of almost all biochemical processes and most industrial chemical processes.

　　A catalyst provides a new and easier pathway for reactant molecules to be converted into product molecules. By analogy, consider instead of reactant molecules a group of climbers crossing a mountain range, breaking ground slowly over the steep crest. Alternatively, they might be guided rapidly along a less direct pathway, experiencing gentle ups and downs but circumventing the crest and crossing a low pass to reach the opposite valley in a short time. According to this rough analogy, the guidance along this new pathway —more roundabout and complicated but faster —is provided by the catalyst.[2] The catalyst participates in the reaction by somehow combining with the reactant molecules so that they rearrange into products (and regenerate the catalyst) more rapidly than they could if the catalyst were not present.

A catalyst is by definition a substance that increases the rate of approach to equilibrium of a chemical reaction without being substantially consumed in the reaction.[3] A catalyst usually works by forming chemical bonds to one or more reactants and thereby facilitating their conversion —it does not significantly affect the reaction equilibrium.

The definition of a catalyst rests on the idea of reaction rate, and therefore the subject of reaction kinetics is central, providing the quantitative framework. The qualitative chemical explanations of catalysis take the form of reaction mechanisms.[4] These are models of reactions accounting for the overall stoichiometry, identifying the sequence of elementary reaction steps, and (insofar as possible) explaining, in terms of chemical bond strength and geometry, the interactions of the catalyst with reactants.

Catalytic reactions take place in various phases: in solutions, within the solutionlike confines of micelles and the molecular-scale pockets of large enzyme molecules, within polymer gels, within the molecular—scale cages of crystalline solids such as molecular-sieve zeolites, and on the surfaces of solids. This list of phases in which catalysis occurs forms a progression from the simplest toward the most difficult to characterize in terms of exact chemical structure. A given catalytic reaction can take place in any of these phases, and the details of the mechanism will often be similar in all of them.

A full account of how a catalyst works requires a description of how reactant molecules are transported to the catalyst and of how product molecules are transported away. Because the reactants and products are often concentrated in a phase separate from that holding the catalyst, it is necessary to consider transport between phases by diffusion and convection and to determine how these transport processes affect the rates of catalytic reactions. For example, in the ammonia synthesis, the reactants H_2 and N_2 are concentrated in the gas phase flowing through the reactor, but the catalytic reaction occurs on the surface of the iron particles. Therefore, the rate of the reaction depends not only on what happens on the surface but also on how fast the H_2 and N_2 are transported to the surface and how fast the ammonia is transported away. The reaction occurs on the surface in the steady state at just the rate of transport of the reactants to the surface and the rate of transport of the products from the surface.[5]

Some of the essential ideas defining catalysis can be learned from preliminary consideration of an example. The reaction of ethylene and butadiene in solution to give 1, 4-hexadiene is of industrial importance in the manufacture of the polymer nylon. The reaction has been suggested to proceed via the cycle of elementary steps. The species entering the cycle are H, NiL_4 (a complex of Ni with unspecified ligands L), ethylene (symbolized by the double bond), and butadiene (symbolized by 1,4-butadiene). The species leaving the cycle are the hydrocarbon products, namely, three isomers of hexadiene. At this point it is not important what structures are formed from the reactants and the nickel complex. What is important is that the catalyst is formed from the reactants and the nickel complex and then converted cyclically through the various forms. The nickel is not consumed in the reaction once it has entered the cycle, but is repeatedly converted from one form to another in the cycle as the reactants are converted into products.

Catalysis always involves a cycle of reaction steps, and the catalyst is converted from one form to the next, ideally without being consumed in the overall process. The occurrence of a cyclic reaction sequence is a requirement for catalysis, and catalysis may even be defined as such an occurrence.

A catalyst for a particular reaction always provides at least one pathway for conversion of reactants that is kinetically significant. The catalyst virtually always provides this pathway as a consequence of its becoming chemically bonded to reactants.

An inhibitor slows down a catalytic reaction; a competitive inhibitor slows down the reaction by competing with the reactants in bonding to the catalyst. A very strong inhibitor, one that bonds so strongly that it virtually excludes the reactants from bonding with the catalyst, is called a poison.

A quantitative measure of how fast a catalyst works is its activity, which is usually defined as the reaction rate (or a reaction rate constant) for conversion of reactants into products. Often products are formed in addition to those that are desired, and a catalyst has an activity for each particular reaction. A ratio of these catalytic activities is referred to as selectivity, which is a measure of the catalyst's ability to direct the conversion to the desired products. For a large-scale application, the selectivity of a catalyst may be even more important than its activity. In practice, catalysts are inevitably involved in side reactions that lead to their conversion into inactive forms (those not appearing in the catalytic cycle). Therefore, a catalyst is also chosen on the basis of its stability; the greater the stability, the lower the rate at which the catalyst loses its activity or selectivity or both. A deactivated catalyst may be treated to bring back its activity; its regenerability in such a treatment is a measure (often not precisely defined) of how well its activity can be brought back.

From *Catalytic Chemistry*, by Bruce C. Gates

New Words and Expressions

catalysis [kə'tælisis]　*n.* 催化（作用）
equilibrium [ˌi:kwi'libriəm]　*n.* 平衡，均衡
reactor [ri(:)'æktə]　*n.* 反应器
nitrate fertilizer　含氮肥料
assimilate [ə'simileit]　*vt.* 吸收（食物、思想、文化）；*vi.* 被吸收，同化
macromolecular [ˌmækrəu'məu'lekjulə]　*n.* 大分子
roundabout ['raundəbaut]　*a.* 迂回的，不直接的，胖的
rearrange ['ri:ə'reindʒ]　*vt.* 重新安排；*vi.* 重排
facilitate [fə'siliteit]　*vt.* 使容易，使便利，推进促进
account for　解释，说明
catalytic [ˌkætə'litik]　*a.* 催化的
molecular scale　分子范围
ethylene ['eθili:n]　*n.* 乙烯，次乙基
butadiene [ˌbju:tə'daii:n]　*n.* 丁二烯
hexadiene [ˌheksə'dæi:in]　*n.* 己二烯
polymer nylon　尼龙
inhibitor (inhibiter) [in'hibitə(r)]　*n.* 禁止剂，抑制剂，抑制因素
selectivity [silek'tiviti]　*n.* 选择性
inactivate [in'æktiveit]　*vt.* 钝化，使减少活性

Notes

1. 在此句中使用了被动句式，这是科技英语里表达一种现象或事实时常用的语态。再看下句：Both the synthesis reaction and the catalysis itself have been extensively studied to achieve an understanding of the reaction mechanism and the factors controlling the efficiency of the overall reaction.

2. 两句中的破折号的作用是不同的。第一句中它用来对 catalyst 进行解释说明，第二句中它表示插入，对 pathway 加以修饰。

3. 句中"by definition"用来定义催化剂，是一种对物质或事物下定义的方法。还有其他表达法：

We define the catalyst as a substance that ....

A catalyst is defined as ....

The substance that could accelerate or decline the reaction rate of a certain reaction could be named (called) as catalyst.

4. This sentence could be paraphrased as the following:

The reaction mechanisms could explain the catalysis behavior qualitatively with chemical language.

5. 参考译文：反应在物质表面以稳定状态进行，反应速度恰是反应试剂传送到物质表面的速度，也是产物离开物质表面的速度。翻译时将"at the rate of"译为另一句子，使句子衔接流畅，并加了主语"反应速度"。

Exercises

I. Comprehension

1. A catalyst is by definition a substance that increases the rate of approach to equilibrium of a chemical reaction ____ in the reaction.
   A. without being substantially consumed   B. not at all consumed
   C. with decreasing significantly   D. with the change of it's composition

2. Catalytic reactions take place in various phases: the following locations except ____.
   A. in solutions
   B. within the solution like confines of micelles and the molecular-scale pockets of large enzyme molecules
   C. within polymer gels   D. in the inside of solids

3. A catalyst for a particular reaction always provides at least one pathway for conversion of reactants that is ____ significant.
   A. both kinetically and thermodynamically
   B. not kinetically and thermodynamically
   C. thermodynamically   D. kinetically

4. A quantitative measure of how fast a catalyst works is its activity, which is usually defined as ____ for conversion of reactants into products.
   A. reaction time   B. the reaction rate
   C. reaction passage   D. reaction temperature

5. In practice, catalysts are inevitably involved in side reactions that lead to their conversion into inactive forms, which means ____.
   A. that materials produced in side reactions are poisoning to catalysts
   B. that inactive catalysts are useful to side reactions
   C. that the side reaction lead to catalysts being inactive
   D. that catalysts are active in the side reactions

II. Problem

1. In some catalytic reactions the species formed may adsorb more strongly than the reacting gas. This is the case, for instance, in the catalytic decomposition than the ammonia on platinum at 1000℃. As a first step in examining the kinetics of this type of process, show that the rate of ammonia decomposition should follow $-dp/(NH_3)/dt = k_c p(NH_3)/p(H_2)$ in the limit of very strong adsorption of hydrogen. Start by showing that

when a gas J adsorbs very strongly, and its pressure is p (J), that the fraction of uncovered sites is approximately $1/K_p$ (J).

2. Ammonia was introduced into a bulb at a pressure 200mmHg. At 856℃ it was found that a tungsten catalyst brought about a pressure change of 59mmHg in 500s, and 112mmHg in 1000s. What is the order of the catalysed decomposition? Account for the result.

III. Question for discussion
(1) Give the technology to describe the catalyst property and its behavior.
(2) Why can the catalyst accelerate the reaction?
(3) Can it change the reaction equilibrium?

IV. Translate the following sentences into English
(1) 定义活性为催化剂催化作用的大小。
(2) 催化反应在不同的相中均可发生，其机理大致相同。
(3) 酶是人体中最有功效的蛋白质，用于加速人体新陈代谢的进行。

V. Change mood of the following sentences
(1) The use of radar in a car in order to warn the driver of obstacles or possible targets on the road is discussed ahead in this chapter. （提示：在译文中可加"本章"）
(2) Oil is pumped up from the pan at the bottom of the engine and is sent in stream to all bearings and other moving surfaces in the engine. （提示：可译为"将"）
(3) Stress must be laid on the development of the electronic industry. （提示：可将主语与谓语合译而成无主语）

VI. Translate the following into English
反应平衡	重复性	基元反应步骤	稳定性	催化循环	活性
定量分析	选择性	新陈代谢反应	化学能	反应机理	尼龙
定性分析	分子筛	管式反应器	阻抑剂	计量化学	

Reading Material

Catalyzed Reactions

Reactions catalyzed in solution

Catalysis takes place in solutions, on surfaces, and in environments that are microscopic phases, such as molecular-scale cages. Catalysis in solutions is the best understood, and therefore the logical starting point, because of the uniformity of the catalytic species and of the environment around the species participating in a reaction. The structures of reacting species, possibly including short-lived intermediates, may be determined by methods such as infrared, ultraviolet, and nuclear magnetic resonance (NMR) spectroscopy, and the dependence of rates of reaction on the concentrations of reactants and catalysts may be relatively easy to determine.

To understand how catalysts function in solutions, it is helpful to consider the organization of molecules in solutions. The fluids with the simplest structure are gases; in gases of low density, the interactions between molecules are negligible except when molecules in random motion collide. A collision between two molecules may result in no more than a transfer of energy between them, but occasionally it may lead to the forming or breaking of chemical bonds or both.

Chemical reactions in a liquid involve ions and molecules as reactants and catalysts.

Since solvent-solute interactions are often strong, solvents often influence catalysis strongly, affecting the interactions between reactants and catalysts. Consequently, rates of catalytic reactions can be regulated by the choice of a solvent.

The most common solvent is water. Water is unique because the molecules are small and strongly polar, and water therefore dissolves many ionic and polar compounds. The structure of liquid water is determined by the hydrogen bonds between the molecules. Hydrogen bonds are not strong (the magnitude of the enthalpy of formation of a hydrogen bond is about 5 kcal/mol), but each water molecule can participate in several such bonds simultaneously. The hydrogen bonds in pure water are like those in aqueous solutions of alcohols and carboxylic acids.

Solutions containing ions may also contain ion pairs and weakly organized environments of polar molecules surrounding positively and negatively charged ions. Nonionic solutions also have structure. For example, polar molecules have an affinity for other polar molecules; hydrogen-bonded structures like those of Fig. 21.1 are typical. The protons in these structures are highly mobile, which is of great importance in catalysis proceeding via cycles of proton transfer steps.[1]

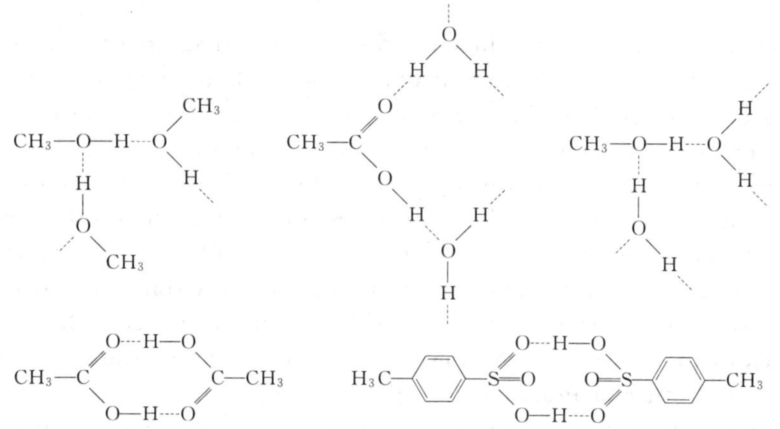

Fig. 21.1 some structures existing in liquids which involve hydrogen bonds

When polar solute molecules such as CH_3CO_2H are present in nonpolar solvents, the hydrogen bonding between them is pronounced, since the solute molecules themselves are the only candidates for polar interactions. Sometimes the affinities of molecules for each other are so strong that they form a separate phase, which may be an ordinary liquid but which also may be a microphase, such as a micelle.

Acid-base catalysis is the most thoroughly developed part of solution catalysis. The essential steps of acid-base catalysis are often protonic transfers. The protons in hydrogen-bonded structures are highly mobile because the proton mass is so low. Consequently there is a rapid interconversion of related structures as a proton moves; in water, for example, a proton moves from the O atom of one molecule toward the O atom of a neighbor, and this motion is compensated by the motion of other protons to and from the corresponding O atoms, as shown in Fig. 21.2. The rapid proton jumping accounts for the electrical conductivity of water and of ice. Many reactions catalyzed by acids and bases in water proceed via such proton transfers, and the catalytic cycles often involve water. Many of the transformations of acid-base catalysis are analogous to the structural rearrangements shown in Fig. 21.2.

Reactions Catalyzed by Enzymes

Enzymes are gigantic molecules with typical molecular weights ranging from about 6000 to more than 600000. Moreover, enzymes are much more complex structurally than the catalysts considered thus far in the section, and their catalytic sites are far more intricate. Enzymes have evolved by the life process to be extremely specific catalyst; each enzyme is a catalyst for only one biological reaction or, sometimes, one class of reaction. The typical enzyme has a catalytic site that bonds specifically to a single reactant and activates it. The catalytic site is multifunctional, bonding to the reactant at more than one position, almost to the exclusion of all but closely similar molecules (often products), and these similar molecules are reaction inhibitors.[2] Enzymes catalyze conversion of biological molecules with very high selectivities and at high rates, typically in the range of 10 to 10^3 molecules/(enzyme. s).

Fig. 21.2 a schematic representation of proton transfer in a hydrogen-bonded chain of water molecules

Each enzyme has a unique three-dimensional structure that usually includes a pocket or cleft presenting an array of functional groups positioned to bond to complementary functional groups of the reactant molecule.[3] The region of the cleft is a three-dimensional microenvironment, and the bonding of the reactant is comparable to a highly specific chemisorption. Nature's process of Darwinian selection has led to the biosynthesis of individual enzyme molecules each of which is in essence a unique multifunctional catalytic site that allows bonding and conversion of a particular reactant or class of reactants. Other chemical properties of enzymes besides those of the catalytic site are important also: the functional groups on the outer surface, for example, determine the enzyme's affinity for particular locations in the biological cell, such as the aqueous environment of the cytoplasm or the hydrophobic environment of a cell wall or other membrane.

Enzymes catalyze biological reactions; and since living organisms usually exist only at relatively mild temperatures, most enzymes function only under these conditions. Enzymes are delicate and do not retain their structures under conditions much outside the range characteristic of living organisms, although they may function *in vitro* in atypical environments such as nonaqueous solvents. Some organisms, such as those living in hot springs, have adapted to relatively high temperatures, and they could not exist without enzymes that are stable and active at these temperatures.

There is a great variety of biological reactions, including, for example, (i) the breakdown of proteins and sugars occurring in the digestive tracts of animals, (ii) the biosynthetic reactions that lead to growth and replacement of living organisms, (iii) photosynthesis, and (iv) oxidations that proceed by intricate pathways that convert food (e. g., sugars, proteins, etc.) into CO_2 water and energy in a biologically useful form.

Many enzyme-catalyzed reactions take place in biological cells.

The contents of cells are organized into well-defined domains. The cytoplasm is an aqueous biological soup with many molecules, including reactants, products, and enzymes in solution. The membranes are much more highly structured. Enzymes are also present in membranes and in cellular subunits called organelles. These bound enzymes are sometimes present in arrays that can be described as assembly lines. Evidently, the product of reaction in one enzyme is transported to the next enzyme in line so that a sequence of reactions takes place efficiently. Nature's catalysts function in highly sophisticated reactors.

Enzymes are usually named for the reactions they catalyze. For example, lysozyme catalyzes reactions that lead to the breakdown by hydrolysis (lysing) of polysaccharides; iosmerases catalyze isomerization reactions; dehydrogenases catalyze dehydrogenation reactions; and so forth. More specifically, alcohol dehydrogenases catalyze alcohol dehydrogenations, and L-lactate dehydrogenase catalyzes the dehydrogenation of L-lactate (to give pyruvate). Because the composition and structure of one kind of enzyme from one plant, animal, or bacterium may be different from those of the same kind of enzyme from another plant, animal, or bacterium, a further specification includes the source, for example, horse liver alcohol dehydrogenase.

From *Catalytic Chemistry* by Bruce C. Gates

New Words and Expressions

intermedium [ˌintə(:)'mi:diəm] (*pl* intermedia)   *n.* 中间体，媒介物
negligible ['neglidʒəbl]   *a.* 可忽略的，微不足道的
negligent ['neglidʒənt]   *a.* 疏忽的，粗心大意的
compensate ['kɔmpənseit]   *vt.* 补偿，赔偿，酬报
compensator ['kɔmpenseitə]   *n.* 补偿器，补助器
gigantic [dʒai'gæntik]   *a.* 巨大的，庞大的
three-dimensional structure   三维结构
cleft [kleft]   *n.* 裂缝，裂口
biosynthetic [baiousin'θetis]   *a.* 生物合成的
biosythesis [baiou'θi:sis]   *n.* 生物合成

Notes

1. 参考译文：这些结构中质子高度移动，这对于通过质子转移循环的催化过程有很大的重要性。对这一点的理解，可从课文中后面部分体会。

2. 参考译文：催化活性中心是多功能的，不止一个位置与反应物发生键合。除了与反应物非常相似的分子（常常是产物）以外，催化活性中心不与其他分子键合，而这些相似的分子是反应的阻抑剂。

3. 参考译文：每个酶具有独特的三维结构，通常包括了表示官能团排布的空穴或裂缝。这些官能团与分子的补充官能团相键合。

Unit 22 Cosmetics Introduction

Cosmetics are important to both men and women. They help us present an image not only to others but to ourselves. In a study of hair coloring and makeup, in which photographs were attached to fictitious work records for possible employment, it was found that hair coloring and makeup had a beneficial effect on offered salaries.[1] The amount averaged 12 percent greater when the photograph showed the prospective employee after receiving the cosmetic treatment rather than before. Most of us have more self-confidence facing others when we think we look our best. Cosmetics can cover skin blemishes and graying hair and can emphasize our best features.

But what is a cosmetic? What's in it? How safe is it? Is it worth its price?

The Food, Drug and Cosmetic Act defines a cosmetic as:

(1) Articles intended to be rubbed, poured, sprinkled or sprayed on, introduced into, or otherwise applied to human body or any part thereof for cleansing, beautifying, promoting attractiveness, or altering the appearance and (2) Articles intended for use as a component of any such articles, except that such terms shall not include soap.

To the United States Government, a cosmetic improves appearance, whereas a drug diagnoses, relieves, or cures a disease.[2] However, things are not quite that simple. A product may be both a cosmetic and a drug if it is intended to cleanse, beautify, or promote attractiveness by affecting the body or if a cosmetic is also intended to treat or prevent disease. Examples of products that, by law, are drugs as well as cosmetics are dandruff shampoos, antiperspirants that are also deodorants and suntanning preparations intended to protect against sunburn. This has caused consternation among regulators and the regulated because, for example, a sunscreen is considered a drug because it may protect against skin cancer and premature aging, whereas a tanning preparation is considered a cosmetic.

Another gray area is hormone-containing lotions. If the product affects the structure or function of the skin, then it is a medication. If the hormones are present in such small amounts that they have no effect, then it is sold under false pretenses because of the lack of effectiveness and the product should be considered misbranded.

Cosmetics have traditionally received little attention because it has been wrongly assumed that such products do not really affect our health and safety. The skin was believed to be a nearly perfect barrier that prevented chemicals applied to it from penetrating into the body. This belief went unchallenged until the 1960s when the much-heralded—but unmarketed—miracle drug DMSO proved its ability to carry substances with it through the skin and into the body's tissue and bloodstream.[3] Until it was shown that rabbit's eyes were adversely affected by the drug, DMSO was being promoted as a through-the-skin carrier of all sorts of medications. In fact, an increasingly popular new way to deliver drugs today is "transdermally." Medications to prevent seasickness or to treat angina (chest pains) are placed in an adhesive disc for delivery through the skin.

It has now been accepted that all chemicals penetrate the skin to some extent, and many do so in significant amounts. There are good tests for skin penetration available, yet they are rarely used for cosmetics. Tests to determine the systemic effects or metabolic degradation of an ingredient are rarely performed either. And the most frequent cosmetic culprits were fragrances, preservatives, anolin and its derivatives, p-phenylenediamine, and propylene glycol.

The most difficult issue in the identification of ingredients and contaminants in cosmetics concerns cancer-causing agents. A number of cosmetic ingredients now in use have been shown to be carcinogenic in animals or to cause mutations in the Ames Test, which uses bacteria to determine genetic breaks in cells. Testing for mutagenicity—breaks in the genetic material of bacteria—can screen many chemicals inexpensively and rapidly. Almost all chemicals known to be carcinogenic in humans have been shown to be mutagens in these systems. However, not all mutagens are necessarily carcinogenic. Thus animal studies—which cost approximately $ 300000 to thoroughly test an ingredient are needed.

All agents that cause cancer in humans cause cancer in rats and mice, with the exception of trivalent arsenic. Whether all chemicals that cause cancer in animals also cause cancer in humans is not known, but many scientists in the cancer field believe they do.

Two contaminants found in cosmetic products have been shown to cause cancer. One is N-nitrosodiethanolamine (NDELA), which penetrates easily through the skin when in a fatty base. It is a contaminant that appears to be produced by the interaction of two otherwise safe ingredients—for example, the amines (surfactants, emulsifiers, and detergents) and nitrites or nitroso compounds, such as in the preservative 2-bromo-2-nitro-propane-1, 3-diol (BNPD). The other carcinogen is 1, 4-dioxane, a contaminant of raw materials. It is believed that about one-third of the emulsion-based cosmetics containing polyoxyethylene derivatives have it in amounts ranging from one percent to over 25 percent.

After a brief introduction of cosmetics, we give shampoo as an example of cosmetics. Nowadays shampoos constitute one of the main products for personal care used by all strata of the population (age, sex...). In 1977 shampoos represented 43 percent of the total US haircare market.

Defined as " suitable detergents for the washing of hair, packaged in a form convenient for use ", they have since undergone drastic changes in design and technology in order to respond to multiple requirements, from the most sophisticated to the simplest and which go much beyond the single purpose of cleaning.

As early as 1955, a panel reported that " women want a shampoo to clean and also to rinse out easily, impart gloss to the hair and leave it manageable and non-drying. " At the same time, it was also stressed that " the principal trend evident in shampoo formulation is toward surfactants which have a milder effect on the skin, complete elimination of any sting if the product gets into the eye is the objective.

Conventional detergents of the anionic type seem, to cause unpleasant after-effects to the hair roughly in proportion to their grease removing power, but many other materials which remove grease will cause no apparent deterioration in the hair condition. Thus, if the hair is extracted with ether or trichloroethylene it can rapidly be made essentially grease-free, but its condition will be found almost unchanged. The hair will still be smooth, lustrous, and easy to comb and set. Even among detergents, there will be found some which remove relatively little sebum, but leave the hair in bad condition, and others which wash quite thoroughly without harming the hair. So no cause-effect relationship is likely to exist between residual oil and hair condition and it is up to the cosmetic chemist to find the right balance between adequate soil removal and desirable hair condition.[4]

This balance between cleaning and conditioning must be chosen with care, and it must also take into account the type of market to be supplied. People with greasy hair are highly critical of a shampoo which produces effects lasting only for three or four days, while those with dry hair may be more easily satisfied. However, many dry-haired people also use dressings of an oily character which must be removed, and in any case there is a deep-seated feeling, among women in particular, that the process of shampooing is a cleansing, purifying activity, designed to free them from daily accumulation and maturation of grease, dirt, perspiration, cooking smells, dandruff, environmental pollution and so on. In fact, it seems sensible to retain the definition of a shampoo as a suitable detergent for washing the hair with the corollary that it should also leave the hair easy to manage and confer on it a healthy look.

These are the two basic attributes of the types of shampoo described here and it is these requirements, known as "conditioning effects" and "mildness", that shampoo formulators nowadays provide as the indispensable cosmetic counterpart to the original "cleaning" function.

However, no matter how grand a shampoo may be, its primary function remains that of cleansing the hair of accumulated sebum, scalp debris and residues of hair-grooming preparations. Although any efficient detergent can do this job, cleansing should be selective and should preserve a quantity of the natural oil that coats the hair and, above all, the scalp. Undesirable side-effects have been shown to occur when using some of the best cleansers and indeed some authors include cleansing among the functions of shampoo only as an afterthought. The view that shampoos should be "inefficient" detergents arises mainly from the theory that the after-effects of shampooing-difficulty in combing the hair, roughness to the hand, lack of lustre and "fly" when the dry hair is combed—are due to excessive removal of oil from the hair. This assumption is at first sight quite reasonable but further examination shows that it is very much oversimplified: if sebum somehow fulfils a natural function of protection, and enhances the lustre and lubricity of the hair, it also possesses the dangerous drawback of attracting and trapping dust and dirt and has a potentially deleterious effect on the maintenance of set and the 'feel' of hair.

From *Harry's Cosmetology* 7th by J. B. Wilkinson, R. J. Moore

New Words and Expressions

cosmetic [kɔz'metik] n. 化妆品；a. 化妆用的，整容的
coloring ['kʌləriŋ] n. 着色（法），色彩，色调，面色，颜料
makeup ['meikʌp] n. 组成，构造，化装用品
fictitious [fik'tiʃəs] a. 虚构的，杜撰的，假造的
blemish ['blemiʃ] vt. 有损……的完美，玷污；n. 污点，瑕疵
sprinkle ['spriŋkl] vt. 洒，喷淋，撒布；vi. 洒，喷淋
diagnose ['daiəgnəuz](pl: diagnoses) v. 诊断（疾病），分析
antiperspirant ['ænti'pə:spirənt] n. 防汗剂
suntanning ['sʌntæniŋ] n. 防晒剂
suntan ['sʌntæn] n. 阳光晒黑后皮肤上出现的褐斑
consternation [ˌkɔnstə(:)'neiʃən] n. （极度）惊愕，惊恐
premature [ˌpremə'tjuə] a. 早熟的，不成熟的；n. 早产的婴儿；vi. 成熟，生长
misbrand ['mis'brænd] vt. 贴错（药品，食品）标记，贴假标签于
transdermally [træns'dʒ:məlli] ad. 经过真皮的
dermal ['dʒ:məl] a. 真皮的，皮肤的，表皮的
seasickness ['si:ˌsiknis] n. 晕海，晕船
seasick ['si:sik] a. 晕海，晕船
angina [æn'dʒainə] n. 心绞痛
preservative [pri'zə:vətiv] a. 有保护力的，防腐的；n. 防腐剂，防腐料
p-phenylenediamine ['fenəliːn'daiəmin] n. 亚苯基二胺
carcinogen [kɑː'sinədʒən] n. 致癌物

mutagen [ˈmjuːtədʒən] *n.* 诱变
mutagenic [ˌmjuːtəˈdʒenik] *a.* 诱变的
contaminant [kənˈtæminənt] *n.* 沾染物
surfactant [səːˈfæktənt] *n.* 表面活性剂
emulsifier [iˈmʌlsifaiə] *n.* 乳化剂，乳化器
emulsion [iˈmʌlʃən] *n.* 乳胶，乳浊液
detergent [diˈtəːdʒənt] *a.* 使干净的，使清洁的；*n.* 清洁剂，去垢剂
1，4-dioxane [daiˈɔksein] *n.* 1，4-二环氧乙烷
rinse [rins] *vt.* 冲洗，清洗（发，手）；*vi.* 漂净
trichloroethylene [traiˌklɔːrəuˈeθiˌliːn] *n.* 三氯乙烯
sebum [ˈsiːbəm] *n.* 皮脂，脂肪
perspiration [ˌpəːspəˈreiʃən] *n.* 排汗
cosmetology [ˌkɔzməˈtɔlədʒi] *n.* 整容术

Notes

1. 参考译文：在头发染色剂和化妆品的有关研究中，发现在应聘者所持的看上去不真实的工作记录中，如附有应聘者经过这些物质的化妆后所拍的照片，将对他们可能获得更高的雇佣工资有益。

2. 注意此句中"whereas a drug diagnoses"为插入状语，指"relieve"和"cure"结论的由来。英语中的"a cosmetic" "a disease"在翻译时应译通称。而不是"一种化妆品"或"一种疾病"。此为英语中名词若可数，应有数量词或冠词限制而来。参考译文：美国政府研究认为化妆品可以美容，而药物可以减轻或治愈疾病。

3. 注意："went unchallenged"是人们始终未怀疑这种想法。翻译时应指出"this belief"所指代的内容，即 the skin can prevent chemical penetrating into the body.

4. 句中"be up to"为短语，译为"这是……的责任（工作）"。在口语中"it is up to me"用于饭后付账时，指"由我付账"或"记在我头上好了"。也可用"it is on me."表示。

Exercises

Ⅰ. Comprehension

1. Which following sentence is not true for cosmetics. ____
   A. Medications to prevent seasickness or to treat angina (chest pains) are placed in an adhesive disc for delivery through the skin.
   B. Cosmetics have traditionally received little attention because the skin was believed to be a nearly perfect barrier that prevented chemicals applied to it from penetrating into the body.
   C. Cosmetics have traditionally received little attention because it has been wrongly assumed that such products do not really affect our health and safety.
   D. Cosmetics have traditionally received much attention because it has been assumed that such products do really affect our health and safety.

2. Two contaminants found in cosmetic products have been shown to cause cancer. One is N-nitrosodiethanolamine, ____.
   A. which penetrates easily through the skin when in a fatty base
   B. which penetrates easily through the skin when in a fatty acid
   C. which penetrates easily through the skin when in an unsaturated acid
   D. which does not penetrate easily through the skin when in a fatty base

3. This balance between cleaning and conditioning must be chosen with care, and it must also take into account the type of market to be supplied. Which sentence of the following is not true.

A. People with greasy hair are highly critical of a shampoo which produces effects lasting only for three or four days.

B. People with dry hair may be more easily satisfied.

C. Many dry-haired people also use dressings of an oily character which must be removed

D. People with greasy hair are highly critical of a shampoo which produces effects lasting for long time.

4. Shampoo's primary function remains the following except ____.

A. cleansing the hair of accumulated sebum
B. cleansing the scalp debris
C. cleansing the residues of hair-grooming preparations
D. leaving the hair easy to manage and confer on it a healthy look.

5. True or false

(1) Cosmetics, to some extent, are drugs because they can relieve the agony of the patients and can cure their diseases.

(2) It's DMSO that made people realize that the cosmetics have some side effects to the body.

In fact, every kind of cosmetic is carcinogenic, so we shouldn't promote its appearance in daily affairs.

6. Questions for discussion:

(1) Do you agree that the cosmetics could promote the chances for hunting a good job?

(2) Describe the functions of cosmetics.

II. Fill in the blanks with the proper words given below

affect   focused on   particular   considerations   commitments
using   boosting   proposed   price   different

As we know, marketing strategies have ____ the market or customer-oriented approaches. Enterprises are ____ their sales by developing special offers that cater to the needs and desires of customers with ____ backgrounds and specific customer groups. This kind of ____ is called "market segmentation". Product ____, of course, is one of the main factors to ____ the customer's purchasing behaviors. ____ budget segmentation, the cosmetics industry should make ____ to developing various price-based product collections so as to provide more customized or specialized commodities for ____ requirements. In the following, when price effects are considered, several rules are ____.

III. Put in proper prepositions or adverbs into the blanks

1. It faced many challenges including regulatory changes, product safety concerns, calls for scientific data to document product claims, increasing environmentalism, desire ____ natural ingredients, pressure ____ the growing animal rights movement, as well as economy and market channels for product distribution.

2. This means that customer orientation is the main concern for investigating market segmentation according ____ customers' attributes, preferences, and personal factors.

3. Cosmetic products are a kind of collection products, which include different cosmetic products and functions ____ specific usage stages in order to fulfill customer needs.

4. Fourthly, ____ a demand chain, the focus is clearly customer-centric, as defined early by Brace.

5. This paper proposes the association rules ____ data mining ____ extract customer and

market knowledge on product and transaction data from database.

IV. Answer the following questions

1. Hydrogenation reactions, processes in which H is added to a molecule, are usually catalyzed. An excellent catalyst is a very finely divided metal suspended in the reaction solvent. Tell why finely divided rhodium, for example, is a much more efficient catalyst than a small block of metal.

2. Sketch a reaction energy diagram for an exothermic reaction that proceeds through two steps, with the second step rate determining. If the first step were rate determining, how would your diagram change?

V. Translate the following into Chinese

p-pheylenediamine ____　　degradation ____　propylene ____　dandruff　　lotion
N-nitrosodiethanolamine　　carcinogenic　　premature ____　shampoo　　hormone
antiperspirant ____　　mutageniccity　　deodorant ____　corollary　　glycol

VI. Translate the following into English

表面活性剂　　环境污染　　乳化剂　　副作用
污垢　　　　　去垢剂　　　排汗　　　防腐剂

Reading Material

The History of Perfumery

The gratification of his senses is peculiar to man, and it is to this trait that we are indebted for all the arts.[1] The activities which aimed at the gratification of the eye and ear developed into the creative arts and music, and in like manner human endeavor directed toward the stimulation of the sense of smell has in our time assumed the proportions both of an art and a science;[2] for it was nothing but the advancement of chemistry that made it possible to fix all the pleasant odors offered by nature and to create new perfumes by the artistic combination of these scents. The preparation of perfumes is a very ancient art that is met with among all peoples possessed of any degree of civilization. It is particularly the ancient nations of the Orient which had in truth become masters in the manufacture of numerous perfumes.

The first perfume was the fragrant flower; it has continued to be so to the present day: the sprig of dried lavender flowers which we lay in the clothes-press was probably used for the same purpose by the contemporaries of Aristotle. In the Orient, which we may look upon as the cradle of the art of perfumery, the idea suggested itself early to substitute for the delicious fragrance of the flowers some substances of lasting odor; various sweet-scented resins supplied the material for this purpose. The use of these aromatic resins must have been very extensive: the ancient Egyptians alone consumed extraordinary quantities for embalming their dead. How highly the Oriental peoples in general prized perfumes can be learned from the Bible: the Jews (like the Catholics to the present day) employed an aromatic gum-resin (olibanum, frankincense) in their religious ceremonies; in the Song of Solomon mention is made of Indian perfumes, for instance, cinnamon, spikenard, myrrh, and aloes.

Altogether, incense played a prominent part in the religious ceremonies of the ancient Western Asiatic nations—among many peoples under a theocratic government it was even believed to be sinful to use incense for other than religious purposes. The Bible teaches us that Ezekiel and Isaiah protested against it, and that Moses even prescribed the preparation of certain kinds of incense for use in the tabernacle.

Among the most highly civilized people of antiquity, the Greeks, a large number of fragrant substances, as well as oils perfumed with them—that is to say, perfumes in the same sense as we still understand the term—was known; this will be no surprise to those familiar with the culture of this remarkable people. The odor of violets was the favorite among the Greeks; besides this they used the scent of the different mints, thyme, marjoram, and other aromatic plants. This was carried so far as to become a matter of fashion for the Greek fop to use only certain odors in the form of ointments for the hair, others for the neck, etc. In the order to prevent this luxury which was carried to such an excess, Solon even promulgated a law that interdicted the sale of fragrant oils to Athenian men (the law did not apply to the women).

The Romans, who were the pupils of the Greeks in all the arts, carried the luxury with perfumes perhaps even farther. In ancient Rome there was a very numerous guild of perfumers called *unguentarii*; they are said to have had a street to themselves in Capua. A Patrician Roman anointed himself three times daily with precious, sweet-scented oils which he personally took along into his bath in golden vessels of exquisite workmanship, so-called narthecia. At the funeral of his wife Poppaa, Nero is said to have used as incense more odorous substances than could be produced in one year in Arabia, at that time the only reputed source of perfumes. This luxury went so far that during the games in the open amphitheatres the whole air was filled with sweet odors ascending from numerous censers arranged in a circle. The apartments of well-to do Romans always contained large and very valuable urns filled with dried blossoms, to keep the air permanently perfumed.

Roman extravagance with perfumes was carried to such an excess that under the consulate of Licinius Crassus a law was passed which restricted the use of perfumery, there being good reason to fear that there would not be enough for the ceremonies in the temples.[3]

With the migration of the almost savage Huns and Goths, the refinement of morals ceased, progress in civilization was retarded for centuries, and at the same time the use of perfumes disappeared entirely in Europe; but it was otherwise in the Orient. As an instance we may mention the prophecy of Mohammed, who promised in the Koran to the faithful in paradise the possession of black-eyed houries whose bodies were composed of the purest musk.

The Arabs, the ancient masters of chemistry, were also the first founders of the art of perfumery. Thus the Arabian physician Avicenna, in the tenth century, taught the art of preparing fragrant waters from leaves, and Sultan Saladin, in 1157, on his triumphal entry, had the walls of the mosque of Omar washed with rose water.

It was the intercourse with the Orient brought about by the Crusades that made Europeans again more familiar with the art of perfumery, and a number of new odors rapidly became known. Italy and France, in those times the representatives of culture, were the countries in which the preparation of perfumes was carried on on a large scale. Thus, for instance, we find the name of a Roman family preserved to the present day because one of its members had combined a sweet-scented powder, called Frangipanni after its inventor, which is still in favor, and because his grandson Mauritius Frangipanni had made the important discovery that by treating this powder with spirit of wine the fragrant substance could be obtained in a fluid form.

The fact has been frequently related and repeated, that Catherine de Medici, the wife of Henry II, had made use of the fashion of perfuming the body for the purpose of ridding herself of objectionable persons, by giving them scented gloves prepared and at the same time poisoned by a Florentine named René. We think this tale to be simply a hair-raising fable—modern chemistry knows no substance the mere touch of which could produce the effect of a fatal poison; and it is scarcely credible that such a material had been known at that time and lost sight of since.

In the sixteenth century, especially at the court of Queen Elizabeth, perfumes were used with great extravagance; in fact, were looked upon as one of the necessaries of life. This luxury was carried still farther at the courts of the sumptuous kings of France; Louis XV. went so far as to demand every day a different odor for his apartments. A lady's lover always used the same kind of perfume she did.

It is well known that among the Oriental nations perfumes are used so largely that even food is flavored with rose water, musk, etc.; and Indian and Chinese goods always possess a peculiar aroma which is so characteristic for certain products that it was considered to be a sign of genuineness; this was the case, for instance, with the patchouly odor which always adheres to Indian shawls.

A shawl-maker of Lyons, who had succeeded in perfectly imitating Indian shawls with reference to design and colors, spent a fabulous sum to obtain possession of the plant used by the Indian weavers for perfuming their wares. Despite the great outlay caused by the search for this plant, the manufacturer is said to have done a flourishing business with his "genuine" Indian shawls.

In more recent times the wider range of commerce has resulted in the appearance of many new and valuable natural odorant materials and the scientific study of their extraction and preparation has made them available in more convenient form.[4] The culture of the perfume bearing plants has not been neglected and the yield of perfume has been in many cases notably increased. On the other hand, chemistry has added many new notes to the odor scale and has made the production of cheaper but still desirable perfumes possible. The consequent extension in the use of perfumes has led to placing the industry on a higher and more scientific plane and is in a fair way to make it even more important than it is today.

If empiricism is still the rule in the blending of odorous materials it is only because Science is still incapable of measuring accurately such an imponderable quantity as odor value. Yet it may be predicted that the time is not far off when a rational theory of odor values will be advanced on which can be founded experimental work which will result in placing the art of perfuming on a more scientific basis than it can claim today.

At present France claims supremacy in the perfume field and aided as she is by a plentiful supply of native raw material and by the natural artistic genius of her people. But the American perfumer yields place to none, and if our tariff policy allows him the unrestricted access to a quality of raw materials such as is enjoyed by his Gallic competitor he can easily hold his own. Even now the demand for imported perfumes is a matter of vogue and not of superior quality.

From *Perfumes and Cosmetics* 5th, by George William Askinson

New Words and Expressions

endeavor [in'devə]　　*vt.* 努力，尽力，努力，尽力，力图
sprig [sprig]　　*n.* 小枝，小枝状饰物，用（小枝）枝状物装饰
lavender ['lævində]　　*n.* 熏衣草，干熏衣草的花，用熏衣草熏香
spikenard [ə'spaikna:d]　　*n.* 甘松，甘松香油
myrrh [mə:]　　*n.* 没药，没药树，没药树脂
aloe [mə:]　　*n.* 芦荟

extravagance (extravagancy) [ikˈstrævəgəns]   n. 奢侈，浪费，铺张
objectionable [əbˈdʒekʃənəbl]   a. 引起反对的，令人不愉快的，讨厌的
shawl [ʃɔːl]   n. 长方形的围巾（披巾）用围巾（披巾）包裹
empiricism [emˈpirisizəm]   n. 经验主义

Notes

1. 参考译文：人们对感觉的满足是人类特有的，正因为这个特点，我们才感谢所有的艺术。

2. 参考译文：人们用来满足眼睛、耳朵的活动发展成为创造性的艺术、音乐，这样人们对嗅觉追求付出的努力在我们这个时代就占据了一门艺术、一门科学的位置。

3. 参考译文：罗马人对香水是如此奢侈，以至于在 Licinius Crassus 的作用下通过了一部法律限制人们使用香水。对此一个很好的理由是担心在圣坛举行仪式时香水不够用。

4. 参考译文：近来更广泛的香水贸易导致出现了许多新的、有价值的香味材料，对这些物质的提取、制备的研究使人们能够以更便利的方式来得到香水。

Unit 23　Research of Vitamin E

During the last almost 90 years since its discovery, research on vitamin E has focused on different properties of this molecule, the focus often depending on the specific techniques and scientific knowledge present at each time. For giving a brief overview and introduction about vitamin E for this special issue of " Molecular Aspects of Medicine ", it is therefore most convenient to follow the major research directions with a historical perspective (Fig. 23. 1).

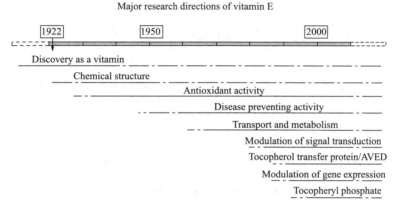

Fig. 23. 1　major research directions of vitamin E

Discovery of vitamin E

Vitamin E has been discovered as " factor X " by Evans and Bishop while investigating dietary factors that are essential for reproduction in rats (Evans and Bishop, 1922). Similar experiments were performed by Sure, who then called the substance " vitamin E " (Sure, 1924). At about the same time Mattill and Conklin investigated whether milk represents a " perfect food ", and they came to the conclusion that milk may contain a substance that inhibited reproduction (Mattill and Conklin, 1920). Notably, the diet given in these experiments usually contained relatively high amounts of lard (10%～22%), and Mattill later proposed that fats from animal sources are susceptible to auto-oxidation (Mattill, 1927). Subsequent expansion of this research showed that vitamin E can prevent the oxidation of lipids, and thus acts chemically as an antioxidant molecule (Cummings and Mattill, 1931). The discovery of the biological activity of vitamin E, its chemical structure and its antioxidant and non-antioxidant functions have been recently reviewed in detail (Mason, 1977; Ricciarelli et al., 2002; Rosenfeld, 1997; Wolf, 2005).

Research on the chemical structure of vitamin E

Natural vitamin E comprises eight different forms, the α-, β-, γ-, and δ-tocopherols and the α-, β-, γ-, and δ-tocotrienols (Fig. 23. 2). The tocotrienols have an unsaturated isoprenoid side chain, whereas the tocopherols contain a trimethyltridecyl tail with three chiral centres which naturally occur in the RRR configuration. Only recently novel natural vitamin E analogues have been discovered; palm oil contains also small amounts of α-tocomonoenol, and some marine organisms contain also marine derived tocopherol (MDT), with a single unsaturated bond at the end of the side chain, which is assumed to be the result of cold-water adaptation (Fig. 23. 2).[1] The phosphorylated form of α-tocopherol, α-tocopheryl phosphate (Fig. 23. 2), was synthesized already in the 1940s; however, only recently after developing a novel isolation method, it was shown to occur naturally in foods and in animal as well as in human tissues, acting possibly as a storage molecule, as transport form, or as "lipid messenger" for the modulation of signal transduction and gene expression.

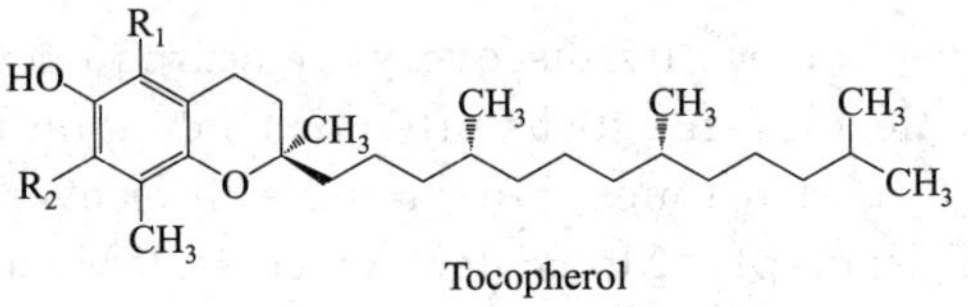

Tocopherol

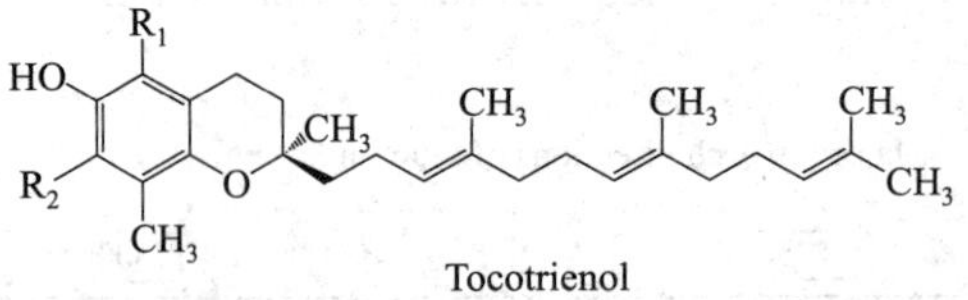

Tocotrienol

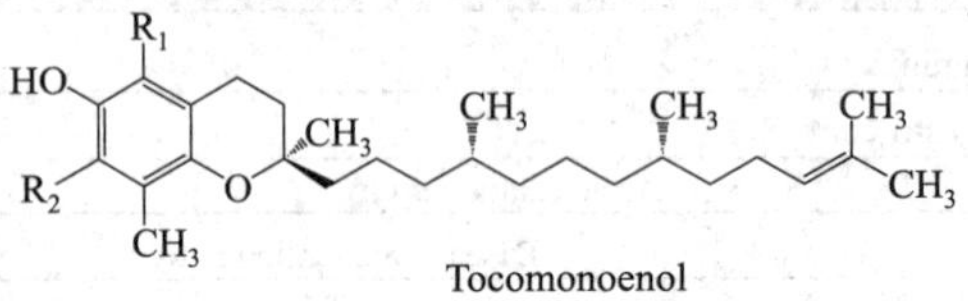

Tocomonoenol

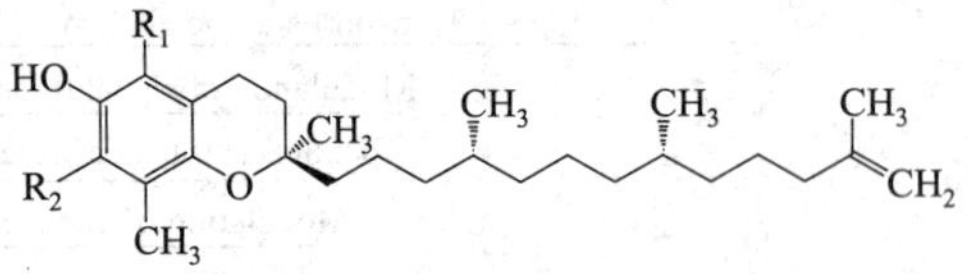

Marine Derived Tocopherol(MDT)

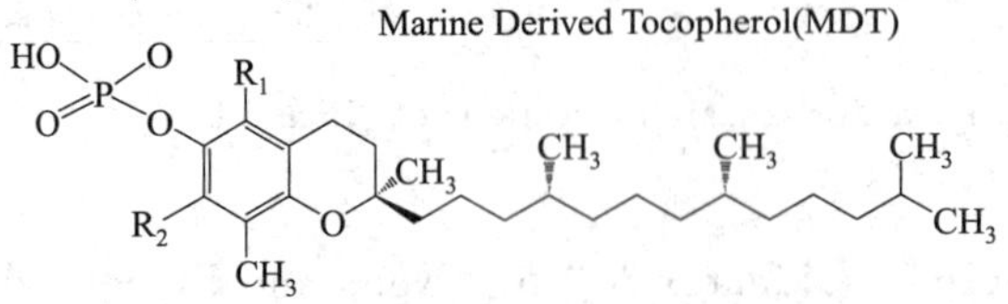

Tocopheryl Phosphate

R_1	R_2	
CH_3	CH_3	α
CH_3	H	β
H	CH_3	γ
H	H	δ

Fig. 23.2 natural vitamin E analogues

Research on the biosynthesis of vitamin E in plants

The tocopherols are exclusively synthesized in photosynthetic organisms including higher plants; significant amounts are found in all green tissues but predominantly occur in seeds. Plant derived oils represent the major sources of vitamin E in the human diet, and because these oils contain the four tocopherols in different relative amounts, the overall intake of each vitamin E analogue depends in large on the dietary oil preferences in different countries. The major vitamin E analogue in olive and sunflower oils is α-tocopherol, corn oils contain mainly γ-tocopherol, and oils derived from soy beans contain relatively high amounts of δ-tocopherol. The tocotrienols are the major vitamin E components of palm oil, significant amounts are also found in barely, oat and rice bran. In the last decade, the genes involved in biosynthesis of vitamin E in plants have been identified and genetic engineering was used to elevate the tocopherol content in leafs and seeds. Several important functions for vitamin E in plants were described, such as the prevention of non-enzymatic lipid oxidation during seed storage, germination, and early seedling development, and the abilities of vitamin E to prevent photo-oxidative stress, to adapt to low temperature, and to modulate signal transduction in plants by influencing jasmonic acid levels.

Research on health benefits of vitamin E

Potential health benefits of vitamin E supplementation that are in addition to the essential effects on reproduction were suggested already in the 1950s.[2] In particular, the neurological symptoms associated with vitamin E deficiency were reported to improve with vitamin

E supplementation. Although therapeutic properties of vitamin E against cardiovascular disease were proposed very early, they remained controversial until a first epidemiological study was described suggesting that vitamin E supplementation can protect against cardiovascular disease. Since then the possible beneficial effects of vitamin E supplementation, that may go beyond its essential function, were studied with many diseases; in particular with atherosclerosis and other cardiovascular diseases.

Vitamin E is also commonly used in cosmetic and skin care products, and experimental evidence suggests that topical and oral vitamin E has anti-tumorigenic, photoprotective, and skin barrier stabilizing properties, albeit large controlled clinical studies for specific dermatological indications such as atopic dermatitis or photocarcinogenesis are still lacking. Many of the above diseases are caused, aggravated or associated with inflammatory events, and as reviewed in this issue, vitamin E (in particular α-and γ-tocopherol) can interfere with inflammation either by scavenging reactive oxygen and nitrogen species, by modulating the synthesis of inflammatory lipid mediators, or by influencing signal transduction and the expression of specific cytokines, chemokines and other inflammatory molecules.

All these studies are based on the finding that vitamin E levels can be increased by extra dietary supplementation, implying that pathways involved in vitamin E uptake and body distribution are often not saturated. Plasma vitamin E concentrations could vary in different individuals as a consequence of consumption, e. g. by excessive production of oxidants, or of a deficient uptake and transport into plasma and tissues. Certain diseases, like abetalipoproteinemia, chronic cholestatic liver disease, cystic fibrosis, chronic pancreatitis, progressive systemic sclerosis, shortbowel syndrome or several other lipid malabsorption syndromes are associated with a low efficiency of vitamin E uptake, that can at the extreme lead to similar symptoms as in AVED. These symptoms clearly can be prevented and in some situation reversed by supplemental vitamin E.

Whereas in cell culture models and animal studies the health benefits of vitamin E supplementation in diseases such as atherosclerosis, inflammation, cancer and neurodegenerative diseases have been clearly demonstrated, with a few exceptions most recent human epidemiological and clinical studies often gave neutral or disappointing results. Nevertheless, although recent meta-analyses showed slightly increased all-cause mortality with high doses of vitamin E supplementation, there is little evidence for negative side effects of vitamin E and C in adults when taken below the tolerable upper intake level (1000 mg/day for vitamin E and 2000 mg/day for vitamin C, as suggested by the Food and Nutrition Board of the Institute of Medicine). Moreover, in a recent follow-up study of the α-tocopherol, β-carotene cancer prevention study surveying 29092 Finnish male smokers (the ATBC-study), higher baseline serum concentrations of vitamin E were reported to be associated with lower total and cause-specific mortality.

As shown for hyperlipidemic mice, vitamin E works best against experimental atherosclerosis in situations of severe vitamin E deficiency induced by knockdown of the liver α-TTP gene, an effect that is independent of preventing lipid oxidation in the vessel wall, and probably similar statements could be made for other diseases, such as Alzheimer's disease. Several factors have been proposed to explain the often negative outcome of human studies, in particular the relatively short duration of treatment, the presence of vitamin E in the normal diet sufficient to prevent disease symptoms, and a number of other reasons. In addition to that, supplemented vitamin E may gain relevance during local depletion of vitamin E occurring during inflammatory processes, infection, smoking or UV irradiation, suggesting that potential health effects may become evident only under specific environmental and patho-physiological circumstances.

Taken together, it has to be clearly distinguished whether vitamin E is supplemented at supra-physiological doses aimed to systemically increase vitamin E plasma and tissue levels and to reverse local vitamin E depletion, or whether vitamin E supplementation is used to reverse systemic vitamin E deficiency syndromes. In the first case, the potential benefits of vitamin E supplementation may be detectable only with difficulty and possibly reflect the scavenging of damaging reactive oxygen and nitrogen species produced locally during the disease process; in the second case it is well documented that vitamin E deficiency syndromes can clearly be prevented and in some situations reversed by supplemental vitamin E, possibly resulting from some of the essential molecular and cellular activities of vitamin E discussed in this issue of "Molecular Aspects of Medicine".

From *Vitamin E*: *An overview of major research directions by Jean-Marc Zingg*

New Words and Expressions

lipid ['lipid, 'laipid]　*n*. 脂质，油脂［脂肪，乳酪］
oxidant ['ɔksidənt]　*n*. 氧化剂
isoprenoid [,aisəu'prenɔid]　*a*. & *n*. 类异戊二烯（的）
trimethyltridecyl [trai'meθil trai'desil]　*n*. 三甲基十三烷基
phosphorylate ['fɔsfərileit]　*vt*. 使磷酸化
gene [dʒi:n]　*n*. 因子，基因
neurological [njuərəu'lɔdʒikəl]　*a*. 神经学上的
therapeutic [θerə'pju:tik]　*a*. 治疗的，治疗学的；*n*. 治疗剂，治疗学家
cardiovascular [,kɑ:diəu'væskjulə]　*a*. 心脏血管的
atherosclerosis [,æθərəuskliə'rəusis]　*n*. 动脉硬化症
topical ['tɔpikəl]　*a*. 论题的，局部的
oral ['ɔ:rəl]　*a*. 口头的
clinical ['klinikəl]　*a*. 临床的，病房用的
atopic [ə'tɔpik]　*a*. 遗传性过敏症的
inflammatory [in'flæmətəri]　*a*. 煽动性的
inflammation [,inflə'meiʃən]　*n*. 炎症，发炎
plasma ['plæzmə]　*n*. 血浆，乳浆，等离子体，等离子区
chronic ['krɔnik]　*a*. 慢性的，延续很长的
cystic ['sistik]　*a*. 胞囊的；膀胱的，胆囊的
fibrosis [fai'brəusis]　*n*. 纤维症，纤维化
pancreatitis [,pæŋkriə'taitis]　*n*. 胰腺炎
sclerosis [skliə'rəusis]　*n*. 硬化症，硬化，硬结
syndrome ['sindrəum]　*n*. 综合病症
infection [in'fekʃən]　*n*. 传染，传染病，影响，感染

Notes

1. 参考译文：只是最近才发现新型的天然维生素 E 的类似物，棕桐油也含有少量。一些海洋生物也含有在侧链末端带有一个不饱和键海产生育酚（MDT），声称这是适应冷水的结果。

2. 句中，"in addition to"在科技英语中作加和理解，意思为除了……以外，还有……；也可翻译成另外……。参考译文：维生素 E 的补充除了早在 1950 年就发现的对生殖有重要影响外，对健康也有潜在的益处。

Exercises

I. Comprehension

1. Natural vitamin E comprises eight different forms, the α-, β-, γ-, and δ-tocopherols and the α-, β-, γ-, and δ-tocotrienols. Which sentence for natural vitamin E is not true? ____
   A. The tocotrienols have an unsaturated isoprenoid side chain.
   B. The tocopherols contain a trimethyltridecyl tail with two chiral centres which naturally occur in the RRR configuration.
   C. The tocopherols contain a trimethyltridecyl tail with three chiral centres which naturally occur in the RRR configuration.
   D. The tocotrienols have a trimethyltridecyl tail with three chiral centres which naturally occur in the RRR configuration.

2. The tocopherols are exclusively synthesized in photosynthetic organisms including higher plants; significant amounts are found in all green tissues but predominantly occur in ____.
   A. seeds   B. leaves   C. stem   D. root

3. Vitamin E is also commonly used in cosmetic and skin care products, and experimental evidence suggests that topical and oral vitamin E has the following properties except ____.
   A. anti-tumorigenic property   B. photoprotective property
   C. skin barrier stabilizing property   D. anti-oxidative property

4. Vitamin E can interfere with inflammation either by scavenging reactive oxygen and nitrogen species, by the following passages except ____
   A. modulating the synthesis of inflammatory lipid mediators
   B. influencing signal transduction
   C. the expression of specific cytokines, chemokines and other inflammatory molecules
   D. only expression of chemokines

II. Answer the following questions

(1) Who first discovered vitamin E and when did they found it?
(2) How many forms does natural vitamin E have, and what are they?
(3) What is the major vitamin E analogue in olive and sunflower oils? Then write down its structural formula.
(4) Please summarize the research on health benefits of vitamin E.
(5) Why is vitamin E commonly used in cosmetic and skin care products?

III. Fill in the blanks with the proper form of the word given at the end of the sentence

(1) This third requirement makes α-TTP selective for the 2R-isomers of ____ α-tocopherol, as has also been demonstrated in α-TTP null mice. (synthesis)

(2) The ____ binding of RRR-α-tocopherol by α-TTP is reflected in the 3-fold greater half-life of RRR-α-tocopherol (57h±19h) compared to the half-lives of SRR-α-tocopherol or γ-tocopherol. (preferential)

(3) The mechanism by which α-TTP maintains plasma α-tocopherol remains under intense ____. (investigate)

(4) It is clear that in the ____ of α-TTP the default pathway results in lysosomal accumulation of α-tocopherol and its ultimate excretion rather than the secretion of α-tocopherol into the plasma, as shown in patients with defective α-TTP. (absent)

(5) ____ of vitamin Es appears to also play a major role in hepatic regulation of vitamer

concentrations. (metabolic)

(6) Additionally, it should be noted that the fully ____ chromanol ring of α-tocopherol prevents adduct formation at the positions that are not ____ in the non-α-tocopherols. (methyl)

IV. Problem

(1) Addition of ethanol or other organic solvents to an aqueous "solution" of a globular protein brings about denaturation. Such treatment also tends to break up micelles of, say, soap. What basic process is at work in both cases?

(2) An amino group can be protected by acylation with phthalic anhydride to form an N-substituted phthalimide. The protecting group can be removed by treatment with hydrazine, H_2N-NH_2 without disturbing any peptide linkages. Write equations to show how this procedure could be applied to the synthesis of glycylalanine and alanylglycine.

V. Translation the following words and expressions into English

维生素   生育酚   抗氧化剂   酯类物   甲基化反应   氧化反应   刺激物

VI. Translation the following sentences into English

(1) 种抗氧剂的相互作用使抗氧剂的保护作用的水平如此之高使在正常的环境下氧化的之类物的含量是可以控制的。

(2) 维生素E，作为过氧化自由基的清道夫来终结链反应，其抗氧化功能是大家都知道的，并且被各类化学家所描述。

(3) 应该指出的是α-生育酚的氧杂奈满酚环的完全甲基化可以防止在天然非α-生育酚没有甲基化位置上加合物的形成。

(4) 香烟是一种许多反应性的氧和氮物种以及炎性刺激物的外界生成的来源。

(5) 生育酚只有在光合反应的生物，包括高级的植物中被合成。

Reading Material

Vitamin E and Antioxidant

Vitamin E was discovered in 1922 by Evans and Bishop as a necessary dietary factor for reproduction in rats. Subsequent studies showed that the presence of rancid fat in the experimental diets fed to rats and chickens was the causative agent of various pathologies in these animals and that these abnormalities could be "cured" by wheat germ oil concentrates that later were demonstrated to contain tocopherols.

Vitamin E antioxidant activities

The curiosity is that all of the naturally occurring vitamin E forms, as well as those of synthetic all-rac-α-tocopherol, have relatively similar antioxidant activities, so why does the body prefer α-tocopherol as its form of vitamin E? Vitamin E's antioxidant function, as a peroxyl radical scavenger that terminates chain reactions, is well-known and well-described by various chemists. There are important differences between the various vitamin E forms with respect to their antioxidant activities. Whether they are measured in organic solution such as chlorobenzene or in detergent supported lipids (to mimic biological membranes), the rank order of the tocols remains the same and the greater potency of α-tocopherol versus the other vitamers is approximately constant.[1] Surprisingly, this is true across the different chemical systems, as well as different investigators. These results are due to the relative H-atom-donating ability of the different tocols, which increases in efficiency with greater ring methyl substitution. The differences in potency of α-tocopherol versus other tocols in vivo.[2]

are due to hepatic discrimination favoring α-tocopherol, as well as the preferential metabolism of non-α-tocopherol forms.

What has not been established is whether non-α-tocopherols follow the same rank order of antioxidant efficiency when in biological membranes. In actual membranes, the antioxidant power would include the H-atom-donating ability, location (penetration) and movement within the membrane, plus the efficiency of tocopheroxyl radical recycling by cytosolic reductants, such as ascorbate.[3] Attempts have been made to compare α-tocopherol and α-tocotrienol; in microsomal membrane systems the conclusion was that tocotrienols are better antioxidants, but in more chemical systems they are said to be near equivalent.

Additionally, it should be noted that the fully methylated chromanol ring of α-tocopherol prevents adduct formation at the positions that are not methylated in the non-α-tocopherols. For example, the formation of 5-nitro-γ-tocopherol has been touted as a marker of the benefit of γ-tocopherol scavenging reactive nitrogen species. Provocatively, Tafazoli et al. reported that the order of vitamin E analogues in catalyzing hepatocyte cytotoxicity, lipid peroxidation, and GSH oxidation was δ-tocopherol > γ-tocopherol > α-tocopherol > PMC. The toxic prooxidant activity of vitamin E analogues was therefore inversely proportional to their antioxidant activity. The in vivo preference for α-tocopherol may then also rest on the potential "toxic" activity of the vitamin E analogues.

Human vitamin E deficiency

Human vitamin E deficiency symptoms began to be reported in the 1960s in various case studies of patients with lipoprotein abnormalities and subsequently in fat malabsorption syndromes, but because these patients had malabsorption of other nutrients, especially long-chain fatty acids, it was not clear the extent to which various symptoms could be attributed to lack of vitamin E. In the early 1980s case studies and various reports of unique humans with vitamin E deficiency symptoms without fat malabsorption began to appear in the literature. Subsequently, the cause of this form of human vitamin E deficiency was shown to be a defect in the gene for the α-TTP.

The peripheral neuropathy of vitamin E deficiency in humans is described as a progressive dying back of the nerves. Interestingly, the symptoms observed in these patients are similar to the abnormalities observed in patients with Friedreich ataxia, a genetic disorder caused by a mutation in the gene for frataxin, a mitochondrial iron-binding protein. Thus, free iron in mitochondria could cause lipid peroxidation, an increased need for a lipid-soluble antioxidant and therefore a decrease in α-tocopherol. The dying back of the sensory neurons in both ataxias is likely caused by insufficient nerve vitamin E resulting in apoptosis. So is this a sign of vitamin E signaling that cells should undergo apoptosis, or an oxidative stress due to lack of vitamin E antioxidant function? We are currently studying the question, but do not have an answer.

Oxidative stress in humans

Does vitamin E act as an antioxidant in humans? In general, there are numerous studies showing that vitamin E supplements can decrease measures of lipid peroxidation in subjects with oxidative stress, examples include decreasing urinary F2-isoprostanes in hypercholesterolemic subjects and in diabetics. However, normal subjects not under oxidative stress showed no effect of vitamin E supplements on markers of oxidative damage. We believe that the level of antioxidant protection by the interaction of various antioxidants is so efficient that under normal circumstances, the levels of oxidized lipids are kept in check. This contention is supported by studies in selenium-deficient guinea pigs that are subsequently fed a vitamin E-deficient diet, or vitamin C-deficient guinea pigs that are subsequently fed a vitamin E-deficient diet. In both cases, the depletion of two antioxidant systems leads to a rapid system failure and death within days.

To evaluate whether vitamin E acts as an antioxidant in humans, first it was necessary to establish model systems where humans are under ethically accepted modes of oxidative stress. We have used two different model systems, both extreme exercise and cigarette smoking.

Studies in extreme exercisers

An ultramarathon race (50km or 32miles) is run annually in McDonald forest, a research forest belonging to OSU, Corvallis, Oregon. The racecourse is up and down hills, usually taking the runners 5 to 7 h, and the runners expend around 7000 calories during the race. In our first study, we found that both vitamin E disappearance rates and F2-isoprostane concentrations increased in the runners during the race as compared with a rest period. To evaluate whether prior supplementation with antioxidants (vitamins E and C) would prevent the increased oxidative stress, a more extensive follow-up study was carried out in the ultramarathon racers. In this second study, the 50km ultramarathon run again caused oxidative damage measured as increased F2-isoprostane concentrations and DNA damage. Muscle damage was characterized by measures of fatigue, as well as increased circulating muscle damage markers. Circulating inflammatory markers elicited by the run increased in the characteristic progression of cytokine responses to tissue damage and inflammation. Supplementation with both vitamins E and C completely inhibited exercise-induced lipid peroxidation, but had no effect on other parameters, such as inflammation, DNA damage, muscle damage markers, fatigue, or recovery.

Cigarette smokers as examples of oxidative stress in humans

Cigarette smoke is an exogenous source of an enormous number of reactive oxygen and nitrogen species, as well as an inflammatory stimulant. The hypothesis of this study was to determine if the chronic oxidative stress of cigarette smoking would result in a more rapid in vivo disappearance of α-tocopherol. The investigation (10 subjects/group) was conducted among nonsmokers and smokers (>10cigarettes/day). The subjects were healthy, college-aged, nondietary supplement users with normal cholesterol status. The α-tocopherol fractional disappearance rates in cigarette smokers (0.215 ± 0.001) were ~13% greater than in nonsmokers [0.191 ± 0.001 pools/day; $p<0.05$]. Moreover, the smokers with the lowest plasma ascorbic acid concentrations had the fastest α-tocopherol disappearance rates, presumably because vitamin C regenerates vitamin E. To test this hypothesis, smokers and nonsmokers were supplemented for 2 weeks with placebo or vitamin C (1000 mg/day), and then their plasma vitamin E disappearance rates were measured. Using a crossover design, the same subjects were tested again on the opposite supplement. Marginal vitamin C status in smokers was associated with increased rates of vitamin E disappearance from plasma, and these rates were normalized by prior vitamin C supplementation. Importantly, both α-and γ-tocopherols were similarly affected by vitamin C status, suggesting that oxidation of the tocopherols is the mechanism for the faster vitamin E disappearance.

From *Vitamin E, antioxidant and nothing more* by Maret G. Traber

New Words and Expressions

rancid ['rænsid] *a.* 像油脂腐臭味的，腐臭的
causative ['kɔːzətiv] *a.* 原因的，成因的
pathology [pə'θɒlədʒi] *n.* 病理学

abnormality [ˌæbnɔːˈmæliti] n. 变态；n. 畸形，异常性
peroxyl [pəˈrɔksil] n. (=hydrogen peroxide) 过氧化氢
scavenger [ˈskævindʒə] n. 清除剂；净化剂
tocol [ˈtəukɔl] n. 母育酚
potency [ˈpəutənsi] n. 能力
hepatic [hiˈpætik] a. 肝的
cytosolic [ˈsaitəusɔlik] a. 细胞溶质的
ascorbate [ˈæskɔːbeit] n. 抗坏血酸盐
adduct [əˈdʌkt] n. 加合物
malabsorption [ˌmælæbˈsɔːpʃən] n. （营养）吸收障碍，吸收不良
neuropathy [njuəˈrɔpəθi] n. 神经病
selenium [siˈliːniəm, -njəm] n. 硒
guinea [ˈgini] n. 几尼（英国的旧金币，值一镑一先令）
exogenous [ekˈsɔdʒinəs] a. 外因的
ascorbic [əsˈkɔːbik] a. 维生素 C 的
placebo [pləˈsiːbəu] n. 安慰剂

Notes

1. 句中"*versus*"是拉丁语，意思是"……对……"，或"与……进行比较"。参考译文：在有机溶剂例如氯苯或在洗涤剂负载的脂类（模拟生物膜）中抗氧化活性测试表明 tocols 的排序是一样的，α-生育酚比其他维生素能力的提高差不多是恒定的。

2. "*In vivo*" 拉丁语，意思是在体内，自然条件下的实验、化验。

3. 句中的"plus"是连接词，本文中的意思是加和。参考译文：实际的膜中，抗氧剂能力会包括氢原子的给予能力，在膜内的定位（穿透性）和运动，再加上称作为维生素类细胞溶质性还原剂循环生育酚自由基的效率。

Unit 24　The Benefits of Pesticides

The hazards of pesticides are well documented, but their benefits are largely ignored in published literature and the mass media. A recent brief poll of pesticide-related articles in published literature, conducted by the authors, revealed a ratio of over 40 negative articles for each one that took a more positive view. Many point to health or environmental problems from accidental or deliberate exposure to pesticides, particularly pesticides with high mammalian toxicity or those that persist in the environment. These risks should not be ignored, and efforts must be made to minimize them through rigorous regulation and proper training for users, but we should not overlook the positive impacts of pesticide use. When pesticides are used rationally and carefully, in conjunction with other technologies in integrated pest management systems, it is more likely that their use will be justifiable.

This paper does not attempt to quantify or rank the benefits, nor to balance the benefits from pesticide use against any negative consequences. Rather it focuses on the positive outcomes delivered by judiciously used pesticides, in order to inform a more objective assessment of costs and benefits.

Types of positive outcome from pesticide use

There is a large range of positive outcomes from different types of pesticide use. Reduced crop loss resulting from spraying fungicides is an obvious benefit, but some are less obvious either because they occur in the medium or long term, or are subtle or small incremental benefits distributed over a large area. To facilitate a systematic analysis capable of unravelling the many potential benefits of pesticide use, a hierarchical model of outcomes was adopted, comprising effects, primary benefits and secondary benefits.

Effects

Effects are the immediate outcomes of pesticide use—for example killing caterpillars on a cabbage. These are not classed as benefits because the consequences of the effects have not manifested themselves yet. The three main effects of pesticides are:

(1) controlling agricultural pests (including diseases and weeds) and vectors of plant disease;

(2) controlling human and livestock disease vectors and nuisance organisms;

(3) preventing or controlling organisms that harm other human activities and structures.

Primary benefits

These are the consequences of the pesticides' effects—the direct gains expected from their use. For example, the effect of killing caterpillars prevents them feeding on the crop and brings the primary benefit of higher yields and better quality of cabbage.

Secondary benefits

These are the less immediate, less intuitively obvious, or longer term consequences. It follows that for secondary benefits, it is more difficult to establish cause and effect, but nevertheless they can be powerful justifications for pesticide use. For example, higher cabbage yield might bring additional revenue that could be put towards children's education or medical care, leading to a healthier, better educated population.

The benefits of effect

The benefits of effect 1—*controlling pests and plant disease vectors*

Over the last 60 years, farmers and growers have changed the way they produce food in order to meet the expectations of consumers, governments and more recently, food processors and retailers. In doing so, they have made many changes to the way they farm, including the extensive use of pesticides. They have done this principally to prevent or reduce agricultural losses to pests, resulting in improved yield and greater availability of food, at a reasonable price, all year round.

Not only do pesticides prevent losses on existing crops, they broaden the range of viable crop options that a farmer can grow at particular times of year. For example, tomatoes can only be grown in the rainy season in Zimbabwe by using fungicide to prevent late blight—without them, there is usually total crop failure. This rainy season production is also extremely lucrative; tomatoes have a highly elastic price response to demand, with rainy season prices being 10 times dry season prices.

Herbicides are the most widely used type of pesticide since weeds are the major constraint that limit yield in many crops. Herbicides represent around 50% of all crop protection chemicals used throughout the world, compared with insecticides and fungicides that are around 17% each. Without herbicides there would be an estimated 13.3 billion US Dollars loss in farm income in the US.

There are knock-on benefits of these primary benefits. If marketable yields and quality are increasing, farm revenues are also likely to increase. This results in wealthier farmers with more disposable income to stimulate the local economy. Higher yields mean less pressure to cultivate un-cropped land—a wider benefit to biodiversity and the environment as highlighted by McNeely Jeffrey and Scherr Sara. In turn, regional and national agricultural economies become more buoyant and revenues from exports of high quality produce bring in much needed foreign exchange. This last factor is particularly important in some developing countries that export fruit and vegetables to the US and Europe, where the unintended presence of certain flora and fauna in the produce can be a major barrier to international trade.

Pesticides can also improve the quality of the produce including its safety. When stressed or attacked by diseases, many plants, or the pathogenic organisms causing the diseases, produce chemicals that are acutely toxic.[1]

Benefits of effect 2—controlling human/livestock disease vectors and nuisance organisms

The most obvious benefit of controlling the wide range of human and livestock disease vectors is reduced suffering and lives saved that would otherwise have been lost, but reducing the likelihood of international spread of disease is not insignificant. With regard to livestock, controlling disease vectors translates to secondary benefits of additional livestock revenue and reduced veterinary and medicine costs.

There are also substantial benefits to reducing the number of people suffering sub-lethal effects of vector borne diseases. The misery caused by frequent bouts of malaria or the insidious effects of river blindness on eyesight has a debilitating effect on the morale and productivity of communities, not to mention the cash cost of medicines to treat these diseases. Moreover, studies by Hoffman et al. have shown that acute malaria infection increases HIV viral load, and that this increased viral load was reversed by effective malaria treatment. This malaria-associated increase in viral load could lead to increased transmission of HIV and more rapid disease progression, with substantial public health implications.

A less obvious, but still significant benefit is the prevention of misery and disturbance caused by various biting insects, whether they transmit disease or not. This group includes mosquitoes, blackflies, midges, other biting flies, fleas, lice and bedbugs. Studies in Cameroon have found people in some areas being bitten up to 2000 times per day by Simuliid blackflies, effectively preventing them doing any useful agricultural or other outdoor work due to the nuisance and constant irritation.[2] An additional nonlethal but nonetheless disfiguring effect of these bites is depigmentation of the skin, which causes social stigmatization and inability to find life partners. The whining noise of mosquitoes flying—especially Culex species—disturbs people and prevents them sleeping properly.

Benefits of effect 3—*preventing or controlling organisms that harm other activities or damage structures*

In the same way that pests in agriculture and public health cause undesirable effects such as losses, spoilage and damage, various organisms have a negative impact on human activities, infrastructure and the materials of everyday life unless controlled. Pesticides play an important, if often unseen role in preventing this negative impact.

The transport sector makes extensive use of pesticides, particularly herbicides, to ensure that roads, railways and waterways are kept free of vegetation that might otherwise cause a hazard or nuisance. For example, if vegetation is allowed to grow too tall on roadsides, it reduces the drivers' view at junctions, and deposits branches or vegetation onto the road that might be an obstruction or make it very slippery[3]. The use of pesticides to manage this vegetation brings secondary benefits of safer transport systems with fewer accidents and less stress for users.

Pesticides are also used on water craft to prevent the build up of algae, molluscs, and weeds, and deliver secondary benefits of reduced costs of manual cleaning, and increased fuel efficiency from the reduced drag of a smooth hull. Similarly, the pesticides used in domestic gardens enable householders to maintain their plants—edible or ornamental—and protect them from pests and diseases. Gardening is the most popular leisure activity in the United Kingdom and pesticides are helping to facilitate a hugely popular pastime that provides fresh air and exercise for millions of people around the world, contributing to their health, fitness and quality of life. The result of their efforts is reflected economically in several ways. Exercise promotes health and reduces medical needs, and pleasant gardens add significantly to the value of properties.

Insecticides protect buildings and other wooden structures from damage by termites and wood boring insects, thus decreasing maintenance costs and increasing longevity of buildings and their safety. This use also has wider environmental benefits in that timber—a renewable resource that can be produced in an environmentally beneficial way—becomes a more viable construction material. So while there is plentiful evidence linking pesticide effects to primary benefits, in order to link the primary benefits to the secondary and subsequent ones and validate the complete chain of benefits, pesticides must be strictly regulated and used judiciously by properly trained and appropriately equipped personnel, ideally in tight integration with other complementary technologies.

From *The benefits of pesticides to mankind and the environment by Jerry Cooper*

New Words and Expressions

junction [ˈdʒʌŋkʃən]   n. 连接，结合，交叉点，汇合处
assessment [əˈsesmənt]   n. （为征税对财产所作的）估价，被估定的金额
fungicide [ˈfʌndʒisaid]   n. 杀真菌剂
subtle [ˈsʌtl]   a. 狡猾的，敏感的，微妙的，精细的，稀薄的
hierarchical [ˌhaiəˈrɑːkikəl]   a. 分等级的
caterpillar [ˈkætəpilə]   n. 毛虫
cabbage [ˈkæbidʒ]   n. 甘蓝，卷心菜
nuisance [ˈnjuːsns]   n. 讨厌的人或东西，麻烦事，损害

revenue ['revinju:]   n. 收入，国家的收入，税收
blight [blait]   n. 枯萎病，不良影响，打击；vt. 破坏，使枯萎
lucrative ['lu:krətiv, lju:-]   a. 有利的
herbicides ['hə:bisaid]   n. 除草剂
buoyant ['bɔiənt]   a. 漂浮的；有浮力的
flora ['flɔ:rə]   n. 植物群
fauna ['fɔ:nə]   n. 动物群，动物区系，动物志
pathogenic [ˌpæθə'dʒenik]   a. 致病的，病原的，发病的
veterinary ['vetərinəri]   n. 兽医；a. 医牲畜的，兽医的
lethal ['li:θəl]   a. 致命的；n. 致死因子
misery ['mizəri]   n. 痛苦，苦恼，悲惨，不幸，穷困
bout [baut]   n. 一回，一场，回合，较量
malaria [mə'lɛəriə]   n. 疟疾，瘴气
insidious [in'sidiəs]   a. 隐伏的；埋伏的
debilitating [di'biliteit]   vt. 使衰弱，使虚弱
midge [midʒ]   n. 蚊
flea [fli:]   n. 跳蚤
lice [lais]   n. 虱子，白虱
irritation [ˌiri'teiʃən]   n. 刺激
nonlethal ['nɔn'li:θəl]   a. 不致命的
depigmentation [di:pigmən'teiʃən]   n. 退色，脱色
infrastructure ['infrəstrʌktʃə]   n. 下部构造，基础下部组织
craft [krɑ:ft]   n. 工艺，手艺
algae ['ældʒi:]   n. 藻类，海藻
molluscs ['mɔləsk]   n. 软体动物
weed [wi:d]   n. 野草，杂草
edible ['edibl]   a. 可食用的
termite ['tə:mait]   n. 白蚁

Notes

1. 句子中，"When stressed or attacked by diseases"表示的是"many plants"的状态，与"the pathogenic organisms"没有关系。参考译文：杀虫剂可以提高农产品的质量，包括它的安全性。感受到了压力或者疾病的植物或引起疾病的病原生物体都会产生有毒的化学物质。

2. 句子中的分词短语作结果状语，参考译文：在 Cameroon 进行的研究表明，某些地区一些每天被蝇蚋咬 2000 多次的人会因为持续的烦躁而无法进行有效的农业或者其他户外活动。

3. 句子中，"it"指的是"vegetation"，其后面有两个并列的谓语，"reduces"和"deposits"。参考译文：比如说，如果路边的植被长得太高的话，司机看马路交叉口的视野就会减小，掉落的树枝或者植物也有可能成为障碍物或者使路面变得很滑。

Exercises

Ⅰ. Comprehension

1. The main effects of pesticides are the following mentioned except ____.
A. controlling agricultural pests (including diseases and weeds) and vectors of plant disease

B. controlling human and livestock disease vectors and nuisance organisms
C. preventing or controlling organisms that harm other human activities and structures
D. controlling human disease

2. How much of all crop protection chemicals used throughout the world do Herbicides represent?
   A. around 17%   B. around 50%   C. around 15%   D. around 20%

3. Studies in Cameroon have found people in some areas being bitten up to 2000 times per day by Simuliid blackflies, effectively preventing them doing ____.
   A. useful agricultural or other outdoor work due to the nuisance and constant irritation
   B. useful agricultural or industrial work due to the nuisance and constant irritation
   C. homework and other outdoor work due to the nuisance and constant irritation
   D. useful agricultural or other outdoor work due to infectious disease

4. Pesticides can also improve the quality of the produce including its safety. ____ many plants, or the pathogenic organisms causing the diseases, produce chemicals that are acutely toxic.
   A. When stressed or attacked by pests
   B. When stressed or attacked by diseases
   C. When stressed or attacked by infectious diseases
   D. When stressed or attacked by bad weather

II. Answer the following questions

(1) Describe the three main effects of pesticides.
(2) What's the primary benefits of pesticides?
(3) Summary the benefits of effect.
(4) When are herbicides the most widely used type of pesticide?
(5) Please describe the the most obvious benefit of controlling human and livestock disease vectors in detail.

III. Fill in the blanks with the phrases given below

be associated with   due to   arises from   the range of   relevant in
in terms of   as a result of   access to   effect on   resulted in

(1) Secondary penalties would be massive environmental damage ____ the land needs of less productive farming, and a financial cost of around 20 billion US Dollars.

(2) It ____ an extensive literature search, the preparation of a comprehensive review report and the compilation of an electronic database of pesticide benefits for Crop Life International.

(3) Pesticide residues in food, detected at ever-lower levels due to increasingly sensitive laboratory equipment, are perceived to ____ these issues and are lumped together with them as another of the evils of agricultural intensification.

(4) These domains and dimensions are mentioned where ____ the exploration of benefits that follows and the benefits are categorised according to them later in Fig. 5.

(5) Not only do pesticides prevent losses on existing crops, they broaden ____ viable crop options that a farmer can grow at particular times of year.

(6) He concluded that increased agricultural productivity creates direct economic benefits for farming families ____ increased income.

(7) The reduction in the need for manual weeding is particularly significant in sub-Saharan Africa where HIV/AIDS has ____ shortages of labour and many adults being too ill to work.

(8) For example, when rats are introduced onto islands previously free of them, they have a devastating ____ local fauna-in particular, on ground-nesting birds, but also other mammals, molluscs, insects, spiders, amphibians and reptiles.

(9) The World Health Organization claims that without ____ chemical control methods, life will continue to be unacceptably dangerous for a large proportion of mankind.

(10) To some extent, this is an over-simplification ____ trying to categorise the benefits and avoid repetition, for example, the benefit of reduced soil erosion and moisture loss that currently sits in the national benefits area, applies equally to communities.

IV. Fill in the blanks with the proper form of the word given at the end of the sentence

(1) Similarly, few people would deny that medicines can reduce disease and preserve life, but if they are used without care they can be extremely ____. (hazard)

(2) These examples provide parallels with pesticides, being technologies that make our lives better, ____ they are regulated and used in such a way that the benefits significantly outweigh the risks. (provide)

(3) However, the detail of the linkages is less important at this stage than the ____ that there are many and varied positive downstream implications arising from pesticide use—some more obvious, and some less so. (recognize)

(4) ____ nutrition and ____ drudgery clearly both improve the quality of life of rural communities, and while 'quality of life' is imprecise and difficult to define, it is surely what most people are seeking to improve-whether it be through money, work satisfaction, home life or more time for recreation. (improve reduce)

(5) Children are at risk for pesticide ____ from different sources and at levels different than adults in the same ____ scenario. (expose)

V. Problems

(1) Arrange the compounds in each set in order of reactivity toward the indicated reagent. Give the structure and name of the product expected from the compound you select as the most reactive in each set.

(a) NaOH: chlorobenzene, m-chloronitrobenzene, o-chloronitrobenzene, 2,4-dinitro- chlorobenzene, 2,4,6,-trinitrochlorobenzene

(b) HNO_3/H_2SO_4: benzene, chlorobenzene, nitrobenzene, toluene

(2) The insecticide called DDT, 1,1,1,-trichloro-2,2-bis-(p-chlorophenyl) ethane, (p-ClC_6H_4)$_2CHCCl_3$, is manufactured by the reaction between chlorobenzene and trichloroacetaldehyde in the presence of sulfuric acid. Outline the series of steps by which this synthesis most probably takes place; make sure you show the function of the H_2SO_4. Label each step according to its fundamental reaction type.

VI. Translation the following words and expressions into English

有机氯化合物   多氯联苯二噁英   污染物   苯氧羧酸类   去毒作用
毒化作用   协同作用   除草剂   杀虫剂

VII. Translation the following sentences into English

(1) 除草剂是种运用最为广泛的杀虫剂，因为野草是农作物产量的主要限制因子。

(2) 长期以来，苯氧羧酸类除草剂中例如DTT和二氧（杂）芑等有机氯刹虫剂成分引起了人们的关注，因为它的在环境中的持久性，生物累积以及对健康有长期负面影响的毒性——包括癌症和例如先天缺陷等对生殖能力的有害影响。

(3) 我们可以鉴定儿童对杀虫剂毒性的易感性。

(4) 总的来说，最近母乳中的二氧（杂）芑含量有所下降。有机氯水平的地理性差异有被报道过。

(5) 根据结构上的相似性，上述数据表明有机氯类的杀虫剂可能有相似的毒性作用。

Reading Material

Pesticides and Children

For many years now, there has been public concern raised about the potential health effects of pesticides on the developing fetus and in childhood. A fundamental maxim of pediatric medicine is that "children are not little adults". This observation is especially relevant to discussion of children and their exposures to pesticides. Children are at risk for pesticide exposures from different sources and at levels different than adults in the same exposure scenario. Children's respiratory rate, heart rate, and metabolism are significantly different from adults. Food consumption and food consumption patterns place children in a special dietary pesticide risk category. Hand-to-mouth behavior further adds to children's pesticide exposure by the oral route. Children, being low to the ground, may have greater exposure to volatile pesticide vapors, particularly those pesticides that, in the gas phase, have a density greater than air. One prime example is the grain fumigant aluminum phosphide (AlP). After enclosed space application, AlP is converted to the toxicant gas phosphine, the active pest control agent. Human phosphine fatality case reports dealing with children playing on AlP fumigated grain, and another dealing with a fatality of a pregnant woman living near large tarp covered fumigated grain piles, illustrate the potential hazard.[1]

Children's pesticide exposure

Historically, organochlorine pesticides, for example, DDT and dioxin contaminants in chlorophenoxy herbicides, have been a concern in regard to environmental persistence, bioaccumulation, and toxicity related to longer-term adverse health effects, including cancer and adverse reproductive effects such as birth defects. For children, the principal route of exposure for these chemicals is through ingestion from breast milk and diet. In general, levels of dioxins in breast milk have been decreasing in recent times. Geographic variation in organochlorine levels has been reported in studies of human breast milk from lactating women residing in the arctic and subarctic regions of Russia. Similar geographic variation was noted in historical resident-based studies from California.[2] In another study, organochlorine levels in offspring were found to vary directly with the age of the mother pointing to cumulative historic maternal exposure as a major part of the infant's total exposure.

Recent studies of preschool children from the Netherlands demonstrated that alteration of markers of neurobehavioral development and immunologic status were related to higher body burdens or prenatal exposures to dioxins/PCBs. These works imply that more subtle neurobehavioral toxicity can occur in children subject to current dioxin/PCB exposure levels. More careful study of this question is needed.

Children's health and pesticides
Pesticides and childhood cancer

In an earlier comprehensive review of childhood cancer, Zahm and Ward presented a detailed analysis of the available epidemiological data for or against association between pesticides and childhood cancer. In their review, the authors included case reports and case-control studies. Individual case-control studies reported tended to have few subjects and fewer exposed subjects. The studies were further limited by nonspecific pesticide exposure information. Nonetheless, linkage between childhood leukemia and parental exposure or use of pesticides was frequently reported in the studies reviewed. Most studies reviewed also suggested an association between childhood brain cancer and parental pesticide exposure. Fewer studies suggested possible relationships between neuroblastoma, Ewing's sarcoma, and non-Hodgkin lymphoma in childhood and pesticide use.

With regard to cancer in general and childhood cancer in particular, gene-environment interaction becomes a major concern. Population-based case-control studies showed interaction between CYPA1M1 and CYP1AM2 mutations and the occurrence of acute lymphocytic leukemia when women were pregnant or their children had been exposed to insecticides. Other gene polymorphisms examined in this reported work failed to show evidence of gene—chemical toxicant interaction.

Altogether, epidemiological studies reviewed above have provided a beginning for understanding of the relationships between parental and children's exposures to pesticides and the occurrence of childhood cancer. The general lack of specificity of these studies point out the need for laboratory-based studies with specific toxicological endpoints to fingerprint exposure—effect relationships.

Children and neurologic/neurobehavioral effects of pesticides

A number of editorials and reviews identified the need to examine neurobehavioral and neurodevelopmental status of children exposed to toxicants, including pesticides. Studies evaluating possible neurological and neurobehavioral effects of pesticides in children are indeed rare. In this connection, neurobehavioral studies conducted among children exposed to polychlorinated biphenyls have parallel interest. These studies consistently showed PCB dose-related interference with cognitive function during early childhood. On the basis of structural similarities, the foregoing data infer that members of the organochlorine class of insecticides might have similar toxicant effects. Neurobehavioral studies conducted among adults and children inadvertently exposed to chlordane, an organochlorine insecticide, in an apartment complex (216 exposed and 174 control subjects) showed an association between protracted impairment of neurophysiological and psychological function and exposure to chlordane.

Susceptibility to OP intoxication and neurodevelopment may have a basis other than anticholinesterase effects. Polymorphisms of paraoxonase (PON), an enzyme involved in the detoxification of organophos-phorothioate (OP) insecticides, showed very low levels of activity in the human newborn period. In the same review and study, enhanced OP sensitivity was demonstrated in paraoxonase activity-deficient adult (knockout) mice.

Endocrine effects

More subtle and perhaps more important to the developing fetus, child, and adult are endocrine disorders arising out of alteration of thyroid function. If thyroid modulation of organ and tissue form and function are changed, physical and mental retardation and congenital births defects in children, including alterations of the cardiovascular system and musculoskeletal defects, are more likely to occur[3]. In the hypothyroid pubescent child, routine clinical studies demonstrate alterations of the menstrual cycle and onset of menarche, obesity, and failure to develop secondary sex characteristics appropriately.

A number of pesticide products are thought to interfere with thyroid function [acetanilide, ethylene bisdithiocarbamates (EBDCs), nitroanilines, organophosphates, and synthetic pyrethroids]. The reported molecular mechanism of action in terms of thyroid toxicant activity of each of these pesticide classes may differ significantly. Possible synergistic interactions anywhere in the hypothalamic—pituitary—endocrine organ axis among pesticides used in combination add further complexity. Measurable adverse health outcomes due to exposures to endocrine disrupting agents can be diverse. At the governmental level, programmatic progress toward development of effective research tools has been made to reduce the uncertainty that surrounds determination of endocrine disruptive effects in populations.

In the context of this review, the following quote seems applicable: " Although endocrine disruption in humans by pollutant chemicals remains largely undetermined, the underlying science is sound and the potential for such effects is real ". Hormones and hormone effects are low-dose, receptor-driven actions, dependent on local and distant feedback. Normal hormone activities take place over a relatively narrow concentration range[4]. Chemical interference with hormone actions, particularly during neurodevelopment, and consequent effects on cognitive behavior are a current concern. The appropriateness of toxicological screening for detection of endocrine-active compounds continues to be a point of much concerted query and discussion.

Future directions

Much of the research data reviewed here is necessarily descriptive. It is an appropriate effort for epidemiologist and an ancillary role for toxicologist. With the rise of genomics and toxicogenomics and the introduction of sensitive immunoassay and analytic methods capable of being used to measure toxicants levels in humans, mechanism-based human studies are at the horizon. With these tools, population toxicologists can assess differences and similarities between children's and adults' response to pesticide exposure. We can identify children's susceptibility to toxicant effects of pesticides. More importantly, we will be able to better quantify children's risk. In the meantime, it seems prudent to minimize children's exposure to pesticides wherever possible.

From *Pesticides and children by Vincent F. Garry*

New Words and Expressions

fumigant ['fju:migənt]   n. 熏蒸剂
phosphide ['fɔsfaid]   n. 磷化物
phosphine ['fɔsfin]   n. 磷化氢，三氢化磷
arctic ['ɑ:ktik]   a. 北极的，北极区的；n. 北极，北极圈
leukemia [lju:'ki:miə]   n. 白血病
neuroblastoma [,njuərəblæs'təumə]   n. 成神经细胞瘤
lymphocytic [,limfəu'sitik]   a. 淋巴球的，淋巴细胞的
polymorphism [,pɔli'mɔ:fizəm]   n. （同质）多晶（现象）
specificity [,spesi'fisiti]   n. 特异性，特征；种别性
chlordane ['klɔ:dein]   n. 氯丹；八氯化甲桥茚
psychological [,saikə'lɔdʒikəl]   a. 心理（上）的
intoxication [in,tɔksi'keiʃən]   n. 中毒；喝醉
anticholinesterase ['ænti,kəuli'nestəreis]   n. 抗胆碱酯酶（如毒扁豆碱）
endocrine ['endəukrain]   n. 内分泌
cardiovascular [,kɑ:diəu'væskjulə]   a. 心脏血管的
musculoskeletal [,mʌskjuləu'skelitəl]   a. 肌（与）骨骼的
hypothyroid ['haipəu'θairɔid]   n. 甲状腺功能减退者，甲状腺 a. 甲状腺机能减退的
ethylene bisdithiocarbamates (EBDCs):   n. 乙烯双二硫代氨基甲酸盐（或酯）
nitroaniline [,naitrəu'ænilain]   n. 硝基苯胺
organophosphates [,ɔ:gənəu'fɔsfeit]   n. & a. 有机磷酸酯（的）(现广泛用作杀虫剂、抑燃剂等)
pyrethroid [pai'ri:θrɔid]   n. 拟除虫菊酯，合成除虫菊酯
hypothalamic [,haipəuθə'læmik]   a. 丘脑下部的，下丘脑的

pituitary [piˈtju(:)itəri] n. 垂体
ancillary [ænˈsiləri] a. 补助的，副的

Notes

1. 句子中，两处的"dealing with"都是修饰"reports"。参考译文：在封闭空间应用之后，AlP 转化为有毒气体磷化氢——一种正在被使用的除虫剂。磷化氢对人类有潜在的危险，报道过磷化氢致人死亡事件，例如在用 AlP 熏过的谷物堆上玩耍的小孩死亡事件和住在用来遮盖被熏过的谷物堆的大防水布附近的孕妇死亡事件。

2. 句子中，"noted"意为"注意到……"，"发现……"。参考译文：根据来自加利福尼亚长期居住的研究发现相似地理性变化。

3. 句子中，分词短语"including..."作状语，修饰"defects"，而与"retardation"没有关系。参考译文：如果甲状腺对器官和组织形态功能的调控发生了变化，那么行为和思维上的迟缓以及儿童的先天性缺陷-包括心血管系统的变化和肌肉骨骼的缺陷就更有可能发生。

4. 句子中，短语"dependent on…"作补语，进一步描述"actions"。参考译文：激素和激素效应是低剂量，受体驱动的反应，依赖于本地和远距离的反馈。正常的激素活动发生在一个比较狭窄的浓度范围内。

PREFIX AND SUFFIX

-a	……化物	butano-	桥亚丁基
a-	无,不,非	butoxy-	丁氧基
ab-	脱离		
-able	易于……的,可……的	carb(o)-	碳,羰
abs-	相反,不	-carbaldehyde	甲醛
acet(o)-	乙酰	carbamoyl-	酰胺基
acetato-	醋酸合	-carbohydrazide	甲酰肼
-acious	有……性质的,多……的	carbonato-	碳酸合(根)
acyl-	酰基	-carbonitrile	甲腈
-ad	(名词词尾)	-carbonyl halide	甲酰卤
-adiene	……二烯	-carbonyl	羰基,酰基
-adiyne	……二炔	carbonyl-	羰基,酰基
-al	醛	-carboxamide	甲酰胺
alk-	烃类	-carboxamidine	甲脒
allyloxy-	烯丙氧基	carboxy-	羧基
-amide	酰胺	carboxylate	……酸酯
amidino-	脒基	-carboxylic acid	甲酸
-amine	胺	chem(o)-	化学的
amino-	氨基	chloro-	氯化……,氯代……
ammine-	氨化,氨合	chlorosyl-	亚氯酰
amphi-,ampho-	两个,两种	chloryl-	氯氧基
an-	无,不,非	chrom(o)-	铬的
-ane	……烷	-cide	除……剂,防……剂
-aneous	……性质的,属于……的	circum-	周围,环绕,附加
anhydr(o)-	酐,无水,脱水	cis-	顺式
ante-	前,先	co-,col-,com-,cor-	同,共,合
aquo(a)-	水合	cyano-	氰合,氰基
-ar	(形容词词尾)	cyclo-	环
arsa-	砷杂		
-ate	含氧酸盐,……酯	deca-	十,癸
-atriene	……三烯	deutero-	氘代
-atriyne	……三炔	de-	消除,脱去,解,减,除
aza-	氮杂	dexter-,dextro-	右
azido-	叠氮基	di-	双,二,偶
azo-	偶氮	dia-	对穿,横穿,通过,完全
		diacetoxyiodo-	二乙酰氧基碘代
ba-	两,双,二	diazo-	重氮,偶氮
be-	使……,加以……,用……	-dienyl	……二烯基
benzeno-	桥亚苯基	dif-	逆,反,散
benzyloxy-	苄氧基	dihydroxyiodo-	二羟基碘代
bi-	二,双,酸式	-dione	二酮
bis-	双	dis-	否定,相反,分离
bisma-	铋杂		
bora-	硼杂	-ecine	辛因
bromo-	溴代	ef-	出,脱离
but-	丁	electr(o)-	电,电的

-en	变得……,放入……内部,进入……之中	-ine	已因,含氮
endo-	吸收,桥,内	inter-	相互,中间,一起
-ene	……烯	intro-	在内,向内,进入
-enyl	……烯基	iodo-	碘代
ep(i)-	环	iodoso-	亚碘酰
-epine	庚因	iodosyl-	亚碘酰
equi-	相等,平等	iodyl-	碘酰基
-er	……剂	-iridine	丙啶
-ete	四元环	-irine	丙因
ethano-	桥亚乙基	ir-	无,非
etheno-	桥亚乙烯基	-ish	略带……的,微……的
ethoxy-	乙氧基	isopropoxy-	异丙氧基
ethylenedioxy-	亚乙基二氧基	iso-	同,等,异
-etidine	丁啶	-ite	亚酸盐,亚……酯
ex-	由……向外,放出	-ium	(金属元素词尾)
exo-	放出,向外	-ize	使……化
extra-,extro-	再外,外部,离	-ketone	酮
		kilo-	千
ferro-	亚铁	kin(e)-	动,运动
fluoro-	氟代		
-fold	倍	-lactone	内酯
-form	仿	-less	不,无
formyl-	甲酰基	-lysis	分解,消散
-free	无		
		mal-	恶,失,不
germa-	锗因	macro-	大,巨,宏观
gluco-	甜味的	magni-	宏,大,巨大
glyco-	甜味的	mercapto-	巯基,氢硫基
-gram	图,记录,图表,克	mercura-	汞杂
graphy-	……(方)法	meso-	间位,片,杂
		meta-	间,偏,变
halo-	卤素	-meter	……表,……仪,……计
haloformyl-	卤甲酰基	methano-	桥亚甲基
-hedral	……面体的	methoxy-	甲氧基
-hedron	……面体	methylamine-	甲氨(合)
hemi-	半	-metry	……测量法,……度量法
hept(a)-	七,庚	micro-	微,小,百万分之一
hetero-	杂,异,多,	mis-	坏,误,否定
hex(a)-	六,己	mol(e)-	摩尔,分子
homo-	均,同,单	mono-	单,一,独
holo	全		
hydro-	水,氢	nano-	纳
hydroxo-	羟基(合)	neo-	新
hydroxy-	羟基	nitrato-	硝酸合
hydroxyl-	羟基	nitro-	硝基
hyper-	高,超	nitroso-	亚硝基(合)
hypo-	次,低	non-	无,非,不
		nona-	九,壬
-ic	酸的,高价金属离子	nor-	正,正常,降
-ide	……化物,无氧酸盐,酐		
il-	无,非	-oate	……酸盐,酸酯
im-	无,非	-ocene	二茂(金属)化合物
imino-	亚氨基	-ocine	辛因

oct(a)-	八,辛	quadri-quadr(u)-	四
-ode	路,通道,极,管	-quinone	醌
-ohydrazide	甲酰肼		
-oic acid	酸	radio-	放射,辐射
-oid	似……,像……	re-	再,重新,反,回
-ol	醇	retro-	向后,回,反
-olate	……醇……		
-ole	氮杂茂	scopy-	……观察法,……检验法
-olidine	戊啶	selena-	硒杂
olig(o)-	少,低,微	seleno-	硒基
-on	(名词词尾),(非金属元素词尾)	self-	自身,自发,自动
		semi-	半,部分,不完全
-one	酮	sens-	感觉,灵敏
-onine	壬因	-side	苷
-or	剂,体,器	sila-	硅杂
organo-	有机的	spectr(o)-	(光)谱,视觉
ortho-	邻,正,原	stanna-	锡杂
-ose	糖	-stat	恒,不动,固定
osm(o)-	渗透	stereo-	立体,空间
-ous	亚……的,亚	stiba-	锑杂
oxa-	氧杂	sub-	低,亚,次
oxalato-	草酸合	sulfo-	磺(酸)基
-oxide	氧化物	super-	上,超,过,高
oxo-	氧代,氧化		
oxy-	含氧,氧(代)	tellura-	碲杂
-oyl halide	酰卤	telluro-	碲基
-oyl	酰基	tetra-	四
		thermo-	热
para-	对,顺,聚,旁,侧	thia-	硫杂,噻
pent(a)-	五,戊	-tion	(名词词尾,表状态、行为、结果等)
pentyloxy-	戊氧基		
per-	高,过,全,完全,十分	trans-	反式
perchloryl-	氯过氧基,过氧氯基	tri-	三
perhydro-	全	trimethylenedioxy-	亚丙基二氧基
peri-	周围,包围		
phenoxy-	苯氧基	ultra-	极度,超,过度,外
-phile	亲……的,亲……体	-um	(金属元素词尾)
-philic	亲……的,亲……体,亲近	un-	不,未,非,去
phospha-	磷杂	uni-	单,一
photo-	光,摄像		
phthal-	(邻)苯二甲……	vapori-	水蒸气,水雾
plumba-	铅杂	volt(a)-	伏特
poly-	聚,多		
pre-	预先,早,前	-yl	……基
pro-	早,前,先,代替	-ylene	亚基
propano-	桥亚丙基	-yne	炔
propoxy-	丙氧基	-ynyl	炔基

VOCABULARY

ablation [æb'leiʃən] n. 消融，熔损
abnormality [ˌæbnɔː'mæliti] n. 变态；n. 畸形，异常性
absorbance [b'sɔːbəns] n. 吸光率，吸光度
academia [ˌækə'diːmjə] n. 学术界，学术环境
account for 解释，说明
accumulator [ə'kjuːmjuleitə] n. 收集器，蓄电器，存储器
acetamide [æsi'tæmaid] n. 乙酰胺
acetaminophen [ˌæsi'tæminəfən] n. 退热净，对乙酰氨基酚
acetanilide [ˌæsi'tænilid] n. 乙酰苯胺，退热冰
acetone ['æsitəun] n. 丙酮
acetyl ['æsitil] a. 乙酰基，醋酸的
acetylacetonate [ˌæsiti'læsitəuˌneit] 乙酰丙酮盐
acetylene [ə'setiliːn] n. 乙炔，电石气
acetylsalicylic [əˌsitilˌsæli'silik] n. 乙酰水杨酸，阿司匹林
acquisition [ˌækwi'ziʃən] n. 获得，获得物
acrylic acid [ə'krilik] n. 丙烯酸
acute [ə'kjuːt] a. 急性的，剧烈的
adduct [ə'dʌkt] n. 加合物
adequacy ['ædikwəsi] n. 适当，足够
adipic [ə'dipik] a. 己二酸的
adjacent [ə'dʒeisənt] a. 邻近的，接近的
adulterant [ə'dʌltərənt] a. 掺杂用的；n. 掺杂物
affinity [ə'finiti] n. 亲和力
alchemy ['ælkimi] n. 炼金术，炼丹术
algae ['ældʒiː] n. 藻类，海藻
align [ə'lain] v. 使成一线，结盟，调节
alkali ['ælkəlai] n. 碱；a. 碱性的
alkaline ['ælkəlain] a. 碱的，碱性的
alkane ['ælkein] n. 烷烃
alkene ['ælkiːn] n. 烯烃
alkoxy [æl'kɔksi] n. 烷氧基，烃氧基
alkyl ['ælkil] a. 烷基的，烃基的；n. 烷基，烃基
alkyne ['ælkain] n. 炔（烃）
alloy ['ælɔi] n. 合金；vt. 使成合金，减低成色
aloe ['æləu] n. 芦荟
alphabetical [ˌælfə'betikəl] a. 依字母顺序的
alphabetize ['ælfəbitaiz] vt. 依字母顺序排列，用字母标示
aluminium [ə'ljuːminiəm] n. 铝
aluminosilicate [əˌljuːminəu'silikeit] n. 铝硅酸盐
aluminum [ə'ljuːminəm] n. 铝

amide ['æmaid] n. 酰胺
amino ['æminəu] a. 氨基的
amino acid ['æminəu'æsid] n. 氨基酸
aminoethane [ˌæminəu'eθein] n. 氨基乙烷，乙胺
ammonia ['æməunjə] n. 氨，氨水
ammonium ['məunjəm] n. 铵，铵盐
amorphous [ə'mɔːfəs] a. 无定形的；非结晶质的；没有明确结晶结构的
amphiphile [æm'fifil] n. 两亲物，两性分子
amplitude ['æmplitjuːd] n. 广大，充足，振幅
ampule ['æmpuːl] n. 小型密封玻璃瓶，安瓿（装液体的密封小瓶）
analgesic [ˌænæl'dʒiːsik] n. 止疼剂
analyte ['ænəlait] n. 分析物；被分析物
ancillary [æn'siləri] a. 补助的，副的
angina [æn'dʒainə] n. 心绞痛
anhydride [æn'haidraid] n. 酐，脱水物
anion ['ænaiən] n. 阴离子
anionic detergent 阴离子清洁剂
antacid [ænt'æsid] n. 抗酸剂；a. 中和酸性的，抗酸性的
anthocyanin [ˌænθə'saiənin] n. 花青素，花青苷，花色素苷
anticholinesterase ['æntiˌkəuli'nestəreis] n. 抗胆碱酯酶（如毒扁豆碱）
anticipate [æn'tisipeit] vt. 预期，期望
antioxidant ['ænti'ɔksidənt] n. 抗氧化剂，硬化防止剂，防老剂
antiperspirant ['ænti'pəːspirənt] n. 防汗剂
antiprism ['ænti'prizəm] n. 反棱柱体
antiquity [æn'tikwiti] n. 古代，古人，古迹
apatite ['æpətait] n. 磷灰石
aperture ['æpətjuə] n. 孔；缝隙；孔径
approximation [əˌprɔksi'meiʃən] n. 近似
aquation [ə'kweiʃən] n. 水合（作用）水化作用
aqueous ['eikwiəs] a. 水的，水溶液的
arable ['ærəbl] a. 可耕的，适于耕种的
archaebacteria [ˌɑːkiəbæk'tiəriə] n. 太古细菌，原始细菌
archeological [ˌɑːkiə'lɔdʒikəl] a. 考古学的
arctic ['ɑːktik] a. 北极的，北极区的；n. 北极，北极圈
arginine ['ɑːdʒini(ː)n] n. 精氨酸
argon ['ɑːgɔn] n. 氩
Aristotle ['æristɔtl] n. 亚里士多德（古希腊哲学家）

aroma [əˈrəumə] n. 芳香，香气，香味
arsenic [ˈɑːsənik] n. 砷［元素符号 As］
arsenious [ɑːˈsiːniəs] a. 亚砷的，三价砷的
artifacts [ˈɑːtifækt] n. 人工制品
aryl [ˈæril] n. 芳基
ascorbate [ˈæskɔːbeit] n. 抗坏血酸盐
ascorbic [əsˈkɔːbik] a. 维生素 C 的
aspirin [ˈæspərin] n. 阿司匹林，乙酰水杨酸
assay [əˈsei] n. & v. 化验，分析，评估
assessment [əˈsesmənt] n. （为征税对财产所作的）估价，被估定的金额
assimilate [əˈsimileit] vt. 吸收（食物、思想、文化）；vi. 被吸收，同化
astatine [ˈæstətiːn] n. 砹（元素符号 At）
astronomer [əˈstrɔnəmə(r)] n. 天文学家
asymmetric [ˌæsiˈmetrik] a. 不匀称的，不对称的，不均匀的
at trace level   在痕量水平上
atherosclerosis [ˌæθərəuskliəˈrəusis] n. 动脉硬化症
atomic mass unit（amu） n. 原子质量单位, 1 u =1Da
atomic number [əˈtɔmikˈnʌmbə] n. 原子序数（元素在周期表中的排列序号）
atomic weight [əˈtɔmik weit] n. 原子量
atopic [əˈtɔpik] a. 遗传性过敏症的
auxochrome [ˈɔːksəkrəum] n. 助色团
axial [ˈæksiəl] a. 轴的，轴向的
azeotrope [əˈziːətrəup] n. 共沸混合物
back-extraction 反萃取，逆萃取
batch [bætʃ] n. 一批，一组；大量；vt. 分批处理
batchwise [ˈbætʃwaiz] a. 成批的
bathochromic [ˌbæθəˈkrɔmik] shift 化合物的吸收光谱向光谱带的红端移动，红移
bathymetric [ˌbæθiˈmetrik] a. 海深测量的
benzaldehyde [benˈzældiˌhaid] n. 苯甲醛，安息香醛
benzoic [benˈzəuik] a. 安息香的，苯甲酸的
bicarbonate [baiˈkɑːbənit] n. 碳酸氢盐，重碳酸盐
binary [ˈbainəri] a. 二进位的，二元的
biogenic [ˌbaiəuˈdʒenik] a. 源于生物，生物所造成的
biosynthetic [baiousinˈθetis] a. 生物合成的
biosythesis [baiouˈθiːsis] n. 生物合成
bipyramidal [ˌbaiˈpirəmid] n. 双锥（体）；a. 双锥体的
birefringence [ˌbairiˈfrindʒins] n. 双折射（现象）
blemish [ˈblemiʃ] vt. 有损……的完美，玷污；n. 污点，瑕疵
blight [blait] n. 枯萎病，不良影响，打击；vt. 破坏，使枯萎
boiling point   沸点
bomb [bɔm] n. 高压气体储罐，炸弹
bombardment [bɔmˈbɑːdmənt] n. 轰击，炮击
borate [ˈbɔːreit] n. 硼酸酯
borax [ˈbɔːræks] n. 硼砂，$Na_2B_4O_7 \cdot 10H_2O$
boric acid   硼酸
boride [ˈbɔːraid] n. 硼化物
boron [ˈbɔːrɔn] n. 硼
botanist [ˈbɔtənist] n. 植物学家
bout [baut] n. 一回，一场，回合，较量
brine [brain] n. 盐水，海水
bromine [ˈbrəumiːn] n. 溴
bronze [brɔnz] n. 青铜（一种铜锡合金），青铜制品
bulk analysis   全分析
buoyant [ˈbɔiənt] a. 漂浮的；有浮力的
butadiene [ˌbjuːtəˈdaiiːn] n. 丁二烯
butane [ˈbjuːtein] n. 丁烷
butene [ˈbjuːtiːn] n. 丁烯
butyric acid [bjuː(ː)ˈtirikˈæsid] n. 丁酸
cabbage [ˈkæbidʒ] n. 甘蓝，卷心菜
cadaverine [kəˈdævəriːn] n. 尸胺，1, 5-戊二胺
calcium [ˈkælsiəm] n. 钙
calibration curve   校准（定标，标定）曲线
calorimeter [ˌkæləˈrimitə] n. 热量计
calorimetry [ˌkæləˈrimitri] n. 热量测定
camphor [ˈkæmfə] n. 樟脑
capillary [kəˈpiləri] n. 毛细管；a. 毛状的，毛细作用的
carbide [ˈkɑːbaid] n. 碳化物
carbocation [ˌkɑːbəˈkeiʃən] n. 碳阳离子
carbon disulfide [ˈkɑːbən, daiˈsʌlfaid] n. 二硫化碳
carbon tetrachloride   四氯化碳
carbonaceous [kɑːbəˈneiʃəs] a. 碳的，碳质的，含碳的
carbonate [ˈkɑːbəneit] n. 碳酸盐（或酯）
carboxyl [kɑːˈbɔksil] n. 羧基
carboxylate [kɑːˈbɔksileit] n. 羧酸盐，羧酸酯
carboxylic [ˌkɑːbɔkˈsilik] a. 羧基的
carboxylic acid [ˌkɑːbɔkˈsilikˈæsid] n. 羧酸
carcinogen [kɑːˈsinədʒən] n. 致癌物
carcinogenic [kɑːsinəˈdʒənik] a. 致癌物（质）的
cardiovascular [ˌkɑːdiəuˈvæskjulə] a. 心脏血管的
cardiovascular [ˌkɑːdiəuˈvæskjulə] a. 心脏血管的
carnallite [ˈkɑːnəlait] n. 光卤石（$KCl \cdot MgCl_2 \cdot 6H_2O$）
cartridge [ˈkɑːtridʒ] n. （萃取柱）柱体
cascade [kæsˈkeid] n. 阶式蒸发器
cascade [kæsˈkeid] n. 小瀑布，喷流；一连串的阶段、过程、运作或单位
catalysis [kəˈtælisis] n. 催化（作用）
catalytic [ˌkætəˈlitik] a. 催化的
catastrophe [kəˈtæstrəfi] n. 大灾难，大祸
category [ˈkætigəri] n. 种类，部属，范畴

caterpillar ['kætəpilə] n. 毛虫
cation ['kætaiən] n. 阳离子
causative ['kɔːzətiv] a. 原因的, 成因的
CE＝capillary electrophoresis 毛细管电泳
cedar ['siːdə] n. 雪松
centrifugation [senˌtrifjuˈgeiʃən] n. 离心法, 离心过滤
ceramic [siˈræmik] a. 陶器的; n. 陶瓷制品
ceramics [siˈræmiks] n. 制陶术, 陶瓷学, 陶瓷制品
cesium [ˈsiːzjəm] n. 铯
chelate [ˈkiːleit] a. 螯合的, 螯形的
chelation [kiːˈleiʃən] n. 螯合, 螯合物
chiral [ˈtʃirəl] a. 手征（性）的
chlordane [ˈklɔːdein] n. 氯丹；八氯化甲桥茚
chloride [ˈklɔːraid] n. 氯化物
chlorination [ˌklɔːriˈneiʃən] n. 氯化, 用氯处理
chlorine [ˈklɔːriːn] n. 氯
chloroacetophenone [ˌklɔːrəuˌæsəutəufəˈnəun] n. 氯苯乙酮
chloroform [ˈklɔ(ː)rəfɔːm] n. 氯仿
chlorophyll [ˈklɔːrəfil] n. 叶绿素
cholera [ˈkɔlərə] n. 霍乱
cholesterol [kəˈlestərəul, -rɔl] n. 胆固醇
cholesteryl benzoate [kəlˈlestəriˈbenzəueit] n. 胆甾醇苯甲酸酯
chromatographic [ˌkrəumætəˈgræfik] a. 色析法的, 层离法的
chromatography [ˌkrəuməˈtɔgrəfi] n. 层析, 色谱法
chromatography [ˌkrəuməˈtɔgrəfi] n. 色谱
chromogenic [ˌkrəuməˈdʒenik] a. 发色的, 发色体的
chromophore [ˈkrəuməfɔː] n. 发色团, 生色团
chronic [ˈkrɔnik] a. 慢性的, 延续很长的
cinnamaldehyde [siniˈmældihaid] n. 肉桂醛
cinnamic [siˈnæmik] 肉桂酸的, 苯乙烯的
cinnamon [ˈsinəmən] n. 肉桂, 肉桂树, 肉桂色
circulating pump 往复泵
cleft [kleft] n. 裂缝, 裂口
clinical [ˈklinikəl] a. 临床的, 病房用的
colchicum [ˈkɔltʃikəm] n. 秋水仙, 秋水仙制成的麻药
collision [kəˈliʒən] n. 碰撞, 冲突
colorimetry [ˌkʌlɔˈrimitri] n. 比色法
coloring [ˈkʌləriŋ] n. 着色（法）, 色彩, 色调, 面色, 颜料
combustion [kəmˈbʌstʃən] n. 燃烧, 氧化
compensate [ˈkɔmpenseit] vt. 补偿, 赔偿, 酬报
compensator [ˈkɔmpenseitə] n. 补偿器, 补助器
compliment [ˈkɔmplimənt] n. 称赞, 致意; vt. 称赞, 恭维
concentration [ˌkɔnsenˈtreiʃən] n. 集中, 集合, 专心, 浓缩, 浓度

concerted reaction [kənˈsəːtidri(ː) ˈækʃən] n. 协同反应
concomitant [kənˈkɔmitənt] a. 伴随的; n. 伴随物
condensation [ˌkɔndenˈseiʃən] n. 冷凝
configuration [kənˌfigjuˈreiʃən] n. 构型, 结构, 配置, 外形
consistency [kənˈsistənsi] n. 坚固, 浓度, 密度, 一贯
console [kənˈsəul] n. 悬臂, 肘托, 控制台; v. 安慰, 抚慰
consternation [ˌkɔnstə(ː)ˈneiʃən] n. （极度）惊愕, 惊恐
contaminant [kənˈtæminənt] n. 沾染物
coordinate [kəuˈɔːdinit] a. 配位的, 同等的, 并列的
coordination [kəuˌɔːdiˈneiʃən] n. 配位作用
coprecipitate [ˌkəupriˈsipiteit] v. 共沉淀
corollary [kəˈrɔləri] n. 结果, 推论
corrosion [kəˈrəuʒən] n. 侵蚀, 腐蚀
corrosiveness [kəˌrəuˈsivnes] n. 侵蚀, 腐蚀
cosmetic [kɔzˈmetik] n. 化妆品; a. 化妆用的, 整容的
cosmetology [ˌkɔzməˈtɔlədʒi] n. 整容术
countercurrent [ˈkauntəˌkʌrənt] n. 逆流, 反向电流; adv. 相反地
covalent [kəuˈveilənt] a. 共有原子价的, 共价的
crack [kræk] n. 裂缝
craft [krɑːft] n. 工艺, 手艺
crucible [ˈkruːsibl] n. 坩埚
cryolite [ˈkraiəlait] n. 冰晶石, 氟铝酸钠
cryptand [ˈkriptənd] n. 穴状配体
cryptogram [ˈkriptəugræm] n. 密码, 暗记, 暗号
crystalline [ˈkristəlain] a. 晶体的, 晶体状的; 水晶的; n. 结晶体（质）, 晶态
cumbersome [ˈkʌmbəsəm] a. 讨厌的, 笨重的
curcumin [ˈkəːkjumin] n. 姜黄色素, 酸性黄
cyanate [ˈsaiəneit] n. 氰酸盐
cyanide [ˈsaiənaid] n. 氰化物
cylindrical [siˈlindrikl] a. 圆柱的
cystic [ˈsistik] a. 胞囊的; 膀胱的, 胆囊的
cytosolic [ˌsaitəusɔlik] a. 细胞溶质的
Dalton (Da) [ˈdɔːltən] n. 道尔顿（质量单位, 等于一氧原子质量的1/16, 约为 1.65×10^{-24} 克）
debilitating [diˈbiliteit] vt. 使衰弱, 使虚弱
decaffeination [diˈkæfiəˈneiʃən] n. 脱咖啡因, 不含咖啡因
decipher [diˈsaifə] v. 解开（疑团）, 破译（密码）
decouple [diˈkʌpl] n. 分离, 断开, 吸收（核子爆炸）的震力
decoupling [diˈkʌpliŋ] n. 去耦合, 去耦合装置, 退耦
defensible [diˈfensəbl] a. 可防御的; 可辩护的
degumm [diːˈgʌm] vt. 使……脱胶（使……去胶）

dehydrohalogenation [diːhaidrəuˌhæləd ʒə'neiʃən] n. 脱卤化氢（作用），脱去卤化氢
delicate ['delikit] a. 精巧的，精致的，脆弱的，微妙的
denote [di'nəut] vt. 指示，表示
densitometry [ˌdensi'tɔmitri] n. 密度测定法（显像测密术，测光密度术）
depict [di'pikt] v. 描出，描写，描述
depigmentation [diːpigmən'teiʃən] n. 退色，脱色
deposit [di'pɔzit] vt. 沉积，堆积
deposition [ˌdepə'ziʃən, di:-] n. 沉淀，沉淀物
deprotonation [diːprəutə'neiʃən]; n. 去质子化（作用）
dermal ['dəːməl] a. 真皮的，皮肤的，表皮的
detergent [di'təːdʒənt] a. 使干净的，使清洁的；n. 清洁剂，去垢剂
determination [diˌtəːmi'neiʃən] n. 测定，确定
detritus [di'traitəs] n. 残屑，沉渣
diacetate [dai'æsiteit] n. 双乙酸盐（酯）
diagnose ['daiəgnəuz](pl: diagnoses) v. 诊断（疾病），分析
diagonal [dai'ægənl] a. 对角线的，对顶的，斜的；n. 对角线，对顶线
1, 4-diaminobutane ['daiəmin.əbjutein] n. 1, 4-二氨基丁烷
1, 6-diaminohexane [dai'æminəu, heksein] n. 1, 6-己二胺
1, 5-diaminopentane [dai'əminiəupentein] n. 1, 5-戊二胺
dicarboxylic [daiˌkɑːbɔk'silik] a. 二（元）羧基的
dichloromethane [daiˌklɔːrə'meθein] n. 二氯甲烷
dichromate [dai'krəumeit] n. 重铬酸盐
diene ['daiiːn] n. 二烯（烃）
differentia [ˌdifə'renʃiə] n. 差异，特异，种差，特殊性
differentiate [ˌdifə'renʃieit] vt. 区分，区别，使分化，求……微分
diffraction [di'frækʃən] n. 衍射，折射
diisopropyl ether [daiˌaisə'prəupil'estə] n. 二异丙基醚
dilute [dai'ljuːt] v. a. 冲淡（的），稀释（的）
dimensional [di'menʃənəl] a. ……维的
dimethylformamide [daiˌmeθilˌgli'ɔksəl] n. 二甲基甲酰胺
diol ['daiəul] n. 二醇
1, 4-dioxane [dai'ɔksein] n. 1, 4-二环氧乙烷
discipline ['disiplin] n. 纪律，学科；v. 训练
discotic [dis'kəutik] a. 盘柱状的
disinfection [ˌdisin'fekʃən] n. 消毒
dispersion force [dis'pəːʃənfɔːs] n. 色散力，分散力
dissociation energy [diˌsəuʃi'eiʃən'enədʒi] n. 离解能
distill [dis'til] vt. 用蒸馏法提取，蒸馏

distillation [ˌdisti'leiʃən] n. 蒸馏，蒸馏法，蒸馏物，精华，精髓
distribution coefficient 分配系数
do the job 发挥作用
donor ['dəunə] n. 给予（体），捐献者
downfield ['daun'fiːld] n. 低磁场
droplets ['drɔplit] n. 小（微，液，熔）滴；水珠
dry ashing 干法灰化
dual ['djuːəl] a. 双的，二重的，二元的
ductile ['dʌktail] a. 易拉长的，可塑的
duet [djuː'et]; (US) duː'et] n. 二隅体
dyestuff ['daistʌf] n. 染料
dynode ['dainəud] n. [电子]倍增器电极
Earth's mantle 地幔
edible ['edibl] a. 可食用的
efficiency [i'fiʃənsi] n. 效率
eigenvalue ['aigənˌvæljuː] n. 特征值
electrolyse [iˌlektrəlaiz] vt. 电解
electromagnetic radiation 电磁辐射
electron-capture detector 电子捕获检测器
electronegative [iˌlektrəu'negətiv] a. 负电的，带负电的
electronegativity [iˌ'lektrɔn'negə'tiviti] 电负性
electron-withdrawing a. 吸电子的
electrophilic [iˌlektrəu'filik] a. 亲电（子）的
electrophoresis [iˌlektrəfə'riːsis] n. 电泳，电泳分离法
electrospray n. 电喷雾
electrostatic [iˌ'lektrəu'stætik] a. 静电的，静电学的
elimination [iˌlimi'neiʃən] n. 消除作用，消除反应
elixir [i'liksə] n. 长生药，万能药
eluent [eljuent] n. 洗脱液，洗脱剂
empiricism [em'pirisizəm] n. 经验主义
emulsifier [i'mʌlsifaiə] n. 乳化剂，乳化器
emulsion [i'mʌlʃən] n. 乳胶，乳浊液
en route [ɔn'ruːt] adv. & a. 在途中或在沿途
endeavor [in'devə] vt. 努力，尽力，努力，尽力，力图
endocrine ['endəukrain] n. 内分泌
endothermic [ˌendəu'θəːmik] a. 吸热（反应）的，内热的
enrich [in'ritʃ] vt. 使浓缩，加浓，富集
enrichment [in'ritʃmənt] n. 富集，浓缩
enthalpy ['enθəlpi, en'θelpi] n. 焓，热函
entropy ['entrəpi] n. 熵
enzyme mediated assays 酶仲裁分析
epicatechin [ˌepi'kætitʃin] n. 表儿茶素
epidemic [ˌepi'demik] n. （风尚等）流行，流行病
equilibrium [ˌiːkwi'libriəm] n. 平衡，均衡
erroneously [i'rəunjəsli] adv. 错误地，不正确地
ester ['estə] n. 酯，酯类
esterification [esˌterifi'keiʃən] n. 酯化

ethane ['eθein]; n. 乙烷
1，2-ethanediol ['eθeindaioul] n. 1，2-乙二醇
ethanolamine [,eθə'nɔləmi:n] n. 乙醇胺，氨基乙醇，胆胺
ethanoyl ['eθənouil] n. 乙酰基
ethene ['eθi:n] n. 乙烯
ether ['i:θə] n. 醚，乙醚
ethoxyethane [eθɔksi'eθein] n. 乙氧基乙烷，乙醚
ethylene ['eθili:n] n. 乙烯，次乙基
ethylene bisdithiocarbamates（EBDCs）：n. 乙烯双二硫代氨基甲酸盐（或酯）
ethyne ['eθain] n. 乙炔
ethynyl [e'θainil] n. 乙炔基
evaporator [i'væpəreitə] n. （食物干燥）蒸发器
exergonic [,eksə'gɔnik] a. 释出能量的，放热的
exogenous [ek'sɔdʒinəs] a. 外因的
exothermic [,eksəu'θɜ:mik] a. 发热的，放出热量的
exterminator [ik'stɜ:mineitə（r）] n. 消防者，灭火者
extinguisher [ik'stiŋgwiʃə（r）] n. 熄灭者，灭火器
extract [iks'trækt] vt. 萃取，提取，摘选
extraction [iks'trækʃən] n. 抽出，提取（法），萃取法，抽出物
extraction [iks'trækʃən] n. 萃取，提取，摘要
extrapolation [iksɪtræpə'leiʃən] n. 外推（法）
extravagance（extravagancy）[ik'strævəgəns] n. 奢侈，浪费，铺张
fabric ['fæbrik] n. 编织物，结构，组织
facilitate [fə'siliteit] vt. 使便利，推动，促进
facilitate [fə'siliteit] vt. 使容易，使便利，推进促进
far-fetched [fɑ:fetʃt] a. 牵强的，勉强的
fauna ['fɔ:nə] n. 动物群，动物区系，动物志
fermentation [,fɜ:men'teiʃən] n. 发酵
ferric ['ferik] a. （正）铁的，三价铁的
ferrous ['ferəs] a. 亚铁的
fertilizer ['fɜ:tiˌlaizə] n. 肥料（尤指化学肥料）
fibrosis [fai'brəusis] n. 纤维症，纤维化
fictitious [fik'tiʃəs] a. 虚构的，杜撰的，假造的
filtration [fil'treiʃən] n. 过滤，筛选
flammability [,flæmə'biləti] n. 可燃性
flammable ['flæməbl] n. 易燃之物；a. 易燃的，可燃的
flash distillation 闪蒸
flea [fli:] n. 跳蚤
flip [flip] v. 轻击，掷，弹，抽打，迅速翻动
flora ['flɔ:rə] n. 植物群
fluorapatite [fluə'ræpətait] n. 氟磷灰石
fluorescamine [,flu:ə'reskəmi:n] n. 荧光胺
fluorescence [fluə'resns] n. 荧光，荧光性
fluoridisation [,fluərədə'zæʃən] n. 氟化作用
fluorine ['flu(:)əri:n] n. 氟（9号元素，符号F）
fluorogenic ['flu:ərədʒən] a. 荧光团的
fluoromethane ['flu:ərəu'meθein] n. 氟代甲烷
fluorspar ['flu(:)əspɑ:] n. 萤石，氟石
flux [flʌks] n. 助熔剂，流量；vi. 熔化，流出；vt. 使熔融
foldover [fɔ:d'əuvə] n. 重叠，叠影，摺过
forensic [fə'rensik] a. 法院的，公开辩论的；n. 辩论术
forgery ['fɔ:dʒəri] n. 伪造物，伪造罪，伪造
formaldehyde [fɔ:'mældiˌhaid] n. 甲醛，蚁醛
formic ['fɔ:mik] a. 蚁的，蚁酸的
fraction ['frækʃən] n. 小部分，片段，馏分，级分
fractionating column 分馏柱
fracture ['fræktʃə] v. （使）分裂，（使）破裂
fragrance ['freigrəns] n. 芬芳，香气，香味
freeze-dry [fri:z-drai] vt. （冷）冻干（燥）
froth [frɑθ, frɔ:θ] n. 泡沫，起泡，使（啤酒）起泡沫
frothy ['frɔθi] a. 起泡沫的，多泡沫的
fume hood 烟橱，通风橱
fumigant ['fju:migənt] n. 熏蒸剂
fungicide ['fʌndʒisaid] n. 杀真菌剂
fusion ['fju:ʒən] n. 熔化，熔解，熔融
gas chromatography 气相色谱
gas-tight ['gæs'tait] a. 不漏气的，气密性的
gastro-intestinal [,gæstrəuin'testənl] a. 肠胃的
gene [dʒi:n] n. 因子，基因
genome ['dʒi:nəum] n. 基因组，染色体组
gigantic [dʒai'gæntik] a. 巨大的，庞大的
glassy carbon 玻璃化炭黑
glyceride ['glisəraid] n. 甘油酯，脂肪酸丙酯
glycerine ['glisəri:n] n. 甘油
glycerol ['glisərɔl] n. 丙三醇，甘油
glycol ['glaikɔl] n. 乙二醇，甘醇
glycosidic [ˌglaikəu'sidik] a. 糖苷的
glycosylate ['glaikəsileit] vt. 使（蛋白质）糖基化
gradient ['greidiənt] n. 梯度，倾斜度
granite ['grænit] n. 花岗岩，花岗石
graphite ['græfait] n. 石墨
gravimetric analysis 重量分析
greenhouse ['gri:nhaus] n. 温室，花房
grenade [gri'neid] n. 消防弹，灭火弹
guinea ['gini] n. 几尼（英国的旧金币，值一镑一先令）
gyromagnetic ratio 回转磁比率
haemoglobin [,hi:məu'gləubin] n. 血色素，血红蛋白
haemoglobin analysis n. 血红蛋白分析
hafnium ['hæfniəm] n. 铪
halide ['hælaid] n. 卤化物；a. 卤化物的
halogenation [,hælədʒə'neiʃən] n. 卤化（作用），卤代反应

hamper [ˈhæmpə] v. 妨碍，牵制
haphazard [ˌhæpˈhæzəd] a. 偶然的，随便的
helical [ˈhelikəl] a. 螺旋状的
helium [ˈhiːljəm, -liəm] n. 氦
hepatic [hiˈpætik] a. 肝的
herald [ˈherəld] n. 使者，先驱，预兆；vt. 预报，宣布
herb [həːb] n. 药草，香草
herbicides [ˈhəːbisaid] n. 除草剂
heroic [hiˈrəuik] a. 英雄的，英勇的；大小或范围很大的，宏大的
heteroatom [ˈhetərəuˌætəm] n. 杂原子，杂环原子
hexadiene [heksəˈdaiːin] n. 己二烯
hexafluoride [ˌheksəˈfluəraid] a. 六氟化物
hexafluoroacetylacetone [ˈheksəfluərouæsitilæsitəun] n. 六氟化乙酰基丙酮
hexahedron [ˌheksəˈhedrən] n. 六面体
hexamethylenediamine [hekseinˈmeθiliːn. daiəmiːn] n. 1，6-己二胺，亚己基二胺
hexyne [ˈhekˌsain] n. 己炔
hierarchical [ˌhaiəˈrɑːkikəl] a. 分等级的
homogeneity [ˌhɔməudʒeˈniːiti] n. 同种，同质，同次性
homogeneous [ˌhɔməuˈdʒiːnjəs] a. 均匀的，均相的
homologue (homolog) [ˈhɔmələg] n. 同系物，同源染色体，相应物
hormone [ˈhɔːməun] n. 荷尔蒙，激素
hue [hjuː] n. 色彩，色调，颜色
hydrate [ˈhaidreit] n. 水合物
hydration [haiˈdreiʃən] n. 水合，水合作用
hydrocarbon [ˈhaidrəuˌkɑːbən] n. 烃，碳氢化合物
hydrodistillation [ˌhaidrəuˌdistiˈleiʃən] n. 水蒸馏法
hydrogen halide [ˈhaidrəudʒən ˈhælaid] n. 卤化氢
hydrohalide [ˌhaidriˈhelaid] n. 氢卤化物
hydrophilic [ˌhaidrəuˈfilik] a. 亲水的
hydrophobic [ˌhaidrəuˈfəubik] a. 恐水的，狂犬病的
hydrothermal [ˈhaidrəuˈθəːməl] a. 热水的，热液的
hydroxide [haiˈdrɔksaid, -sid] n. 氢氧化物，羟化物
hyperchromism [ˈhaipəˈkrəumizəm] n. 增色
hypochlorite [ˌhaipəuˈklɔːrait] n. 次氯酸根，次氯酸盐
hypochromism [ˌhaipəuˈkrəumizəm] n. 减色
hypothalamic [ˌhaipəuθəˈlæmik] a. 丘脑下部的，下丘脑的
hypothetical [ˌhaipəuˈθetikəl] a. 假设的，假定的
hypothetically [ˌhaipəuˈθetikəli] ad. 假设地，臆说地
hypothyroid [ˈhaipəuˈθairɔid] n. 甲状腺功能减退者，甲状腺；a. 甲状腺机能减退的

hypsochromic [ˌhipsəˈkrɔmik] shift 蓝移
ibuprofen [ˌaibjuˈprəufin] n. 布洛芬（一种镇痛药）
icosahedron [ˌaikəusəˈhedrən] n. 二十面体
imine [ˈimiːn, -in; iˈmiːn] n. 亚胺
immaterial [ˌiməˈtiəriəl] a. 非物质的，无形的，不重要的
immiscible [iˈmisəbl] a. 不能混合的，不互溶的
immune [iˈmjuːn] a. 免疫的
immunoassay [ˌimjunəuˈæsei] n. 免疫测定，免疫分析
impurity [imˈpjuəriti] n. 杂质，混杂物 不纯
inactivate [inˈæktiveit] vt. 钝化，使减少活性
inclement [inˈklemənt] a. 险恶的，严酷的
incline [inˈklain] v. 使倾向于
indigestion [ˌindiˈdʒestʃən] n. 消化不良
infection [inˈfekʃən] n. 传染，传染病，影响，感染
inflammation [ˌinfləˈmeiʃən] n. 炎症，发炎
inflammatory [inˈflæmətəri] a. 煽动性的
infrastructure [ˈinfrəˈstrʌktʃə] n. 下部构造，基础下部组织
inherently [inˈhiərəntli] ad. 天生地，本质上
inhibitor [inˈhibitə (r)] n. 抑制剂，抑制者
inhibitor (inhibiter) [inˈhibitə (r)] n. 禁止剂，抑制剂，抑制因素
inhomogeneity [ˈinˌhəuməˈdʒiˈniːiti] n. 不同类，不同族，不同质
initiation [iˌniʃiˈeiʃən] n. 开始，初始
insidious [inˈsidiəs] a. 隐伏的；埋伏的
insoluble [inˈsɔljubl] a. 不能溶解的
interchange [ˌintəˈtʃeindʒ] vt. 内部交换，交替发生；n. 交换，交替
interfering substance 干扰物质
interhalogen [ˌintəˈhæləudʒən] n. 杂卤素，杂卤化合物
interionic [ˌintəaiˈɔnik] a. 离子间的
intermediate [ˌintəˈmiːdjət] n. 中间体，媒介物
intermedium [ˌintə (ː) ˈmiːdiəm] (plintermedia) n. 中间体，媒介物
interrelate [ˌintə (ː) riˈleit] v. 使相互关联
interstellar [ˈintə (ː) ˈstelə] a. 星际的，星球与星球间的
intimacy [ˈintiməsi] n. 密切，熟悉
intimately [ˈintimitli] ad. 亲切地，密切地
intoxication [inˌtɔksiˈkeiʃən] n. 中毒；喝醉
intriguing [inˈtriːgiŋ] a. 引起兴趣（或好奇心）的，迷人的
intuitive [inˈtjuː (ː) itiv] a. 直观的，直觉的
invoke [inˈvəuk] v. 求助，借助
iodide [ˈaiədaid] n. 碘化物
iodine [ˈaiədain] n. 碘，碘酒
iodomethane [ˌaiədəuˈmeθein] n. 碘甲烷
ion-association 离子缔和络和物

ionization [ˌaiənai'zeiʃən] n. 离子化，电离
ionization energy [ˌaiənai'zeiʃən'enədʒi] n. 电离能
irritation [ˌiri'teiʃən] n. 刺激
isobaric [ˌaisəu'bærik] a. 表示等压的；同（原子）量异序的
isoelectronic [ˌaisəuilek'trɔnik] a. 等电子的
isomer ['aisəumə] n. 异构体
isomerization [aiˌsɔməraiˈzeiʃən] n. 异构化（作用）
isopentylamine [aisuəˌpentil'æmi:n] n. 异戊胺
isoprenoid [ˌaisəu'prenɔid] a. & n. 类异戊二烯（的）
isothermally [ˌaisəu'θə:məli] ad. 等温（线）地
isotope ['aisəutəup] n. 同位素
junction ['dʒʌŋkʃən] n. 连接，结合，交叉点，汇合处
kinetics [kai'netiks] n. 动力学
Krebs cycle 克雷布斯循环
lanthanum ['lænθənəm] n. 镧
lavender ['lævində] n. 熏衣草，干熏衣草的花，用熏衣草熏香
leach [li:tʃ] v. 沥滤；浸提
leather ['leðə] n. 皮革，皮革制品
lethal ['li:θəl] a. 致命的；n. 致死因子
leukemia [ljuː'ki:miə] n. 白血病
leukotriene [lju:ku'triin] n. 白三烯
lice [lais] n. 虱子，白虱
lipid ['lipid, 'laipid] n. 脂质，油脂（脂肪，乳酪）
lipids ['lipid, 'laipid] n. 脂质，油脂
lipophilic [ˌlipə'filik] a. 亲油的；亲脂的
lithium ['liθiəm] n. 锂
lubricant [luː'brikənt] n. 润滑剂
lucrative ['luːkrətiv, lju:-] a. 有利的
lymphocytic [ˌlimfəu'sitik] a. 淋巴球的，淋巴细胞的
macromolecular [ˌmækrəu'məu'lekjulə] n. 大分子
macromolecule [ˌmækrəu'mɔlikju:l] n. 巨大分子，高分子
magma ['mægmə] n. 岩浆
magnetron ['mægnitrɔn] n. 磁电管
magnitude ['mægnitju:d] n. 大小，数量，巨大，广大
makeup ['meikʌp] n. 组成，构造，化装用品
malabsorption [ˌmæləb'sɔ:pʃən] n. （营养）吸收障碍，吸收不良
malaria [mə'lɛəriə] n. 疟疾，瘴气
MALDI = Matrix Assisted Laser Desorption Ionization 基体辅助激光解吸离子化
malleable ['mæliəbl] a. 有延展性的，可锻的
malonic ['mælənik] a. 丙二酸的
mantle ['mæntl] n. 覆盖物
marginalize ['mɑːdʒinəlaiz] vt. 忽视，排斥
marine [mə'ri:n] a. 海的，海产的，航海的
masking agent 掩蔽剂
mass-to-charge ratios (m/z) 质荷比

matrix ['meitriks] n. 矩阵
mechanism ['mekənizəm] n. 机理，进程
membrane ['membrein] n. 薄膜，隔膜
mercury ['mə:kjuri] n. 水银，汞
mesh [meʃ] n. 筛眼，每平方英寸的网孔（筛眼）数
metabolic [ˌmetə'bɔlik] a. 新陈代谢的
metabolism [me'tæbəlizəm] n. 新陈代谢（作用）
metabolist [me'tæbəlist] n. 新陈代谢者
metaborate [ˌmetə'bɔ:reit] n. 偏硼酸盐 MBO_2
metallurgy [me'tælədʒi] n. 冶金学，冶金术
metastable [ˌmetə'steibl] a. 亚稳的，准稳的
methaemoglobinaemia [meθi:məugləubi'ni:miə] n. 正铁血红蛋白血症
methodology [ˌmeθə'dɔlədʒi] n. 方法学，方法论
methoxide [meθ'ɔksaid, -sid] n. 甲醇盐，甲氧基物
4-methoxyoctane ['meθəksi'ɔktein] n. 4-甲氧基辛烷
methyl ['meθil, 'mi:θail] n. 甲基
methyl acetanilide 甲基乙酰苯胺
2-methylbutanal [meθilbju:tinəl] n. 2-甲基丁醛
methylene ['meθili:n, -lin] n. 亚甲基
2-methylpropene [tuː'meθil'prəupi:n] n. 2-甲基丙烯
microenvironment ['maikrəuin'vaiərənmənt] n. 小环境
microgram ['maikrəugræm] n. 微观图，显微照片
microscopic ['maikrə'skɔpik] a. 微观的，细致的
microtube [maikrəutju:b] n. 微管
midge [midʒ] n. 蚊
minicolumn ['mini'kɔləm] n. 小型柱
misbrand ['mis'brænd] vt. 贴错（药品，食品）标记，贴假标签于
miscibility [ˌmisi'biliti] n. 溶混性
miscible ['misibl] a. 易混合的
misery ['mizəri] n. 痛苦，苦恼，悲惨，不幸，穷困
mobile ['məubail] a. 可移动的，易变的
mobile phase 流动相
modulation [ˌmɔdju'leiʃən] n. 调整
molal ['məuləl] a. 摩尔的
molarity [məu'læriti] n. 摩尔浓度
molecular scale 分子范围
molluscs ['mɔləsk] n. 软体动物
monatomic [ˌmɔnə'tɔmik] a. 单原子的
monoglyceride [ˌmɔnəu'glisəraid] n. 单酸甘油酯
mother liquor 母液
muffle furnace 马弗炉，套炉，回热炉，膛式炉，隔焰炉
multideck ['mʌltidek] n. 多层（板）
musculoskeletal [ˌmʌskjuləu'skelitəl] a. 肌（与）骨骼的
mutagen ['mju:tədʒən] n. 诱变

mutagenic [ˌmjuːtəˈdʒenik] a. 诱变的
myrrh [məː] n. 没药,没药树,没药树脂
nanogram [ˈneinəˌgræm] n. 毫微克,纳克
nanometer [ˈneinəˌmiːtə] n. 纳米
naphthalene [ˈnæfθəliːn] n. 萘(球),卫生球
nebulize [ˈnebjulaiz] vt. 雾化,使(液体)化为细的喷雾;喷为雾状
negligent [ˈneglidʒənt] a. 疏忽的,粗心大意的
negligible [ˈneglidʒəbl] a. 可忽略的,微不足道的
nematic [niˈmætik] a. n. 向列相(的),丝状的
neon [ˈniːən] n. 氖
neonatal [ˌniːəuˈneitəl] a. 新生的,初生的;新生儿的
neonatal screening n. 新生儿筛选
neuroblastoma [ˌnjuərəblæsˈtəumə] n. 成神经细胞瘤
neurological [ˌnjuərəˈlɔdʒikəl] a. 神经学上的
neuropathy [njuəˈrɔpəθi] n. 神经病
neutralize [ˈnjuːtrəlaiz] v. 使中性,使(溶液)呈中性;中和
neutralize [ˈnjuːtrəlaiz;(US) nuː-] vt. 使中立,使中和
Newtonian [njuːˈtəunjən, -niən] a. 牛顿的,牛顿学说的
nicotine [ˈnikətiːn, -tin] n. 烟碱,尼古丁
nitrate [ˈnaitreit] n. 硝酸盐
nitrate fertilizer 含氮肥料
nitroaniline [ˌnaitrəuˈænilain] n. 硝基苯胺
nitrogen [ˈnaitrədʒən] n. 氮
nitrogenous [naiˈtrɔdʒinəs] a. 氮的,含氮的
nitroimidazole [ˈnaitrəuˌimiˈdæzəul, -dəˈzəul] n. 硝基咪唑
nitroso [naiˈtrəusəu] a. 亚硝基的
noble metal [nəubl ˈmetl] n. 贵金属,惰性金属
nomenclature [nəuˈmenklətʃə] n. (系统)命名法
nominally [ˈnɔminəli] adv. 有名无实地,名义上地
nonionic [ˌnɔnaiˈɔnik] a. 在溶液中不分解成离子的;非离子的
nonlethal [ˈnɔnˈliːθəl] a. 不致命的
nonmagnetic [ˌnɔmdjuˈleiʃən] a. 非磁性的;n. 非磁性物
nonpolarizable [nɔnˈpəuləraizəbl] a. 不可极化的
nonprescription [ˌnɔnpriˈskripʃən] a. 非处方的,无医生处方也可买到的(药)
norgestrel [nɔːˈdʒestrəl] n. 甲基炔诺酮,18-甲炔诺酮
nucleophile [ˈnjuːkliəʃail] a. 亲核试剂
nucleophilic [ˌnjuːkliəuˈfilik] a. 亲核的,亲质子的
nuisance [ˈnjuːsns] n. 讨厌的人或东西,麻烦事,损害
nutrient [ˈnjuːtriənt] a. 有营养的
objectionable [əbˈdʒekʃənəbl] a. 引起反对的,令人不愉快的,讨厌的
obstacle [ˈɔbstəkl] n. 障碍(物)
octahedron [ˌɔktəˈhedrən] n. 八面体
octene [ˈɔktiːn] n. 辛烯
octet [ɔkˈtet] n. 八隅体
octyne [ˈɔktin] n. 辛烷
oleoresin [ˌəuliəuˈrezin] n. 含油树脂;精油树脂;松脂
oligonucleotide [ˌɔligəuˈnjuːkliəutaid] n. 低(聚)核苷酸,寡核苷酸
onion [ˈʌnjən] n. 洋葱
optimizing [ˈɔptimaiziŋ] n. 充分利用,有效利用
oral [ˈɔːrəl] a. 口头的
orbital [ˈɔːbitl] n. 轨道,轨函数
organometallic [ɔːgənəumiˈtælik] a. 有机金属的
organophosphates [ˌɔːgənəuˈfɔsfeit] n. & a. 有机磷酸酯(的)(现广泛用作杀虫剂、抑燃剂等)
orientation [ˌɔ(ː)rienˈteiʃən] n. 方向,取向,倾向性
orifice [ˈɔrifis] n. 锐孔;喷嘴(管,口)
orthophosphate [ɔːθəuˈfɔsfeit] n. 正磷酸盐
outermost [ˈautəməust] a. 最外面的,最远的,价电子层的
Overhauser [ˈəuvəhed] 奥佛豪塞(人名)
overhead [ˈəuvəhed] n. 塔顶馏出物的;a. 高出地面的
oxalic [ɔkˈsælik] a. 醋浆草的
oxalis [ˈɔksəlis] a. 酢浆草
oxidant [ˈɔksidənt] n. 氧化剂
oxidation [ˌɔksiˈdeiʃən] n. 氧化(作用)
oxidize [ˈɔksiˌdaiz] v. (使)氧化
oxoacid [ˌɔksiˈæsid] n. 酮酸,含氧酸
oxoanion [ˌɔksiˈænaiən] n. 含氧阴离子
oxonium [ɔkˈsəunjəm] n. 氧鎓(离子)
oxyanion [ˌɔksiˈænaiən] n. 氧离子
oxymoron [ˌɔksiˈmɔːrɔn] n. 矛盾修饰法
oyster [ˈɔistə] n. 牡蛎
PAHs = polycyclic aromatic hydrocarbons 多环芳烃,稠环芳烃
pancreatitis [ˌpæŋkriəˈtaitis] n. 胰腺炎
parameter [pəˈræmitə] n. 参数
particulate [pəˈtikjulit, -leit] n. 微粒;a. 微粒的
pasture [ˈpɑːstʃə] n. 草原,牧场
pathogenic [ˌpæθəˈdʒenik] a. 致病的,病原的,发病的
pathology [pəˈθɔlədʒi] n. 病理学
PCBs = polychlorinated biphenyls 多氯化联(二)苯
peculiarity [piˌkjuːliˈæriti] n. 特性,怪癖
pentachloride [ˈpentəˈklɔːraid] n. 五氯化物
pentafluoride [ˌpentəˈfluəraid] n. 五氟化物
pentahydrate [ˌpentəˈnaidrəid] n. 五水合物
pentoxide [ˌpenˈtɔksaid] n. 五氧化物

peptide ['peptaid] n. 缩氨酸
perchlorate [pə'klɔːreit] n. 高氯酸盐（或酯）
peroxide [pə'rɔksaid] n. 过氧化物，过氧化氢
peroxodisulphate [pəˈrɔksəudisalfeit] n. 过二硫酸盐
peroxyl [pə'rɔksil] n. （＝hydrogen peroxide）过氧化氢
perpendicular [ˌpəːpən'dikjulə] a. 垂直的，正交的
perplexed [pə'plekst] a. 困惑的，不知所措的
perplexity [pə'pleksiti] n. 困惑，茫然
perspiration [ˌpəːspə'reiʃən] n. 排汗
pesticide ['pestisaid] n. 杀虫剂，农药，防疫药
pharmaceutical [ˌfɑːmə'sjuːtikəl] n. 药物；a. 制药（学）上的
pharmacokinetics [ˌfɑːməkəuˌkai'netiks] n. 药物（代谢）动力学
pharmacology [ˌfɑːmə'kɔlədʒi] n. 药理学
phenol ['fiːnəl] n. （苯）酚，石炭酸
phenolic [fi'nɔlik] a. 酚的，石炭酸的
phlogiston [flɔ'dʒistən] n. 燃素
phosphide ['fɔsfaid] n. 磷化物
phosphine ['fɔsfin] n. 磷化氢，三氢化磷
phospholipid [ˌfɔsfəu'lipid] n. 磷脂
phosphorus ['fɔsfərəs] n. 磷（元素符号 P）
phosphorylate ['fɔsfərileit] vt. 使磷酸化
physicochemical [ˌfizikəu'kemikəl] a. 物理化学的
pictogram ['pikəgræm] n. 皮（可）克，微微克（10^{-12} g）
pigment ['pigmənt] n. 色素，颜料
pitch [pitʃ] n. 程度，斜度
pituitary [pi'tjuː(ː)itəri] n. 垂体
placebo [plə'siːbəu] n. 安慰剂
plague [pleig] n. 瘟疫，灾祸；vt. 使染瘟疫，烦扰
plasma ['plæzmə] n. 血浆，乳浆；等离子体，等离子区
plate theory 塔板理论
platelet ['pleitlit] n. 血小板
plumbing ['plʌmiŋ] n. 管道（制品）
polarizability ['pəuləˌraizə'biləti] n. 极化性，极化率，极化度
polarizable ['pəuləraizəbl] a. 可极化的
polarization [ˌpəulərai'zeiʃən; -ri'z-] n. 偏振（现象），极化（作用）
pollutant [pə'luːtənt] n. 污染物，污染源
polyatomic [ˌpɔli'ətɔmik] a. 多原子的
polyfunctional [ˌpɔli'fʌŋkʃənəl] a. 多功能的
polyhalogen [ˌpɔli'hælədʒən] n. 多卤素
polyhedra [ˌpɔli'hiːdrə] (polyhedron 的复数形式); n. 多面体［形］
polyhedron [pɔli'hedrən] n. 多面体
polymer nylon 尼龙
Polymerase ['pɔləməreis] n. 聚合酶

polymerization ['pɔliməraizeiʃən] n. 聚合（作用）
polymorphism [ˌpɔli'mɔːfizəm] n. （同质）多晶（现象）
polyvinyl [ˌpɔli'vainil] a. 聚乙烯的
porcelain ['pɔːslin, -lein] n. 瓷器，瓷；a. 瓷制的，精美的，脆的
pore [pɔː] n. 毛孔，小孔，气孔
post-translational modification n. 遗传转译模式
postulate ['pɔstjuleit] n. 假定，基本条件，公理；vt. 要求，假设
potassium [pə'tæsjəm] n. 钾（19 号元素，符号 K）
potency ['pəutənsi] n. 能力
potential-energy [pə'tenʃ(ə)l'enədʒi] n. 势能
potentiometry [pəˌtenʃi'ɔmitri] n. 电势［位］测定法
p-phenylenediamine ['fenəliːn'daiəmin] n. 亚苯基二胺
prebiotic [priːbai'ɔtik] a. 生命起源以前的
precautionary [pri'kɔːʃənəri] a. 预防的
precellular [ˌpri'seljulə] n. 前细胞的
precipitation [priˌsipi'teiʃən]; n. 沉淀，沉淀作用
precoat ['priːkəut] vt. 预涂（预敷，预浇）；n. 预涂层（预敷层）
predominantly [pri'dɔmineit] ad. 占优势的
premature [ˌpremə'tjuə] a. 早熟的，不成熟的；n. 早产的婴儿；vi. 成熟，生长
preservative [pri'zəːvətiv] a. 有保护力的，防腐的；n. 防腐剂，防腐料
probe [prəub] n. 探针，探测品；v. 探查，穿刺
propanal ['prəupənæl] n. 丙醛
1,2-propanediol [prə'pænədiəul] n. 1,2-丙二醇
propanetricarboxlic ['prəupəntrica, bɔksilik] n. 三羧基丙烷
propanol ['prəupənɔl] n. 丙醇
propene ['prəupiːn] n. 丙烯
prophylactic [ˌprɔfi'læktik] a. 预防疾病的；n. 预防药，避孕药
propyne ['prəupain] n. 丙炔
protagonist [prəu'tægənist] n. （戏剧，小说中的）主角，领导者
protonation [ˌprəutə'neiʃən] n. 质子化（作用）
provoke [prə'vəuk] vt. 引起，惹起，驱使
pseudothermodynamic ['sjuːdəu'θəːməudai'næmik] a. 假热（力）学的
psychological [ˌsaikə'lɔdʒikəl] a. 心理（上）的
putrescine [pjuː'tresiːn, -in] n. 腐胺，丁二胺
pyrethroid [pai'riːθrɔid] n. 拟除虫菊酯，合成除虫菊酯
pyridine [ˌpirə'dainə] n. 嘧啶
pyrites [pai'raitiːz] n. ［矿］硫化铁矿
quadrupoles ['kwɔdrəˌpəul] n. ［物］四极
qualitative ['kwɔlitətiv] a. 定性的，性质上的
quantitate ['kwɔntiteit] v. 测定（估计）的数量，用数量来表示

quantitative [ˈkwɒntɪtətɪv] a. 定量的，数量的
quenching [ˈkwentʃɪŋ] n. 淬火，猝灭
rancid [ˈrænsɪd] a. 像油脂腐臭味的，腐臭的
random [ˈrændəm] a. 随机的，随意的；n. 随机，随意
reactant [riːˈæktənt] n. 反应物
reactor [rɪ(ː)ˈæktə] n. 反应器
rearrange [ˌriːəˈreɪndʒ] vt. 重新安排；vi. 重排
rearrangement [ˌriːəˈreɪndʒmənt] n. 重排
reboiler [riˈbɔɪlə] n. 再沸器
receptor [rɪˈseptə] n. 接受器，感受器，受体
recipe [ˈresɪpi] n. 处方，制法，
reciprocal [rɪˈsɪprəkəl] a. 倒数的
reconcentration [ˌriːkɒnsenˈtreɪʃən] n. 再浓缩
recondensation [ˌriːkɒndenˈseɪʃən] n. 浓缩，凝结
Recondense [ˌriːkənˈdens] v. 再浓缩，再凝结
rectification [ˌrektɪfɪˈkeɪʃən] n. 精馏，矫正，纠正
rectify [ˈrektɪfaɪ] vt. 精馏，矫正，纠正
reflux [ˈriːflʌks] n. 回流
refraction [rɪˈfrækʃən] n. 折光，折射
regulatory agency 管理机构
rehybridize [ˌriːˈhaɪbrɪdaɪz] vt. 重新杂化，再杂化
reminiscent [remɪˈnɪs(ə)nt] a. 回忆往事的
repulsive [rɪˈpʌlsɪv] a. 推斥的，排斥的
residue [ˈrezɪdjuː] n. 残余，剩余，渣滓
resonate [ˈrezəneɪt] vt. vi. （使）共鸣，（使）共振
resurrect [ˌrezəˈrekt] v. 复活，重新使用
retention [rɪˈtenʃən] n. 保持，保留，保持力
revenue [ˈrevɪnjuː] n. 收入，国家的收入，税收
reversibility [rɪˌvɜːsəˈbɪlɪti] n. 可反转性，可逆性
rheumatoid [ˈruːmətɔɪd] a. 风湿症的，患风湿症的
rhubarb [ˈruːbɑːb] ;n. （植物）大黄
rinse [rɪns] vt. 冲洗，清洗（发，手）；vi. 漂净
rival [ˈraɪvəl] n. 竞争者，对手
roundabout [ˈraʊndəbaʊt] a. 迂回的，不直接的，胖的
rubidium [ruːˈbɪdɪəm] n. 铷
rugby [ˈrʌɡbɪ] n. 橄榄球
runaway [ˈrʌnəweɪ] a. 不受控制的，摆脱控制、限制或局限的
runaway reaction 失控反应
salicylic [ˌsælɪˈsɪlɪk] a. 水杨酸的
saline [ˈseɪlaɪn, səˈlaɪn] a. 盐的
saltpeter [sɔltˈpiːtə] n. 硝石，硝酸钾
sample introduction 进样
sandwich [ˈsænwɪdʒ, -tʃ] v. 插入，夹入
saponification [səˌpɒnɪfɪˈkeɪʃən] n. 皂化（作用）
scavenger [ˈskævɪndʒə] n. 清除剂；净化剂
scenario [sɪˈnɑːrɪəʊ] n. 剧情
schematically [skɪˈmætɪk] ad. （用图等）示意性地
scintillation [ˌsɪntɪˈleɪʃən] n. 闪烁（现象）

sclerosis [sklɪəˈrəʊsɪs] n. 硬化症，硬化，硬结
seasick [ˈsiːsɪk] a. 晕海，晕船
seasickness [ˈsiːsɪknɪs] n. 晕海，晕船
sebum [ˈsiːbəm] n. 皮脂，脂肪
segregate [ˈseɡrɪɡeɪt] vt. 分凝，分异，成熟分裂时等位基因分离
selectivity [sɪlekˈtɪvɪti] n. 选择性
selenium [sɪˈliːnɪəm, -njəm] n. 硒
semi-continuous [ˌsemɪkənˈtɪnjʊəs] a. 半连续的，断断续续的
separation coefficient 分离系数
separatory funnel 分液漏斗
sewage [ˈsjuː(ː)ɪdʒ] n. 污水，下水道
shawl [ʃɔːl] n. 长方形的围巾（披巾）用围巾（披巾）包裹
shield [ʃiːld] n. 护罩，盾，盾状物；v. 保护，防护
sieve-plate column 筛板柱
signature [ˈsɪɡnɪtʃə] n. 签名，署名，信号
silicon [ˈsɪlɪkən] n. 硅
sinusoidal [saɪnəˈsɔɪdəl] a. 正弦波的；n. 正弦
slope [sləʊp] n. 倾斜；v. 倾斜
smectic [ˈsmektɪk] a. 近晶相的
soap [səʊp] n. 肥皂，脂肪酸盐
soda [ˈsəʊdə] n. 苏打
sodium [ˈsəʊdjəm, -dɪəm] n. 钠
sodium bicarbonate [ˈsəʊdjəm, baɪˈkɑːbənɪt] n. 碳酸氢钠，小苏打
solubility [ˌsɒljuˈbɪlɪti] n. 溶解度，溶解性
solubilize [ˈsɒljubɪlaɪz] v. （使）溶解，（使）增溶
solvate [ˈsɒlveɪt] n. 溶质，被溶解物，溶剂化物
solvation [sælˈveɪʃən] n. 溶液，溶解
solvent [ˈsɒlvənt] n. 溶剂
solvolysis [sɒlˈvɒlɪsɪs] n. 溶剂分解（作用）
soybean [ˈsɔɪbiːn] n. 大豆，黄豆
species [ˈspiːʃɪz] n. （物）种，种类
specificity [ˌspesɪˈfɪsɪti] n. 特异性，特征；种别性
spectral [ˈspektrəl] a. 幽灵的，鬼魂的
spectral signature 光谱信号
spectrometer [spekˈtrɒmɪtə] n. 分光计
spectrophotometry [ˌspektrəʊfəʊˈtɒmɪtri] n. 分光光度测定法，分光光度技术
spectroscopic [ˌspektrəˈskɒpɪk] a. 分光镜的，借助分光镜的；光谱（学）的
spectroscopy [spekˈtrɒskəpi] n. 光谱学，波谱学
spectrum [ˈspektrəm] n. 光谱，型谱，频谱
speculation [ˌspekjuˈleɪʃən] n. 思索，推测，投机
speculative [ˈspekjʊlətɪv] a. 推测的，投机的
spice [spaɪs] n. 香料，调味品，
spikenard [əˈspaɪknɑːd] n. 甘松，甘松香油
sprig [sprɪɡ] n. 小枝，小枝状饰物，用（小枝）枝状物装饰
sprinkle [ˈsprɪŋkl] vt. 洒，喷淋，撒布；vi. 洒，

喷淋
standpoint ['stændpɪnt] n. 立场观点
starch [stɑːtʃ] n. 淀粉；vt. 给……上浆
stationary phase 固定相
stem [stem] n. 母体词，词干
steric ['stiərik, 'sterik] a. 空间的，位的
steric ['stiərik, 'sterik] n. 立体的，空间（排列）的
steroid ['stiərɔid] n. 类固醇
steroid ['stiərɔid] n. 类固醇，甾族化合物
still [stil] n. 蒸馏室，蒸馏器；v. 蒸馏
strip [strip] vt. 剥去，剥夺，使去色（化），通过蒸馏去除挥发组分
strip [strip] vt. 清除，剥去
subcritical [sʌbˈkritikl] a. 次临界
subdivide [ˈsʌbdiˈvaid] vt. 区分，把……细分，把……分成几份
sublime [səˈblaim] v. （使）纯化，（使）升华
substituent [sʌbˈstitjuənt] n. 取代（基）
substitution [ˌsʌbstiˈtjuːʃən] n. 取代作用，取代反应
substrate [ˈsʌbstreit] n. 底物（被试剂进攻之物）
subtle [ˈsʌtl] a. 狡猾的，敏感的，微妙的，精细的，稀薄的
succinic [səkˈsinik] a. 丁二酸的，琥珀酸的
sulfate [ˈsʌlfeit] n. 硫酸盐，硫酸根，硫酸酯
sulfite [ˈsʌlfait] n. 亚硫酸盐
sulfur [ˈsʌlˈfjuːrik] n. 硫［元素符号 S］
sulfuric [ˈsʌlfə] a. 硫的，含硫的
sulfuric acid [sʌlˈfjuərikˈæsid] n. 硫酸
sulphur [ˈsʌlfə] n. 硫（元素符号 S）；a. 含硫的
suntan [ˈsʌntæn] n. 阳光晒黑后皮肤上出现的褐斑
suntanning [ˈsʌntæniŋ] n. 防晒剂
supercritical [ˌsjuːpəˈkritikəl] a. 超临界的
supercritical [ˌsjuːpəˈkritikəl] a. 超临界的
supersaturate [sjuːpəˈsætʃəreit] vt. 使过饱和
supersaturation [ˈsjuːpəˌsætʃəˈreiʃən] n. 过饱和（现象）
supersaturation zone 过饱和区
surface analysis 表面分析
surfactant [səˈfæktənt] n. 表面活性剂
surfactant [səˈfæktənt] n. & a. 表面活性剂（的）
sweep [swiːp] n. 扫除，掠过；v. 打扫，吹走
swirl [swəːl] vt. 旋动，使打旋，涡动，漩涡
symmetrical [siˈmetrikəl] a. 对称的，匀称的
syndrome [ˈsindrəum] n. 综合病症
tabulate [ˈtæbjuleit] vt. 把……制成表格
tandem [ˈtændəm] mass spectrometers n. 串联质谱计
tartar [ˈtɑːtə] n. 酒石（酿造葡萄酒时酒桶底的沉淀物质，为酒石酸的原料）
tartaric [tɑːˈtærik] a. 酒石（酸）的
t-butyl [ˈbjuːtil] n. 叔丁基

tellurium [teˈljuəriəm] n. 碲
termite [ˈtəːmait] n. 白蚁
tertiary [ˈtəːʃəri] a. 第三的，三级的，叔的
tetraborate [ˌtetrəˈbɔːreit] n. 四硼酸盐
tetracarboxylic [teˈtri, kæːbɔksilik] a. 四羧基的，四羧酸的
tetrahedral [ˌtetrəˈhedrəl] a. 有四面的，四面体的
tetrahedron [ˌtetrəˈhedrən] n. 四面体
tetramethylenediamine [ˌtetriməθiliˈndaimiːn] n. 丁二胺，腐胺，四亚甲基二胺
Thales [ˈθeiliːz] n. 泰利斯（古希腊哲学家，数学家，天文学家）
thallium [ˈθæliəm] n. 铊［元素符号 Tl］
theorem [ˈθiərəm] n. 定理，原则
therapeutic [ˌθerəˈpjuːtik] a. 治疗的，治疗学的；n. 治疗剂，治疗学家
thermodynamics [ˈθəːməudaiˈnæmiks] n. 热力学
thionyl [ˈθaiənil] n. 亚硫酰（基）
thionyl chloride [ˈθaiənilˈklɔːraid] n. 二氯亚砜
three-dimensional structure 三维结构
throughput [ˈθruːput] n. 生产量，生产能力，吞吐量
thyroid [ˈθairɔid] a. 甲状腺的；n. 甲状腺
titration [taiˈtreiʃən] n. 滴定
tocol [ˈtəukɔl] n. 母育酚
tocopherol [təuˈkɔfərəul] n. 生育酚，维生素 E
toluidine [təˈljuidin] n. 邻甲苯胺
topical [ˈtɔpikəl] a. 论题的，局部的
topology [təˈpɔlədʒi] n. 拓扑学，拓扑
toxicant [ˈtɔksikənt] n. 有毒物，毒药
transdermally [trænsˈdəːməli] ad. 经过真皮的
transition [trænˈziʒən, -ˈsiʃən] n. 转变，过渡，跃迁
trial-and-error [ˈtraiəl-ændˈerə] n. 反复试验法
tricarboxylic [traiˌkɑːbɔkˈsilik] a. 三羧酸的
trichloroethylene [traiˌklɔːrəuˈeθiliːn] n. 三氯乙烯
triene [ˈtraiiːn] n. 三烯（烃）
trifluoride [ˌtraiˈfluəraid] n. 三氟化物
triiodide [ˌtraiˈaiədaid] n. 三碘化物
trillion [ˈtriljən] num. 万亿，等于 10^{12}
trimethyltridecyl [traiˈmeθiltraiˈdesil] n. 三甲基十三烷基
triol [ˈtraiɔl] n. 三元醇
trioxide [traiˈɔksaid] n. 三氧化物
triple [ˈtripl] a. 三倍的，三重的；n. 三倍数
tunable [ˈtjuːnəbl] a. 悦耳的
turbid [ˈtəːbid] a. 浑浊的，雾重的
turbidity [təːˈbiditi] n. 浑浊，混乱，混浊度，含沙量
typhoid [ˈtaifɔid] n. 伤寒症，伤寒的
ultraviolet [ˌʌltrəˈvaiəlit] a. 紫外（线）的；n. 紫外线辐射
unimolecular [ˌjuːnimɔuˈlekjulə] a. 单分子的

unshared [ˌʌnˈʃeəd] *a.* 非共享的，独享的
upfield [ʌpfiːld] *n.* 高磁场
vacant [ˈveikənt] *a.* 空的，空白的，未被占用的
valved [vælvd] *a.* 有阀的
vanish [ˈvæniʃ] *vi.* 消失，变成零
vaporize [ˈveipəraiz] *vt/vi.* （使）蒸发，（使）汽化
vent [vent] *n.* 通风孔，出烟孔，出口
vesicle [ˈvesikl] *n.* 小囊，水泡
vestige [ˈvestidʒ] *n.* 遗留物，残余
veterinary [ˈvetərinəri] *n.* 兽医；*a.* 医牲畜的，兽医的
vicinity [viˈsiniti] *n.* 附近，接近，邻近，附近地区
vinyl [ˈvainil, ˈvinil] *n.* 乙烯基
vinyl chloride [ˈvainil-ˈklɔːraid] *n.* 氯乙烯

viscosity [visˈkɔsiti] *n.* 黏性
volatile [ˈvɔlətail] *a.* 挥发性的，反复无常的
volumetric [vɔljuˈmetrik] *a.* 测容量的，容量的，
volumetric analysis 容量分析
waterborne [ˈwɔːtəbɔːn] *a.* 水中的，水传播的
wavelength [ˈweivleŋθ] *n.* 波长
weed [wiːd] *n.* 野草，杂草
weep [wiːp] *vt.* 渗出液体，（水珠的）渗出滴下
withdraw [wiðˈdrɔː] *vt.* 收回，撤回；*vi.* 撤退
withdrawal [wiðˈdrɔːəl] *n.* 收回，取回，提款，撤销
XRF＝X-ray fluorescence   X射线荧光
xylene [ˈzailiːn] *n.* 二甲苯
zeroth [ˈziərəuð, -rəuθ, ˈziː-] *a.* 零的
zirconium [zəːˈkəuniəm] *n.* 锆
zwitterions [ˈtsvitəraiən] *n.* 两性离子